Being Human: the Problem of Agency

Humanity and the very notion of the human subject are under threat from postmodernist thinking which has declared not only the 'Death of God' but also the 'Death of Man'. This book is a revindication of the concept of humanity, rejecting contemporary social theory that seeks to diminish human properties and powers. Archer argues that being human depends on an interaction with the real world in which practice takes primacy over language in the emergence of human self-consciousness, thought, emotionality and personal identity – all of which are prior to, and more basic than, our acquisition of a social identity.

This original and provocative new book from leading social theorist Margaret S. Archer builds on the themes explored in her previous books *Culture and Agency* (1988) and *Realist Social Theory* (1995). It will be required reading for academics and students of social theory, cultural theory, political theory, philosophy and theology.

Being Human: the Problem of Agency

Being Human: the Problem of Agency

Margaret S. Archer

University of Warwick

CAMBRIDGE
UNIVERSITY PRESS

PUBLISHED BY THE PRESS SYNDICATE OF THE UNIVERSITY OF CAMBRIDGE
The Pitt Building, Trumpington Street, Cambridge, United Kingdom

CAMBRIDGE UNIVERSITY PRESS
The Edinburgh Building, Cambridge CB2 2RU, UK   www.cup.cam.ac.uk
40 West 20th Street, New York NY 10011-4211, USA   www.cup.org
10 Stamford Road, Oakleigh, Melbourne 3166, Australia
Ruiz de Alarcón 13, 28014 Madrid, Spain

First published 2000

Printed in the United Kingdom at the University Press, Cambridge

Typeface Plantin 10/12   *System* QuarkXPress™   [SE]

A catalogue record for this book is available from the British Library

ISBN 0 521 79175 8 hardback
ISBN 0 521 79564 8 paperback

Contents

Figures

Produced under the aegis of an ESRC
Research Fellowship

Acknowledgements

I owe many debts to those who have given me various kinds of support when writing this book. It was produced under the terms of an ESRC Research Fellowship and I am extremely grateful for being given three years of uninterrupted research.

In the Department of Sociology at the University of Warwick, I would like to thank all of those who collaborated on our joint venture, 'Challenging Rational Choice Theory'. The seminars, which have been running over a two-year period, provided a fund of ideas and represented collegiality at its best. Particular thanks are owing to Simon Williams for his detailed comments on the two chapters dealing with the emotions, which enabled me to avoid sundry potholes. Without the constant good humour of Frances Jones and Mandy Eaton over my computing deficiencies, the manuscript would never have seen the light of day.

My friends in the Centre for Critical Realism have provided continuous support and comment. They are too many to name, but I must thank Andrew Collier, Alan Norrie and Tony Lawson for reading chapters and for our discussions in the Camden Head, Islington, where ideas are grilled mercilessly. Roy Bhaskar and Doug Porpora have been constant travelling companions through this field of ideas, and once again Roy supplied a bolder title for the book than I would have dared.

Much of the argument is a debate with the spirit of Martin Hollis. I hope that I have not misrepresented him, for my respect for his contribution has grown in this writing, and my regret at no longer being able to exchange views with him in person says much about what we all have lost.

Finally, my main thanks must go to Ninian McNamara and our ongoing research into exports from the Isle of Islay, over which many of these ideas were distilled. His generous diurnal activities as a reader of drafts have done much to clarify ideas and defend the purity of the English language. The many remaining faults are entirely my responsibility.

Introduction

Twelve years ago, the idea of writing a book about human agency did not strike me as a defensive project. After all, the 'problem of structure and agency' was widely acknowledged to lie at the heart of social theorising. This could only be the case if there were a difficulty about how to link two sets of properties and powers; those belonging to the parts of society and those belonging to the people. Certainly, as I examined this linkage, first for culture (*Culture and Agency*, Cambridge University Press, 1988), and then for the structure (*Realist Social Theory: the Morphogenetic Approach*, 1995), it was very clear that some short cuts were being taken. These I called forms of 'conflation'. They were strong tendencies, rooted in classical sociology, either to let the 'parts' dominate the 'people' (downwards conflation), or alternatively, to allow the 'people' to orchestrate the 'parts' (upwards conflation). However, in terms of the philosophy of social science, these two fallacies were embedded in the old debate between Methodological Holism and Methodological Individualism, which thankfully seemed to be largely defunct. Indeed, it appeared to have been superseded by a new debate between Structuration Theorists and Social Realists. Despite their undoubted antinomy, the central task of both was to advance a framework which linked 'structure and agency'. There were hugely important differences between the 'duality of structure', advanced by structurationists, and the 'analytical dualism', advocated by critical realists, and these will continue to divide practical analysts of society. Nevertheless, they address the same problem of how to link the 'parts' and the 'people'.

Since then, there has been a full frontal assault upon agency itself, in which Modernity's 'Death of God' has now been matched by Postmodernism's 'Death of Humanity'. If one is neither a modernist nor a postmodernist, which these days does tend to mean one is a realist, then we are not funeral-goers. However, we are on the defensive. Just as over a decade ago, realists wrote books with titles like *Reclaiming Reality*[1] and

---

[1] Roy Bhaskar, *Reclaiming Reality*, Verso, London, 1989.

Reality at Risk,[2] so now it is our job to reclaim Humanity which is indeed at risk. At least, it is at risk in the Academy, where strident voices would dissolve the human being into discursive structures and humankind into a disembodied textualism. Outside of Academia, ordinary people act in undemolished fashion – they confront the world, meaning nature and practice rather than just society, for, as functioning human beings, they cannot endorse the 'linguistic fallacy'; in confronting their environment they feel a continuous sense of the self who does so, for they cannot live out their dissolution; they have cares, concerns and commitments which they see as part of themselves, for they cannot accept the 'identity' of demolished men and women; and they have social positions, which most of them would like to rectify, in at least some respect, and are unconvinced that social improvements merely depend upon discursive changes.

All this stuff of life needs confirming. This is not because lay agents are infallibly right about their agency. Indeed they are not, or there would be much less discrimination, injustice, alienation, oppression, materialism and consumerism around, and much more emancipatory collective action. However, they are hanging on to the bare bones of agency, which are the necessary pre-conditions for human activity rather than passivity. It is those that need reinforcing. This is not because I think that the emergence of postmodernist beings is a real possibility: far from it, they are such a contradiction in terms that they could never get out of bed. On the contrary, given the way in which we are constituted, the way in which the world is made, and the necessity of our interaction, I believe we are all realists – naturalistically.

Because of this, we cannot be ontologically undermined, in the same sense that natural reality never itself needed reclaiming, for it is self-subsistent. It is prevalent ideas about both which need resisting, because the spread of an epistemology of dissolution can have serious repercussions for one of our most distinctive human properties and powers – our reflexivity. Although our continuous sense of self is, I will argue, ontologically inviolable, our personal and social identities are epistemologically vulnerable. Both hinge upon our ultimate concerns and commitments. Both then can be undermined by a reflexivity which repudiates concern as anything other than ephemeral, and which thus repulses the solidarity of self and its solidarity with others, which is necessary for commitment. The reflexive turn towards inconstancy would effectively make us passive: our instant gratification may give the illusion of hyperactivity, but we would not care enough, or long enough, about anything to see it through. There is a default setting on the human being: if we do not care enough

---

[2] Roger Trigg, *Reality at Risk*, Harvester Wheatsheaf, London, 1989.

about making things happen, then we become passive beings to whom things happen.

Part I of this defence (chapters 1, 2 and 3), begins by scrutinising theories about the dissolution of humanity. It argues that the intransitive properties of human beings cannot be dissolved into the transitivity of language. The path followed by postmodernists is one which progressively tries to sever the relationship between language and the world, and then to hold the resulting sign system to be a closed one. People are reduced to nodal points through which messages pass, and the self becomes dissolved into discursive structures. The basic defence against this, which is developed throughout the book, is that the relationship between human beings and the world never can be severed. The way we are organically constituted, and the way in which the world is, together with the fact that we have to interact with the world in order to survive, let alone to flourish, means that an important part of being human is proofed against language. Specifically, to anticipate the argument developed in part II, our continuous sense of self, or self-consciousness, emerges from our practical activity in the world. It therefore cannot be demolished by any linguistic theory, for the simple reason that our sense of selfhood is independent of language.

No one of postmodernist persuasion would accept this primacy which I am defending of practice, because of their 'exorbitation of language'. Nevertheless, the postmodernist project hesitates before the total demolition of humanity. Demolished 'man' is just that, and because of it, 'he' is entirely passive. Yet certain major thinkers wanted signs of life from 'him', which amounted to significant activity. Thus, Foucault held on to the human capacity for resistance, and Rorty to the human ability for self-enrichment. Yet neither resistance nor enrichment could be coherent without a human self who engaged in them. Thus, in their thought, the postmodernist project turns full circle, and acknowledges that the human being cannot be dispensed with. However, if re-humanisation was admitted to be a necessity by some, this was with a grudging minimalism about the human properties and powers allowed back on board. Human beings were necessary, but they were not necessarily very much, in fact just a pouch which held their projects together like loose change.

In the face of this postmodernist onslaught upon humanity, minimalism became the hallmark in dealing with humankind. Just how few properties and powers could be allowed to people, in order for them to function as agents, within any alternative theoretical framework? Thus, even the opposition contributed to the impoverishment of humanity. This is the theme of part I. Firstly, 'Modernity's Man' (chapter 2), as the projection of the Enlightenment tradition, worked strenuously at stripping-down the human being until he or she had one property alone, that of rationality. Rationality was treated as pre-given, and therefore none of our relations with the world contributed anything to making us what we are. Yet, this model of *homo economicus* could not deal with our normativity or our emotionality, both of which are intentional, that is they are 'about' relations with our environment – natural, practical and social. These relationships could not be allowed to be, even partially, constitutive of who we are. Instead, the lone, atomistic and opportunistic bargain-hunter stood as the impoverished model of 'man'. One of the many things with which this model could not cope, is the human capacity to transcend instrumental rationality and to have 'ultimate concerns'. These are concerns which are not a means to anything beyond them, but are commitments which are constitutive of who we are, and an expression of our identities. To anticipate part III, 'Modernity's Man', 'who knows the price of everything and the value of nothing', lacked the wherewithal to acquire strict personal identity, which is a matter of determining our ultimate concerns and accommodating others to them.

Standing opposed to 'Modernity's Man', was 'Society's Being' (chapter 3). This is the social constructionists' contribution to the debate, which presents all our human properties and powers, beyond our biological constitution, as the gift of society. From this viewpoint, there is only one flat, unstratified, powerful particular, the human person, who is a site, or a literal point of view. Beyond that, our selfhood is a grammatical fiction, a product of learning to master the first-person pronoun system, and thus quite simply a theory of the self which is appropriated from society. This view elides the concept of self with the sense of self: we are nothing beyond what society makes us, and it makes us what we are through our joining society's conversation. However, to see us as purely cultural artefacts is to neglect the vital significance of our embodied practice in the world. This is crucial because it is these practical exchanges which are held, in part II, to be the non-linguistic sources of the sense of self. Of the many features of human beings which present difficulties to the constructionist, the most intransigent is our embodiment. Bodies have properties and powers of their own and are active in their environment, which is much broader than 'society's conversation'. The resultants of our embodied relations with the world cannot be construed as the gift of society. Constructionism thus impoverishes humanity, by subtracting from our human powers and accrediting all of them – selfhood, reflexivity, thought, memory and emotionality – to society's discourse.

Of course, what emerges in these two approaches as they impoverish humanity, are conventional forms of conflationary theorising. Conflation

How do people live in history? How do people live in history

Introduction   5

in social theory has been the critical target of this whole trilogy. Basically conflationists reject the stratified nature of social reality by denying that independent properties and powers pertain to *both* the 'parts'of society and to the 'people' within it. I have used the term conflation in preference to reduction for two reasons. The first is simply in order to accentuate the *effects* of witholding emergent properties from either agents or society. In Upwards Conflation the powers of the 'people' are held to *orchestrate* those of the 'parts': in Downwards Conflation the 'parts' *organise* the 'people'. Thus, in the cultural realm, in the Upwards version, Socio-Cultural interaction *swallowed* up the Cultural System as a group or groups dominated and directed a completely malleable corpus of ideas. In the Downwards version, Cultural Systems (logical relations between bodies of ideas like theories and beliefs) *engulfed* the Socio-Cultural level (causal relations of influence between groups) through the basic processes of regulation and socialisation. In the structural domain the same effects were encountered. Either the state and nature of 'social integration' upwardly *moulded* 'system integration', or the state and nature of 'system integration' downwardly *shaped* 'social integration'. Now, in dealing with agency, the same two unacceptable forms of conflating two real levels of analysis are readily apparent and have the same effects. 'Modernity's Man' is old-style Upwards conflation, in which the single property of rationality is held to *make* both human beings and also their society. Conversely, 'Society's Being' is old-style Downwards conflation, in which the effects of socialisation *impress* themselves upon people, seen as malleable 'indeterminate material'.

Obviously, since both forms of conflation hold that *either* the properties and the powers of the 'parts' *or* of the 'people' are epiphenomena of the other, then they are reductionist theories. Downwards conflation means that the properties of the 'people' can be 'upwardly reduced' to properties of the system, which alone has causal powers. Upwards conflation means that the properties of the 'parts' can be 'downwardly reduced' to properties of the 'people', who alone have causal powers. This may seem to introduce unnecessary terminological confusion, but these *methodological* procedures for reduction do not really capture the downward weight of the systemic upon the social, or the untramelled freedom of the people to make structure, culture and themselves, which play such a prominent part in conflationary theorising. Nevertheless, conflation and reduction rest upon exactly the same ontological bases. That is *either* the 'parts' *or* the 'people' are held to be the *ultimate constituents* of social reality, to which the other could be reduced. Therefore, were all that were at stake a matter of *picturing* how epiphenomenalism works in actual theories, rather than methodological charters, then the introduction of the term 'conflation' (and its directionality) might be considered an unwarranted source of confusion.

However, there is another and more compelling reason for introducing it. This is because there is a third form of conflation which does not endorse reductionism at all. There is Central conflation which is *a*reductionist, because it insists upon the inseparability of the 'parts' and the 'people'. In other words, the fallacy of conflation does not *depend* upon epiphenomenalism, on rendering one level of social reality inert and thus reducible. Epiphenomenalism is not the only way in which the 'parts' or the 'people' are deprived of their emergent, autonomous and causally efficacious properties and powers, and that in consequence their interplay is denied. Any form of conflation has the same consequences. Hence, conflation is the more generic error and reductionism is merely a form of it, or rather two particular cases of it.

This is demonstrated by Central conflation, where elision occurs in the 'middle'. This directional approach, which is reflowering at the moment, interprets neither the 'parts' nor the 'people' as epiphenomena of one another. Indeed, it is precisely their opposition to reduction which is the prime article of faith among modern proponents of Central conflation. Instead, what happens is that autonomy is withheld from *both levels* because they are held to be mutually constitutive. These theories have been encountered before when examining those who elide culture and agency[3] and structure and agency.[4] As mutually constitutive, the two elements cannot be untied and therefore their reciprocal influences cannot be teased out, which is held to be their major defect and one which severely limits their utility in practical social research. They will be encountered again during the present examination of agency itself, particularly in the theorising of Giddens and Bourdieu. Their respective approaches to human practices generically preclude one from disengaging the properties and powers of the practitioner from the properties and powers of the environment in which practices are conducted – and yet again this prevents analysis of their interplay. Instead, we are confronted with amalgams of 'practices' which oscillate wildly between voluntarism and determinism, without our being able to specify the conditions under which agents have greater degrees of freedom or, conversely, work under a considerable stringency of constraints.

What realism needs to do is not to re-animate the old debate between Upwards and Downwards conflationism, although both fallacies will be

---

[3] See Margaret S. Archer, *Culture and Agency*, Cambridge University Press, 1988, Chapter 4.
[4] See Margaret S. Archer, *Realist Social Theory: the Morphogenetic Approach*, Cambridge University Press, 1995, chapter 4.

found to be alive and well in 'Modernity's Man' and 'Society's Being', respectively. Nor should social realists dally with the ranks of Central conflationists, even though they share a critique of reductionism, because they do so on diametrically opposed grounds. The elision of the 'parts' and the 'people' in Central conflation is *a*reductionist: realism, which stresses the independent properties and powers of both is firmly *anti*-reductionist. Therefore, social realism should continue where it is going, namely struggling on to link the 'parts' and the 'people', without conceding for a moment that their respective properties and powers can be reduced to one another, or should be regarded as inseparable and mutually constitutive .

The direct implication then, is that social realists have to be a good deal more precise about these properties and powers of human beings, and how they emerge through our *relations* with the world, which cannot be narrowly construed as 'society', let alone as 'language', 'discourse' and 'conversation'. This task is begun in part II, which deals with our *continuous sense of self*, or self-consciousness. It has to begin there, because without a continuous sense that we are one and the same being over time, then even the two impoverished models just introduced cannot get off the ground, let alone a more robust conception of humanity. 'Modernity's Man' needs this sense of self if he is consistently to pursue his so-called fixed preference schedule, for he has to know both that they are his preferences and also how he is doing in maximising them over time. Similarly, 'Society's Being' also needs this sense of self, rather than a grammatical fiction, in order to know that social obligations pertain to her, rather than just being diffuse expectations, and that when they clash, then it is she who is put on the spot, and has to exercise a creativity which cannot be furnished by consulting the discursive canon. Unscripted performances, which hold society together, need an active agent who is enough of a self to acknowledge her obligation to perform and to write her own script to cover the occasion.

The realist approach to humanity thus begins by presenting an account of this sense of self, which is prior to, and primitive to, our sociality. Self consciousness derives from our embodied practices in the world. Because acquiring a continuous sense of self entails practices, then it also involves work. This is what sets it apart from the pre-given character of 'Modernity's Man'. Because it emerges at the nexus of our embodied encounters with the world, this is what sets it apart from 'Society's Being'. One of the most important properties that we have, the power to know ourselves to be the same being over time, depends upon practice in the environment rather than conversation in society. Instead, the sequence which leads to the emergence of our selfhood derives from how our species-being interacts with the way the world is, which is independent of how we take it to be, or the constructions we put upon it. Each one of us has to discover, through embodied practice, the distinctions between self and otherness, then between subject and object, before finally arriving at the distinction between the self and other people. Only when these distinctions have been learned through embodied practice can they then be expressed in language.

Chapter 4 draws upon Merleau-Ponty's account of how our embodied encounters instil the sense of self and otherness. This is a continuous sense of self to him, because of the necessary continuity of the relations which people have to sustain with the natural environment throughout their lives, that is even after they become fully social beings. To Merleau-Ponty it is our embodied memories which give us the sense of our own continuity. This is highly compatible with Locke's conception of the self, where the continuous sense that we are one and the same being over time hinged upon the body and our memories. Locke has always been vulnerable to the charge that he made the continuous sense of self depend upon perfect recall, which is manifestly defective in most of us. However, modern neurobiology now views memory as a living storage system, which would be dysfunctional if everything were retained, and this therefore means that total recall is not what we should expect to find in the non-pathological human being. Instead, neurobiology gives evidence of our durable powers of recognition, our lasting and distinctive eidetic memories and the indelibility of our performative skills. Significantly, none of these are language dependent, yet together they are sufficient to supply a continuous sense of self, which is unique to each individual and thus anchors their strict self-identity.

The primacy of practice, rather than of language, has thus been defended in relation to that prime human power, our self-consciousness. To possess this power also implies that we are reflexive beings, for to know oneself to be the same being over time, means that one can think about it. The final stage of the argument about embodied practice as the source of the sense of self is completed by seeking to demonstrate the primacy of practice in the development of thought itself. Here, Piaget's experimental demonstrations that it is the child's own practical activities which serve to instil the logical principles of identity and non-contradiction, show our powers of thinking and reasoning to be neither pre-given nor to be the gift of society – they have to be realised in and through practice.

However, it could be rejoined that all I have defended is the primacy of practice in early childhood development. Thus it could be countered that once we become fully part of society's conversation, it takes over the baton in directing our lives, and practice falls into the background. Chapter 5 is devoted to anticipating this objection. Firstly, it seeks to show that practical relations are life-long because we all have ineluctable relations with nature and with material culture. In short we never cease, and never can cease, to sustain relations with all three orders of reality – natural, practical and social. We are incapable of living life as solely discursive beings, and what we make of our lives cannot thus be captured on the Hamlet model. More ambitiously, this chapter seeks to show not only that practice is enduring, not only that it is indispensable to human comportment in the world, but also that it is pivotal to the knowledge which we gain from nature and from society, which have to be filtered through practice – the fulcrum of knowledge. Thus we remain embedded in the world as a whole, and cannot be detached from the other orders of reality to become 'Society's Being'. Conversely, the discursive order, far from being independent and hegemonic, remains closely interdependent with nature and with practice.

The fact that, as human beings, we necessarily live out our lives in all three orders of reality, natural, practical and social, provides the bridge to part III. This moves on from human beings as the bearers of a *continuous sense of self*, a property which they acquire early on in life, to their active acquisition of a *personal identity* at maturity. Our selfhood is unique, but it can largely be constituted by the things that have happened to us. Certainly, it entails active interplay with the environment in which individuals find themselves, but it cannot be pro-active in selecting this environment. Personal identity, however, hinges precisely upon the emergence of a mature ability to take a reflective overview of the three orders of reality in which we are ineluctably engaged. Because of our constitution in relation to the constitution of the world, we cannot ignore any of these three orders with impunity: nevertheless, we can prioritise where our predominant concerns lie and accommodate our other concerns to them. It is the distinctive patterning of these concerns which is held to give people their unique personal identities.

Thus chapter 6 defends the proposition that we live, and must live, simultaneously in the natural, practical and social orders. It presents our emotions as the commentaries made upon our welfare in the world. Distinctive emotional clusters represent different types of commentary upon the inexorable human concerns attaching to these three orders in which we live out our lives. The three kinds of emotional imports relate to our physical well-being in the natural order, our performative achievement in the practical order and our self-worth in the social order. Here, there is a major dilemma for every human being, because their flourishing depends upon their attending to all three kinds of emotional commentaries, and yet these do not dovetail harmoniously: attention to one can jeopardise giving due heed to the others. For example, to respond to physical fear may constitute cowardice in our social roles and incompetence in exercising our practical skills. Because no one can live satisfactorily by simply heeding the strongest emotional commentary *seriatim*, then everyone is constrained to strike a balance between our trinity of inescapable human concerns. This means prioritising our concerns, but without neglecting those pertaining to other orders: these can be relegated but they must be accommodated. Which precise balance we strike, and what exactly features as our ultimate concerns is what gives us our strict identity as particular persons – our personal identity.

The way in which this is achieved is examined in chapter 7, which explores the role of the 'inner conversation' as the process which generates our concrete singularity. The internal dialogue entails disengaging our ultimate concerns from our subordinate ones and then involves elaborating the constellation of commitments with which each one of us feels we can live. The 'inner conversation' is about exploring the terms of a liveable degree of solidarity for the self in its commitments, and the unique *modus vivendi* to emerge is what defines the uniqueness of personal identity. Whereas self-identity, the possession of a continuous sense of self, was held to be universal to human beings, personal identity is an achievement. It comes only at maturity but it is not attained by all: it can be lost, yet re-established.

In short, we are who we are because of what we care about: in delineating our ultimate concerns and accommodating our subordinate ones, we also define ourselves. We give a shape to our lives, which constitutes our internal personal integrity, and this pattern is recognisable by others as our concrete singularity. Without this rich inner life of reflection upon reality, which is the generative mechanism of our most important personal emergent property, our unique identity and way of being in the world, then we are condemned to the impoverishment of either 'Modernity's Man' or 'Society's Being', neither of whom play a robust and active role in who they are. They have been rendered passive because they have been morally evacuated; since they themselves are not allowed to play a major part in the making of their own lives. Realism revindicates real powers for real people who live in the real world.

However, we do not make our personal identities under the circumstances of our own choosing. Our placement in society rebounds upon us, affecting the persons we become, but also and more forcefully influencing the social identities which we can achieve. Personal and social identity must not be elided, because the former derives from our relations with all three orders of reality, whilst our social selves are defined only in social terms. Nevertheless, the emergence of the two are intertwined, which is the subject of part IV.

Chapter 8 begins the account of the path trodden by all people towards the social identity that they may ultimately achieve. It starts with our involuntary placement as Primary Agents. At birth we are assigned to positions on society's distribution of resources, which means that we become members of *collectivities* who share the same life-chances. As such, the 'I', the subject of self-consciousness, discovers the 'Me' as the object of society, who is involuntarily either privileged or non-privileged. Such positions are entirely objective, but their transformation depends partly upon the subjective reflexivity of Primary Agents in seeking to play an active part in the re-shaping of society's resource distribution. In large part, their success depends upon their capacity to realise collective action and to transform themselves into Corporate Agents. The articulation of aims and the development of organisation to achieve them, is an emergent power which enables Corporate Agency to become strategically involved in shaping social change. However, socio-cultural configurations have their own emergent properties and powers, and the deterrent effects of morphostatic formations constrain the ability of Primary Agents to become Corporate Agents, whilst morphogenetic scenarios positively enable such collective action. The configurations stretching from Pre-Modernity, through Modernity, to High Modernity are presented as increasingly enabling the disengagement of more and more Corporate Agents, which leaves a much reduced and residual category of those condemned to the passivity of Primary Agency – to accepting the characteristics of the 'Me' which they have been involuntarily assigned.

Thus, there is a historical movement from the 'Me', which seeks to make out *within* the confines of the existing socio-cultural structures, towards the 'We' which together seeks strategically to *transform* such structures. Corporate Agency transforms itself in pursuing social transformation. Primarily it does this, in the course of its struggles, by inducing the elaboration of the institutional role structure. New roles are created, and these constitute new positions in which more people can willingly invest themselves. Corporate Agency alone does not represent strict social identity, since participants are still merely members of a group. However, the elaboration of the role structure which it introduces provides the bridge towards attaining social identity for increasing sections of the population.

In this way, in chapter 9, the Agent is presented as the parent of the Actor. Strict social identity is achieved by assuming a role(s) and personifying it, by investing oneself in it and executing it in a singular manner. Reasons for incumbency are found within Agency itself, since the roles adopted will narrow the gap between the 'I', whom an individual seeks to become, and the 'Me', whom they have previously been constrained to be. Here, the problem has always been, *who* does this personifying: *who* is sufficient of an individual to produce a unique performance in a role? Particularly if their social identity is held to derive *from* the role, then this cannot be the source of their unique execution of it. Thus we need to introduce personal identity to supply at least sufficient concrete singularity for this to be brought to the role. People will of course change with the experience they acquire in living out the role, which is why the final consolidation of personal identity and social identity are dialectically related. The moments of their interplay are disentangled, but it is concluded that social identity remains a sub-set of a much broader personal identity. This is because our personal identities are forged in the three orders of reality – natural, practical, as well as social. Therefore, it is ultimately the person who determines where the self-worth, that he or she derives from their social roles, stands in relation to their other commitments in the world as a whole. It is also the person who arbitrates upon the relative importance of their multiple social roles and between their greedy demands. Once again it is the person who strikes the balance *within* their social concerns and *between* them and other concerns. They can only do this by prioritising their ultimate concerns, which will determine *how much* of themselves is invested in their social identities, and therefore *what* they will bring to living them out.

Our commitments, which define us as persons and also define what kinds of social Actors we become, are subject to continuous internal review. Thus we return to the inner conversation which never ceases. In it, the 'I' whom I have become, periodically re-visits the 'Me' and evaluates its (newly) acquired and objective characteristics. The judgement reached then tendentially influences the 'We', with whom one will work in solidarity, to induce further social transformations. Finally, the 'You', the maker of the future, is constantly subject to inner deliberation about the continuity of its commitments. Together, the 'I' and the 'You' may re-endorse, revise or renege on their prime concerns at any time. The self, in solidarity, must determine whether and how to project forward its existing social identity, according to the priority which it is assigned within the overall personal identity. Personal identity is an accomplishment, but it has to be reconstituted from day to day by a re-affirmation and renewal of our concerns. Such active continuity makes us recognisable to others in our concrete singularity and consistent as social Actors through the consistency of our personified conduct in our social positions.

It has been suggested that 'two stories' are involved in the subject matter of this book. Some have maintained that there will always be an 'outsiders' account, dealing with the external socio-cultural factors which position us and predispose us to various courses of action. On the other hand, there is the 'insiders' hermeneutic account of what agents believe they are doing in their activities. The implication is that we can begin with either agential reasons or social causes, but that at best each story will be filled in from the other side. Because realism does not accept this division between 'reasons' and 'causes', I have maintained that there is only one story to tell. Society enters into us, but we can reflect upon it, just as we reflect upon nature and upon practice. Without such referential reality there would be nothing substantive to reflect upon; but without our reflections we would have only a physical impact upon reality. This is why there is only one story. It is the long account of how human beings are constituted, how the world is made, and of the necessity of their mutual interaction.

Part I

The impoverishment of humanity

1   Resisting the dissolution of humanity

Humanity is seen as the linchpin of agency in general and is therefore crucial to how one side of the 'problem of structure and agency' is conceptualised.[1] Too often we are presented with reductionist accounts, which either make all that we are the gift of society or, conversely, which claim that all society is can be derived from what we are. Instead, both humanity and society have their own *sui generis* properties and powers, which makes their interplay the central issue of social theory for all time. This book is concerned with the emergence of our human properties and powers. They are relational: stemming from the way our species is constituted, the way the world is and the necessity of their mutual interaction. The relations between the two, being universal, supply the anchor which moors our elaborated human forms as Selves, Persons, Agents and Actors, and thus sets limits to their variability. Humanity, as a natural kind, defies transmutation into another and different kind. It is this which sustains the thread of intelligibility between people of different times and places, and without it the thread would break. It is this too which underpins our moral and political responsibilities to humankind *despite* the socio-cultural differences of groups – for these are never big enough for them to leave the human family and dispense us from our obligations to family members.

Another way of putting this is that human interaction with the world constitutes the transcendental conditions of human development, which otherwise remain as unrealised *potentia* of our species. However, it must be stressed from the start that there is more to the world than society (which until recently would have been unnecessary), and that all of its constituent orders contribute to our human being and to what it is to be human in the world. Indeed, my key argument maintains that it is

---

[1] Although these large claims were made in the first two parts of this trilogy (*Culture and Agency*, Cambridge University Press, 1988 and *Realist Social Theory: The Morphogenetic Approach*, Cambridge University Press, 1995), their justification was postponed until this last volume. This book is intended to redeem the promissory notes scattered through the previous ones.

precisely because of our interaction with the natural, practical and transcendental orders that humanity has prior, autonomous and efficacious powers which it brings to society itself – and which intertwine with those properties of society which make us social beings, without which, it is true, we would certainly not be recognisably human. This book will confine itself to working on our feet of clay, that is our relations with the natural and practical orders of reality, because these are all that are needed for the defence of humanity as *sui generis* within sociology.

My stress upon the transcendental necessity of relations with nature for the possibility of being a human, should clearly serve to separate this view of common humanity from the Enlightenment model of intrinsically rational 'Man', characterised by 'his'[2] mastery over nature. Here the natural relations of people are neither ones confined to instrumental rationality nor ones which can be captured by notions of mastery. Indeed our most basic practices, basic in terms of our physical survival, are better portrayed as our embodied accommodation to the mercy of nature, and not the other way around. As we accommodate, we do indeed learn things, *inter alia*, about means and ends but these come after the event; they cannot be construed as part of our natural attitude in advance.

It should be clear that my objective is to reclaim the notion of common humanity, even if its practical grounding has not yet been explicated. Although the present work distances itself from the Enlightenment concept of man, it does not do so by the radical device of de-centring, dissolving or demolishing the human subject. Because the aim is to salvage a workable notion of humankind, this book is also hostile to the postmodernist mood, where the inclination of theorists is to distance themselves from the metaphysics of modernity by scrapping humanity. I wish to reclaim human beings as the ultimate *fons et origio* of (emergent) social life or socio-cultural structures, rather than subjugating humanity, as if it were the epiphenomenon of social forces.

The following quotations from leading postmodernists (their immediate predecessors and fellow-travellers) reflect not only the 'death of Man' but also the method of his demise. What could appear on the death certificate is 'asphyxiation by social forces'.

'I believe the ultimate goal of the human sciences to be not to constitute, but to dissolve man.' (Lévi-Stauss)[3]

---

[2] Rational 'Man' was the term current in Enlightenment thinking. Because it is awkward to impose inclusive language retrospectively and distracting to insert inverted commas, I reluctantly abide with the term Man, as standing for humanity, when referring to this tradition, its heirs, successors and adversaries.

[3] C. Lévi-Strauss, *The Savage Mind*, London, 1966.

(Humanity) that 'spongy referent, that opaque but equally translucence reality, that nothingness' an 'opaque nebula whose growing density absorbs all the surrounding energy and light rays, to collapse finally under its own weight'. (Baudrillard)[4]

'Man would be erased, like a face drawn in sand at the edge of the sea.' (Foucault)[5]

'With the spread of postmodernist consciousness we see the demise of personal definition, reason, authority, commitment, trust, the sense of authenticity, sincerity, belief in leadership, depth of feeling and faith in progress. In their stead, an open slate emerges on which persons may inscribe, erase and rewrite their identities as the ever-shifting, ever-expanding and incoherent network of relationships invites or permits.' (Gergen)[6]

'Identities are points of temporary attachment to the subject positions which discursive practices construct for us. They are the result of a successful articulation or "chaining" of the subject into the flow of discourse.' (Stuart Hall)[7]

'A *self* does not amount to much.' (Lyotard)[8]

'Socialisation . . . goes all the way down.' (Rorty)[9]

This displacement of the human subject and celebration of the power of social forces to shape and to mould is the epitome of what I have termed Downwards conflation. For 'a *self* does not amount to much'[10] is a view redolent of the human being seen as 'indeterminate material' by Durkheim. To both, the epiphenomenal status of humankind deflects all real interest onto the forces of socialisation. People are indeed perfectly uninteresting if they possess no personal powers which can make a difference. Of course, if this is the case then it is hard to see how they can offer any resistance, for even if it is ineffectual it has to stem from someone who at least amounts to the proportions of an irritant (and must thus be credited minimally with the personal power to challenge). Foucault was to face the problems set up by this one-dimensional, sociocentric account and there is evidence in his later work that he began to reinstate a more robust self concept, one strong enough to restore the 'problem of structure and agency' which the notion of resistance

[4] J. Baudrillard, *In the Shadow of the Silent Majorities*, New York, Semiotext(e), 1983.
[5] M. Foucault, *The Order of Things*, New York, Random House, 1970, p. 387.
[6] Gergen, *The Saturated Self*, New York, Basic Books, 1991.
[7] Stuart Hall, 'Who Needs Identity?', in Hall, S. and Du Gay, P. (eds.), *Questions of Cultural Identity*, London, Sage, 1996.
[8] J-F. Lyotard, *The Postmodern Condition*, Minneapolis, University of Minnesota Press, 1984.
[9] Richard Rorty, *Contingency, Irony and Solidarity*, Cambridge University Press,1989, p. 185.
[10] Lyotard, *The Postmodern Condition*, p. 15.

ineluctably implies. In short the programme of dissolution turns out to be circular in that it returns grudgingly to examine the *two* terms and the interplay between them in order to account for outcomes. Explanation of these is, of course, the charter of the Analytical Dualism[11] advocated here, but there are crucial reasons why there can be no *rapprochement* with post-modernism which goes deeper than the fact that not all postmodernists have followed Foucault's re-turn.

There is a much more profound circularity running through post-modernist thought if it is to be regarded as a contribution to social theor-ising rather than a prolongation of the fiesta of May 1968: that is as an investigator of events rather than a participator in the *évènements*. This circularity concerns the stance taken towards anthropocentricism. Below I will consider three questions about the postmodernists' view of human-ity whose answers ultimately tend to a very different conclusion from the brutalist presentation of humankind contained in the cluster of dismissive quotations just given. If we consider sequentially, (a) *why* this de-centring of Man?; (b) *how* was humanity dissolved?, and; (c) *what* personal self this leaves for sociological investigation and theorising?; the progression of answers comes full circle. And this is a vicious circle both for post-modernist consistency and for utility in social analysis.

The basic answer to 'Why de-centre?' was in order to demolish the anthropocentricism explicit in Rational Man as master of all he surveyed, with consciousness thus being the source of history. The answer to how he was dethroned was by installing an anti-humanism which made him the recipient rather than the maker of history. But when we come to what kind of consequences this has for the social 'sciences' there are three pos-sible responses. The first sometimes tells us that we, as sociologists, have perished with humankind, washed away with the face of Man, for 'All that remains to be done is to play with the pieces' now that 'history has stopped.'[12] We can make art but not sociology (who remains to appreciate these aesthetics we will leave to Rorty to tell). Ultimately, author-less texts without referents swing free as the product of disembodied forces, not the cumulative production of succeeding agential generations of critics. What we make of them is our game in the here and now.

The second bids us engage in an idealist reification of process-without-a-maker or discourse-without-a-speaker or texts-without-an-author, which ironically turns out to be anthropocentric for it installs the inter-preter in a position of rhetorical authority in place of the absented inten-tional agent. Perhaps this accounts for its popularity, but it makes it a

---

[11] See, *Realist Social Theory*, ch. 6.
[12] Baudrillard, 'On Nihilism', *On the Beach*, 6, 1984, pp. 24–5.

thoroughgoing form of anthropocentricity, even though an intergenerational one, since successive interpreters must endlessly defer to their successors and their successors to their children's children's interpretations.

Yet there is a third answer, forthcoming externally from those disinclined to shake their sandals free of postmodernism and yet who seek instead a rescuable account of reason, truth and self embedded in it which can still sustain the sociological enterprise. The paradox is that this version recommits the anthropocentric fallacy with a vengeance. It concurs with the 'Death of God' at the price of resurrecting Man. For if a 'God's eye view' can provide no knowledge of the world, told in disembodied worldspeak, then our only recourse is to knowledge generated from our own human perspectives – incarnational and perspectival knowledge which has to reinvoke the human point of view. Both the circularity and the fallacy consist in now over-privileging people's emergent properties (PEPs), for our access to the social is via what human beings can tell us of it. Since they are not merely fallible (as we all agree) but necessarily limited in their perspectives, then structural and cultural emergent properties (SEPs and CEPs) are under-privileged because they can only be grasped through what people say. This is quite a different statement from the activity-dependence of social forms stressed by social realists. That never presumes full knowledgeability on the part of agents (we cannot discover the nature of social structure by administering questionnaires), whereas this does assume full agential discursive penetration. Or if it does not, it condemns the investigator to the same ignorance of social processes as their subjects. The reason is that we shall find this analysis to be confined to the Humean level of the event, for only the actual rather than the real is accessible to direct human perception from the human perspective.

As a social realist, I would seek to rescue social theory from both the postmodernists and their charitable humanistic defenders. For we must neither under- nor over-privilege human agency in our analytical approach. In contesting both the original and the derivative positions on humanity and its role in society and sociology alike, the realist does not seek to prop-up modernity's model of Man. We are just as critical of such attempts, represented by the Rational Choice theorists' model of the utility maximising bargain-hunter, as of demolished Man. Such latter-day proponents of the Enlightenment model are fully anthropocentric in their Upward conflation, for it is some property of people (usually their in-built rationality, though sometimes modified by social additives such as normativity) which is held to account for the entirety of the social context – by a process of aggregation. The deficiencies involved in reducing structure (SEPs) and culture (CEPs) to aggregate properties, rather than emergent ones with their own causal powers, have been rehearsed in *Realist Social Theory* (ch.2), but it is the sourceless, fully asocial, rational abstraction which stands for agency which is criticised here (see chapter 2).

Instead of rehabilitating Enlightenment Man with his incorporeal consciousness, or any equally mentalistic portrayals of humanity, social realism makes our real embodied selves living in the real world really load-bearing. It constitutes a naturalistic account of consciousness rather than taking the latter as an *a prioristic* endowment. Nevertheless, contra postmodernism, this is an account of consciousness with a real history which, in turn, ultimately accounts for there being real world history. Far from being groundless, it is firmly grounded in the natural praxis of humanity; ways of being in the world without which the species would not survive as a natural kind to develop its potential properties – all of which at conception only exist *in potentia*. These natural relations are the source not only of consciousness but also of our distinctive self reflexivity, whose origins are equally practical. It should be noted, to complete this aerial view, that this insistence upon natural praxis does not align the humankind conceptualised by realists with the ontology of praxis held by Central Conflationists, such as advocates of Structuration Theory.[13] For their 'ontology of praxis' would deny the autonomy, priority and causal efficacy of natural relations, since every practice is held to draw upon socio-structural properties. It therefore also denies questions about the interplay between natural and social practices, which cannot even be addressed from within that framework.

I   Social imperialism and linguistic terrorism

However, to return to postmodernism as the *apogée* of Downwards conflation, let us trace through my contentious claim that this most avowedly anti-humanist stance actually does come full circle to advocate an unacceptably anthropocentric position. We begin by returning to the three questions listed above.

Why de-centre humanity?

Postmodernists usually pay their intellectual respects to Nietzsche. In particular they align themselves with him in attacking the Enlightenment for having allowed the 'death of God' to issue in titanic Man (as if thought abhors a vacuum in the cult of personality). Thus with the secularisation

---

[13] See *Realist Social Theory*, ch. 4.

of modernity went a progressive humanistic endorsement of human self-determination, of people's powers to come to know the world, master their environment and thus control their own destiny as the 'measure of all things'. This lies at the heart of humanism, a tough doctrine not to be confused with secularised humaneness: it is not the latter gentle belief that 'people matter', but the more strident doctrine that nothing matters at all except in so far as it matters to man.

As Kate Soper puts it, this 'Humanist thought is very commonly described as "anthropocentric": it places Man at the centre. But there are different ways of doing so. One is to assume from the outset an opposition between an "external", objectively existing world on the one hand, and human subjects possessed of consciousness, on the other. In this view, "Man" is conceived as standing "outside" the reality which is given him in consciousness. It is a standpoint that promotes and endorses an instrumental conception of the relations between humanity and the non-human or "natural" world: Nature exists for Man, who by means of an objective knowledge of its workings, harnesses it in the service of human ends.'[14] This seems a very fair encapsulation of the Enlightenment model of the modern self. Not only does this self stand outside nature as its master, it also stands outside history as the lone individual whose relations with others are not in any way constitutive of the self, but are merely contingent accretions, detachable from our essence. Thus the modern self is not contingently made but is universally given. Because all that is contingent can be stripped from this self, it can step forward as a purely logocentric being whose consciousness, freed from any embedding in historical circumstances, can pellucidly articulate the cosmic story. As the 'Pure Visitor' in Gellner's terms,[15] logocentric man is by nature the perfect recorder (he does not have the moral struggle of honest Chroniclers, condemned in advance to fail in eradicating their subjective biases). The metaphysics of modernity thus adduced a model of instrumentally rational man who could attain his ends in the world by pure *logos*, a rationality working through the formal manipulation of linguistic symbols to generate truth.

Yet the very quest for truth is dismissed by postmodernists as a human *folie de grandeur*. It was dismissed in part (the one that concerns us here) because of the fundamental error entailed in holding human consciousness to be the mirror of nature. The human subject is not the 'origin' of knowledge, nor is meaning derived from what is self-evident to the human mind. Indeed, since there is no progressive mastery, either

[14] Kate Soper, *Humanism and Anti-Humanism*, London, Hutchinson, 1986, p. 24.
[15] Ernest Gellner, *Thought and Change*, London, Weidenfeld and Nicolson, 1964, pp. 105–13.

epistemological or ontological, neither is there a story to be told about the mastery of progress. With the anathematisation of such historical meta-narratives came the explicit concern with the whole status of history, and who, if anyone 'made it'. To privilege human makers is to misconstrue historical thought as humanist mythology: it is to throw up the Cartesian *cogito* onto the big screen and backwards over time. Instead, to Lévi-Strauss, history has neither meaning, nor subject, nor object – 'We have only to recognise that *history is a method with no distinct object corresponding to it* to reject the equivalence between the notion of history and the notion of humanity which some have tried to foist on us with the unavowed aim of making historicity the last refuge of a transcendental humanism.'[16]

Where then does that leave humankind? Not as the makers of history, because history as metanarrative is dead, not as the honest chronicler because truth is dead, and not as the external observer because our refer-ential language is dead too. These fatalities spell the dethronement of the previous masters of nature, but what status do they now occupy? Those who previously harnessed nature and made history progress are now themselves harnessed and subjugated. Instead of being the subjects who mediated these realities through their consciousness and rationality, the fact that referential reality has died the death too means that they are sub-jected to the play of meanings which are all that remain. Demoted from being makers of something real, true and progressive, once all of these terms have been contested, humankind itself figures among the 'made'. Meanings now become constitutive of humanity itself and not vice versa. Our status is that of semiological objects, *homo significans*, or cultural sub-jects. And culture itself has shrunk: there is neither the cultural cut and thrust amongst groups with real interests, nor the continuous elaboration of the Cultural System with internal relationships of contradiction and complementarity as its emergent properties, which impinge causally upon interested parties, as was described in *Culture and Agency*. Instead, to Lacan, 'culture could well be reduced to language'.[17]

The postmodernist denies human subjects any form of external mastery over society's development and form, in opposition to the Enlightenment model which gave them complete sway. The intermediate position where structure and agency conjointly determine society's tra-jectory, whose shape is an unintended consequence conforming to the exact desires of no one, is passed over. If humankind cannot be the master of society it becomes the slave of one of its sub-systems, culture, restric-tively presented as language. In the next section, which deals with how

[16] C. Lévi-Strauss, *The Savage Mind*, London, 1966, p. 269. My italics.
[17] J. Lacan, *Ecrits*, London, 1997, p. 148.

humanity was lost, we will find a common thread uniting structuralist, post-structuralist and full-blown postmodernist thought, namely 'the concern is with the universal inscription of humankind within language and systems of codification which regulate all human experience and activity, and therefore lie beyond the control of either individuals or social groups.'[18] However, in trying to answer why humanity was de-centred in terms of a revulsive reversal of the primacy assigned to it by the Enlightened model, a major difficulty has already been encountered. Since all that now constitutes our selves are local contingencies, then this presages the collapse of any concept of self identity *qua* human beings. The de-centring of the Enlightenment concept of the human being leads directly to an actual dissolution of the self which is then kaleidoscopically shaped by the flux of historical contingencies. References to the human being become indefinite, since contingency deprives them of a common denominator, and thus any coherent idea of *human* identity is lost. To return to the quotations at the beginning of this chapter, it seems as if humankind will not be mourned: but as we will see a little later, some of the jobs performed by human beings in social theorising will be so indispensable as to make them subjects of attempted resuscitation.

The dissolution of humanity

The human being, as a causally efficacious subject was exposed to a linguistic terrorism which intensified over the stages of thought paving the way to postmodernism – structuralism, post-structuralism and textualism. Rather than being the source of referential meanings in the real world, humanity was increasingly turned into an entity constituted by language – a movement from subject to subjectification and subjugation.

This represents the most radical form of Downwards conflation encountered in these studies, because postmodernism not only asserts the primacy of (linguistic) structure over human agency, it ultimately seeks to dissolve the human subject entirely. This tough anti-humanism insisted upon the priority of circumstance over will in opposition to the Enlightened humanist emphasis on the primacy of will over circumstances.[19] This opposition is general when these two convictions confront one another: what was distinctive was that the *only* circumstances given consideration were *linguistic* ones. Noting this from the beginning is crucial, because such persuasiveness as these views carry is crucially dependent on what they leave out and encourage us to ignore by their own silences. Specifically what is omitted is that the causal powers of

---

[18] Kate Soper, *Humanism and Anti-Humanism*, p. 97.   [19] Ibid., p. 151.

social and cultural structures are of a different order from language, which is in no sense paradigmatic of them. As Anderson has argued, the exchange of words in no way models the exchange of women in kinship structures or of goods in the market economy for the latter cannot be 'defined in terms of exchange at all: production and property are always prior.'[20]

Certainly, the terms in which modern metaphysics had been cast since Descartes introduced a dualism between brute matter (what was there) versus human consciousness (what to do), which served to facilitate this one-sided concentration on the latter term amongst its postmodernist opponents. Realism, instead, challenges the dualism itself, particularly our inheritance of the is/ought distinction from it. As Collier argues, one could not make sense of the simplest intentional action, like making tea, unless it was taken for granted that the way things are does provide grounds for action.[21] In general, realists would claim priority for practice over language, which is the theme to which this whole book is devoted, but modernist metaphysics, rooted in the Cartesian *cogito*, begins from the opposite and non-practical conception of consciousness and experience and this non-practicality has ironically passed directly on to postmodernism. Yet the normal place of thought is as an aspect of practice. It can never be independent of reality as Cartesian thought is, since if it confronts no other, it cannot evade the concepts, theories, beliefs and so on which are lodged in the Cultural System. And the C.S. contains a whole series of emergent relationships between items which cannot be reduced to the relations between words, because once they have developed they can be expressed in an unlimited number of alternative words (consider the limitless semantic forms in which propositional contradictions between religious and scientific convictions can be expressed). It is not the word-to-word relationship which matters, but the logical relations of contradiction and complementarity in the 'systemic register' since these impinge upon the fundamental activity of holding an idea.

Saussure's 'exorbitation of language',[22] follows the path of nonpracticality by severing the relationship between language and the world and holding the sign system to be a closed one. Signs are not prior to the relations between them, but themselves arise out of the play of differences between them. The system of *langue*, thus constituted, is 'radically arbitrary' to the world of objects. Therefore linguistic terms acquire identity, not by consistency of reference, but only in so far as they are

---

[20] Perry Anderson, *In the Tracks of Historical Materialism*, London, 1983, p. 43.
[21] Andrew Collier, 'Language, Practice and Realism, in Ian Parker (ed.), *Social Constructionism, Discourse and Reality*, London, Sage, 1998, p. 53.
[22] Perry Anderson, *In the Tracks*, p. 40.

differentiated from other signs by their differences. Hence the subject is no longer constitutive of *langue* by endowing words with meaning, that is referring to objects to which he has access. Rather meaning is now autonomous, it is not the creation of speakers who instead merely and 'passively assimilate' the system produced by the interplay of signifiers. In short, consciousness is necessarily mediated by discourse which transcends the human subject who has no exit from the linguistic system.

However, there are various ways in which Saussure's theory of meaning, as the play of differences between signifer and signified, was not hermetically sealed against the real world or the subjects' practical activity within it. Firstly, reality was not entirely banished. Signs after all signify something, and, although Saussure sought to confine these referents to 'ideas and concepts', reality kept obtruding, for how could the arbitrary nature of the signifiers 'boeuf' and 'ox' be articulated without the fact that these two terms referred to the same animal in reality? Secondly, he does not in fact manage to sustain the argument that all linguistic values stem entirely from differences, because which differences *count* depends upon the *practical* interests *of the subjects involved*. Thus in his famous 'Paris–Geneva–Train' example, this retains its identity for the passenger, although every carriage and engine changes, so long as it departs on that route approximately on schedule, but not for the trainspotter or maintenance staff. In short the barrier which was meant to exclude real world objects and the practical involvement of subjects proved ineffectual. Finally, the argument that words gain their meanings from their relation to other words, through the differences established, does nothing whatsoever to show that difference itself related to nothing in the world or that it is not our practical interests which prompt the establishment of differences. The numerous Inuit words for snow encode differences between impactable and powdery substances and only proliferate among a population which has a practical interest in such matters. These differences disclose information of utility to any who have an interest in *learning* them, even a trivial one like snowballing. Since real referents and practical human interests keep surfacing, Saussure had not produced a linguistic theory which demoted the subject from being the mediator of meaning and subordinated her to passively assimilating all meaning through discursive mediation.

Saussure had attempted to advance an anti-realist theory of meaning, uncoupled from any referential theory, since 'differences' were not meant to point to referents. Since what counted in language was the distinction between 'signifier' (word) and the 'signified' (concept), the subject was reduced to a very secondary role in the generation of meaning, since priority was accorded to the 'differences' themselves. However we have seen that neither referents nor subjects were effectively excluded. The common denominator of the various structuralists, who linked back to Saussure, was to assign the subject to a more firmly based subordinate status. In the work of Lévi-Strauss, Althusser and Lacan, subordination consisted in conceptualising subjects as constituted by social forces beyond their control (whether the grid of the human mind, the forces and relations of production or the unconscious) and whose very subjectivity was constructed in language. Such forces render human consciousness irrelevant since it is now presented as the effect of a determinism which is outside both our conception (as lay actors) and control (as investigators).

The significance of Lévi-Strauss lay in his direct challenge to the notion that 'men make history' and its attempted replacement by autonomous processes, consisting of binary codes of signifiers (such as 'raw' and 'cooked'), which owed nothing to the intentional creation of meanings by human beings.

History, in short, does not record or discover meaning; it does no more than provide a catalogue which can serve as a point of departure in the quest for intelligibility. We must understand, that is, that there has been no progress of the kind that humanist historians suppose, no development of cognition, no dialectical process at work in human society, but merely the reformulation in numerous different guises of an essential structure of human knowledge – a structure which is, according to Lévi-Strauss, a closed system. Historical thought is simply the humanist mythology by means of which the 'civilised' or 'developed' world relates to the discontinuous, objective and immutable structure of brain and psyche.[23]

Therefore all forms of humanism are considered to be 'ideological' since they distortedly take our wholly superficial subjectivity seriously and thus deflect attention from the underlying social forces which alone have causal efficacy to Lévi-Strauss.

An identical process of transcending subject and object is inscribed in Althusser's two basic propositions: that individuals are not themselves constitutive of the social process or history but are only its *träger*, and that the consciousness or subjectivity of the subject is constructed in ideology. The former insists that we are not the 'makers of history' but only the supporting material which energises the process. Thus it is that the

structure of the relations of production determines the *places* and *functions* occupied and adopted by the relations of production, who are never anything more than the occupants of these places, insofar as they are the supports (*Träger*) of these functions. The true 'subjects' (in the sense of constitutive subjects of the process) are therefore not these occupants or functionaries, are not, despite all appearances, the 'real men' – *but the definition and its distribution of these places and functions. The true 'subjects' are these definers and distributors: the relations of produc-*

[23] Kate Soper, *Humanism and Anti-humanism*, p. 99.

tion (and political and ideological social relations). But since these are 'relations', they cannot be thought within the category *subject*.[24]

Secondly, everything about the concrete historical individual(s) and their experience is actually subject*ed* to these relations and therefore human subjectivity is the subordinate product of these social forces. Subjectivity and the misrepresentation of ourselves *as* subjects are ideological constructs, ways in which we are formed and from which we cannot escape. Here Althusser is careful to specify that we are not directly produced by effects of the economy, but rather by functional ideological apparatuses whose task is to produce subjects whose consciousness is appropriate to the positions they occupy. This is not the place to start questioning what hidden hand ensures the *functionality* of ideological (or repressive) state apparatuses in providing the non-material pre-conditions of production. But it is the point to note why Althusser advances two distinct but related theses, the first about social positions and functions and the second about ideological mediation which equips people for these roles.

Now both Mepham[25] and Collier[26] have argued that the force of the first argument is that it is collective class action which 'makes history', rather than individuals, and this gels with Althusser's own protestation that he never sought to deny the existence of human beings. The use of '*Träger*' applied not to concrete reality, but to deeper structural mechanisms which could only be grasped by this abstraction of our being to become nothing but 'carriers'. Yet the problem remains, for who now does the 'grasping'? It looks as though real human beings have been readmitted (in concrete reality though not in functional theoretical abstractions), in which case why are they not deemed the real history-makers? Alternatively, if we can *only* reflect upon ourselves as *Träger*, then how can we (collectively is irrelevant) attempt to transform the structures dominating us? If that is the only way we can experience our existence, then how is it possible to talk about individuals being in need of liberation from such domination? *Träger* are not *human* beings, but without humanity they must lack any real interests in being liberated. It seems as though the human being gains readmission, but the price of that is to accord him the power of 'making history'.

This is the dilemma, either complete structural determinism where people are quite irrelevant to political change has to give way, or the beings who are deemed to be so constituted have to be affirmed as non-human, in which case why does it matter what happens to puppets?

---

[24] L. Althusser, *Reading Capital*, p. 180.
[25] John Mepham, 'Who Makes History', *Radical Philosophy*, 6, 1973.
[26] Andrew Collier, *Scientific Realism and Socialist Thought*, Hemel Hempstead, Harvester Wheatsheaf, 1989, ch. 3.

Certain British neo-Althussarians like Paul Hirst[27] have taken the latter tack by denying that we are a 'unity of consciousness', but in the process have had to sacrifice any reason for advocating socio-economic change. The case for 'letting the men back in' is logically and politically strong, but it is incompatible with a structuralism in which they only feature as systemically constituted effects.

The same dilemma is found in Lacan's linguistic Freudianism, where the sign is given sovereignty over the mind itself and its desires. He maintains that we only become human by a socialised induction into a cultural order, which is linguistic in form. Thus, for example, gender differences are discursively constructed, but its bearers are only gendered subjects by courtesy of the cultural order and thus via their subordination to language. Once again, if it is not by reference to a prior and non-discursively constituted humanity, how can he consistently condemn the victimising effects of socialisation? The 'subjects' so constituted are incapable of knowing their victimisation and *who* is the Jacques Lacan who reveals it, and *where* epistemologically is there for him to stand in the terms of his theory?

The advent of the post-structural and eventually postmodern dispute with structuralism challenged its residual humanistic premises and sought to eliminate problems like the above which stemmed from a 'lurking subject' which had not been thoroughly expunged. Once again the prime device was a reconceptualisation of language to eradicate any notion of it as the transparent source of representation which derived from some determinate relationship between consciousness and reality. (For, as has been seen, nothing precluded Saussure's 'differences' from being referential or human practical interests from disclosing this.) Now Foucault declared that 'the question of language seems to lay siege on every side to the figure of man.'[28]

However, this siege involved four consecutive moves on the part of Foucault, Derrida and Baudrillard. Firstly, an ontological denial of the relationship between discourse and reality, which effectively blocked any access to reality, meaning of course natural reality (since things social were transmuted, as is typical of idealism, into discourse itself). This move entailed a radical version of the 'epistemic fallacy' where ontology is collapsed into epistemology, such that what is, becomes synonymous with knowledge claims about it (or being is subordinated to knowing). The second move then cut any epistemological connection between discourse and truth and between discourse and linguistic referentiality. The third involved detaching textual 'knowledge' from a 'knowing subject' and

---

[27] Paul Hirst, *Law and Ideology*, London, 1979.   [28] M. Foucault, *The Order of Things*.

severed all links between traditional philosophical anthropology and culture. Finally, having eliminated the human subject, it was then possible to 'de-structuralise' completely because, unconstrained by human properties of the 'subject' with which it deals, theoretical discourse was no longer limited by any call to 'order'.

It is worth looking briefly at each move, particularly to pinpoint where some hesitated whilst others moved on. The latter were willing to demolish the social sciences in any recognisable form as a simple corollary of the 'death of man'. Others sought to re-cast these disciplines and, equally necessarily, had to re-consider a stay of execution. This division is crucial to my argument, which at this stage can be presented as a parting of the ways between Foucault and Derrida. Since the first two moves find them in considerable unanimity, neither can have anything in common with realist social theory. Nevertheless, their subsequent differences represent very different challenges to it.

Firstly then, we find ontology suspended in Derrida's aestheticising of language where all texts have no more grounding in reality than the literary genre. Foucault is equally willing to endorse the 'epistemic fallacy' when he argues, in connection with mental illness, that the point is to 'dispense with things' in favour of 'things said', that is discourses which have no limitation by virtue of the way things are. The severing of epistemology from truth is also shared via the nature of what discourse is held to be. Thus, Foucault can claim that his lengthy disquisition on the Panopticon was metaphor rather than penal history, whilst Paul de Man has rightly argued that in Derrida's thought 'literature turns out to be the main topic of philosophy and the model of the kind of truth to which it aspires'.[29] Indeed the whole practice of deconstruction deprives theoretical texts of cognitive content and thus truth claims, hence according them the status of rhetorical devices, indistinguishable from rhetoric in literature.

The third point is the crucial one. To Derrida, the 'text' swings free from the 'knowing subject', for it has no determinate meaning which depends upon its authorial origin. Neither does it carry any unequivocal meaning, but is only the source of 'differences' and their alteration. Thus all signification is relieved of a signified, of any particular concept or idea which had its genesis in a human subject: instead the 'subject is subordinated to the endless play of difference'.[30] The early Foucault endorsed this conclusive demotion of subjects from constitutive to constituted status and rendered them impotent as 'knowing subjects', since what was available to be known was independent of these socially created

---

[29] See Christopher Norris, *Deconstruction: Theory and Practice*, London, Methuen, 1982, p. 21.   [30] Alex Callinicos, *Against Postmodernism*, Oxford, Polity Press, 1989, p. 75.

knowers. Hence his argument that 'The individual is not a pregiven entity which is seized on by the exercise of power. The individual, with his identity and characteristics, is the product of a relation of power exercised over bodies, multiplicities, movements, desires, forces.'[31] What he knows, or even that he knows, has nothing to do with his powers as a 'knower', for the only property left to the subject is epistemological malleability. Their very subjectification is therefore a social gift which is predicated upon their subjection to social forces: what they think they know is what they have been disciplined to believe.

Where the fourth move bids to take us need not detain us here, namely into Baudrillard's 'hyperreality'. 'With distinctions dissolved between objects and their representations we are left only with "simulacra". These refer to nothing but themselves. Media messages, such as TV ads, are prime examples. This self-referentiality goes far beyond Max Weber's fears for a disenchanted, detraditionalised world. Signs lose contact with things signified; the late twentieth century is witness to unprecedented destruction of meaning. The quest for some division between the moral and the immoral, the real and the unreal is futile.'[32] Since as a realist, I agree about this futility, I am much more interested to return to the third move and to examine Foucault's hesitations over making it. If he refused to do so, having already made the first two moves, where does that leave human subjects and the disciplines which ultimately deal with them?

In the seventies Foucault had forcefully claimed that the individual is not a pregiven entity seized upon by the exercise of power: power operates by a process of constitution of people and thus he effectively denies that 'there remains any progressive political potential in the idea of an autonomous subject'.[33] Simultaneously, however, he vituperates against the 'carceral' society which subordinates them. His condemnation of this form of our constitution does seem to call for an 'anthropology' which is at odds with the disciplinary culture operating in this manner. Especially if resistance is to have a locus, then this needs to be predicated upon a self which has been violated, knows it, and can do something about it. Yet his early work precluded precisely this. In order to account for why power can be and is resisted, and thus to retain his own critical stance towards it, he has to reintroduce premises about the natural desires of people which means withdrawing the earlier view that humanity is in no respect an entity – in place of a being, one of whose properties is to resist those things done to it which are contrary to its nature.

[31] M. Foucault, *Power/Knowledge: Selected Interviews and Other Writings*, Brighton, Harvester, 1980, pp. 73–4.
[32] David Lyon, *Postmodernity*, Buckingham, Open University Press, 1994, p. 16.
[33] Peter Dews, 'The New Philosophers', *Radical Philosophy*, 24, 1980, p. 87.

In his last writings, Foucault appears to have bitten the bullet and spat out 'move three' above, by now accepting an anthropological entity, a real subject, which confronts culture as a 'knowing subject', capable of agential resistance. In a late essay on 'The Subject and Power', he conceded that 'power is exercised only over free subjects, and only insofar as they are free. By this we mean individual or collective subjects who are faced with a field of possibilities in which several ways of behaving, several reactions, and diverse comportments may be realised.[34] This re-turn to the 'philosophy of the subject' is increasingly marked in the second and third volumes of the *History of Sexuality*, published in the year of his death.

He characterised this as a 'theoretical displacement' away from the conflated 'power/knowledge' complex and towards 'truth-games in the relation of self to self and the constitution of oneself as a subject'.[35] In exploring the idea that the truth concerning the subject is found in sexuality and thus tracing the history of changing sexual conceptions (as in Greek practices of self-mastery), he introduces new notions of 'arts of existence' or the 'technology of the self'. Some[36] have sought to 're-discipline' this work into the foucauldian mainstream. They argue that these are demonstrations of variable subjectivities whose very relativity to changing social forms only underscores the absence of a prior and universal human nature. However, this interpretation cannot sit well at all with Foucault's last preoccupation, namely that 'everyone's life become a work of art' – a democratic version of Nietzsche's aim.[37] Yet in both thinkers, what is there to form (and how can the self play any part in this formation) unless the existence of a prior self, primitive to this process, is finally conceded? If there is no antecedent self, one cannot become 'someone' but only 'something' and this again collapses back into a passive process of socialisation and subjugation.

Yet, as Callinicos argues, the readmission of the human self means conceding a great deal. By 'thus acknowledging the irreducible distinctness of persons, however, we have gone a long way towards setting limits to the process of self-creation. My particular characteristics circumscribe my likely achievements. If I am tone-deaf or blind then I cannot appreciate, let alone produce music or painting respectively. My past actions – an act of personal or political betrayal, for example – may give a shape to the rest of my life which is, quite simply, inescapable. My bad temper may bedevil

---

[34] M. Foucault, 'Afterword' to Dreyfus and P. Rabinow, *Michel Foucault: Beyond Structuralism and Hermeneutics*, Brighton, Harvester, 1982, p. 221.
[35] M. Foucault, *L'Usage des Plaisirs*, Paris, 1984, p. 12.
[36] L. Ferry and A. Renaut, *La Pensée 68*, Paris, 1985, pp. 150f.
[37] M. Foucault, 'On the Genealogy of Ethics', in P. Rabinow, *The Foucault Reader*, New York, Pantheon, 1985, p. 350.

my personal life, helping to undermine my most important relationships with others . . . the process of making sense of one's life . . . is constrained by the facts of one's character and history.'[38] This then takes one of poststructuralism's central thinkers full circle back to the point where Foucault readmits the autonomous human subject, since 'he' has proved indispensable to resistance, to progressive political potential and to creativity – all of which assume people doing things rather than having things happen to them.

Now 'the body +' is a fairly standard anchorage of the human being (leaving aside those like Parfit who deny we have a unique physical identity; only the psychological continuity of our mental states over time).[39] The contentious element is 'plus what?' With the readmission of the autonomous self into postmodern theorising we can explore the answer which is reluctantly given by Rorty. He takes up the late foucauldian project of self-formation and self-enrichment within the same confines of moves one and two (anti-realism and a pragmatic view of truth).

In parallel he wishes to conceptualise the self anti-foundationally, that is without any fixity of human nature, but only one plastically constituted in discourse. Because he completes the design which Foucault only gestured towards, we can examine his project of making oneself conversationally. In it I will seek to establish two propositions:

  (i) that the project of aesthetic self-redefinition and self-enrichment is *logically* incoherent without a self to unify this enterprise,
  (ii) that *substantively* there is an inescapable appeal to the notion of the human being, which does underpin his argument.

II   Rorty: the ineradicable face of humanity

I want to establish that, despite Rorty's post-foundational picture which is in full communion with the French movement to 'decentre the subject', the move cannot be completed. The aim is to replace the 'I', of the *cogito* by the 'we' of conversation, so that we exist as intersections of transient public interpretations, but there 'is nothing which *has* these interpretations, just as there is no uninterpreted reality these are interpretations *of*'.[40] In other words, the self is dissolved into discursive structures and would seem to be denied agency if the 'I' is merely a conversational construct and not something given. It cannot be given because there are no 'essential features' of life, no timeless truths about the human condition,

---

[38] Alex Callinicos, *Against Postmodernism*, p. 90.
[39] Derek Parfit, *Reasons and Persons*, Oxford University Press, 1984.
[40] Charles B. Guignon and David R. Hiley, 'Biting the Bullet: Rorty on Private and Public Morality', in Alan Malachowski (ed.), *Reading Rorty*, Blackwell, Oxford, 1996, p. 344.

our own or any one else's. Since life is 'a tissue of contingent relations, a web which stretches backward and forward through past and future time', it is not 'something capable of being seen steady and whole.'[41] Thus there is nothing of ourselves to 'discover'. If all our insights are culled from current language-games, it follows that our own self-interpreting activities are transitory. This is the consequence of Rorty's 'ubiquity of language'.

His definition of the self re-echoes this decentring, for it is simply 'a network of beliefs, desires, and emotions with nothing behind it – no sub-strate behind the attributes'. A self 'just *is* that network' which is also 'a network constantly reweaving itself',[42] in a 'hit or miss way' in the face of environmental pressures. There are major problems here. To begin with, Rorty wishes to make this reweaving the heroic action of 'strong poets', yet in denying the existence of a 'master weaver', which as Hollis points out used to stand for our self-consciousness, how does agency pertain to a network which *passively* adjusts to its environment, let alone it being accorded heroic moral responsibility for what it becomes?[43] Simultaneously, the process of 'reweaving' is presented as *hyperactive*, for as we have no internal fixity, then we can envisage ourselves being completely transformed. Yet as Bhaskar has rightly argued, a 'total trans-formation would leave the discursive agent and her community without the linguistic resources to recognize or refer to her achievement; nor could it be literalized in the community unless there were some continuity or overlap in usage. "Overcoming" is always piecemeal and partial-trans-formation, not replacement; and it respects the existential intransitivity of the self or past to be overcome.'[44]

However, Rorty never makes the essential distinction between things (including people) which do change (to some degree), and therefore require a new description which may be incommensurable with the old, and things which remain unchanged (including people) but which can be re-described in potentially incommensurable ways. It is crucial not to conflate these two, the transitive and the intransitive. Rorty wants to incline towards the former (all is transitive), but sometimes has to mean only the latter because of our intransitive embodied continuity, amongst other things. Yes, we undergo certain changes, such that I hope I can describe myself as a 'wiser woman' than the 'ingenue' who lived a quarter

[41] Richard Rorty, 'The Contingency of Selfhood', *London Review of Books*, 8, May 1986, pp. 14–15.
[42] Richard Rorty, 'Postmodern Bourgeois Liberalism', in Robert Hollinger (ed.), *Hermeneutics and Praxis*, Notre Dame University Press, Notre Dame, 1985, p. 217.
[43] Martin Hollis, 'The Poetics of Personhood', in Alan Malakowski (ed.), *Reading Rorty*, p. 249.
[44] Roy Bhaskar, *Philosophy and the Idea of Freedom*, Blackwell, Oxford, 1991, p. 66.

of a century ago, but both relate to the same bodily entity: and how could I suffer the future indignity of incontinence, were I not reproaching the same body which had never previously let me down in this way. Similarly, 'we' simply do not have the power to redefine our society's structural properties (SEPs) as our linguistic community pleases. We remain rich or poor, powerful or powerless, privileged or underprivileged in the (relatively enduring) intransitive dimension, which takes more than talk to change it.

However, this distinction between the transitive and the intransitive is impossible to Rorty. He could accept, for example, biological intransitivity *qua* human beings as organic parcels, but he denies us the ability to inspect bodily change mentally, from the standpoint of someone with a continuous sense of self. Instead, he insists that 'there is no such thing as getting outside the web which constitutes oneself, looking down upon it and deciding in favour of one portion of it rather than another'.[45] This then produces an unworkable split in selfhood, between the self who is the web and the self who reweaves it; between the passive 'I am' and the active 'I will be'. Now these two have necessarily to be united in an emergent, active self-consciousness which embraces both, for otherwise how can the self be a 're-weaver'? Such a self may be able to garner external discursive materials for self-elaboration, but how does it make something new or know that it has done so? Unless it is granted a sufficient degree of internal self-consciousness over time, its linguistic heroics may merely be transitive re-descriptions of completely routine actions, beliefs, desires and so on. This point will become crucial when we turn to the question of self-enrichment: for you have to know what you are to determine whether you have been enriched by something or not.

What Rorty proffers in place of this continuous sense of self is a variety of 'quasi-selves', different internal clusters of belief and desire, amongst which there is no inner conversational relationship since they lack the internal coherence to constitute one unified person who is self-conscious about her own constituents. He draws this picture from his reading of Freud, to whom our unconscious inhabitants mean that 'we are "lived" by unknown and uncontrollable forces'[46] and are thus constituted by more than one self. As each one tells its own story there are no correct accounts about what happened to me in the past or who I am now, independent of the optional interpretations produced by these different inner denizens. There is no 'inner core', which persists when accretions are stripped away, or which struggles against inclinations which are hostile to its integrity.

---

[45] Richard Rorty, 'A Reply to Six Critics', *Analyse & Kritik*, 6, 1984, p. 95.
[46] S. Freud, *The Ego and the Id*, W. W. Norton, New York, 1962, p. 13.

In the light of this, the ideal which makes most sense is that of 'self-enlargement', that is 'the development of richer, fuller ways of formulating one's desires and hopes, and thus making those desires and hopes themselves – and thereby oneself – richer and fuller'.[47] To Rorty, Freud's heritage is to herald the aesthetic life by presenting us as 'centreless, as random assemblages of contingent and idiosyncratic needs rather than as more or less adequate exemplifications of a common human essence'.[48] So his major legacy is a licence for *homo ludens* who can play with all manner of vocabularies without ever asking 'which of these shows us how things really are' or 'which of these things matters most to (a non-existent) me?' This is self-creation, rather than the self-knowledge of modernist philosophy. Freud's patrimony is read like a charter of supreme indulgence for the uncontrolled 'id', since perversion and obsession can now be read as 'the private poem of the pervert, the sadist or the lunatic: as richly textured'[49] as is any life.

Firstly, this seems to hang on a serious misreading of Freud, who was underwriting neither the stern voice of the 'super-ego' nor complete indulgence for the 'id', but describing the balancing act which the 'ego' had to accomplish, on the reality principle, in relation to getting by intact in the world. As Shusterman argues, this 'unified self is not a uniform self, but nor can it be an unordered collection of egalitarian quasi selves inhabiting the same corporal machine'. Rorty's confederacy (rather than centralist union) of quasi selves thus seems less the formula for a Freudian ideal or self-perfection than the recipe for a Freudian pathology of schizophrenia for 'Freud implicitly realised what a pricelessly important and yet perhaps fragile achievement the unity of self was, how difficult and painful such a unified self or self-narrative was to construct, and yet how necessary it was to lead any plausible version of a good or satisfying life in human society.'[50]

Secondly, although Rorty does not have much time for emancipation, neither does he for constraints. The picture which he paints of our various incommunicado 'quasi selves', each heroically enlarging themselves through nothing but word-play, comes up against reality in a different way from the Freudian Ego's confrontations. The latter surveys the current social scene and strikes the most generous balance amongst its internal clamourings that it can get away with. The Ego's job is 'passing' in society,

[47] Richard Rorty, 'Freud and the Moral Revolution', in Joseph H. Smith and William Kerrigan (eds.), *Pragmatism's Freud: The Moral Disposition of Psychoanalysis*, The Johns Hopkins Press, Baltimore, 1986, p. 11.   [48] Ibid., p. 12.
[49] Richard Rorty, 'The Contingency of Selfhood', p. 14.
[50] Richard Shusterman, 'Postmodern Aestheticism: A New Moral Philosophy', in *Theory, Culture and Society*, 5: 2–3, 1988, p. 350.

getting by in the structure and culture it finds itself in without doing too much inner damage: Rorty's 'quasi-selves' lack this restraint, they seek to transform the world (as discourse) to conform to their ambitions. The former is realistic in its accommodations; the latter is anti-realist in its ambitions. His 'quasi-selves' can only be so because Rorty takes the typically liberal stance towards society (inadmissibly cut-off from nature) of the methodological individualist. It is made up of nothing but 'other people', as in Watkins classic formulation,[51] and thus all is up for conversational redefinition between members. Realism, of course insists that we are considerably more trammelled by socio-cultural structures whose durability serves to constrain and shape our conversations and whose transformability depends upon more than how the community talks about them (see Casto's example).[52] As Bhaskar puts it 'social structures may be just as objective, and transfactually efficacious within their geo-historical domain, as natural laws. Moreover, both alike typically impose limits and constraints upon the kinds of action (including speech action) possible to human beings.'[53]

However, my reservations are not limited to the fact that living the aesthetic life is impossible in society with its resistant structures, but extend to the proposition that this aestheticisation project is logically incoherent without a self to unify the enterprise. This project stands against an ethics of purity and a futile quest for self-knowledge, and stands for one of 'self-enrichment' and 'self-enlargement'. It expresses the 'desire to embrace more and more possibilities, to be constantly learning, to give oneself over entirely to curiosity'[54] and involves both an 'aesthetic search for novel experiences and (for) novel language' to redescribe them – hence extruding the experience and enlarging the experiences. Thus through our radicalised vocabularies, each dizzily replacing its predecessor in this voracious search for novelty in experience and expression, people 'make their lives works of art'.[55]

Now this notion of both 'a life' and a 'work of art' are significantly in the singular, implying some kind of unity, yet Rorty consistently celebrates the absence of any centre. He thus explicitly denies precisely that coherence which is essential to a life and a work alike by insisting upon a self made up of 'a plurality of persons' each with 'incompatible systems of belief and desire'.[56] Thus 'the only constancy that he in fact prescribes is

[51] J. W. N. Watkins, 'Methodological Individualism and Social Tendencies', in May Brodbeck (ed.), *Readings in the Philosophy of the Social Sciences*, Macmillan, New York, 1968. This is discussed in my *Realist Social Theory*, p. 34–46.
[52] Margaret S. Archer, *Realist Social Theory*, pp. 76–9.
[53] Roy Bhaskar, *Philosophy and the Idea of Freedom*, p. 73.
[54] Richard Rorty, 'Freud and Moral Reflection', p. 15.   [55] Ibid., p. 11.   [56] Ibid., p. 19.

the constancy of change, of novel alternative self-descriptions and narra-
tions, the constancy of inconstancy which essentially nullifies the unity
and integrity of the self'.[57] It also nullifies the kind of *Bildungsroman* he
would like to celebrate: for this life needs its narrator, who is the same
story-teller (even if she undergoes great life-changes) in order to hold it
together as the story of one life. It neither remains one if the different
voices disavow their common anchorage in one and the same human
being (in the same body), nor is comprehensible as a story if the various
chapters are written in incommensurable vocabularies whose radical
novelty defies translation. This incoherence rebounds on the teller as
much as the story. As Shusterman puts it, 'without such a self that is
capable of identity through change or changing description, there can be
no self capable of self-enrichment or self-enlargement, and this would
nullify the Rortian aesthetic life of self-enrichment by rendering it mean-
ingless'.[58] It makes his whole project of self-enrichment basically incoherent by denying that there is any relatively persisting and coherent self
there to be enriched.

This works both ways: for the anti-foundationalist story, the only
form of narrative self-constitution which remains also implodes into
incomprehensibility on this account. As Shusterman continues, if we
abandon 'the aim of a unified or consistent self-narrative for Rorty's dis-
cordant chorus of inconsistent "quasi-selves" constituted by alternative,
constantly changing, and often incommensurable narratives and vocabularies, with no complex narrative able to make them all hang together,
then the project of self-enrichment becomes mythical and incoherent
with the myth and incoherence of a single self collecting these riches
together'.[59] When Cronin wrote *Three Loves*, described in the languages
of sexual, maternal and spiritual love, these were recognisably parts of the
same life of the same woman by virtue of the communality of their very
single-minded possessiveness and extravagant self-investment. These
linked the three loves together and simultaneously to her, which are the
dual requirements for coherence.

There is a third such requirement: because lives are lived and narratives are recounted in society, they must also be coherent with their
context. Now as we have seen, Rorty is both a methodological and a
liberal individualist. Hence his advocacy of the aesthetic life is concerned
with individual gratifications and is not a project for public welfare.
However, when he advances this 'private morality' he also maintains it to
be beneficially compatible with the public domain and particularly with

---

[57] Richard Shusterman, 'Postmodernist Aestheticism', p. 350.   [58] Ibid., p. 346.
[59] Ibid., p. 349.

social solidarity. Many, like Nancy Fraser,[60] have voiced severe doubts about their complementarity. I see a more basic difficulty here, which is logical rather than substantive, namely how can one speak of making commitments, which by definition are not fleeting, without someone who has sufficient continuity to sustain them? Rorty's assertion that selfhood is a 'matter of decision rather than knowledge, an acceptance of another being into fellowship rather than a common essence',[61] makes our decisions about solidarity with others revokable given narrative changes in ourselves. Yet transient impulses of fellowship which can be revoked are not the stuff of solidarity. As Hollis maintained, the 'fellowship needed for a broadening franchise is precisely one of beings who recognise a common essential sameness in others'.[62]

If we take enfranchisement, manumission or civil rights literally, these are determinations that similarities outweigh differences and constitute a good reason for emancipatory practice: they are not revisable (withdrawing the vote or re-enslaving) just because some new self-wrought difference acquires sudden salience in our aesthetic project. Thus 'we must ask with puzzlement, where is the coherent integrated individual narrative (among the myriad inconsistent narratives of quasi persons) which we wish to bind with others in a project of solidarity? Where is there a self that is unified and firm enough not only to allow a momentary self-satisfied glimpse of convergence with others but to guide the narrative enactment of continued and deepening bonds of solidarity? The Rortian self needs to get its own act together, attain its own narrative solidarity and coherence, before it can hope to cohere with others in more than a fleeting cohabitation of the same geography or language-game.'[63]

Now my final point is that so strong is this logical requirement that Rorty does in fact concede it substantively. Although aestheticisation was meant to go all the way through and 'socialisation all the way down'; and both declared war upon essentialism, nevertheless Rorty (dis)continuously endorses a significant list of properties as inherent in or common to human beings. I am fully in agreement with Norman Geras[64] that such a list is sufficiently extensive to constitute a notion of human nature, which therefore proves to be ineradicable from Rorty's work. His argument repays following through, because it shows Rorty finally coming full circle

[60] Nancy Fraser, 'Solidarity or Singularity? Richard Rorty between Romanticism and Technocracy', in Alan Malakowski, *Reading Rorty*.
[61] Richard Rorty, 'The Contingency of Selfhood', pp. 11–15.
[62] Martin Hollis, 'The Poetics of Personhood', p. 252.
[63] Richard Shusterman, 'Postmodernist Aestheticism', pp. 350–1.
[64] Norman Geras, *Solidarity in the Conversation of Humankind*, Verso, London, 1995.

back to re-endorse humanity, as I started out maintaining was the case for the postmodernist enterprise.

Firstly, Geras presents Rorty's clear statement of the need to 'avoid the embarrassments of the universalistic claim that the term 'human being' . . . names an unchanging essence, an ahistorical natural kind with a permanent set of intrinsic features'.[65] Thus he seems clearly to reject any notion of a universal human nature made up of shared intrinsic characteristics. However, it is not to Rorty that there are no such properties, only that there are none which are distinctively human. Thus he agrees that people have the inherent quality 'to suffer and inflict pain',[66] but this is not exclusive to humans as we share it 'with the brutes'. The important point here is that even if what is common to human beings is not a specifically *human* nature, why does this disqualify it as being part of our nature, especially since its existence means that there are some constraints which are independent of socialisation and which this process has to confront as irreducible properties which it can only partially reform and channel?[67] No durable social arrangements can be indifferent to the amount of pain they entail or allow to be inflicted. Even behaviourists like Skinner depend upon a judicious mixture of pleasure and pain in the process of social conditioning. Our inescapably incarnational nature presents society with non-negotiable intolerances which are no less salient for the societal enterprise because they are not species-specific. Bhaskar is thus correct in stressing that 'Rorty neglects the material embodiment of human nature in an untenable distinction between the physical and the personal'.[68]

This distinction implies a stratification of our properties and powers *qua* organic bodies, versus those we possess in virtue of being socialised beings. There are relations of complementarity and contradiction between the two which cannot be ignored because of *their* impact upon any social project – which is a universal statement about human nature *inter alia*. To Geras this is 'a reminder that there is that distinction, irreducibly – as there would not be if socialisation really did go all the way down'.[69] Certainly historical pressures can modify the most basic bodily needs, as in different cultural shapings of *how* we eat and sleep, but these have to work within the confines of the fact *that* we must eat and sleep. Thus rather than rejecting human nature because it has a significant degree of malleability, Rorty would do better to accept that '(i) it always

[65] Richard Rorty, *Essays on Heidegger and Others*, Cambridge University Press, 1991, p. 77.
[66] Richard Rorty, 'Feminism and Pragmatism', *Radical Philosophy*, 59, 1991, p. 4.
[67] Norman Geras, *Solidarity in the Conversation of Humanity*, p.51.
[68] Roy Bhaskar, *Philosophy and the Idea of Freedom*, p. 81.
[69] Norman Geras, *Solidarity in the Conversation of Humanity*, p. 62.

manifests itself in some historically specific and mediated social form, and (ii) it is and must always be known under some historically particular – and therefore potentially transformable – description'.[70] But neither the transitivity of description nor the intervention of social shaping can nullify the intransitive, and therefore transfactual, nature of the real human quality itself.

Secondly, Rorty indeed goes further and accepts that we do possess species-specific qualities, in particular 'that special sort of pain which the brutes do not share with the humans – humiliation'.[71] Now the human capacity to be ridiculed and belittled is predicated upon further proper-ties which we have and the brutes lack, such as values, beliefs, a capacity for symbolic inventiveness, for poetry and for individualisation itself *on these bases*. Yet Rorty reinforces his point in stating that 'man is always free to choose new descriptions (for, among other things, himself)'.[72] Animals are not, so does that not make the capacity for discourse the essence of humankind? The only hedge here is that Rorty insists upon these as being *potentials* which we possess (and therefore ones which may remain unreal-ised in various circumstances), a fact which therefore nullifies their uni-versal manifestation. This cuts little ice because *all* of our human properties (e.g. our capacities to walk, to reproduce, to make things man-ually, to become language speakers) exist only *in potentia*: adverse circum-stances can jeopardise every one of them. Although the development of each does depend upon an appropriate (and often) social setting, these properties are then realised without their being a pure social endowment. As Sayer argues 'human beings must have a particular make up or nature for it to be possible for them to be conditioned by social influences in con-sistent ways'.[73] Even in cases where the biological is socially mediated in every instance (such as holding a pen), *what* is mediated remains irre-ducibly biological. As Geras comments, it is not through lack of socialisa-tion that 'the brutes' do not read Heidegger.

Therefore, thirdly, it seems that what Rorty may be denying is purely the normative usage of human nature, such that this would be 'a set of characteristics common to human beings that provided also a moral reference point: for shaping or constraining our thinking about human dignity, how to live well, our moral obligations, and so on'.[74] Yet Rorty's claim that 'cruelty is the worst thing that we can do' (especially that 'very cruel' practice of causing that special kind of pain, humiliation) turns on

[70] Roy Bhaskar, *Philosophy and the Idea of Freedom*, p. 69 n. 7.
[71] Richard Rorty, *Contingency, Irony and Solidarity*, Cambridge University Press, 1989, pp. 91–2.   [72] Richard Rorty, *Philosophy and the Mirror of Nature*, Oxford, 1980, p. 377.
[73] Andrew Sayer, *Method in Social Science: A Realist Approach*, Routledge, London, 1992, p. 121.   [74] Norman Geras, *Solidarity in the Conversation of Humanity*, p. 55.

that to which humans are uniquely susceptible. If this is the very *worst* thing that we can do to one another, this moral judgement is reliant upon human vulnerability to humiliation, and it is this which underpins his own normative commendation of tolerance as indispensable in human affairs.

Finally, Geras collects together the properties and powers of people which Rorty has sequentially conceded and poses the following question. 'By what criterion or in what context, bearing on the understanding of the ways of human beings, is a notion of their nature according to which they are susceptible to pain and humiliation, have the capacity for language and (in a large sense) poetry, have a sexual instinct, a sense of identity, integral beliefs – and then some other things too, like needs for nourishment and sleep, a capacity for laughter and for play, powers of reasoning and invention . . . and more shared features yet – not substantial enough?'.[75] He then asks specifically why this susceptibility to pain and humiliation is not as substantial as any properties which are usually at stake when human nature is in dispute, such as natural greed and competitiveness or universal beneficence? Furthermore, if pain and humiliation are the worst things that can befall us, but we have the capacity to make up our own natures, then why have we not gone in for redescriptions which make us proof against all of that? Certainly Geras agrees, we do adapt as far as possible to make our unavoidable suffering more bearable, but there are limits to human adaptability in oppressive circumstances, such that life becomes intolerable, or at the limits we die. Here Geras concludes that the language of emancipation, one so uncongenial to Rorty, is far from inappropriate. 'The idea of setting free from restraint or bondage, here, of beings of a particular, not infinitely flexible, nature'[76] can never be irrelevant as long as the world is replete with oppression, hunger, persecution and discrimination.

If we assent to this, we are not only endorsing an idea of human nature, we simultaneously have to answer how humankind can be 'unchained'. This is where mere acts of redescription are impotent in the face of structural and cultural properties and powers, which retain their constraining qualities in the face of our full discursive penetration and any redescriptions we proffer, individually or collectively (e.g. the effect of inflation upon those with fixed incomes which negatively affects their buying power, whether or not they are aware of the cause, and regardless of how they define it). As Bhaskar maintains about such social emergent properties (SEPs and CEPs), 'the identification of the *source* of an experienced injustice in social reality, necessary for changing or remedying it, involves

---

[75] Ibid., p. 66.   [76] Ibid., p. 68.

much more than redescription, even if it depends on that too centrally. It is a matter of finding and disentangling webs of relations in social life, and engaging explanatory critiques of the practices that sustain them.'[77]

In short, Rorty has not expunged the human being from his account and I have argued that there are logical and substantive reasons why this cannot but be the case. What should not surprise us is that as the human face reappears, as the irreducible and far from completely malleable anchorage of agency, then the problem of structure and agency resurfaces simultaneously. This is necessarily the case, for just as humankind cannot be dissolved in a solution of linguistic redescriptions, neither can the properties and powers of socio-cultural systems be reduced to linguistic terms. Postmodernism as a whole represents the most extreme account of Downwards conflation yet encountered, with linguistic terrorism supporting sociological imperialism. When it is argued, on the contrary, that all we are as humans is not thanks to society by courtesy of language – and I have maintained that Foucault and Rorty concede the point – then the parallel argument opens up, namely that all that is social in kind is not linguistic in nature. This brings us back to the charter of realist social theory, that in structure and agency we are dealing with two irreducible strata which make for a stratified social world, and to the charter of analytical dualism, namely that we must examine the *interplay* of their respective properties and powers to explain the outcome for either and both.

III   The anthropocentric turn

I want to conclude by pointing up a strange twist in the postmodernist project. So far, this chapter has tracked the fate of anti-humanism which intensified after Saussure, whose linguistics neither excluded the practical interests of language users nor references to the real world by way of differences which could accord with features of it. Yet one step short of full-blown textualism, certain major figures hesitated and began to re-introduce human properties, albeit rather grudgingly, but as necessary in order to anchor such agential activities as 'resistance' and 'solidarity'. However, that is not quite the end of the story.

The last instalment concerns those commentators who hold firm to this tentative re-humanisation of the social world, but remain deeply impressed by the radical anti-foundationalist stance of the postmodernists and share their critique of the scientism of the Enlightenment, especially because things human cannot be captured by a language of matter-in-motion. They then seek to put these two elements together and

---

[77] Roy Bhaskar, *Philosophy and the Idea of Freedom*, p. 72.

ask whether an anti-foundationalist idea of truth can be combined with the linguistic notion of perspectivism, namely that what we say about the world is deeply embedded in the community of discourse that we inhabit. When the answer is 'yes', it is completely dependent on the idea of truth from a human perspective, as opposed to Modernity's quest for a God's eye view of the world.

In briefly following this through, the aim is to show that this humanist perspectivism yields an anthropocentric view of the world because it is based upon our experience, talk and common sense which cannot be transcended. This anthropocentricism is a turn too far for the realist, for it confines truth about the world to that which can be experienced and discussed, thus limiting the enterprise to an actualism which can never progress to the real – in the physical and social worlds alike. Although on this new line of thought we do not make truth in our own image (for it works with a metaphysical distinction between truth and judgement rather than committing the epistemic fallacy and taking what we know about the world to be how the world is), nevertheless the truths we can enunciate are limited by the experiences we can have from a human perspective.

Basically, the realist has two reservations about this rehabilitation of postmodernism which will be developed in these last few pages against this new version of 'critical empiricism'. Firstly, the 'fallibility of experience' leads necessarily to a distorted actualism which is often simply wrong. Secondly, because experience necessarily deals with observables, then it is shackled to the perceptual criterion for making ontological judgements and cannot embrace the causal criterion which can establish real but non-observable mechanisms at work. In short, critical realists would criticise postmodern critical empiricists for reinvoking Humean anthropocentricism.

Critical empiricism can be seen as a selective salvage operation performed on postmodernism. It wants to save it from the anti-rationalism which inevitably ensues if language-games are fully incommensurable, for then relativism commits us to the view that it is our different human perspectives, as members of different communities of discourse, which makes things 'true for them'. The rescue operation thus depends on finding universally shared languages which 'might be true, or be capable of talking the truth, because they are universally accepted as necessary in order to make sense of experience'.[78] Those like Luntley are not despondent that such universals can be found: all cultures are held to play the science game for they all talk about, for example, the motion of physical

[78] Michael Luntley, *Reason, Truth and Self*, Routledge, London, 1995, p. 124.

bodies, engage in object talk, know that apples fall from trees or that balls roll downwards on an inclined surface. Those like Wiggins,[79] do not despair that we can extract a sparse notion of truth in this context, that is the true idea that apples go on falling and the grass remains green independently of our presence or of our thinking this is the case. But, if there is truth to be had within these shared frameworks, it will be truth from a human perspective and not absolute knowledge told in a universal transparent language. 'It is knowledge and truth about the world as seen by us. It is not the world according to God or whoever is supposed to sit at the Archimedean point enjoying the point of view of the cosmos. It is the world according to us.'[80] And they are not depressed about finding such truths, but rather exhilarated by the prospect of humanistic truths about the facts of the matter concerning, for instance, the state of our bank balances, which could never feature in Modernity's language which is restricted to matter in motion.

Now the concept of simple truth is given legitimacy by using a transcendental argument. It is one quite different from that employed by realists who frequently ask, what needs to be the case for a practice (like the rush hour) to be possible. Instead, the argument is inverted. Now it starts from if X *is* the case, then certain things Y must also be accepted. Thus rather than the external world being a necessary condition for the possibility of experience, it is our experiences which commit us to believing in the existence of the external world. Thus, for example, thought and talk about material objects (X) commits us to the metaphysical model of objects persisting in space and time (Y) and is a condition of our thinking and talking about physical objects which is not falsified by our experience.

Thus the procedure to establish that certain things exist independently of us, begins and ends with experience. This is its weakness and there are two large categories of instances where our human perspective may well be fallacious. The catch is that we cannot know this from within our human perception, for our direct experience is the worst possible guide. On the one hand, there are all the well-rehearsed examples of where actualism goes wrong. Human perceptual experience alone would indeed make Ptolemaics of us all as well as flat earthers (for visual evidence of the ship's mast being the last part of it to disappear over the horizon does not establish the counter-experiential curvature of the earth's surface, it merely 'shows' that things drop off the edge quite slowly or that the edge itself is a gentle gradient). Thus, critical empiricists will accept this, that

[79] David Wiggins, *Needs, Values and Truth*, Blackwell, Oxford, 1991.
[80] Michael Luntley, *Reason, Truth and Self*, p. 120.

no observations can finally arbitrate between interpretative differences, but they take some cold comfort from the fact that both are watching the same thing (ships in relation to the horizon).

However, what of cases where we cannot even argue about what we see or experience? Thus, instances of pervasive ideological distortion lead us to think, talk about and experience various 'X's, such as a 'fair wage', 'one's station in life' or any tenet of racism or sexism, which in turn legitimate things like the 'market economy', 'feudalism' or 'racial differences in intelligence'. That is their purpose, but not as part of a transcendental argument! If experience is the judge, but ideology is presenting the case, then if it does its work well we the jury will simply not have many (if any) counter-factual experiences. Its effect will be that practices of gender discrimination ensured that we did not encounter sufficient practising women engineers to question this being a man's world. Exceptions of course confirm the rule and this leads one to question the authority which common sense is accorded on this post-modern view. The perspective of common sense seems to hedge its bets. Yet the advocates of human perspectivism depend on the notion that having any sort of thought also involves having some sort of notion about what would make the thought false, a state of affairs which would lead us to retract the judgement. Even when we do entertain falsifiers, human perception is also selective perception and, judging by their expletives, some male motorists have not yet encountered a critical mass of competent women drivers. Selective perception works on the verification principle, it is not on the look out for falsificatory instances. Common sense celebrates verification. Contradictions are only intolerable when we have to confront them, but human experiences can pick and mix, with proverbs to cover conflicting eventualities: depending upon where you stand and in relation to what, 'it's never too late to learn' or 'you can't teach an old dog new tricks'.

The second objection concerns the fact that if knowledge is about our lived human experience, then nothing unobservable can be known. Let us get at this through the perspectivists' notion of the world being coloured. They wish to assert two things (contra Modernism), that it is coloured independently of anyone being there to see it, but also that it is only those with human (or human-like) perceptual equipment who are capable of seeing it. The world is and appears coloured to us because of what we are like: it does not appear so to bats. Now I have no trouble with either statement, but how can a human perspectivist working on the basis of experience, know this about bats? We cannot because the bat's experiences are defined by sensory qualities characterising them but not us. From our perspective of what we perceive of their behaviour at dusk, why should we not conclude that they simply have excellent night vision, for what could falsify this experientially? Conversely, what could be observed from our human perspective which would evidence their possession of a sonar echo system? Here we have to leave common sense behind and accept that we are all playing the advanced science game, one of whose moves is to improve instrumentation so that we are no longer confined to observations made from our human perspective by virtue of our human endowments. Thus scientists from Brown University got out of their human skins this week to inform us (a) that bat experiences mean they can distinguish two objects, the width of a pencil line apart, using their sonar, and that (b) from our point of view, their powers are three times better than any sonar equipment we make. Satellite photographs, particle physics, electron-microscopes, body scans and key-hole surgery are presumably among the reasons why Rorty has not given up on science, but they have everything to do with the game which enlarges and often transcends our human perspective.

We transcend, not only when we can tell with what precision a bat discriminates, but every time we introduce a non-observable factor, such as heat conduction as the causal mechanism accounting for the second law of thermodynamics, or planetary forces to account for their (counter-experiential) movements. What is crucial about many examples of non-observables, especially social ones, is that their detection does *not* depend upon instrumentation. Some of the non-observable social factors which concern us may be open to humanistic hermeneutics (my motives in writing this book or yours in reading it), but frequently we just are dealing with non-observables which remain that way (i.e. they are distinct from a psycho-analyst's attempts to help clients to awareness of something unconscious). In this category would go international finance markets, institutional contradictions, ecological imbalance, third dimensional power or ideological mystification. We can observe their effects and, using the causal, not the perceptual criterion, postulate their necessary existence. But this procedure leads us fully back into the traditional form of transcendental argument, for human experience, limited by definition to the level of events, can never alone reveal these transfactual generative mechanisms.

In short, the human perspective would limit us to some very simple truth claims and, on the perceptual criterion, we could well be wrong about them. The insertion of the epistemological word 'critical' before the ontological descriptor 'empiricist' certainly reminds us of the fallibility of our experience, but is of little help when two human views, interpretations or theories clash. No amount of empiricism or even empirically grounded 'guesses' can purge the indexicality of the competing accounts; one group can persist in their selective perception and the other in theirs.

Anthropocentricism binds us intransigently to indexicals even though it wants these to be as big as the human race. But often it is not the case that humanity shares a universal language which is accepted as necessary in order to make sense of experience, and even if we do we might be wrong because the game we are playing might be that of global actualism. Thus knowledge from a *universal* human perspective may only represent globalised fallibility. After all this is what Enlightenment thinkers held the pervasive religious language of the antecedent period to be: it is also how postmodernism reflects upon the generalisation of the Enlightenment project itself in the language of Modernity.

Conclusion

This is why the anthropocentric turn will not do. It does not lead via relativism and nihilism to the anti-rationalism of textualism, but both strands of postmodernism end up in different cul-de-sacs. What we need instead, in order to avoid these two brick walls is a strong, but still anti-foundational account, of how the way the world is *constrains* our language about reality, and especially of how direct (that is socially unmediated) contact with the world shapes our languages, so that they are not just about the human communities to which we belong. It is the latter task in particular to which this book is devoted, to our human relations with practical reality. Because neither our humanity, which anchors our selves, nor practical reality through which our human potentials are developed, can be dispensed with, our task is necessarily to examine the interplay between these two irreducible components.

As Trigg sums up the matter:

The real world is not a dream-world under my control, a fiction my language has created and can mould to my convenience. Reality is more resistant. At many levels, things are not always as I want them to be, or conceive them to be. Realism has to start with the realization that I or anyone else can be wrong. Fallibility is part of the human condition. Any view which denigrates reason, and the possibility of truth, and which even doubts our identity, is in fact saying that there is no way in which we can be mistaken, either individually or collectively. Each epoch will have its own views, its fictions and even that view will be a fiction. Even the notion of fiction collapses, since there will be nothing left to contrast it with. If we cannot be right, we cannot be wrong, and if we cannot be wrong, we cannot be right. When everything is linguistically constructed, language itself will collapse. *So far from the differentiation between subject and object being the consequence of a concentration on language, language itself depends on it. The self cannot be constituted by language. It is presupposed by it.*[81]

---

[81] Roger Trigg, *Rationality and Religion*, Blackwell, Oxford, 1998, p. 159 (my italics).

That is what this chapter has argued, by showing that postmodernism cannot dispense with the human being.

It is a different question from how our humanity should be conceptualised. The next chapter considers accounts that regard it as *pre-given* and which view rationality as our most distinctive human endowment. Chapter 3 presents the opposite social constructionist account, which holds the human self to be *socially derivative*. These lead up to the next section on 'The Emergence of Self-Consciousness' which puts forward a realist account of the human being as neither pre-given nor socially constituted. Realism construes our humanity as the crucial emergent property of our species, which develops through practical action in the world. Our continuous sense of self, or self-consciousness, is advanced as emerging from the ways in which we are biologically constituted, the way the world is, and from the necessity of our human interaction with our external environment.

2   Modernity's man

The particular interest of the Enlightenment's 'model of man' is that it represents a being whose fundamental constitution owes nothing to society. It is this metaphysical individual which we have just seen late twentieth-century thought seeking to demolish and deconstruct by dissolving him as the solute in society's conversation. Although I maintained that some kind of human animal was generally snatched back out of the jaws of textualism, it was one whose rugged individualism had been battered out of him, leaving a frail social dependant, prone to disaggregate into a plurality of discursive 'quasi-selves'.

Modernity's man was much more like the Clint Eastwood of the eighteenth century, the lone stranger who walked tall through the townships of the western world: the man from nowhere who arrived on the scene ready-made, imposed the order which he taciturnly deemed justified, and strode off into the sunset, unchanged by his encounter. The major question about this stranger was why he should have any concern, however temporary, for the well-being of others who were never discovered to be constitutive of himself? Well, if the justification of moral action in Westerns boiled down to 'a man's gotta do what a man's gotta do', the Enlightenment did not entirely disagree with the sentiment, for Modernity's man had to be rational in his doings and was merely expected to be a good deal more articulate in supplying reasons for his moral and political actions.

Rationality not sociality was humankind's distinguishing feature. From the beginning, the paradigm of rational action was one of rational choice in a weak sense. Modernity's man was necessarily a chooser, because he was no longer embedded in, let alone constituted by, tradition. As has often been noted, once tradition comes under scrutiny, which implies an alternative stance from which to scrutinise it, its binding power, which rested upon its unquestioned status, has gone for ever. Such durability as it may show is a matter of choice, not necessity, and the chooser is now a differentiated individual rather than a member of a culturally homogenous collectivity. In tribalism what was indisputable was belonging, which meant that the ends of life were pre-selected for the group and the means for achieving them were normatively prescribed. With Modernity's man what is beyond dispute is his individual choice of ends, but there is now scope for discussing the adequacy of those reasons advanced as means for reaching these goals. The traditional normative domain of established custom and practice had been replaced by rational instrumental actions. The model of decision-making is no longer obedience to traditional precept, nor are deviations from it inspected (and punished). Instead the new model of reasoning is similar to formal logical deduction and can be criticised for deductive errors. The cultural deviant has been superseded by the defective maximiser.

In this sense Modernity's man has become logocentric: in so far as he owes the community anything (instead of owing everything to the community), it is a rational account of his actions. Whilst the post-traditional community cannot prescribe his ends, it can proscribe his means of attaining them as rationally sub-optimal. Nevertheless it is important to emphasise that the rational chooser of the Enlightenment was only such in a weak instrumental sense, for although the choice of ends came under the purview of *individual* choice, an end in itself was not a matter of *rational* choice. Fully rational man was not born in the eighteenth century. Indeed he is still coming to maturity as a substantive chooser of ends, which is one justification for speaking of the 'Enlightenment project' as unfinished business. Until the rational conspectus can embrace *Wertrational* as well as *Zweckrational* action, rational man is not fully developed. This is why Habermas would argue that it is premature to condemn him – he might yet learn to formulate his means *and* ends in a context of an ideal-speech situation.

Meanwhile it is crucial to stress that Modernity's man did not start off life as an exemplary symbolic juggler. He lacked that integrity and has not yet fully attained it: all he had shed was that traditionalistic integrality where thinking and feeling (the instrumental and the expressive) were of one piece. He had ceased being Durkheim's clansman whose solidary values arose from collective emotional effervescence in a communal rite. Instead his rationality (instrumental) had been prized apart from his sensibility (expressive). The weakly rational man of the Enlightenment was distinctly Humean; a creature whose ends were governed by *pathos* but whose means were regulated by *logos*. What gave him integration, as opposed to integrity, was the connection posited between the two such that reason operated as the 'slave of the passions'. This saved him from schizophrenia, but left him weakly rational because still in thrall to this passionate make-up.

As far as his rational choice is concerned, Modernity's man has remained shackled to his sensibilities. By 'the passions', Hume's *Treatise* leaves us in no doubt that he was talking of strong emotional beer. Thus although he could allow of benevolence and sympathy for others as motives to our will, equally he wrote that, when 'I receive any injury from another, I often feel a violent passion of resentment, which makes me desire his evil and punishment, independent of all considerations of plea- sure and advantage to myself'.[1] In other words 'the passions' had the emotional strength to cancel out the later utilitarian ethic. Choice of ends was thus handed over to our passionate emotional faculties, which became a matter of taste, and where such are concerned *de gustibus non est disputandum*.

Passions, or desires as they became less evocatively known, are things which we simply have, and have in a way which is beyond rational dis- agreement or moral dispute. In the traditional interpretation of Hume, there is really no moral knowledge as such, for the individual determines and defines the good life internally. That which is known internally is 'hot' knowledge, emotionally formed. Thus rationality does not have the power to select our passions for us or to evaluate our desires. All it can do is act as an ingenious 'slave' which serves them.[2] The ends are selected by *pathos*, and all that *logos* can do is to seek the best instrumental way of real- ising the desired state of affairs. Reason is busy, precisely because the pas- sions are plural. The job description of this slave is to ensure that the means chosen for satisfying a lower passion are carefully selected to prevent them from pre-empting the satisfaction of a higher one. In other words, reason's first task is to rank the passions and its second is to devise those courses of action which will maximise our overall satisfaction by producing the highest pay-off over the full set.

'Economic man' has already entered the scene, endowed with an instrumental rationality which will strive to drive the best bargain, such that he never pays more than he needs and never settles for less satisfac- tion than he can get. The world through which he moves is the global market place in which everything, unless it be a desire itself, is open to negotiated exchange. To the bargain-hunter this includes our relation- ships, for nothing intrinsic to them precludes them from exchange, if market prices make their exchange part of the best bargain. Thus, instead of the traditional picture in which people are partly constituted by their relationships, it is now only in the case of personal attachments that any

---

[1] David Hume, *Treatise on Human Nature*, Oxford University Press [1740], 1978, p. 464.

[2] 'Reason alone can never be a motive to any action of the will . . . reason is and ought only to be the slave of the passions and can never pretend to any other office than to serve and obey them', David Hume, *Treatise*, Book II, Part III, Section 3.

relationship can be saved from commodification, i.e. because someone's individual emotion has chosen it as an end – and while ever his tastes do not change. Hence the picture of the lonely stranger of modernity who selects his relationships in the same manner as his other purchases and who can know no loyalties because all his loyalty is vested in his own internal desires. This makes him selfish even when his behaviour appears otherwise, for such 'altruism' as he displays merely corresponds to his inner desire to behave benevolently. *Homo economicus* can have a taste for philanthropy, in which case it is the task of his reason to make him a well satisfied philanthropist, a cost-benefit effective benefactor and a philanthropic maximiser. If his high ranking preferences run to charity, then let the cats' home or the refugee agency be the best run of charities.

This is the trouble with 'the passions'. They are so full-bloodedly unruly that they can make fools out of us. After all it is said, what is more foolish than a man or a woman of a certain age being ruled by passion – to which the response has to be 'to be ruled by it for life', a lifetime in which the age of reason is never attained. This is what stuck in the craw of second generation utilitarians who could not swallow that the happy pig was in a state to be preferred to Socrates' unhappiness. There must surely be a qualitative difference which commends itself to our reason, some means by which rationality could work loose the judgement that someone was happier with his pushpin than the Golden Treasury. Yet to economists and later still, Rational Choice theorists, even building in measures allowing for the intensity of preferences (replacing mere ordinal ranking by various measures of cardinality or lexicographic preference schedules)[3] still could not banish those strong emotional feelings which continued to set-up the preference set.

My argument throughout the rest of this chapter is that over the last century there has been a sustained attempt to take the emotional heat out of Modernity's man – to encroach upon his 'hot' decisionary goals with the 'coolness' associated with instrumental reason. Yet the assault could not be full-frontal, since *de gustibus non est disputandum* was itself unquestioned and remained the unquestionable credo of individualism. It is not often recognised that rationality and individualism can sometimes be at odds, yet of course, were there to be such a thing as an ideal-speech situation, then the fact that the force of the better argument prevailed would simply mean that the individual has to cede his case to it.[4] Rational

---

[3] See S. Hargreaves Heap et al. (eds.), *The Theory of Rational Choice*, Blackwell, Oxford, 1992.
[4] Habermas too has been rightly criticised for his neglect of the emotions. See Nick Crossley, 'Emotion and Communicative Action: Habermas, Linguistic Philosophy and Existentialism', in Gillian Bendelow and Simon Williams (eds.), *Emotions in Social Life*, Routledge, London, 1998.

Choice theorists cannot afford for Modernity's man to grow up in this way, for robbed of methodological individualism their whole aggregative edifice collapses. Microeconomics and more than a hundred years' worth of elegant equations would be the first to hit the deck. If this was unthinkable, then the only alternative was to work to make individuals more rational without making them any the less individual. The solution was very English as a method for dealing with unwanted passions, namely cold baths. Regular administration of such douches gradually took the passion out of the preferences, leaving behind that cooler disposition, taste, whose imperturbability was so much better for the equations.

At the same time I want to argue that this emotional purification of Modernity's man and his replacement by the risk discounting and profit-maximising bargain-hunter leaves us with a less recognisable and an impoverished human being. The argument is not merely that we do not recognise our own faces in the mirror which Rational Choice holds up, though that is both true and important, it is also that in being stripped of our emotionality, the cold baths have simultaneously dampened what has variously been called by Frankfurt 'the importance of what we care about'[5] or by Charles Taylor the 'significance feature'[6] in humankind. In short I will be maintaining that our emotions are essential adjuncts to the pursuit of the morally good life, not in terms of emotivism but by way of vision and commitment. Cold bathing is not conducive to morality – a fact now regretfully acknowledged in our public schools.

Taking the passions out of the preferences

This is a long drawn out process that can be summarised in four stages which are roughly chronological. Overlaps occur because the practitioners of several disciplines (philosophy, economics, politics and sociology) all worked to the same end – that of excising emotion from desire such that the remaining preferences could be drawn into the ambit of rational choice. Already the utilitarians had shifted semantically from 'passions' to 'pleasures', as the intrinsic value sought by all and as that which, when maximised for the greatest number, represented the ethical standard. Nevertheless most nineteenth-century Utilitarians were still dealing with human happiness in its emotionally unexpurgated form and struggling to sum it by means of 'felicific calculus'.

[5] Harry. G. Frankfurt, *The Importance of What We Care About*, Cambridge University Press, 1988, ch. 7.
[6] Charles Taylor, 'Consciousness', in Paul F. Secord (ed.), *Explaining Human Behaviour: Consciousness, Human Action and Social Structure*, Sage, London, 1982.

(1) The first radical shift came at the hands of the economists and consisted in the reconceptualisation of 'pleasures' as 'preferences'. In empiricist terms, this had the advantage of turning an unobservable human quality into observable and measurable behaviour. 'Preference has a positivistic respectability that pleasure lacks: we can tell what a person prefers by offering him a choice and seeing what he does.'[7] Yet positivism is never innocent and here it entailed substituting for a generative causal mechanism which was internal to the person (the pursuit of pleasure), his external behaviour (choosing) whose reality could be readily ascertained on the perceptual criterion. Now the satisfaction of preferences could in principle be synonymous with the successful pursuit of happiness or even emotional feelings of well-being, but this was not the case. Instead the 'standard here is the satisfaction of preferences, not the satisfaction of people'.[8] It is crucial to recognise the extent of the divergence between the two.

This is a radical break because 'pleasure' and 'preference' can diverge to a point where the two are antithetical, where the quest for the satisfaction of preferences is the enemy of happiness. In fact the single-minded pursuit of certain preferences could only proceed at the expense of subordinating feelings of happiness and thus acting in a counter-Utilitarian manner. If an author's highest stated preference is for posthumous fame, then we are being asked to accept that she will suffer greatly without any happiness accruing to her, even if she is successful. Similarly 'a jealous husband may even prefer a "fool's hell" in which his suspicions rage but his wife is in fact faithful, to a "fool's paradise" in which his suspicions are allayed but in fact he is unknowingly cuckolded. In that case even though he experiences more satisfaction in the fool's paradise than in the fool's hell, his preferences themselves are more fully satisfied in the fool's hell than in the fool's paradise.'[9] Which he would 'really prefer' is impossible to tell *ex ante*, but once we have disturbed his 'fool's paradise', there is no returning to it *ex post*.

The move to take preferences as the standard of human welfare, rather than the degree to which humans report themselves to be satisfied and happy, simply will not do to settle what is best for people. This view assumes that whatever course of action a person prefers is shown *by the fact of his choice* to be better for him. It reached its *apogée* in Samuelson's theory of 'revealed preference'. If a basket of goods could have been bought, within the budget of an individual, yet he was observed to purchase another basket x, then it is presumed that he has revealed a prefer-

---

[7] Allen Gibbard, 'Interpersonal Comparisons: Preference, Good and the Intrinsic Reward of a Life', in Jon Elster and Aanund Hylland (eds.), *Foundations of Social Choice Theory*, Cambridge University Press, 1986, pp. 167–8.   [8] Ibid.   [9] Ibid., p. 169.

ence for x over y, with preferences being inferred from the observed choices. This, Samuelson argued, enabled him to 'develop the theory of consumer's behaviour freed from any vestigial traces of the utility concept'.[10] Presumably by this he means that his overt behaviourism has obviated any need to peer into people's heads to find out what they think they are doing, or into their hearts to discover what they feel they are doing. This shopper has certainly been divested of strong feelings, but we immediately need them back in order to explain why his choosing y over x on one occasion, and x over y on another is *not* inconsistent. Most of us do shop differently for birthdays compared with weekdays and frequently we 'let ourselves be extravagant', with a treat for self or others. Secondly, revealed preference leads directly into the Prisoner's Dilemma since following their self interest leads solitary prisoners to make confessions which produce longer sentences than would have resulted from collaborative or altruistic non-confession. Is this 'choice' of more years in prison a reliable guide to their underlying preferences?[11]

(2) Among those who said 'no' to this question were those neo-Utilitarians whose next move was to clean up our preferences and to purify them from their defective subjectivity by shifting over to talk about our 'ideal preferences'. In other words 'one reason for rejecting the subjectivist conception or taking special care with its formulation is that a person's preferences can be defective in ways which discredit them as a measure of his welfare'.[12] Hence, enter 'ill-informed preferences', 'irrational preferences', 'poorly cultivated preferences' and 'malconditioned preferences', as contrasted with 'rectified preferences', namely ones which are better for a person and which they would prefer were they fully and vividly aware of everything involved. What is significant here is that among the things to be cleaned up are the emotions and emotional interference, which now appear on the 'belief' side of the equation (Desires + Beliefs = Preferences + Action). Situating them there makes it easier for reason to get a grip on them by the innocent means of being supplied with better information.

This is Harsanyi's strategy. For it to be credible we need to be convinced that we do have passionately irrational beliefs (rectifiable), but that our emotionality does not extend to our desires. We also would need to accept that emotion is a thoroughly bad thing in preference formation.

---

[10] P. Samuelson, 'A Note on the Pure Theory of Consumers' Behaviour', *Economica*, 5, 1938, p. 71.

[11] See Amartya Sen, 'Behaviour and the Concept of Preference', *Economica*, 40, 1973.

[12] Thomas Schwartz, 'Human Welfare: What it is Not', in H. B. Miller and W. H. Williams (eds.), *The Limits of Utilitarianism*, University of Minnesota Press, Minneapolis, 1982, p. 195.

Now it is easier to accept this as formulated for a defective belief, which is demonstrable in a way in which to call a desire defective seems always to remain contentious. Thus he writes, that it

> is well known that a person's preferences may be distorted by factual errors, ignorance, careless thinking, rash judgements, *or strong emotions hindering rational choice etc.* Therefore, we may distinguish between a person's *explicit* preferences, i.e. his preferences as they actually *are*, possibly distorted by factual and logical errors – and his *true* preferences, i.e. his preferences as they *would be* under 'ideal conditions' and, in particular after careful reflection and in possession of all the relevant information. In order to exclude the influences of irrational preferences, all we have to do is define social utility in terms of individuals' 'true' preferences, rather than in terms of their explicit preferences.[13]

This is probably the Utilitarians' best move, but it rests on two questionable assumptions which threaten its workability. It seeks to retain the (rectified) link between subjectivity and welfare and can account for the fact that it is possible that what is good for a person nevertheless violates her preferences. The difficulties are two-fold: it is asserted that 'nondefective preferences are more felicifically efficient (other things being equal) than defective ones: their satisfaction is more satisfying. Not only is this not obviously true; it is not obvious how to tell if it is true.'[14]

It might seem that to encourage someone to clean up their irrational beliefs was something no rational agent should resist, because the injunction must come with a demonstration that the belief in question is misinformed. My aim is not to champion 'happy fools', but is to stress (i) that there is no necessary correlation between the passion with which a belief is held and its erroneousness, and (ii) that many of our deepest held beliefs (religious, political, ethical) simply cannot be demonstrated to rest upon defective information. The corrigible beliefs of the discerning shopper are not the appropriate model for the contestable beliefs upon which our lives are run.

(3) If working upon our beliefs to make them more rational, and thus to increase the quotient of rational action, were difficult, then to do the equivalent with our desires might appear to be a non-starter. Yet this has been the main contribution of political science. It is significant that Jon Elster has sometimes called his work 'studies in the subversion of rationality', and he agrees that it is a 'nonstandard move' to consider what induces 'irrational *desires*'.[15] As these studies have progressed, it has become clearer that emotions and addictions (it being no accident that they are examined together) are regarded as the main sources subverting

[13] John Harsanyi, 'Rule-Utilitarianism and Decision Theory', *Erkenntis*, 11, 1977, my italics.   [14] Thomas Schwartz, 'Human Welfare', p. 198.
[15] Jon Elster, *Strong Feelings*, MIT Press, Cambridge, Mass., 1999, p. 179.

the rationality of desires. Hence, 'by virtue of the high levels of arousal and valence they induce, emotions and cravings are among the most powerful sources of denial, self-deception, and rationalisation in human life'.[16] It is they which need cleaning up for Modernity's man finally to succeed to rational autonomy, roughly meaning that he has the inner freedom to plan his desires in relation to the possible.

'Strong feelings' result in discontent, an unhappiness which is more diabolical than divine. Rational desires do not result in happiness, that link has been broken for good, but they do issue in that sober protestant contentment associated with living within one's means and making virtues out of necessities. Thus to Elster 'there is a respectable and I believe valid doctrine which explains freedom in terms of the ability to accept and embrace the inevitable'.[17] This is deeply embedded in the way he defines 'rational desires' and the main question it raises is why social conditions should be treated with such inevitability by agents and why those who refuse to do so are branded as irrational? Thus to Elster the 'definition of a rational desire would include, first, an optimality property: that of leading to choices which maximise utility. If people very strongly desire what they cannot get, they will be unhappy; such desires, therefore, are irrational. A rational desire is one which is optimally adjusted to the feasible set.'[18] Maximum utility is thus defined and delimited within the politics of the possible, for the 'feasible set' is a complete list of actions which do not contravene constraints, such as wealth.

It is that which is really (ontologically) possible to which the rational actor has to accommodate her desires, not her perception of possibilities (epistemological) to which she has to adapt her utilities. All desires have causal origins but some have 'the wrong sort of causal history and hence are irrational';[19] they are under the sway of strong feelings rather than being coolly and deliberately chosen. Thus there is a rationality 'condition on the process whereby this adjustment is achieved. If the adaptation of desires to possibilities is brought about by some unconscious mechanism of dissonance reduction, as exemplified in the fable of the fox and the sour grapes, we would hardly call the result a paradigm of rationality. Our intuitions would rather suggest the opposite conclusion: to be under the sway of opaque psychological forces is a mark of irrationality. To be rational, the adjustment of desires to possibilities would have to be freely and consciously willed.'[20] Thus over-adaptive preference formation (sour grapes) or under-adaptive preferences (Ulysses

---

[16] Ibid., p. 200.   [17] Jon Elster, *Sour Grapes*, Cambridge University Press, 1983, p.119.
[18] Jon Elster, 'Introduction', to his (ed.) *Rational Choice*, Basil Blackwell, Oxford, 1986, p. 15.   [19] Jon Elster, *Sour Grapes*, p. 16.   [20] Jon Elster, *Rational Choice*, p. 15.

unbound)[21] result from a 'hot' rather than a 'cold' process,[22] from 'unconscious drives', from 'non-conscious psychic forces' which are incapable of that cool deferred gratification which is cognisant of the reality principle.[23] Hence 'rational desires' are ones which display an optimal adjustment to what is feasible and thus generate the maximum utility which is realistically possible.

Yet there seems to be something both inherently and unacceptably conservative about defining the rationality of desires in terms of the social *status quo* at any given time. Basically, why is it more rational only to entertain those desires which are attainable within existing social constraints rather than to envisage the transformation of such constraints in a better society? After all, the former attitude is what Marx would simply have called 'false consciousness' and the treatment of social arrangements as immutable would to him have been a matter of (irrational) reification. Nevertheless, this seems to be what is entailed by Elster's notion of rational character-planning. Thus he comments that 'whereas adaptive preferences [Sour Grapes] typically take the form of downgrading the accessible options, deliberate character planning would tend to upgrade the accessible ones'.[24] The message is that rationality in our desires is a matter of getting reconciled: if you don't get the wanted promotion, then change your lifestyle to benefit from the greater leisure opportunities of the less prestigious position.[25] However, suppose you are convinced that the promotion was refused because you were female or black, or spoke with a working-class accent, why is it rational to become reconciled to discrimination? Why is the anger inappropriate, or the passionate commitment to working for a more egalitarian state of affairs an irrational response? Why are our most reasonable preferences those which are 'causally shaped by the situation'?[26] After all, the choice is not restricted to either acquiescence to external constraints or succumbing to internal, hedonic 'psychic forces' – unless freedom-fighting is illegitimately assimilated to the latter!

Because freedom is defined as the autonomy enjoyed only by the 'realistic' character-planner, Elster obviously dissents from Berlin's formulation of the conditions of freedom which puts matters the other way round: 'it is the actual doors that are open that determines the extent of

---

[21] Jon Elster, *Ulysses and the Sirens*, Cambridge University Press, 1979, deals with akrasia, that is weakness of the will as a source of irrationality, and praises Ulysses' 'pre-commitment' in having himself bound to the mast to overcome his akrasia.

[22] Jon Elster, *Sour Grapes*, p. 26.

[23] These unconscious drives are 'conceived of as non-conscious psychic forces that are geared to the search for short-term pleasure, as opposed to conscious desires that may forego short-term pleasure to achieve some longer-term gain'. Ibid., p. 25.

[24] Ibid., p. 119.   [25] Ibid., p. 123.   [26] Ibid., p. 121.

someone's freedom, and not his own preferences'.[27] This Berlin argued is because 'some doors are much more important than others – the goods to which they lead are far more central in an individual's or a society's life'.[28] Precisely: but to Elster this is wrongly to stress the things that one is free to do, irrespective of whether one wants to do them.[29] Yet, his insistence upon defining the rationality of desires in terms of only that which one is free to entertain within social constraints, has the perverse effect of welcoming closed doors. If at a particular time, no one happened to exercise freedom of speech or association, must we conclude that they do not value these freedoms? Moreover, if they value them passionately in times and circumstances when they do not exist, must their attempts to kick the doors open be written off as instances of irrational desires? One of the conclusions to be drawn in the next section is that Elster's rational choice, and rational choice theory in general, cannot cope with the phenomenon of social movements.[30] In part this is due to the socially constrained definition of rationality and in part it is due to the methodological individualism which can only see society being changed through aggregate actions rather than by collective action. In part too, it derives from that purging of the emotions which condemns them as sources of irrational 'wish-fulfilment', rather than allowing that they can foster the vision and commitment which rationally support social movements pursuing the fulfilment of wishes.

(4) In the fourth stage, the attempt is made to rid the theory of these tumultuous emotions by fully incorporating them into rational choice, as items considered alongside others when people maximise their utility. Thus in *Accounting for Tastes*, Becker introduces the proposition that 'Forward-looking individuals consider how their choices affect the probability of developing rewarding emotional relations.'[31] Such relations turn out to be those which save us money, if we avoid them in ourselves, and bring us monetary reward if we inculcate them in other people. One difficulty is the very limited range of emotions Becker considers, which gives one pause to wonder whether the same principle is held to operate over the four hundred or so emotions discriminated in the English language?

---

[27] See Jon Elster's disagreement with Isaiah Berlin, *Sour Grapes*.   [28] Ibid., p. 191.

[29] Jon Elster, *Sour Grapes*, p. 127.

[30] Typical of this is the following methodological individualist statement. 'The real bottom line is that there are individual actions, that there are outcomes of these actions, and that individuals *choose actions in terms of their outcomes*, using some decision rule or another. This is the heart of rational choice theory, and it does not admit of the possibility that groups of individuals choose actions in some way that is fundamentally more than an interactive product, however complex, of the choices of individual members of the group'. Michael Laver, *Private Desires, Political Action*, Sage, London, 1997, p. 28.

[31] Gary Becker, *Accounting for Tastes,* Harvard University Press, Cambridge, Mass., 1996, p. 131.

What then follows is some good mercantile advice about monitoring one's movements in order to minimise the pains of guilt or love. Encounters with beggars make (most of) us feel guiltily uncomfortable, feelings which we would rather avoid; and the stronger the beggar's appeal, the larger the contribution elicited from us. Hence, evasive action is recommended, so that by 'anticipating the negative effects of begging on their utility, guilty contributors may be able to avoid harmful shifts in their preferences'.[32] Similarly, his marriage guidance counselling advises that rather than placing oneself in a position where generous love finds one willingly making financial transfers to a poorer spouse, it is better to stick to those neighbourhoods and clubs which will supply partners from the same class, who do not occasion such expensive sentiments.[33] However, this may well conflict with another injunction, namely to invest highly in children's education, since exposing them to university also broadens their marriage market. Presumably the implication must then be to invest in the most elitist university affordable, thus increasing the costs of evading potential marital generosity.

Nevertheless, there is the expectation of recouping these outlays upon children by ensuring transfers of income back to the parents in their old age. This is part of manipulating other people's emotions so that cost-benefit sums end up being positive. Thus Becker advocates 'investment in guilt' by which parents financially promote the acquisition of 'merit goods' in their offspring, with the intention of inducing sufficient guilt in them to ensure that they themselves are cared for, in return, in their later years. Yet this assumes that parents are actuated by investment considerations, rather than genuinely caring for their children, and that the latter are guiltily responsive later on, rather than simply angry at having been manipulated. In all of this, emotions like love and caring within the family have been subordinated to cost-benefit calculations which will later be cashed-in.

More generally, in society, the development of norms and the formation of preferences entail emotional involvement, so the simple advice here is to buy the appropriate values through indoctrination. Thus the provision of churches for the lower classes is recommended, where the poor are compensated for lending themselves to the inculcation of beliefs because the rich subsidise expensive buildings and the clergy. Compensation is limited to start-up costs, because once the norm of churchgoing is established, the poor will police one another in these socially useful religious practices.[34] A major difficulty here is that indoctrination must not be seen as such, hence 'the rich' cannot do it

---

[32] Ibid., p. 233.   [33] Ibid., p. 236.   [34] Ibid., pp. 229–30.

directly but needs must work through clergy who actually are religious believers. Yet even if these clergymen are not averse to financial contributions, what ensures that the donors' 'message' is prominently preached or prevails in the conflict with religious values of compassionate caring? Nothing does, unless the assumption is made that religious commitments, like all others, have their price-tag.

This fourth strategy which subjects emotions to the process of rational choice itself, necessarily commodifies them. When they were treated as externalities of the market, as in Becker's earlier work, they could impinge, positively or negatively, upon people's welfare, but in their own terms. Now that they are chosen (or deselected for) alongside other commodities, then they must be presumed to be commensurable. Becker does not hesitate to make this assumption and to make cash the common denominator between emotions and anything else which is rationally chosen. It means that he is presuming that emotional 'returns', like the love and regard of others can be bought. I would simply deny that these are commodities or that they are for sale. Instead, they are some of our deepest human concerns, ones which are constitutive of who we are, rather than being instrumentally rational means to yet further ends – to some indefinitely deferred point at which we 'forward-looking individuals' become 'better off'. Yet, if considered as 'ultimate concerns', as I will try to show in the final section, then these emotional states are not commodities which can be costed, but rather should be considered in the guise of commitments which are quite literally priceless. On the contrary, emotions can only be tamed and finally brought within the ambit of rational choice if they are forced to take up their abode in the market place.

The return of the exile

So far, I have represented the upbringers of Modernity's man as four generations of carers, all of whom were determined that he came to maturity a good deal more rational than he started off life. They did this progressively by taming his passions into preferences, then working on the beliefs with which these operated in order to purge him of 'defective preferences' and finally by attempting to purify his utilities until these became matters of 'rational desires'. What were exiled to the nursery were the temper tantrums associated with his 'hot' emotional 'I want's', so that his coming of age was the emergence of a 'cool' reasoner capable of dispassionate 'character planning'. Then Modernity's man would have become a fully rational chooser and thus the ideal subject for rational choice theory. Yet the trouble is that this theory aspires to give us not only a 'model of man' as the rational actor but also to derive complex social structures directly from him and those like him, i.e. from some property pertaining to this (idealised) human being. In other words, as Hollis put it, this second Adam was intended to be a 'sovereign artificer' not only of himself, but together with those like him, of his society.[35] Since Adam is the topic of this book and his society-building was dealt with in its predecessor, I will only make a brief detour to comment on his abilities in making his social environment before returning to the assessment of his character. The point of this excursion is to show that rational choice theorists themselves came to regret the exiling of the emotions and sought the repatriation of 'emotional man' as a necessary partner in the building of society.

The first contender as a society-builder was 'rational man' of classical economics, whose calculus, consistency and selfishness, resulted in choices which summed to produce social reality. The trouble was that this model of 'rational man' could not cope with manifest social phenomena like voluntary collective behaviour or the voluntary creation of public goods. Only the offer of selective incentives or the imposition of coercive measures should persuade the 'free-rider' of rational grounds for co-operating in collective action.[36] Nevertheless, it was admitted that 'irrational' forces such as ideological inspiration, altruism or personal commitment could do the trick of reforming the free-rider. This led some who conceded 'rational man's' inability to deal rationally with the Prisoner's Dilemma or free-riding to complement him with an inner running mate, rather than abandoning him to his paradoxical fate. Enter 'normative man', who shifts to a different logic of action under circumstances in which he realises that he is dependent upon others for his welfare. This is someone who will act in terms of normative expectations and social duty and thus becomes subject to a sense of interdependence when public non-divisible goods are desired. However, inexplicable macro-level effects still remained, and 'emotional man' joined the team to mop up structural and cultural properties which were based upon expressive solidarity or a willingness to share. Above all he was needed to account for social stability deriving from solidarity and for instability resulting from collective protest. Thus as 'a "loving" participant in collective action, emotional "man" contributes to the creation of public goods, and as a creator of corporate actors, to the stabilisation and regulation of otherwise intermittent and fleeting feelings, but also to a general emotional restraint'.[37] On the other hand, emotional action 'represents the

---

[35] Martin Hollis, *The Cunning of Reason*, Cambridge University Press, 1987, ch. 1.
[36] M. Olsen, *The Logic of Collective Action*, Harvard University Press, Cambridge, Mass., 1965. pp. 61–5, 106–8.
[37] Helena Flam, 'Emotional "Man": I The Emotional 'Man' and the Problem of Collective Action', *International Sociology*, 5:1, 1990.

volte-face potential in, or outer limits of, everyday normative or calculating behaviour. As an angered participant in collective protest, emotional "man" is a source of social change and political instability.'[38] Thus, those emotional qualities on whose expunging so much effort had been devoted were now brought back out of exile as necessary components in explaining what held societies together or precipitated them towards transformation.

What was being done, however, was to multiply the incommensurable situational logics to which human beings were responsive. The technique was to multiply the denizens of every human being with these different 'men' all harmoniously cohabiting one body – 'rational', 'normative' and 'emotional' – without the previous fear that one undermined the other, because they were now confined to different spheres of action and were supposed to know their social place. Thus Helena Flam wrote that it was her intention 'to propose a model of the emotional "man" as a *complement* to the models of rational and normative man' and 'not to argue that the mode of emotional action should replace either of the other two. Rather it is to advocate model pluralism in lieu of the present model duopoly. The model of the emotional "man" is useful because it helps to explain some aspects of collective action which the rational and normative man models cannot handle.'[39]

There are problems with this multiplication of complements, all inhabiting the same being. The first concerns Adam's own mental health. What is it that ensures that the complements *do* know their proper place? Once they have been housed in the same body, what prevents one from usurping another? Supposedly they await the appropriate external social cues for activation, but why should we not suppose instead that there is some internal effort after personal integration? If on occasions one can be either dutiful or loving, why should one not strive to be lovingly dutiful? That does not sound too bad: but when instead we try being angrily rational all the old problems of impetuousness which supposedly dogged Modernity's man resurface. Yet, if they do not, if the complements keep themselves to their socially compartmentalised space, then sociologically the key principle of methodological individualism has given way, and philosophically the basic principle of 'one person per body' seems to have been violated!

The second problem with these complements making up the same human being is that it eventually comes full circle ending up with the 'multiple self',[40] and the suggestion that we treat 'man' like an organisation. Yet this is a completely vicious circle: some sort of 'man' was wanted

[38] Ibid., p 42.   [39] Ibid., p. 39.
[40] Jon Elster, *The Multiple Self*, Cambridge University Press, 1988.

to explain that which was problematic, namely social organisation, but now we are enjoined to use the explanandum in order to conceptualise the explanans, the nature of man! Matters are now getting out of hand: *homo sentiens* can neither be left in exile nor can he be repatriated on rational choice soil without doing untold mischief. Hence my suggestion that the upbringing of Modernity's man might fare better if we left him with his emotions intact and allowed them to develop with him. Certainly, I am going to maintain that he will not then much resemble either *homo economicus* or *homo sociologicus*, but he does stand more chance of presenting a human face.

Homo economicus and the circumstances not of his choosing

Fundamentally what accounted for the gradual development of this 'multiple self' with its plurality of inner personas – rational, normative and emotional – is what always goes wrong with methodological individualism's individual. He begins as ruggedly autonomous, radically atomistic, a man whose individual dispositions plot his actions and life course. As Watkins stated the matter, 'According to this principle [methodological individualism], the ultimate constituents of the social world are individual people who act more or less appropriately in the light of their dispositions and understanding of their situation.'[41] Thus, it must follow that if the crucial facts about people are their dispositions, then statements about things other than individuals are excluded as are statements which are not about their dispositions. Yet methodological individualists immediately break with both these requirements of their position, since the facts about people which are allowed to figure in rock-bottom explanations are neither solely individual nor solely dispositional. Instead Watkins allows that acceptable predicates can include 'statements about the dispositions, beliefs, resources and inter-relations of individuals' as well as their 'situations . . . physical resources and environment'.[42] Some of these, of course, are not individual and some are not dispositional, and it is arguable that none are both. What this move permits, however, is that those socio-cultural features to which it is indispensable to refer for explanatory purposes have now been incorporated by making them part of the individual's own constitution.

This is exactly what is going on with the multiplication of inner complements inhabiting Rational Choice Theory's man. Because eco-

---

[41] J. W. N. Watkins, 'Methodological Individualism and Social Tendencies', in May Brodbeck (ed.), *Readings in the Philosophy of the Social Sciences*, Macmillan, New York, 1968, p. 270.   [42] Ibid., pp. 270–1.

nomic choices are obviously constrained by our spending power, the social distribution of wealth is disaggregated into what you or I have laid our hands on and then is incorporated into us as our 'budget'. Thus preferences, a dispositional term, can now be expressed individualistically in the market-place 'within our budget'. Similarly, because our actions are often constrained by normative expectations, these social duties are also disaggregated into a personal sense of co-operative interdependence when individual welfare depends upon co-operation. The creation of public goods can now be dispositionally explained in voluntaristic fashion because there is no longer any need to introduce external normative constraints, since the work they do has been taken over by the individual's recognition of his own good. Finally, because social solidarity frequently seemed to exert a Durkheimian binding force over us, this too is disaggregated into a personal willingness to share or to collaborate, which depends upon individual emotionality. Thus, generous emotional dispositions account for the voluntary creation of public goods and angry men make for collective protest.

In all three cases, those aspects of the social context which are indispensable for explanation – the social distribution of resources, the social pattern of normative expectations and the social condition of solidarity – are themselves incorporated into individual terms. As Lukes puts it, 'the relevant features of the social context are, so to speak, built into the individual'.[43] There are two serious ontological objections to this procedure. On the one hand, in what recognisable sense are we still talking about 'the individual' when he or she has now been burdened with so many inalienable features of social reality? On the other hand, can the social context really be disaggregated in this way, such that solidarity and protest are purely interpersonal matters, normative beliefs are only what certain people hold in their own interests, and resource distributions are just what each of us has on personal deposit? There is a further methodological problem due to this 'desperate incorporation' of social factors into the individual which Gellner expressed as follows. '"Algy met a bear, the bear was bulgy, the bulge was Algy"; the individual may consume what Durkheim and others have called social facts, but he will bulge most uncomfortably, and Algy will still be there. I suspect that actual investigators will often . . . prefer to have Algy outside the bear.'[44] I agree, and want to show good reasons why it is distinctly preferable to keep *homo economicus* and his 'circumstances' clearly differentiated from one another. To

[43] Steven Lukes, 'Methodological Individualism Reconsidered', *British Journal of Sociology*, 19:2, 1968, p. 125.
[44] Ernest Gellner, 'Holism Versus Individualism', in May Brodbeck, *Readings in the Philosophy of the Social Sciences*, pp. 267–8.

anticipate the conclusion, Adam's circumstantial context is not just a neutral medium in which he expresses his preferences, but a series of constraints whose overthrow he may seek with passion. Far from accepting the methodological moral that these things are part of his own constitution, he pursues social transformation in order to generate radically changed circumstances in which he can be himself. What he seeks is a social identity which expresses what he most cares about in himself, and what he repudiates is that he can attain such an identity by self-improvement and self-help within the current alienating context.

The first reason concerns the relationship between 'preferences' and 'circumstances', or rather its absence in rational economic man. Preferences are assumed to be given, current, complete, consistent and determining. Here I want to argue that the societal distribution of resources actually has an *independent* effect upon each of these elements and one which is badly obscured by the process of disaggregation. Economists typically deal with *given* preferences: they freeze the frame in the present tense and generically take no interest in their source or formation. In Becker's extreme version of these, 'tastes neither change capriciously nor differ importantly between people. On this interpretation one does not argue over tastes for the same reason that one does not reason over the Rocky mountains – both are there, will be there next year, too, and are the same to all men.'[45] Others of course allow for changes over time and for inter-personal variability. Nevertheless a normal given preference (of the shopper rather than the addict) is supposed to show price elasticity. Thus those on low pay will stock up with the supermarket's cheapest offer on baked beans, but if their incomes rise they will head for the luxury lines, their basic preference being for the best food they can afford. Now nutritionists may have their doubts about whether sudden wealth does produce good eating, but the bizarre diet of Elvis Presley is just where the economist would invoke *de gustibus non est disputandum*. But the sociologist remains rightly worried when she suspects the converse, namely that it is circumstances which are forming people's preferences. Working-class parents were not being good bargain-hunters when they used to declare a greater preference for the secondary modern school over a free grammar school place, on the grounds that the latter was 'not for the likes of us': and Bourdieu showed middle-class parents to be exceedingly good at winkling-out educational safety-nets which protected against their children's social demotion.[46] Is this difference in economic manhood merely a non-disputatious question of tastes, in which case why is there a class-

[45] Gary Becker, *Accounting for Tastes*, p. 24.
[46] Pierre Bourdieu and Jean-Claude Passeron, *La Reproduction*, Les Editions de Minuit, Paris, 1970.

patterning? Alternatively, is it a highly contentious effect of generations of educational discrimination?

Similar difficulties attach to the requirement that a preference order should be both complete and consistent, meaning that for any given x and any given y, the individual prefers one to the other, or rates them equally, but must have an overall ranking of all alternatives. Necessarily this means that agents must know their preferences for experiences which they have not yet tried and which might alter them considerably if they did so, for relationships which they have not yet undergone, but which, like mother-hood, there is no going back upon, and for ways of living which they have not sampled but which, like early school leaving, will alter their life-chances if they do. Here, information cannot be first-hand yet the distrib-ution of second-hand information is as socially skewed as are other distributions of resources. Appeals to family and friends, the availability of role models and the advice given by teachers will be filtered through their own cultural capital and perhaps reflectively adjusted to the cultural assets of the inquirer. This works to keep our aspirations up as well as down: once I joined the long queue at the local college for the course in Basic English, to be informed that I had come to the wrong desk, before being able to register our *au pair*. Again the differential social accessibility of information plays a role in shaping preferences which is presumed by Rational Choice theorists to work in the opposite direction – preferences lead us to raid a common information bank for which everyone has a PIN number.

Consistent preferences are ones whose ranking shows 'transitivity', namely a ranking such as if A is preferred to B, and B to C, then A must also be preferred to C. It is immaterial what coinage is used to order these incommensurables, hence the handy word 'utility', but it is needed in order to know what is being rationally maximised, or for rational action *tout court*. Difficulties start immediately, because although my current preference may be for A (going straight up to university), I might still rather choose B (taking a gap year) as I know that otherwise this option will be *irretrievably* foregone. And if the choice of B does not enter through the gate of my current preferences, then, like all forms of deferred gratification, it is hard to see how it gets in on the act, especially as this example is not a matter of discounting the future.

Secondly, imperfect information makes a second appearance, affecting our preference *ordering* as distinct from their formation. Think of the thou-sands now agonising over their choice of university. Suppose they have come down to three criteria, 'league position', 'location' and 'course content', all of which are considered equally important. Then an applicant grades university A as 3, 2, 1 (meaning 'excellent', 'good' and 'acceptable' on these criteria), whilst university B scores 1, 3, 2 and university C gets the scores 2, 1, 3. Were the applicant to consider only a difference of two points in any category to be significant enough to dismiss an institution, but that one point difference is unreliable, then transitivity is broken.[47] Thus A would be preferred to B (for decisive superiority on the 'league table'), B to C (for decisive superiority in terms of location), and C to A (for decisive superiority in course content). Our applicant has now violated the Bayesian choice axioms, and yet she is not indifferent to these universities as if they were regarded as equal. Rather than behave like Buridan's ass, our applicant can do many things. She could behave impeccably and introduce a tie breaker like 'accommodation'. Yet, why should she, for her main concern is to pick a university, not to establish a transitive preference order. So she is just as likely to pour over the brochures, meet some congenial people at one particular Open Day, or to ask her friends for their opinions. None of these are irrational reactions, but neither are they 'rational choices'. In fact this is where we remain deplorably ignorant, for though we can invoke 'luck', or 'contingency' which sounds better, what we do not know is where she turns, what she takes into account and how she weighs it in her own personal balance.

This fundamental problem becomes even more acute when we move onto the determining force which preferences are supposed to exert. On our common understanding, the idea of 'choice' is an active process of choosing in which the agent weighs the pros and cons, in terms of whatever weights and measures she employs, and then comes up with her decision. Of course some regularities are to be expected amongst those similarly placed, precisely because the circumstances of those differently placed attach different costs to the execution of the same project. All of this is familiar in realist social theory which sees the constraints and enablements emanating from the societal distribution of resources as being mediated to agents through the situations which they confront and the opportunity costs associated with different courses of action to those who are differently placed. However, realism requires an active agent who reflectively weighs his or her current circumstances against the attainment of his or her goals and who alone determines whether he or she can afford the price. This is very different from the passive man of rational choice theory, for there, 'If we recall that preferences are given, then it will be seen that the agent is simply a throughput.'[48] Determination of a course of action is a matter of the hydraulic pushes and pulls which prices exert on preferences.

[47] See Max Black, *Perplexities*, Cornell University Press, Ithaca and London, 1990, pp. 148–9.   [48] Martin Hollis, *The Cunning of Reason*, p. 68.

The difference between the active chooser and the passive throughput can be seen if we consider bright working-class Sharon who left school early, took her City and Guilds and became a hair stylist. For a time she is buoyed up by her pay packet and progress up the salon hierarchy, but she becomes increasingly frustrated with her job. Now this initial choice is corrigible, but further costs are attached, some necessary and some contingent, for life goes on as corrective preferences are contemplated. The trouble is that whilst on day release she met and later married Darren, who is unenthusiastic about the sundry costs which would fall on him if Sharon pursues the University Access course which a client has just mentioned to her. His concerns are allayed by the birth of Warren, but Sharon's costs of extricating herself have now redoubled. She has acquired new vested interests in her family and home, which constitute new obstacles to enrolment on the Access course. It can still be done, but presented with these situational constraints, not too many will be undeterred and decide that they have good reason to do so at that time and under those circumstances. Suppose that Sharon does not abandon the project entirely, but postpones it until the children are at school: she finally enters the university as a mature student and, in an uncertain job market, has collected another penalty for being older. Moreover, not only does Sharon now have to juggle childcare and study requirements, but in realising her abilities she is also acquiring a new set of friends and outlook, which bode ill for her marital stability. Divorce is another common price to accrue, often leaving Sharon as a single-parent family, with a course to complete and an uncertain occupational future.

The moral of this story is not meant to deter our mature students. On the contrary, they have triumphed over their circumstances, but as extremely active agents they leave us with the question of what made them battle uphill and what exactly they were weighing in their balances which made these sacrifices worthwhile to them. What will not do is to render Sharon passive, and to write off her determination as being due to the effects of 'socially random influences', in the words of one rational choice theorist.[49]

Neither, on the other hand, is reproduction (which in this case replicates the well-known socio-economic differences in educational attainment) merely a matter of routinisation. For let us now take Karen's story of capitulating to her circumstances. Far from being an account of a hydraulic process, this entailed reluctant resignation, strenuous exertion against the odds and a bitter failure to meet the costs of overcoming

---

[49] Diego Gambetta, *Were they Pushed or did they Jump?*, Westview Press, Boulder, Colorado, 1996, p. 186.

situational constraints. To have tried and failed does not mean that she had a different preference schedule from Sharon. Now, routinisation might appear as a more appropriate characterisation of the perpetuation of structural privilege, but this would be deceptive because it requires an active and reflective cooperation with enablements. Habitual action may be highly inappropriate for cashing them in. Enablements are advantageous for allowing people to stay ahead, not to stay where they are, and the former means being ready and able to innovate with new courses and openings, which is beyond the wits of passive man.

Since, as has been seen, the rational choice theorist aspires to explain both the choices we make and the social context in which we make them, it is a fair question to ask for an account of *homo economicus*'s circumstances which are not of his choosing. Rational choice's diachronic account construes enablements as the 'winnings from previous games' and constraints as their losses, as if the privileged and underprivileged come from the lines of good and bad card players respectively. This has a certain plausibility, until it is recalled that the 'games' of game theory have pretty stringent regulative and constitutive rules attached to them (there would be no Prisoner's Dilemma without assuming prison sentencing, criminal justice or solitary confinement). But what are the rules of the 'Life Chances' game? The social distribution of resources was not brought about by our ancestors playing 'Modernist Monopoly', for new players could enter and change the rules (of Constitution, enfranchisement, habeus corpus or combination) and new strategies could not be ruled out (of professionalisation or unionisation). Nor can the present generation of the privileged and under-privileged be construed as playing some 'Us and Them' game. The terminology is empty and metaphoric: to take it literally would be as bad as assuming that when the Third Estate took the Tennis Court oath, they were binding themselves to the rules of tennis.

The alternative synchronic solution to explaining and incorporating constraints is Becker's invocation of 'personal' and 'social' capital. The former is roughly where our childhood sins and virtues are accumulated: 'For example, investment may depend on smoking, attending church, or playing tennis because these types of consumption build up stocks of habitual capital.'[50] Conversely, 'an individual's stock of social capital depends not primarily on his own choices, but on the choices of peers in the relevant network of interaction',[51] plus his ethnicity, family history, nationality and religion, because culture changes so slowly and with such a low depreciation rate that it is effectively 'given' to the individual for life.

[50] Gary Becker, *Accounting for Tastes*, p. 7.   [51] Ibid., p. 12.

This then enabled him to deal with (what he agrees are) 'neglected constraints' in the following manner: 'Preferences and constraints no longer have independent influences on behaviour since personal and social capital *are constraints that operate through preferences*'.[52] What is happening here is the typical methodological individualists' manoeuvre of 'desperate incorporation' of group variables (class, status and power) into the individual person, as was discussed at the start of this section pp.66–68. We thus do not confront constraints like Marx's 'alien powers'; rather they constitute us and thus we involuntarily 'prefer' to reproduce them. Presumably we should neither congratulate Sharon nor commiserate with Karen, since both were only expressing their preferences. At most we should look for an educated role model or encouraging teacher in Sharon's biography and expect to find that all Karen's family and friends spent their school days smoking behind the bicycle shed. Well this may or may not be a way of putting flesh on those 'socially random influences', but it is a long way from regarding the struggles of both girls as real and their outcomes as dependent upon their own, and still opaque, reasons for choosing.

Finally *homo economicus* is passive in another important sense. Because he and others like him are passionless, atomistic individuals, the formation of a social movement is beyond him. It was of course to enable him to engage in collective action that Flam had complemented him with Emotional Man. This was the final way of incorporating into the individual those properties which were needed to make his looks and behaviour approximate to the manifest abilities of social agents. Although it is true that social agents need to have their passions involved before participating in social movements, otherwise all would have reason to be free-riders, this makes collaborative action depend upon 'collective effervescence' alone. Instead, we need to introduce the objective conditions for collective action and the objective goals which 'corporate agents'[53] pursue. After all every social movement is *for* something, even if its ends are imperfectly articulated and its organisation is strategically uncertain about the most effective means to employ.

The missing elements, which are necessarily lacking on a methodologically individualistic account, are *interests* and *identity*. As social agents, collectivities of people are involuntaristically pre-grouped at birth in relation to the social distribution of scarce resources. For simplicity these are

---

[52] Ibid., p. 21. My italics.
[53] These are agents who are organised as social movements and have articulated their goals, as opposed to 'Primary agents' who are simply collectivities of those with similar life-chances. See, Margaret Archer, *Realist Social Theory*, Cambridge University Press, 1995, ch. 8.

called the 'privileged' and the 'non-privileged' and the latter confront plenty of daily exigencies, given their poor life chances. They thus have vested interests in common in ameliorating their position and hence the best of reasons for struggling to develop collective organisations (unionisation, franchise, civil rights movements and feminism), to achieve together what they cannot bring about alone. Their promotive activities are too innovative to be construed as 'games' for there was no nineteenth-century game called 'winning the franchise', no regulative rules governing political conflict (repressive strategies changed all the time), and any constitutive rules were *ex post* since they entailed constitutional changes as a product of this conflict itself.

If we ask, what generically such movements seek to achieve, the answer is a structural change which enables the underprivileged to gain access to new social identities through a form of 'citizenship' which will give access to positions in which agents can be themselves. What the introduction of the collective social movement allows is something which rational choice theory cannot supply, namely an account of how agents are not condemned to a static distribution of life chances and an equally static array of accessible positions. In other words, the picture of individual agents 'living within their budgets' is transformed when we introduce processes through which they collectively alter the structural principles of budgetary allocation. But we cannot do this without also allowing that the inegalitarian distribution of life-chances furnishes *interests* in their transformation and that collective passions fuel what some term 'identity politics'.[54] Neither can be accommodated on a model of *homo economicus*, as an individualistic passive agent whose circumstances push and pull him around, but who lacks the capacity to combine in order to change them.

Homo sociologicus and normative constraints

Greenwood seems correct that the mere mobilisation of collectivities to obtain civil rights or women's rights does not solve the problem of acquiring a social identity. 'Being black does not itself fix any form of identity, any more than being a woman or a man does.'[55] It cannot, because the mere acquisition of new rights does not secure strict numerical identity, whose criteria cannot be satisfied by more than one candidate, and thus never by being members of a social movement with others sharing the same interests. What the successful movement does do is to open doors to new parts of society's role array which were formerly inaccessible to them.

[54] Craig Calhoun (ed.), *Social Theory and the Politics of Identity*, Blackwell, Oxford, 1994.
[55] John D. Greenwood, *Realism, Identity and Emotion*, Sage, London, 1994, p. 131.

'What the feminist movement has done, to a greater or lesser degree, is to open up a number of alternative moral careers that were either closed to women or difficult for them to enter or succeed in (such as the professions, including the army, organised religion, literature, politics and the like).'[56] In other words the social movement is the stepping stone to acquiring a social identity through taking on a role(s) in which people can invest enough of themselves to feel at home with what they have become.

However, here is the rub for rational choice theory. Those who take on social roles are subject to normative expectations. In so far as their conduct is subject to social norms, they act out of a sense of duty rather than according to a rational man's self-interest. Attempts to deal with norms within this theory have often taken the form that norms are merely grist to strategic manipulation, such that people invoke them as a cloak to legitimate their self interest whilst not really subscribing to them. This seems impossible because if no one believed in the norms, they could hardly be manipulated through them. Alternatively it is the avoidance of the sanctions associated with norm-breaking which, on a cost-benefit analysis, makes rational man obedient to them. Against this Elster regards the following arguments as supplying sufficient refutation. 'First some norms are followed in the absence of any observers who could sanction violations. Many people vote even when nobody would notice that they do not.'[57] Secondly, we have to ask why anyone would want to impose the sanctions. Perhaps they follow a metanorm to sanction people who violate first-order norms, but then we have to ask whether it is rational to follow that norm. 'In the regress that now arises, there must come a point at which the cost of expressing disapproval is more than the cost of receiving disapproval for not expressing it, since the former cost is approximately constant while the second goes rapidly to zero.'[58]

Because the efficacy of social norms cannot be denied but neither can they be reduced to the machinations of individuals' rationality, Elster himself agrees that 'among the alternatives to rational choice theory, the (as yet underdeveloped) theory of social norms holds out most promise'.[59] But he gives the warning that were rational and normative behaviour to be successfully combined, this could only be in such a manner that rationality would still retain its privilege in an account of action. This combination is what Martin Hollis set out to explore in what

[56] Ibid.
[57] For ingenious but unconvincing attempts to explain ' the paradox of voter turnout', see, Donald P. Green and Ian Shapiro, *Pathologies of Rational Choice*, Yale University Press, New Haven and London, 1994, ch. 4.
[58] Jon Elster, *Solomonic Judgements*, Cambridge University Press, 1989, p. 34.
[59] Ibid., p. 35.

he called 'a negotiated settlement between the standard *homo economicus* and the standard *homo sociologicus*, whose terms are a fresh notion of rationality.'[60] But he too gave a warning that he was going to leave a loose end, namely the 'weight to be finally attached to the actors' own view of what they are doing',[61] a thread which when pulled finally unravels the settlement.

There is much that is very attractive in Hollis's account, especially the arguments developed from *Models of Man* that a role is both a source of reasons for action and a vehicle which gives a person control over his own social life. The chain of rationality is not broken by the subsumption of action under normative expectations, because cultural dopery is avoided by asserting that the reasons for action associated with a role, move an actor only when they are adopted as his own good reasons. This does imply an overtly contractarian view of role taking, from which I dissent, but it has the advantage of not slipping back into the passive mode where an actor has no reasons for whose sake the role is played, beyond citing role requirements themselves. Thus 'real interests are acquired within a social contract. The initial choice of position, non-rational in prospect, can be rational in retrospect, or if irrational in retrospect can be rationally corrected'.[62] Altogether this choice of position(s) is too unconstrained, and I would want to build back in some of Karen's opportunity costs.[63] Nevertheless, the great attraction to be retained is the manner in which Hollis conceptualises roles as 'intelligent stewardship' and their require- ments as entailing something both more involving and demanding than a mindless reading of the small print. In short, since roles are not fully pre- scribed, it is better to think of individuals as personifying roles, that is monitoring themselves in order to bring the character to life, rather than extinguishing themselves by simply impersonating characters. This makes them into loyal servants rather than subservient dopes, and it has the supreme advantage of conceptualising social selves for Adam and Eve which, whilst dependent upon society, also enable them to meet the strict criteria of identity as particular persons. Thus through choosing (and being chosen) to be Professor of Sociology at Warwick University, I per- sonify the role in my own fashion which makes me distinct from all others who hold the same job contract. My obligations I accept as mine, but their execution, far from swamping me, are used to define me myself.

Why do the attractions of this settlement prove to be its undoing, as Hollis maintains is the case? What stops the bargain-hunter from being

---

[60] Martin Hollis, *The Cunning of Reason*, p. 147.   [61] Ibid.
[62] Martin Hollis, *Models of Man: Philosophical Thoughts on Social Action*, Cambridge University Press, 1977, p. 105.
[63] See Margaret S. Archer, *Realist Social Theory*, pp. 276f.

turned into a creature of norms is that, basically, in seeking to preserve our discretion, Hollis is not prepared to have us become a creature at all if that simply means becoming a hybrid of our rational calculations and our normative obligations. If *homo economicus* is crossed with *homo sociologicus*, although 'each of the two models explains how actions are programmed, then they cannot be combined to explain why action is not programmed.'[64] Yet if we truly personify roles, then we bring to them something other than the normative stuff out of which roles are made. If we can do this, then the missing ingredient must come from our personal identity since it cannot derive from our social identities which depend upon what we do to the roles we assume. What we bring is judgement of a kind 'more like moral judgement than like either ready reckoning or rifle drill. It consists in acting intelligently for reasons which a role-player can justify.'[65] From there on we have to try and understand the man who is both more than a pursuer of his preferences and who animates his roles above and beyond their normative obligations. Who is he? As we have seen, the answer which latter-day rational choice theorists were tempted to give was *homo sentiens* and in the sense that the return of the exile was necessary, they were not too far wide of the mark. The difference is that there his repatriation was needed to do some mopping up: here he is required in order to give real animation to the 'man of judgement' who has more than an eye to the main chance and is something better than word-perfect in the parts he plays.

Basically, the settlement between *homo economicus* and *homo sociologicus* unravels because to a 'strong actionist' like Hollis, both notions give us a passive actor who plays no part in morally shaping his own life. Rational man, the bargain hunter looks more active than he is because of his remorseless pursuit of self-interest. However if he is pre-programmed by a fixed preference schedule, he is deprived of the ability to reflect morally upon his preference-set. Thus he could not do any of those things which Elster advises in order to modify our undesirable or addictive preferences by 'pre-committing' ourselves in ways which outsmart our weakness of will. Ulysses needs to be a morally active agent to ask his sailors to bind him to the mast so that he can hear the Sirens without being drawn to his doom by them. Yet, if he is such an agent, then there is more to him than a programmed robot. However, that which is 'more' than his appetites, because it can control them, cannot be filled in by social norms. For one thing the Classical Sea Captains' manual did not contain the instruction 'immobilise yourself when in the vicinity of beguiling Sirens', because roles cannot be scripted for every contingency. Therefore the successful

---

[64] Martin Hollis, *The Cunning of Reason*, p. 172.   [65] Ibid.

role player cannot sink into the passive follower of normative instructions, whose only reasons for action are located in the role itself, or because satisfactory performance gives access to further roles. Even role-theory's explanation of social change, which is rooted in role-clash, requires an active agent with the capacity to determine what to do under these circumstances because the 'cultural dope' will simply be paralysed. In the first case, we needed a person of sufficient depth to monitor his appetites, but 'normative man' cannot supply this deficiency. Anyway, he also needs to be someone of sufficient breadth to execute his roles creatively, which he cannot do by passively consulting the rule-book.

Hence, the temptation in sociology is to follow Goffman's path and to celebrate the highly knowledgeable actor in order to get away from the oversocialised 'culture dope', who only does things because required to do so by the roles occupied. Instead, agents in their lifeworld play out their positionings with style, skill and distance. Yet if they can perform socially with such virtuosity they must have a personal identity, but one which is not thrust upon them, by prior social conditioning and/or cultural processes of socialisation. Thus we need to know who this 'self' is, which owes nothing to society but is so thoroughly conversant with its ways, and how it came to be. This is a debt which Goffman left unsettled by his question-begging definition – 'a self is a repertoire of behaviour appropriate to a different set of contingencies.'[66] Goffman owes us a theory of his feisty self as a social subject and this too goes unpaid, for his second definition only proffers an organic parcel: 'by "personal identity" I mean the unique organic continuity imputed to each individual, this established through distinguishing marks such as name and appearance.'[67] Goffman's subject has too much autonomy, for it operates in a social arena by merely donning and doffing masks behind which its mysterious private business is conducted, without becoming anything through the social relations it sustains (too much self: too little of the social). Conversely 'normative man' becomes so sunk in his roles that he has too little autonomy and lacks the wherewithal to respond to unscripted exigencies (too much society: too little of the self). This is a problem which cannot be solved by endowing him with a fixed preference schedule for he could neither monitor that reflectively for himself, nor for his role performances, which cannot be reduced to public means to private ends if they are granted to be binding in some sense (too little self *and* too little of the social).

That is the trouble with the steps which in real life are supposed to

---

[66] E. Goffman, *The Presentation of Self in Everyday Life*, Doubleday, New York, 1959.
[67] E. Goffman, *Relations in Public*, Penguin, Harmondsworth, 1971, p. 189.

induce rational man to contract into social norms. He only does so because they are in his enlightened self-interest: he does not accept them as binding but endorses them calculatively. Thus our rogues playing a series of Prisoner's Dilemmas will both calculate that acting according to the 'no-grassing' rule and keeping silent leaves them both better off, until they both later calculate that cheating on this rule leaves each best-off. 'No-grassing' is normatively unstable and deteriorates iteratively into the regular, although sub-optimal, 'tit for tat.'[68] Hence there can be no contractarian ethics because these rogues' codes do not bind morally and the rogue will revert to free-riding or side-dealing provided he calculates that he can get away with it. In other words, authentic ethical behaviour can only work if persons are not ultimately motivated by personal gain, but by something other than the satisfaction of their own preferences. On the other hand, over-binding them so that they become normatively dopey does not do the moral trick either, since it produces socially conventional behaviour rather than that moral sensitivity which bridges the gaps in conventions or copes when they clash.

In both cases what is lacking, yet needed, is a character who is capable of making moral commitments and who has a reason for keeping them which derives from his involvement in society (which means more to him than a public means to his private ends). Hollis works towards this notion of social commitment, which stems from an active agent who does the committing (passive agents being puppets of socialised committal), through asking what people are doing in trying to become 'better-off'. In other words what are their 'pay-offs' and in what currency are they dealing? We need to know the human 'weights and measures' applied in relation to the ultimate ends that they seek. Here, in judging actions, 'it is not enough to know that the agent prefers its expected consequences. We also need the measure of value being applied, including the end allegedly better served.'[69] When we seek to be loved, regarded and respected, not only are these things not for sale, but also they are something like a terminus in that they do not lead on to further ends which could be achieved by an additional dose of instrumental rationality. Ends like these, to which we are ultimately committed, are those things which we care about most. As such they are *both* extensions and expressions of ourselves, but also ones which *can be* irreducibly social. In other words, those social relationships to which we are committed as our deepest concerns (marriage, family, career, church, community) are not for any agent the 'means to his flourishing but its constituents'.[70] Here there is no sense in asking why it

---

[68] See A. Rapoport and A. M. Chammah, *Prisoner's Dilemma*, Ann Arbor, Michigan, 1965.
[69] Martin Hollis, 'Honour among Thieves', *Proceedings of the British Academy*, I.xxv, 1989, p. 174.   [70] Ibid.

pays someone to give their partner a birthday present or to help their friends out, for these actions are expressive of their relationship, not matters of investment and *quid pro quo*. Moral commitment of this kind is neither calculative nor socialised, yet it is both reasoned and social, for our relations to these significant others are expressive of who we are and where we belong.

This serves to cut through both the calculation and the individualism of rational man and to keep him social without his becoming over-socialised. Thus 'a rational agent's ultimate reference group cannot be himself alone. He needs some group to identify with in relationships whose flourishing is a measure of his flourishing.'[71] By necessity, this has to be authentic because when another's interests are part of one's own, short cuts which simply give the appearance of belonging are self-defeating to a person whose real need is really to belong. What this implies is that Weber's *Wertrationalität*, far from being expelled from a disenchanted world, remains part of our lifeworld, which cannot be reduced to the bargain-hunter's bazaar. This has the advantage of allowing back in genuine heroism and self-sacrifice which is unlike those ersatz attempts of latter-day rational choice theorists to make a home for them through the reproductive advantages which characteristics like trustworthiness are supposed to confer.[72] Nor does commitment represent some blind leap of faith, disregarding of how it is served or with what consequences. As Weber argues in 'Politics as a Vocation', considerable thought has to be given to service of a principle. In other words, the honourable have to work out what the honourable course of action is, just as a good marriage needs substantive shaping, rather than relying upon formal fidelity, and intelligent departmental citizenship means striking a balance between contributions to RAE and TQA.

Yet in many ways Weber is not our best guide to commitment or the moral career, which I have just begun to sketch in, for his own Kantianism,[73] in which the stern voice of duty has the task of overriding our passions, also makes Calvinists of us all in our lifeworlds. What fuels our commitments is left entirely obscure because of the firm conventional line which Weber draws between value-rational and emotional action. Emotions are viewed as uncontrollable forces, not themselves subject to our deliberations, yet capable of subverting our evaluative determina-

---

[71] Ibid., p. 179.
[72] See Robert Frank, *Passions within Reason: the Strategic Role of the Emotions*, Norton, New York, 1988.
[73] Martin Albrow, *Max Weber's Construction of Social Theory*, London, Macmillan, 1990, ch. 2.

tions.[74] Nevertheless our commitments have to draw upon something if they are going to be able to fit the job description which Hollis has (rightly) given them. The job which they were needed for was to define the relational constituents of our flourishing as ourselves. The wellsprings of that cannot be our calculative rationality (or, unintelligibly we are trapped into instrumental relations with ourselves) nor can it be an imposed sociality (or, again unintelligibly, we are trapped into a normativity which swamps our personhood). It thus looks as though the time has come for reinstating our *pathos* alongside our *logos*, for letting the 'passions' back in to give us the shoving-power to make our commitments.

Homo sentiens and *homo sapiens*: their reunion

To state the obvious, the more rational we could be made by Rational Choice theorists, the better the human species fitted the theory. Hence the sequential moves which have been traced to subordinate our passions to our reason. Thence the two hundred years of trying to bring up Modernity's man as a good rationalist who has put away those childish things, his Humean passions. His biography is therefore a dualistic one of his head growing whilst his heart contracted, and we have noted that this aim to cultivate his reason at the expense of his emotions has constantly taken the pattern of two steps forward and one step back. Not only did the emotions obtrude themselves but they actually needed to be called upon and annexed to do certain jobs like explaining social solidarity, sharing and collective action. So what ensued was not their suppression, but their subordination: a place was found for them, but they had better know their place. However, they were notoriously bad at keeping their noses out of the things we cared about and the moral judgements we passed. This leads me to question whether the experiment has not gone on sufficiently long to be deemed another failure of dualism?

Perhaps we can begin to transcend it by refusing to join the traditional

---

[74] 'What we find in the *Protestant Ethic and the Spirit of Capitalism* is typical of the conventional understanding of emotion. It is held that rational action is undermined by emotion, and that rationality opposes and suppresses emotion. It also emerges that particular emotions or 'attitudes' may function to define purposes which become subject to rational realisation. Weber, no more than other adherents to the conventional view, does not deal with the obvious question which arises from this characterisation of his position: the ultimate impossibility of the rational suppression of emotion in general and the requirement of particular emotions for deliberatively formed motives. Indeed, the obfustication of the real contribution of emotions in goal-defining practices, by incorporating them in the concept of attitude, reflects the limitations of a general opposition of reason and emotion', J. M. Barbalet, *Emotion, Social Theory, and Social Structure*, Cambridge University Press, 1998, p. 38.

battle lines between Kantian rationalism and Humean emotivism; lines which in any case have become increasingly faint in the give and take of skirmishing.[75] Rather less obviously, a useful place to begin is by asking whether fully Kantian man would really have fitted the Rational Choice theorists' bill? Kant's paradigm rests upon a particular set of motives which form moral imperatives and are not reducible to, or instrumental towards, or derivative of, or explicable by any other. Yet in Rational Choice theory this is exactly what our motives can never be since they *are* reducible or instrumental to, derivative from, or explicable by our preferences. Even if these become as rational as possible, they do not become moral imperatives. Rational choice theory lacks the utilitarian twist which explains the moral in terms of non-moral ends. The utilitarian imperative only binds in the Kantian manner when each person puts general utility before other considerations, but Rational Choice theorists are only half-hearted utilitarians. They believe in something like 'enlightened' self interest, but lack the conviction that things will sum well, let alone that one should act for the best of summations. Consequently preferences remain just preferences and egotistically ours: any Kantian moral impetus to assess them as candidates for universalisation would bring them into the area of public dispute and bring down Rational Choice's prime tenet that *de gustibus non est disputandum*. Preferences would indeed be open to moral dispute because Rational Choices sum badly into 'Leviathan traps' (where force is needed to instil the common good), rather than being orchestrated by a hidden hand to produce the greatest good of the greatest number.

Hence Rational Choice theorists cannot be good Kantians, whilst they maintain that at most you can rationally inform a preference but not transform one: fixed preferences remain at best amoral and, at worst, may be thoroughly vicious. As is often remarked, Kantian man has nothing which explains his will's choices: Rational man has his preferences, but nothing can make these moral. Perhaps if his reason cannot make a moral chap of him, because of his intransigent preferences, he had better settle for life as a sub-Humean, who at least in Bernard Williams's hands can allow rational beliefs to upgrade his 'subjective mental set' provided that they have something subjective which provides leverage. But this battering-on process effectively means that reason is sieved by the emotions which leaves decision-making too 'hot' to handle. Rational man is too selfish for Kant and too cold for Hume: we can neither approve of him nor

---

[75] See Bernard Williams, 'Internal and External Reasons', in his *Moral Luck*, Cambridge University Press, 1981 for the neo-Humean position, and T. Nagel, *The Possibility of Altruism*, Oxford University Press, 1970, on the neo-Kantian side. The debate is economically summarised by Martin Hollis in ch. 6 of *The Cunning of Reason*.

warm to him, so perhaps the time has come to look for a different character as a maker of decisions and one who does not have to figure on one
side or the other of this old debate.

Instead, it has been argued that people have ultimate concerns which
are expressive of who they are, and therefore are *not* a means to some
further end. Firstly, therefore, what is crucial are the things that people
care about (which includes their fallible knowledge of them).[76] Secondly,
however, we would not say that someone was committed to anything
unless they were also emotionally involved. Terms like commitment,
dedication, devotion and caring have to have an affective component, otherwise they mean something different like 'assent'. However, we can
assent to many things (like the rules of arithmetic) without caring much
about them. Thus assent alone will not govern our lives. Emotion is
needed as part and parcel of 'caring'; to provide the shoving-power to
move us (contra Kant) to devote *ourselves* to our concerns which are not
(contra-Hume) just blind impulses or feelings. Consequently, there is
nothing counter-intuitive about the head and the heart being in cahoots,
rather than at loggerheads.

Thus, what people commit themselves to in society is the key to their
social identity and one which involves considerable affect. This is what
Weber (rather inconsistently) insists upon when he says 'nothing is
worthy of a man unless he can pursue it with *passionate devotion*.'[77] As
Frankfurt puts it, a 'person who cares about something is, as it were,
invested in it. He *identifies* himself with what he cares about in the sense
that he makes himself vulnerable to losses and susceptible to benefits
depending upon whether what he cares about is diminished or
enhanced.'[78] What we are committed to thus shapes our lives and determines our pay-offs. Thus a pupil who is devoted to youth culture will
count it a benefit if she can get to pop festivals, and as no loss if her
involvement adversely affects her school performance. Significantly, such
pupils tend to record that they found school 'irrelevant' or 'pointless',
something regarded as a simple waste of time when set against their passionate commitments, and, at the time they are indeed invulnerable to the
school's negative judgements.

Such commitments bind people to careers which are more lasting than
particular decisions, since someone who only cared for something
momentarily would be indistinguishable from one who acted upon
impulse. Instead when a commitment is actively guiding their life course,

[76] See Andrew Collier, *Being and Worth*, Routledge, London, 1999.
[77] Max Weber, 'Science as a Vocation', in H. H. Gerth and C. W. Mills (eds.), *From Max Weber*, London, Routledge and Kegan Paul, 1948, p. 135.
[78] Harry Frankfurt, *The Importance of What We Care About*, p. 83.

it is its vision which will affect their decisions. When explaining what they decide, then it is their commitments which supply their own 'weights and measures'. Without a knowledge of what is moving them we simply do not know what *counts* to them as a cost or a benefit or how strongly it counts.

Now the Rational Choice theorist will presumably object here that committed people are still acting with instrumental rationality, it is simply that we have dug a bit deeper into their preferences. This would be mistaken because with a commitment, means and ends are not separate: the things we care about profoundly affect *how* we honour our commitments. Thus someone does not forgo a blood transfusion in order to be a Jehovah's Witness: the forgoing is an *expression* of being one. Commitments are a way of life 'in the round' which affect means as well as ends. Thus a 'green' cannot be indifferent to the types of investment which fund ecological movements. Where commitments are concerned you cannot be a simple bargain hunter. Politicians often seem tempted to try, and to take funding from anywhere to win an election, but importantly this backfires when they are revealed to have tapped sources which are incongruent with what they are supposed to stand for. Christians know they cannot wheel and deal their way to heaven. Again goals and means are importantly inseparable though it is truer to say that the former informs rather than determines the latter. However, we will not understand the precise means selected unless we comprehend the *relationship* which a person sees between their goals and means, and this is something which can only be understood in expressive and not calculative terms. When we care for our children by giving time to play with them, this is expressive of our relationship with them, it is not a means of gaining their affection, nor is it conformity to the norms of good parenting, which are just as well satisfied by leaving them at a play-group. Instead and 'especially with respect to those we love and with respect to our ideals, we are liable to be bound by necessities which have less to do with our adherence to the principles of morality than with integrity and consistency of a more personal kind. These necessities constrain us from betraying the things we care about most and with which, accordingly, we are most closely identified. In a sense which a strictly ethical analysis cannot make clear, what they keep us from violating are not our duties and obligations but ourselves.'[79]

When emotions are incorporated, as expressive of our personal commitments, this is to argue that we are not engaged in a means–ends calculus and that the instrumental shopper is no model for people like caring

[79] Ibid., p. 91.

parents, friends of the earth, religious believers or anyone who finds fulfilment in their work. This is not because they are or may be altruistic, for a philanthropist could be a sharp bargain hunter, but because they are not behaving instrumentally at all. I thus denied that what mattered most to us could be subject to instrumental rationality and therefore attacked the *logocentric* nature of Modernity's man and sought to replace this by his expressive commitment. By corollary this also denies his lonely individualism in which all his social relationships are detachable and thus play no part in making him what he is. Instead, I have maintained that neither can his relations be construed as means to ends for they are partly constitutive of who we are and what we do. His *pathos* as much as his *logos* give him an individuality which is not divorced from his sociality. Because *pathos* and *logos* work together, they produce his integrity, rather than him becoming a schizophrenic, who is pulled in different directions by head and by heart. This is how Modernity's man was diagnosed, but the proposed cure of emotional lobotomy had the effect of only leaving us with half a human being.

3   Society's being: humanity as the gift of society

Amongst those who have resisted the postmodernist 'dissolution' of humanity, there is no consensus about how the human being should be conceptualised: no agreement about the properties and powers of humans and no accord about where these come from. The 'great divide' is between those just examined, who present our most important power as our rationality, which is treated as pre-given in the individual, who is portrayed so atomistically that nothing about him or her is in any sense owing to society. On the contrary, society itself is the aggregate consequence of the actions of these instrumentally rational individuals. In short, social structure is derived from agency and the macroscopic from the microscopic. This is why 'Modernity's Man' is a straightforward version of Upwards conflation: all properties of society can be derived from the doings of this rational man, along with others like him. Symmetrically, no properties of this individual are derivative from his or her social context – a proposition which was challenged in various ways in the last chapter.

Opposing 'Modernity's Man' stands 'Society's Being'. This presents all our human properties and powers, beyond those stemming from our biological constitution, as derivative from society. The human power most vaunted here is our ability to manipulate meanings, and thus to act meaningfully: to understand what a human being does, it is necessary to grasp the meanings informing his or her activities. Yet, it is not the individual who originates these meanings: in each generation we are born into an ongoing cultural tradition, from which they are individually appropriated through the process of socialisation. This is why 'Society's Being' is a classic version of Downwards conflation: all the recognisable properties of human beings come from their joining in 'society's conversation'. Symmetrically, no properties of this individual are derivative from his or her natural environment or practical activities – a proposition which will be challenged in the course of this chapter and the next.

The reductionism of both 'Modernity's Man' and 'Society's Being' are resisted in social realism, which fundamentally rejects that structure can be reduced to agency or that agency can be reduced to structure. Instead, it puts forward a *stratified* view, in which distinctive properties and powers pertain *sui generis* to both structures and agents. This ground has already been covered for culture and for social structure in the preceding volumes of this trilogy. However, just as structure and culture were themselves shown to be stratified, so the same is the case for 'agency' here.

The properties and powers of the human being are neither seen as *pre-given*, nor as *socially appropriated*, but rather these are emergent from our relations with our environment. As such, they have relative autonomy from biology and society alike, and causal powers to modify both of them. In fact, the stratified view of humanity advocated here sees human beings as constituted by a variety of strata. Each stratum is emergent from, but irreducible to, lower levels because all strata possess their own *sui generis* properties and powers. Thus, schematically, mind is emergent from neurological matter, consciousness from mind, selfhood from conscious-ness, personal identity from selfhood, and social agency from personal identity. The latter three forms of emergence are dealt with sequentially in the three following parts of the book.

The concern here is with selfhood, with that continuous sense of self shared by every human being, who believes himself or herself to be the same self over time. For 'Modernity's Man', this figured amongst the pre-given: the Cartesian *cogito* not only signalled our rationality, but also gave us our self in the 'I' who thinks. 'Society's Being' holds that this very sense of self is a theory which we learn by participating in society's conversation: it is a meaning that we appropriate. To complete the review of theoretical approaches which lead in their different ways to the impov-erishment of humanity, the present chapter will examine Downwards conflation. However, it is also a bridge to the non-conflationary realist approach to self-consciousness. It thus seriously queries whether our social relations are so overpowering that we become nothing but the gift of society, and systematically questions whether our human embodiment does not entail practical relations with the natural world which are broader than our dealings with society, yet crucial for the emergence of our self-consciousness.

The most sophisticated of the downward conflationary approaches on offer is that of Rom Harré. His trilogy, *Ways of Being*, is significant in three respects for present purposes. Firstly, the three volumes, *Social Being*, *Personal Being* and *Physical Being* show by their titles that he is clearly a theorist who accepts the challenge of our sociality and our physicality. Secondly, this order in which they were written does supply a first intima-tion of the order of his priorities. Thirdly, there is a considerable tension between the first two volumes and the last, where various concessions to our physical powers cast doubt on humankind as a purely discursive species. Social constructionism has become more and more Harré's conviction and so *The Discursive Mind* (1994) and particularly *The Singular Self* (1998) intentionally re-visit the scene to reinforce the message that, contra social realism, there is nothing in humankind which lies between us as 'molecules' and as 'meanings'. That both of the latter books are philosophical contributions to psychology is also intended to pre-empt that field for complete invasion by the discursive properties and powers of language.

The leitmotif can be summed up in one quotation taken from *Personal Being*: 'A person is not a natural object, but a cultural artefact.'[1] As this is unpacked in the following pages, it is worth recalling that in his latest book Harré has acceded that his own 'discursive psychology' belongs to the same camp as postmodernist interpretations.[2] In other words, I am not imposing a slant which would be disavowed by the author.

Indeed, a hostility to 'modernism' is the starting point of his whole enterprise. Yet if this is where he begins, the development of his theory depends upon a second assumption, namely that there are no emergent properties occupying the middle ground between the molecules and the meanings. It then involves a systematic attempt to clear this ground, not just of Cartesian mentalistic 'entities', but of any other contenders to ontological status (such as consciousness, reason, intentionality, emotions or self-reflexivity). Unless treated discursively, all of these are dubbed as 'mind stuff'. Since most of us are rightly suspicious of such substances, it could escape attention that relational properties, which can claim reality status due to their causal efficacity, are simultaneously rejected. Correspondingly, it is necessary for this middle ground to be fully cleared before the central assertion can be made that all we are as human beings is a gift of society. It follows directly from the fact that our humanity is held to derive from involvement in society's conversation that the influence of our physical being is downplayed in relation to our discursive selves. Our embodiment is subordinated to language, and our physicality is denigrated in order to enhance the power of sociality. The final point consists in producing a detailed model of how downwards conflation operates through public and collective discourse having primacy over the entirety of human development. It is a tightly argued case which eschews postmodernism's rhetorical devices. Yet its design consistently depends upon ignoring our practical action as embodied beings in the real world, a kind of action which satisfies our needs *qua*

---

[1] Rom Harré, *Personal Being*, Basil Blackwell, Oxford, 1983, p. 20.
[2] Rom Harré, *The Singular Self*, Sage, London and Beverly Hills, 1998, p. 50.

Two ontologies

Ontologies	locative systems	entities	relations
Newtonian	space and time	things and events	causality
Discursive	arrays of people	speech acts	rules and storylines

The Discursive Mind[3]

Figure 3.1 Harré's ontologies of science and society

human beings, and upon whose satisfaction our survival depends if we are to become and remain such beings as discursive ones. In a nutshell, the practice of humanity will be counterposed here to the conversation of humankind, and defended in the usual three realist senses – that practical action has temporal priority, relative autonomy and causal efficacy *vis-à-vis* collective discourse.

Harré's anti-modernism: humanity's involvement in a moral order

Utilisation of the natural science model, with its core objective of establishing causal relations between entities, 'tempts us to think of such concepts as referring to causally potent inner states of people. A closer look shows that the expression makes sense only as a feature of discourse.'[4] This is Harré's fundamental conviction. To him, when we are concerned with the 'tasks' undertaken by people, rather than with the physiological 'tools' which are necessarily employed, then we must swap over to a different and discursive ontology to deal with the relevant components and the relations between them. This he schematises in figure 3.1, which contrasts the Newtonian ontology, representing the mechanical picture of the world, with the Vygotskyan ontology, appropriate to psychology.

The appropriateness of the discursive ontology derives directly from the fact that the relations between 'speech acts' are not ones of causality. On the contrary, Harré maintains that the 'orderly structure of a conversation is maintained by norms of correctness and propriety. This is not a causal theory. In the physical world model, events and things are linked into structures and patterns by causal relations. But one speech-act does not cause another. Rather, one speech-act makes another appropriate or, as they say in this theory, normatively accountable.'[5] Of course, the acceptability of this ontology depends upon our acceding that social life is

---

[3] Rom Harré and Grant Gillett, *The Discursive Mind*, Sage, London and Beverly Hills, 1994, p. 29.   [4] *The Singular Self*, p. 51.   [5] *The Discursive Mind*, p. 33.

purely conversational, and many others besides social realists will want to protest that some of its constituents, like structural properties, cultural constraints and the distributions of resources which underlie them, cannot be reduced to speech-acts, may never even entail them, and yet exert causal influences of a constraining or enabling kind. This would be the case for every emergent SEP and CEP, since they do not require discursive penetration (or necessarily depend upon discursive mystification) to be influential. Thus, generically, resource distributions hinder the aspirations of some and help in the attainment of others, whether those involved discuss this state of affairs or not. Even if they do, their causal influence does not hang upon correct conversational diagnosis: our 'life chances' do not hinge upon our knowledge of them, for discrimination or privilege operate independently of their discursive detection.

In advocating a discursive ontology, Harré makes some extremely controversial assumptions which it is insufficient merely to state. 'I take the array of persons as a primary human reality. I take the conversations in which those persons are engaged as completing the primary structure, bringing into being social and psychological reality. Conversation is to be thought of as creating a social world just as causality generates a physical one.'[6] Justifying this ontological position absorbs the bulk of Harré's work, but this rests on the convincingness of presentation rather than providing a critique of the opposing causal position. Indeed, at only one point does Harré accept that we live in a world of distinct constraints – physical constraints such as doorways, logical constraints such as the law of non-contradiction and cultural constraints such as ideational inconsistencies.[7] Here we are told that 'negotiation and adjustment' will be required, but the only conclusion drawn is that a particular type of discourse is unlikely to hold unbounded sway over the subjectivity of an individual. There is no exploration of 'when', 'where' and 'how', which would re-open the door to at least the combination of causal and discursive analysis.

It is important to note the vastness of the consequential gap between these two ontologies. For Harré, it 'follows that, like every other general psychological theory, it must be assessed, not for verisimilitude, but in relation to some moral order, that is with respect to the kinds of lives belief in it enables people to live'.[8] We are asked then to evaluate it morally, disregarding its truth-content: this invites our normative conversion rather than aiming at our intellectual conviction. Again realists will find the severing of morality from truth concerns wholly unacceptable,[9] as will all who decline the moral permissiveness of postmodernism. In any

[6] *Personal Being*, p. 65.   [7] *The Discursive Mind*, pp. 24–5.   [8] *Personal Being*, p. 284.
[9] See Andrew Collier, *Being and Worth,*Routledge, London, 1999.

case the only kind of academic life a theory enables one to lead cannot be deemed good if the theory itself is found to be flawed.

The first stage in the argument that we are 'cultural artefacts', is to void our 'inner life' in order to vaunt our discursive production. Thus 'I shall be trying to show that what people have called "selves" are, by and large, produced discursively, that is in dialogue . . . Selves are not entities.'[10] This means more than a rejection of Cartesian 'mind stuff' and the inaccessibility of the working of any one mind to others, for it threatens (at least in the later work) our private mental lives of dilemma, deliberation and determination, of curiosity, creativity and contrition, and of anguish, awe and amendment, all of which may be powerful but publicly unavowed, yet they serve to make us what we are in public. Instead there 'is no necessary shadow world of mental activity behind discourse in which one is working things out in private'.[11]

The earlier work does not abolish these private mental activities, it places them quite literally 'behind discourse' as the affordances of public conversation and impossible without it: throughout the 'I' is consistently displaced from being individually sensed to become a socially indexical device. Instead of being a self-referential descriptor, the word 'I' merely displays mastery of the first-person pronoun which indexes one's spatial location and expresses moral responsibility for the utterances made. Thus, if 'self-talk is expressive rather than descriptive then "I" needs to have no referential function, and there need be no object reference which guarantees that the first person is meaningful'.[12]

Instead of a robust 'I', there is the discursive self, the meaning of whose symbol use is a function only of usage in discourse. Thus there is no sense in which a psychological subject or agent has a nature which can be defined in isolation from a conversational context. Hence we become a socio-spatial location, such that 'the study of the mind is a way of understanding the phenomena that arise when different sociocultural discourses are integrated within an identifiable human individual situated in relation to those discourses'.[13] So, just as ethology studied animal behaviour in its environments, so the term 'ethogenics' has been coined for the study of human behaviour in its environment, construed as a normative one made up of the rules and conventions which constitute genres of discourse. Thus, via Wittgenstein, mental activity loses its 'inner' impenetrability and comes out into daylight as public discursive practices, framed within and governed by informal rules.

In this wholesale replacement of causal properties by rule-following,

---

[10] *The Singular Self*, p. 68.   [11] *The Discursive Mind*, p. 27.   [12] *The Singular Self*, p. 44.
[13] *The Discursive Mind*, p. 22.

we are not only led back down the path beaten by the three 'Ws' (Weber, Wittgenstein and Winch), but asked to endorse the even more contentious proposition that our tribal narrative conventions 'are like the "rules of grammar" of our native tongue'.[14] This is doubly difficult, not only because globalisation has weakened tribalism (for there is nothing ludicrous in seeing the human species as a single tribe); but also, even if our Western privileges reduce the realistic scope of solidarity, 'we' of the West are far too cosmopolitan to be bound to the conventions of our mother tongue, if such there be. For just as courtly manners were transnational, so too do football supporters' lack of them cross the frontiers. As is always the case, the temptation to draw an analogy between language and society comes to grief on the dis-analogies which surface.

Be that as it may, such empirical reservations do not undermine Harré's basic claim that discursive activities are involved in a moral order. The strength of this assertion is summarised in the following quotation which is given at length because it stands as a statement of the normativity of the social order.

Discursive activities are always subject to standards of correctness and incorrectness. These standards can be expressed in terms of rules. Therefore a discursive practice is the use of a sign system, for which there are norms of right and wrong use . . . The use of the word 'I' in English is a discursive practice. One of its many roles is in the act of taking responsibility by a speaker for what he or she says and to what he or she is committed to by the saying of it. According to the discursive point of view, in this and similar discursive practices of reflexive talk, I constitute myself as a self, as an embodied moral unit in the world. By using the indexical world 'I', I create my moral individuality for you or anyone else whom I might address.[15]

The point to note at the moment is that this characterisation of discourse as a moral order displaces any notion of social relations as a causal order, and at all levels because Harré is not confining himself to either intra- or inter-personal psychology, since his referents are as big as the English speaking world. It is not even that the two stand alongside one another; the normative now occupies all of the ground which causality once held. In this, the utterance has replaced the act as the primary unit of analysis, and these speech-acts are more firmly tied into a central linguistic value system than ever Parsons envisaged for action.

As in the Parsonian system, what is generated is an 'oversocialised view of man', for everything about us as human beings is derivative from society. What seem to us to be our private lives are internalised from the public moral order because Harré's is 'an ontology in which utterances, interpreted as speech-acts, become the primary entities in which minds

---

[14] Ibid., p. 34.   [15] Ibid., pp. 28–9.

become personalised, as privatised discourses'.[16] It is important to note here that it is not only the contents of our minds which are at all times socially determined (we make no discoveries and think no thoughts which we can call our own, i.e. which are not dependent upon public discourse), but also the form of private thought itself derives from the moral order (our epistemology is confined to the internalised conversation of society and we have no other means of access to knowledge). Both points will be challenged when I consider our practical lives and particularly the non-discursive relationship between our embodiment and natural reality. The same lever will be used to dislodge the view that all the characteristics which make us what we are owe nothing to our natural relations, as sources of creativity (both individual and species-wide), but are again generated under the impress of the public moral order. Thus Harré argues that the 'structure of the discourses in which psychological phe-nomena, such as remembering, displays of emotions, avowals of attitudes, attributions of causality and responsibility, and so on, *are created under the control of conventions of right and wrong performances*'.[17]

Obviously, by making us intrinsically part of the public discursive order, Harré has succeeded in eliminating those 'inner entities' which to him share the dubiety of 'mental substances'. Instead, all has been brought to the surface because there is nothing other than the conversa-tion of humanity, whether in its primary public or derivatively private forms. What this means is that he is advancing a simple two-factor theory. At the individual level, the only powerful particular is the 'person', and at the social level it is the 'discourse'. Now in the previous volumes of this trilogy I have placed great stress upon the stratified nature of culture and of structure respectively and of course refused their reduction to the flatlands of 'discourse'. In this book I want to emphasise that human agency is also stratified, with different properties and powers emerging at different levels, and not all of them from our socio-cultural relations. This case will be constructed gradually and only fully presented in the last chapters. For the moment it is necessary to show more clearly how Harré's discursive constructionism necessarily generates this one flat, unstratified powerful particular – the human person.

The discursive agent: a non-stratified conception of the person

This section entails spelling out precisely what Harré means by 'the ubiq-uitous role of discourse'.[18] Its flattening effect *vis-à-vis* social structure

---

[16] Ibid., p. 36.   [17] Ibid., p. 36 (my italics).   [18] *The Singular Self*, p. 35.

was clearly articulated in *Social Being* where structure was reduced to relational networks constituted through personal interaction as mediated in conversation. Thus the world of work and class relations and that of honour and status hierarchies were secondary products of interpretative linguistic powers, and thus lacked their own *sui generis* emergent properties and powers. Both the parallel flattening of people and the downwards conflationary inflection are evident when Harré summarises his position neatly. 'People and their modes of talk are made by and for social orders, and social orders are people in conversation.'[19]

As far as people are concerned, the one form of reductionism which is resisted is the neurological. Harré signals that the only ontological choice is 'between founding the science of human thought and action on molecules as the basic particulars, and founding it on people as the basic particulars'.[20] In itself this hangs on a rather curious argument about the existence of alternative modes of embodiment (such as our documentary 'file selves'), which leads to the tendentious conclusion that the 'person is prior to embodiment'.[21] At any rate to Harré, there are only two entities in question, bodies whose basic particulars are molecular clusters and discursive resources, or meanings, which serve in personal expression. Between molecules and meanings there is nothing – no inner states, no mental attributes and no personal psychology. There are only persons as powerful particulars and persons have no inner psychological complexity. Indeed our very 'personal singularity is a product of social processes, while the very attributes that characterise the seeming "free standing" person are through and through relational'[22] – a category which includes memory, intentionality, beliefs, rationality and emotions, which are all created performatively in public discourse. Were it objected that many of these predicates apply to pre-linguistic children or indeed to other animate species, the response is that for humans the key to understanding the transformation of these natural potentials into developed powers involves taking part in society's conversation.[23]

Yet many of us would resist the notion that our singularity as individuals reduces to our social specification: in short most people believe themselves to be or to have 'a self'. To Harré, our common feeling of our distinctiveness is not misplaced: we are merely grossly mistaken if we think we possess selfhood. The 'singularity we each feel ourselves to be, is not an entity. Rather it is a site, a site from which a person perceives the world and a place from which to act. There are only persons. Selves are grammatical fictions, necessary characteristics of person-oriented discourses.'[24] Due to

---

[19] *Personal Being*, p. 65.   [20] *The Singular Self*, p. 47.   [21] *Personal Being*, p. 69.
[22] *The Singular Self*, p. 70.   [23] Ibid., p. 127.   [24] Ibid., pp. 3–4.

our embodiment, we occupy a special location which gives us a particular point of view, but this position in time and space exhausts our singularity. Persons then are not like things but like places.[25] The social construction of selfhood is simply a co-ordination of the embodied point of view (site) with grammatical devices, the most important of which is mastery of the pronoun system. Site plus syntax together give rise to the fiction, where 'I' does not designate an entity but merely indexes a location like '39N 77 W' (the co-ordinates for Washington). Beyond that, 'I' does not refer to an individuated speaker, talking from their private inner being, it merely labels a speech-act as mine which carries with it responsibilities within the public moral order. Indeed, the only meaning of 'inner' which Harré will entertain is the literal one of 'inside the skin': what it can never be is a metaphor for 'the private', which has been disposed of through its dependence upon 'the public'.

If we are inclined to hang on to other inner properties yielding our particularity, such as 'consciousness' or 'personality', these again are ontological illusions (beyond the sense of location) which bite the dust along with the Cartesian ego. In place of these proliferating concepts for inner entities to which this gave rise, Harré reckons to have 'condensed this ocean into a drop of grammar'.[26] 'Person' then is the only genuine substantive term designating a real entity. Unsurprisingly, Harré aligns himself with Hume, who when he looked 'inward' could never detect his own self, but only an array of memories and experiences. The self which was sought was unavailable to private introspection and the reason for this, to Harré, was quite simply that there was nothing there to find, since the alleged properties of the Cartesian ego amount to no more than the grammatical rules for using the word 'I', rules which belong to the public not the private domain.

Nevertheless, many of us will still feel unease about this emptying process which leaves nothing of us between the molecules and the meanings, that is our bodily constitution and the stories we tell autobiographically, courtesy of a public medium. We continue to harbour the notion that we have a sense of self, that its continuous nature is what distinguishes me from you, and that the self which eluded Hume's introspection was precisely the self that was doing the searching. Although in his later work, Harré has less and less time for a self-concept (selves become aspects of persons), in *Personal Being* this common intuition is taken very seriously. However the 'self', or the sense of selfhood, cannot be allowed to be an entity or a stratum since personhood remains firmly *un*stratified. So what can it be that does not traduce this proposition and thus would

---

[25] *Personal Being*, p. 61.   [26] *The Singular Self*, p. 178.

not challenge the sole ontological level of 'persons'? The answer is 'a theory'. One which we obtain from society.

Thus 'while "person" is an empirical concept which distinguishes beings in a public-collective realm, "self" . . . is a theoretical concept acquired in the course of social interactions.'[27] As nothing but a theory, this opens the door to querying where we got it from, in exactly the same way that we might ask from where some (nineteenth-century) person learned the theory of evolution, or someone (in the twentieth century) acquired the theory of quantum mechanics.

Well, we learn it in much the same way by being taught it, but this new item, which is rather like acquiring a personal organiser (a mental filofax), has no more secure ontological status than that which Harré accords to scientific theories in general – the stories which scientists tell one another. Here realists would part company with his portrayal of a 'gravitational field', as merely a narrative organising principle, rather than something with reality status on the causal principle, as they would with his analogical treatment of the self. He suggests 'that "I", the first person pronoun, does have a referential force to a hypothetical entity "the self", in much the same way that the gravitational term g refers to a hypothetical entity, the gravitational field'. In other words we can acquire this theory, the holding of it can do organisational work for us, but he has not conceded the existence of a real stratum constituted by our 'selves' because the 'self' remains a theoretical construct. Hence he continues that 'possession of the theoretical concept "self" permits just the kind of organisation of a person's experience that Kant called "synthetic unity" '.[28]

Now Kant termed the locus where experiences are unified, and the element which owns itself to be the focus of expectations, the 'Transcendental Unity of Apperception'. To him it stood not as a hypothetical but as an *a priori* condition for the ordering of experience itself, and whilst not accorded categorical status *per se* it actually functions as the underwriter of all categories. Its existence is established transcendentally, by asking what needs to be the case to anchor the flux of experienced phenomena. Any transcendental argument only establishes (at best) necessity: it does not show how such a need is met empirically. However, it is hard to see how 'through learning a theory' could fit the Kantian bill for the 'self', because on Kant's terms this would just be one more element requiring ordering and would needs call upon his higher order Unity to do just that. It is useful to possess a filofax, but there has to be someone who does so and who uses it to his or her own ends, so the filofax presupposes the real personal organiser! It invokes an intermediate stratum which is ontological and not hypothetical.

---

[27] *Personal Being*, p. 26.   [28] Ibid., p. 82.

Where this comes from is a valid question with far-reaching implications. Harré argues that his 'self' is appropriated from society via pronomial grammar. He then has the tough-minded honesty to confine his personhood to those who do speak, for the pre- and alinguistic represent empty spaces. On the contrary, I will be arguing for the 'self' as real, emergent and, of course, relational. The relation in question will be that pertaining between the body, nature and practice. Thus I will be advancing the case for the naturalistic emergence of the 'self', whilst Harré presents the case for its induction through socialisation. The capacity to use the 'I' in every known culture is precisely what would be expected of a (valid) naturalistic and therefore universalistic theory of the emergent self: but if the 'self' *itself* is a theory, then is it not strange that all cultures, despite their diversity, have shown convergence on this theoretical development? To answer this question rather than scoring a rhetorical point means giving proper attention to Harré's startling assertion that the 'fundamental human reality is a conversation'.[29]

Humanity and society's conversation

Harré coined a motto for his work – 'Nothing in the mind that was not first in the conversation'.[30] In elaborating this statement that all we are as human beings is a gift of society, his argument has three stages. Firstly, he posits the priority of language in human thought and action; secondly, he maintains that all mentation and mental attributes are derivative from conversation and, thirdly, that our private mental activities are parasitic upon public discourse. Taken together they enable him to conclude that 'the minds of individuals are privatised practices condensing like fog out of the public conversation onto material nuclei, their bodies'.[31]

The starting point is explicitly Wittgensteinian, namely it 'is based on the assumption of the priority of language use over all other forms of human cognition'.[32] This then becomes a straightforward doctrine of social construction. He immediately asserts the 'essential linguistic basis for all human practices',[33] which will be challenged fiercely. Due to this he can move on to derive both the degree of universality characterising human beings as language users, and the extent of human diversity due to their using different languages. This is the basis of his general account of how merely animate beings become persons and of his focal account about the sources of personal differentiation, for 'a large chunk of what it is to be a person comes with learning the local language'.[34] Thus we are

---

[29] Ibid., p. 20.   [30] Ibid., p. 116.   [31] *The Singular Self*, p. 50.   [32] Ibid., p. 21.
[33] Ibid., p. 18.   [34] Ibid., p. 29.

what we are (embodiment apart) through the affordances of language, which creates our personal attributes, and we are who we are through theories of the self which are linguistic in origin. Hence Harré's project is nothing short of a complete reorientation of psychology, such that he insists upon 'attributing the properties of mental-predicate ascriptions and avowals to the culture, not to minds'.[35]

Whereas traditional psychology was based on what has been termed the 'faculty model',[36] i.e. that people are bundles of faculties (such as memory, attitudes, cognition, affectivity, etc.), Harré reverses the sequence and next argues how each of these is produced under the aegis of society's conversation. This new psychological paradigm is truly radical, for he hopes 'to show that not only are the acts which we as individuals perform and the interpretations we create of the social and physical world prefigured in collective actions and social representations, but also that the very structure of our minds (and perhaps the fact that we have minds at all) is drawn from those social representations'.[37] What is radical here is not just the large claim that our minds are culturally dependent, but also (i) that the physical world is deemed to be mediated through the cultural conversation rather than impinging upon us directly, and (ii) that it is only in a discursive environment that consciousness comes into existence, with the effect of strictly dividing the human from the animal phyla – since in the absence of (developed) language, animals must be deprived not only of consciousness but of intentionality, intelligence, memory etc. I will be challenging both (i) and (ii) – the amalgamation of the physical to the social world and the great break between species which denies most of our embodied continuity with animal bodies.

For the time being let us simply note what a very large list of attributes, once deemed matters of personal psychology, are now held to be discursively dependent: these include intentionality, rationality, emotionality, the activities of reporting and recounting, and the bundle of skills including intelligence. Basically, the display of any proto-skill takes place in the public domain, where it is subject to commentary and correction according to the moral order. Only after repeated adjustment to convention does the skill become part of an acceptable and thus fixed repertoire. Skills then are construed as displays which earn a public encore, or at least pedagogical encouragement in the form of conversational correction. The implication is that without an encore, the proto-display falls into desuetude – deselected through discursive socialisation. This of

---

[35] *Personal Being*, p. 1.
[36] See Norbert Wiley, *The Semiotic Self*, Polity Press, Oxford, 1994, ch. 1.
[37] *Personal Being*, p. 20.

course is an account of the processes responsible for continuation: it is not an account of genesis, which is either a serious gap in Harré's theorising or one which he might be tempted to plug by seeing the vast array of proto-displays as randomly generated, but systematically selected for by normative goodness of fit.

Since it is impossible to examine the full gamut of 'attributes' with which he deals, let us glance at one, memory, which is held to be 'a cognitive/discursive skill, not a native endowment'.[38] The old model of the memory 'tool' operating in conjunction with experiential properties (such as recency, frequency and intensity) to generate recall (or failure to recall) is replaced by social constructionism. Thus in Coulter's formulation[39] it can be seen how the moral order intrudes at every point:

(a) To remember is to be correct about some past event, not to have a particular kind of experience.
(b) Utterances declaring memories are constructed by reference to the interests and presumed knowledge of the recipient.
(c) There are social norms concerning what one is permitted to remember and to forget.

Attention shifts from some putative mental model of memory, in conjunction with some classification of 'memorable' experiences, to how people represent their pasts in discussion and construct versions of past events in conversation. Thus he gives the example of a memorial interchange between mother and child over an old photo of them, noting how dialogically the parent marks the significance of the pictured event (happy, familiar etc.), cues the child's recall by supplying appropriate descriptions, provides contextual couching for reminiscences (one of many episodes) and positively sanctions the moral right to re-parade the recollection.

We should not accept this plausible account too readily, for the example of a childhood photograph contains elements independent of the social constructions which significant others try to put upon it. Many of us find that our childhood memories are sieved through the photographs available, simply because these visual recordings are there (and themselves assure us that we did indeed ride a donkey on the sands when we were about three), and tend to be looked at periodically, until they outweigh or overlay all the un-snapped moments (of flying a kite at the same age). Equally, the photos supply their own context pictorially and independent of commentary (those wet sands with intriguing rock-pools). Finally, we often go through the albums alone and, whatever accounts we have been given, the visual

[38] *The Singular Self*, p. 143.
[39] J. Coulter, *The Social Construction of Mind*, Macmillan, London, 1979, pp. 56–61.

evidence can still leave us thinking that, contrary to what we had been told, the house seemed rather small and father less than athletic.

The full brunt of the social constructionist account of memory is turned against Locke, who made our continuous sense of self dependent upon our embodiment and memories. Harré changes the basis of this continuity into one of narrative. 'My life is not a sequence of historical events but a story which I tell myself and which is forever being updated and revised'[40] for the purposes of self-presentation or depending upon what is salient at a given juncture. Above all, since 'one's life is lived and told with others, autobiographical story-telling, like all forms of memory work, is essentially social, produced dialogically'.[41] Now it seems to me that this is to conflate the artistic licence we give ourselves when recollecting in public (to aggrandise or to be self-depreciating) with a lack of awareness that we are doing so. Yet, often, we catch ourselves in the act of embroidery (and to Harré who does this catching and against what?). Moreover, objectively these recollections must be among our real memories or otherwise they are pure fantasy.

Now every one of my reservations about Harré's presentation of memory/autobiography as a social construct has hung upon our having private thoughts and private lives. Yet, this is precisely what he firmly repudiates. Public conversation and private thoughts form a continuous web. Put categorically, from 'a discursive point of view the private experience of a human being is shaped and ordered in learning to speak and write . . . This was Vygotsky's great insight. That ordering is expressed in language and other intentional, norm-governed practices. This was Wittgenstein's great insight.'[42] In brief what he takes from both is that inter-subjectivity has primacy over, and is prior to, intra-subjectivity. Indeed, in his Vygotskyan developmental account, the private is always posterior to the public, and, until the public has been internalised, we cannot begin to talk about privatisation. Through symbiosis, the carer supplements the deficient efforts of the child by treating it as if it had the full complement of skills, 'as if it were a fully competent self, seeing and acting upon the world from its own standpoint (and eventually create(ing)) adult human beings'.[43] Only after this partnership of supplementation is the child, aged about three, able to begin to develop the capacity for private discourse. Here, it is of course a secondary ability, as are the powers of self-expression and self-reflexivity. Thus reflexive practices like self-criticism and self-exhortation simply borrow from society's conversation about criticism, exhortation and so on.

[40] *The Singular Self*, p.138.   [41] Ibid., p. 146.   [42] Ibid., p. 42.
[43] *Personal Being*, p. 41.

Not surprisingly, the secondary status assigned to private thoughts is used to attack Locke's account of the subjective sense of identity which we all have of ourselves and which rests upon the continuity of our intra-personal consciousness. Harré's objection is that this seems to make our singularity problematic and in need of criteria (which for Locke our private memories furnish), whereas for Harré our bodily location and use of the first-person pronoun suffices (both of course being publicly observable). His riposte to Locke is that for something to be a memory, it must be a thought about *my* thoughts and actions, thus presupposing the very continuous self it was offered as a criterion to determine.[44] Yet why does Harré think that Locke needs two thoughts, 'a thought about my thought'? The continuity of my thoughts secure my self for Locke. The double-barrelled process is only necessary to Harré himself, because the first thought is public (memories are made of this), whilst the designation 'my' is private and therefore secondary and derivative. Those who allow of an autonomous domain of the private have no such difficulties. Yet this is exactly what Harré disallows, and not just for thought, which is (too readily) presumed to be linguistic, but also for experience which is also held to be secondary to society's conversation. To him, 'the cluster of person concepts that characterise discourses of self play the role of a grammar, the rules that make a discourse of persons possible. They are not the result of abstractions from experience. They are what make experience, as we have it, possible.'[45]

I have logged, without exploring in detail, reservations about thought, memory and reflexivity being secondary to and derivative from discourse. However, when it comes to the large category of experience, which necessarily embraces experiences of practical action in the world, then it will be necessary to maintain strenuously that this is practice directly in the world, and in no way dependent upon a detour through society's conversation. However society's conversation is so much the centre-piece of Harré's socialised conception that it necessarily leads to the exorbitation of human beings as discursive beings, at the expense of allowing that people are ineradicably naturalistic beings – and perhaps they are first and foremost that.

Socialising our naturalistic being

There is no doubt that there is a tension in Harré's work when we consider ourselves as both natural and social beings. This prompts the realist thought that we might well be dealing with two emergent strata. If this is

---

[44] *The Singular Self*, p. 71.   [45] Ibid., p. 72.

the case, analytical dualism would then point to the need to examine the interplay between their different properties and powers. Indeed this would probably have been the first thought of the Harré of *Causal Powers*,[46] but as Shotter argues, I believe correctly, the adoption of social constructionism meant that he had 'abandoned what might be called the "things-ontology" he introduced in his ontological formulations of the concepts of powers – and along with that what is seen as the strength of the realist position: the possibility of appealing, in warranting our claims to knowledge, to structured entities which exist independently of our knowledge or of our experience of them. It is no longer the case that mental powers are or can be ascribed to locatable things or entities in virtue of *their* natures (whatever they are). Their development trajectory must be thought of as originating in (and perhaps terminating in) the diffusely spread-out activities within a collective.'[47] Nevertheless, in his latest work Harré wanted to maintain that his social constructionism is not at odds with social realism, in much the same way that Outhwaite argued the nature of the generative structures themselves was not pre-judged by the realist programme.[48]

In seeking to sustain the compatibility of the two, Harré stresses the background conditions which are transcendentally necessary for the conversation of humanity. As advanced, they have the three properties which are also necessary for disengaging and substantiating the existence of a lower stratum – temporal priority, relative autonomy and causal efficacy. Hence he argues that 'there are some conditions that stand outside any discourse whatever makes that discourse possible. For instance there is the set of conditions that make language itself possible including those natural expressions of feeling, of perceptual point of view and so on without which no symbolic system of any degree of sophistication could even begin.'[49] Now all of these pertain to our natural embodiment and existence in a natural environment. Here I want to demonstrate that although there are tensions within the work (particularly noticeable since *Physical Being* can be read as something of a running critique of the other books), Harré's turn to social constructionism is incompatible with realism. Specifically, he accords no properties and powers to our naturalistic being, which is systematically played down and subordinated to our linguistic being, without itself being accorded ontological status. The point is

[46] Rom Harré and E. H. Madden, *Causal Powers*, Blackwell, Oxford, 1975.
[47] John Shotter, 'Rom Harré: Realism and the Turn to Social Constructionism', in R. Bhaskar (ed.), *Harré and his Critics*, Blackwell, Oxford, 1990, p. 212.
[48] William Outhwaite, 'Realism and Social Science', in Margaret Archer et al. (eds.), *Critical Realism: Essential Readings*, Routledge, London, 1998.
[49] *The Singular Self*, pp. 18–19.

raised not as part of a concern to present the history of Harré's thought, but because of the enormous importance I attach to our socially unmediated relations with nature (including artefacts) in our practical actions.

Let us begin with Harré's approving quotation from William James, which appears to give the body centre-place in the welter of environmental experiences. 'The body is the storm-centre, the origin of co-ordinates, the constant place of stress in all that experience strain. Everything circles round it and is experienced from its point of view. The word "I" then is primarily a noun of position . . . the word "my" designates the kind of emphasis.'[50] How then do we embodied beings make sense of the 'I'/ not-'I' distinction? Sensations themselves cannot do the job, for they are undifferentiated from it, nor can categories since these cannot get a grip without there being a prior differentiation into things which are 'I' and those which are 'not-I'. Now this seems to open up highly profitable considerations of how our embodiment *itself* manages this process of differentiation through the skin's boundary which provides a felt distinction between self and otherness, reliant only upon physiological signification.

For a moment Harré seems inclined to go down this path when he says that 'one must have a sense of a field of things centred on one's own embodied self with which one *is in a material relation*'.[51] However, this practical relation with the world is immediately truncated into something which requires verbal enrichment: it is not allowed to be influential *sui generis*. Thus he proceeds immediately to talk about the indebtedness of 'the origins of a sense of personhood to the manipulative practices with which, *when verbally enriched*, an infant begins to appreciate its world as ordered, with respect to its own position as an embodied being among other things and beings of that or similar sorts'.[52] Enrichment is necessary because manipulative practices, such as grasping and reaching, are held to be developmentally incomplete until language and especially pronoun mastery enable 'one' to ask for 'things' at a distance. Yet, why is such incompleteness (if such it be) therefore judged uninfluential in its own right? To grasp an object is to feel the boundary between one's body and, say, the teddy bear. Is there anything lacking here as a *sense* of self/object differentiation (which is a quite different matter from being able to talk about it or to ask for the bear)? I will be arguing that 'no', nothing!

However, Harré perpetuates a contradiction in Vygotsky's work, such that although cognitive powers are held to be pre-linguistic, it is only after language acquisition that they can re-appear as internal thought using the

---

[50] Quoted approvingly in *The Singular Self*, p. 55.
[51] *The Singular Self*, p. 104 (my italics).   [52] Ibid., p. 104 (my italics).

now appropriated language for private cogitation. Thus '*any function of the child's cultural development appears on the stage twice, on two planes, first on the social plane and then on the psychological*, and then within the child as an *intramental category*'.[53] The confusion seems to arise from the quiet insertion of the adjective 'cultural', qualifying development, for it precludes consideration of that development itself which is not dependent upon emergent cultural properties (CEPs), such as language. Harré seems aware of this distinction between genetic and cultural development when he recognises that what we are pertains not only to our sense of embodiment (point of view) but to our attributes as individual persons (for example, our skills).

This only compounds the problem, for just as our embodiment sets natural boundaries, so too are some of our skills (the development of physical-motor ones) quite independent of their conceptualisation, but are solely reliant on embodied contact with the world (e.g. locomotion, feeding, trial and error manipulation, or avoidance of certain discomforts etc.). There is no need to have the concept of a cot bar to use the skill of withdrawing that part of the body on which it is pressing uncomfortably. Practice may often be 'action according to a rule' without it actively being rule governed. Rather, it is cued by the way we are physiologically made. What I am indicating is that each human being quite literally *develops* such practical skills through their embodiment if they are to survive and flourish in the world. Our bodies embody our needs, some of which we attend to without linguistic mediation.

This view of our primordial and ontogenetic creativity is one through which I open up an epistemological space for naturalistic knowledge. It is precisely what Harré denies. Following Wittgenstein he argues that there 'is no epistemological gap between a feeling and the expression of a feeling'. To be in pain includes the expressive tendency to groan. Yet why not resist this amalgamation on the grounds that groans can be suppressed and that young children can stop crying? When they 'cry themselves to sleep' this does not mean that the pain/need has gone away. More speculatively, children are often seen to desist from or to punctuate their crying, as if 'questioning' its point or 'realising' its pointlessness in a real world which remains unmoved. However, this compacting of experience and expression is used by Harré to argue for an enlarged conception of the role of language in life when he claims that similarly, 'there is no epistemological gap between a sense of self and the expression of that sense in one's use of pronouns and other indexical devices'.[54]

[53] L. S. Vygotsky, 'Development of the Higher Mental Functions', in A. N. Leont'ev, A. R. Luria and A. Smirnov (eds.), *Psychological Research in the USSR*, Progress Publishers, Moscow, 1966, p. 44.   [54] *The Singular Self*, p. 44.

Thus all cognition is rounded-up into a discursive process and crucial matters like formal logic become one among many 'grammars' acquired. Again, this precludes a naturalistic account in which the laws of identity and of non-contradiction are inscribed by the ways in which the body finds the world to be. A bottle cannot be both full and empty: either it has contents which satisfy hunger or it does not; either this is my teddy or substitutes are rejected. Contrary to this (which allows Popper's[55] naturalistic World 1 to play a significant part in the development of our subjective World 2, via the mediation of our embodiment alone), Harré avows that he does 'not believe that the unities that are the basis of selfhood are given in experience'.[56] In contradistinction, the sense of selfhood is nothing naturalistic, it owes nothing to the-body-in-nature, but is the linguistically socialised product of having acquired a theory of the self.

Hence one source (naturalistic) of our selfhood is disallowed, which is why, yet again, all that we are is courtesy of society. This is not the end of our one-dimensionality, for society too is denuded of its stratified properties (CEPs and SEPs), because the social to Harré is a matter only of strictly interpersonal relations. As Shotter puts it, this 'is not a genuinely *social* account of development, but an inter-individualistic one, taking place within a featureless context, devoid of psychological resources or valencies, i.e. in such a non-specific context that it could be situated anywhere'.[57] Thus both the natural background and the foreground of society have been systematically foreshortened to deprive them of stratified properties and powers, in favour of this inter-personal middle ground. The one exception to this is language, or more strictly languages themselves, which afford very different theories of the self, such that the sense of personal identity can be weaker (Eskimo speakers) or stronger (Maori speakers) than our Western self-theories permit. This meaning of the 'social', this down-playing of the natural, and this privileging of the linguistic need to be borne in mind throughout the following presentation of Harré's downwardly conflationary four stages of self development.

Downward conflation in four stages

In this section I will be looking at how Harré explains our acquisition of a sense of self, which to him is a matter of coming to possess a theory. Since the theory of selfhood is enshrined in language, then it can only be acquired derivatively from interacting with existing speakers. Therefore what seems to many of us to be the prime element of our deep private

---

[55] Karl Popper, *Objective Knowledge*, Oxford University Press, 1972, Chs. 3 and 4.
[56] *Personal Being*, p. 22.
[57] John Shotter, 'Rom Harré: Realism and the Turn to Social Constructionism', p. 209.

inwardness in fact turns out to have been appropriated from the external public domain. Now my particular concern, especially in the next chapter, will be to challenge this priority accorded to the public over the private and, in effect, to suggest the reversal of these priorities, both phylogenetically and ontogenetically. In general the argument between us turns on whether our embodiment or our language learning is decisive for acquiring a sense of self – with Harré championing the latter and I the former. Another way of putting this debate is to ask whether practical action provides the necessary and sufficient conditions for the emergence of a sense of self, even if this is later considerably enhanced by language skills, or whether the latter are always indispensable.

Equally it is important to stress what the debate is not about: it is in no way a replay of the nature versus nurture dispute, which lends itself respectively to biological or sociological reductionism. The two of us would, I believe, agree that all human powers only exist *in potentia*. This both implies that action in the world is necessary for their development, but also that we humans have to be the kind of beings who can be developed in this way. In other words, the existence of a biological substratum with the generative powers to produce practical agents or conversationalists, is not at issue, providing that the environment does not intervene to suspend these dispositional states. In both cases sufficiently gruesome experiments have been conducted on sensory and linguistic deprivation, respectively, to show that developmental tendencies to become recognisably human can be overridden by both kinds of deprived environments. It might be concluded from this that each is indispensable for human development, but this again is not something I believe either of us would resist, and again is not the bone of contention. This strictly concerns the sources of the sense of self and what factors and processes should be accorded priority, both at the start of life and throughout it. I will be arguing for the primacy of our embodiment, in practical relation with the natural world, and thus producing a naturalistic account. Harré advances the primacy of our speech-acts in a learning relation to the discursive world, and thus produces a social account. The former emphasises private practice; the latter public involvement.

Since Harré's *Ways of Being* spans our physical, personal and social dimensions, my aim in the remainder of this chapter is to show that the quintessentially social and public stages in the dynamics of our development as selves are seriously challenged by his own discussion of our physical being. In brief, I do not believe that the socio-public account can embrace the affordances supplied by our embodiment and therefore conclude that downwards conflation fails, for all that we are in this respect is not owing to society.

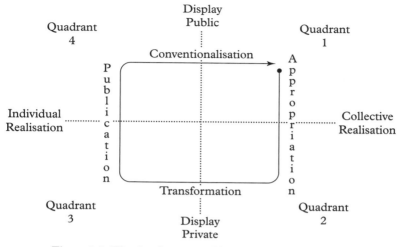

Figure 3.2 The development of Society's Being

In presenting his four stages, Harré sets them out by using two inter-secting axes which produce four quadrants. This then yields the 'Vygotskyan square'. The one axis concerns the public or private per-formance of a mental activity and whether its display is in the public or private domains: the other concerns the realisation of a mental activity and whether this is a property of one or of many – individual or collec-tive. The four quadrants thus look as in figure 3.2, and, to Harré, the dynamics of development consist in moving through them in a clock-wise manner.

Harré makes a fundamental distinction between 'persons' and 'selves' as we have seen, such that 'necessarily all human beings are members of moral orders as persons, social individuals, but the degree of their psychological individuality, their personal being, I take to be contingent'.[58] What it is contingent upon is being taught a theory of the self which is appropriated from the public-collective structure (in developmental transition from Quadrant 1 to Quadrant 2), and is trans-formed into a private-individual sense of self in Quadrant 3. Quadrant 1 is therefore termed the 'primary structure', precisely because it is accorded primacy, and Quadrant 3 the 'secondary structure' because of its derivative status. 'Selves' are therefore secondary to 'persons', because of their contingency, whereas 'person' status is a matter of necessity. They are secondary by virtue of the timing of their appearance in the

[58] *Personal Being*, p. 77.

developmental sequence, and because 'person' is an empirical concept whereas 'self' is a theoretical concept.

In seeking to demonstrate the distinction between 'persons' and 'selves', Harré maintains that every society recognises 'human individuality in the form of persons . . . that is it has a common primary structure; there are wide variations in secondary structure, that is in the degree of singularity with which persons organise their experienced thoughts, feelings, premonitions and plans as their own. The most important evidence of all would be that of a tribe of persons without selves.'[59] Of course, the variation in our 'selves' is to be expected, because as nothing but a theoretical concept, without any real referent, the 'self' may be expected to show conceptual variety on Harré's account. This is because he totally elides the *concept* of self with the *sense* of self. Hence the possibility that members of a tribe may be found (not that they have been) who lack the sense of self *because* they lack a social concept for it. No tribe, I will seek to maintain can ever be found without a *sense* of self possessed by each of its (normal) members.

My own account is precisely the reverse, namely that concepts of 'persons' may show enormous variations between different societies, defining very different obligations for those found at each particular location and exerting pressures which are very different in kind to ensure that they are carried out. This was the force of Durkheim's argument in *Division of Labour*. The early segmented societies, with a low level of differentiation attempted to assure the 'sameness' of persons through the application of repressive law (thus reproducing mechanical solidarity), whilst later co-operative societies, with much higher levels of specialisation, dovetailed 'differences' between persons through the action of restitutive law (which ensured that individuation posed no threat to organic solidarity, based upon mutual interdependence). There is no need to be uncritical of the study to take the basic point. Thus Marcel Mauss[60] traced the historical development of more individualised social conceptions of persons from the Pueblos' ascription of a static repertoire of ancestral roles, through the legal conceptions of personhood in the classical world, to the fully individuated soul which became central with Christianity and was then the focus of finer-grained moral obligations whose execution could neither be checked against tradition nor policed by civil law.

Conversely, Mauss juxtaposed this social process of defining the responsibilities of personhood with the universal sense of self- 'the self

[59] Ibid., p. 85.
[60] Marcel Mauss, 'A Category of the Human Mind: the Notion of Person; the Notion of Self', in M. Carrithers, S. Collins and S. Lukes (eds.), *The Category of the Person*, Cambridge University Press, 1989.

(Moi) is everywhere present' and its universality consists in the fact that 'there has never existed a human being who has not been aware, not only of his body but also of his individuality, both spiritual and physical'.[61] Downward conflationists typically try to absorb the *sense* into the *concept* and thus to credit what is universal to the cultural balance sheet.

Nevertheless, Harré's basic thesis is that animate beings only become 'selves' through acquiring a theory of selfhood: we have to be taught to think that we are 'selves'. In other words 'one who is always presented as a person, by taking over the conventions through which this social act is achieved, becomes organised as a self'.[62] Thus the 'self' is a concept which is secondarily derived from the primary structure. The 'self' is made reliant upon knowing the term 'I', which is derivative through semantic displacement of 'I' when applied to persons. Thus Harré talks of 'an individual private or personal concept of self' derived by Vygotskyan appropriation from 'the social, public-collective concept of "person"'.[63] This thus involves drawing upon Quadrant 1, moving through Quadrant 2, until the appropriated theory can then (and only then) be put to use for private purposes in Quadrant 3. Hence, the contents of Quadrant 3 will depend upon those of Quadrant 1, and thus will reflect variations in the local language game of personhood. Selfhood is therefore a macro-cultural construct which is mediated micro-culturally to the individuals in their symbiosis with carers.

The transformation which takes place between Quadrants 1 and 3 is a phase which 'encompasses processes of development which creates minds that are reflections of linguistic forms and social practices. Mind is formed on the basis of grammatical models and locally acceptable episode structures.'[64] Thus, there are two conclusions which follow from the clockwise movement around the Quadrants, one which concerns origins and the other processes of acquiring a 'self' concept. Firstly, Harré believes that he has furnished 'arguments for the ontological, conceptual and temporal priority of the public-collective realm' for all key aspects of personal psychology[65] – intentionality, rationality and the emotions. Secondly, he concludes that the 'structure of personal psychology has turned out to be the final consequence of the generalisation of the Vygotskyan idea of appropriation'.[66]

Derivatively (and fairly late in childhood), individuals transform their social appropriations and take over their own development within the constraints of the moral order. They come to the reflexivity of self-knowledge, where conscience for example, is seen as the internalisation

---

[61] Mauss, 'Human Mind', p. 3.   [62] *Personal Being*, p. 106.   [63] Ibid., p. 107.
[64] Ibid., p. 256.   [65] Ibid., p. 114.   [66] Ibid., p. 269.

institution of society's moral reproach. In the same way, individuals attain to self-mastery which borrows its thought from the culturally available discourses of command. What we have here is a double endowment by society, rather like the good fairy conferring two gifts at the christening. In the first place, 'Reflexivity is the magic ingredient by which persons are created as self-conscious, self-controlling and autobiographically aware beings. But this is by acquiring a local version of the theoretical concept of "self"'.[67] Secondly, having received this ingredient, its exercise (in the taking over of their own development) is constrained by the conventions of the moral order in which it is exercised. Hence, the gift of reflexivity, which finally creates enough of a self for its workings in the world to become independent, can only work in the kind of world which morally prevents its independence from breaching convention. This is hardly the soil to nurture 'strong poets'.

Not surprisingly then, as we move from Quadrant 3 to 4 which is concerned with 'publication', Harré notes what is undoubtedly the case by this stage, namely that 'efforts to display uniqueness are just one more facet of conformity'.[68] These displays are held to be trebly trammelled; not only by the social gift of a socially acceptable theory of the 'self', not only, in addition, by the conventional moral order, but furthermore by the existing role structure in which the individual has obtained a position. Then, in a manner rather like Hollis's[69] description of how we personify roles by our individualistic enactments of them, to Harré, successful 'publication' consists in convincing (structurally) relevant others that one has the special qualities to which his or her way of performing it laid claim. The scope for creativity has become decreasingly small, is reduced to variations upon an established theme and, crucially, is restricted to the actor-in-her-role: it does not pertain to the agent at large. Not only the 'strong poet', but also the innovative social movement cannot be accommodated in these claustrophobically conventional surroundings.

The last phase, namely where the individual's 'publication' gains an encore, and is assimilated into the moral order of society, is appropriately called 'conventionalisation' (which occurs between Quadrants 4 and 1, thus re-starting the cycle and linking up with *Social Being*). However, this modification of the primary structure over time, through our individual–private creativity, cannot be radical. Partly this is because, as has been seen, the sources of innovation which we find in ourselves (Quadrant 3) are a function of the metaphors available in and appropriated from the

[67] Ibid., p. 264.   [68] Ibid., p. 277.
[69] Martin Hollis, *The Cunning of Reason*, Cambridge University Press, 1987, ch. 10.

primary structure (Quadrant 1). Partly this is because the public-collective realm exercises control via the reception it gives (its moral judgement upon creative offerings emanating from the individual/private domain). At the one and only point where Harré allows that truly subversive wants may surface from privacy, he simultaneously insists upon their bowdlerisation for 'publication' – 'from the dark foundations of the private-individual area there emerge the thrusts of biological imperatives to be clothed in the civilising garb of acceptable interpretations'.[70]

Three problems presented by the body

So far what has been presented is a sociogenic account of both persons and selves, with the 'self' being socially derived from the already socialised person. However, in *Ways of Being*, Harré also devotes a volume to our *Physical Being*. It has not been introduced until now, at the end, because I believe it threatens the coherence of the above account by throwing doubt upon the remorselessly social explanation given. Unsurprisingly, our physiological embodiment does not sit well with social constructionism. Of course, social constructions may be placed upon it, but the body is stubbornly resistant to being dissolved into the discursive. It does not just lie back and allow society to trample all over it. Instead, because it has properties and powers of its own, it is active in the environment and the results of its activity challenge the passivity accorded to it in this account which holds that all we are is a gift of society.

Harré argues that, 'Psychologically speaking, to be human is to be the kind of creature who uses theories to order and so to create the forms of experience.'[71] It is the possession of such theories which distinguishes us from the chimpanzees, not that we have, say, a special kind of perception which is denied to them. Thus, as has been maintained from the start, Harré's is an anthropocentric account, due to the overwhelming importance he attaches to us as language users. Yet his own consideration of the body and its power of physiological signification reveals that its natural environmental relations are not theory neutral. All observation is conceptually formed and the body's naturalistic trial and error learning is no exception to this anti-positivistic rule. That we are dealing with a learning body must cast doubts on the anthropocentric break, for other species' bodies learn too and for precisely the same reason, that they are also engaged in practical action in the world. Of course they cannot articulate it but this is exactly their interest, as a source of theories of inarticulacy: because we have them too, since we also have natural relations.

---

[70] *Personal Being*, p. 284.   [71] Ibid., p. 137.

Yet the theoretical agenda posed by embodiment raises three specific questions which threaten to undermine the imperialism of this sociogenic account. Firstly, there appear to be physiological sources of the sense of self. Secondly, there is that learning which takes place in natural privacy outside the social arena, and thirdly, humans acquire practical knowledge which is non-linguistic in form (though quasi-propositional in kind). These place a serious question mark over their compatibility with the social constructionist account. What they threaten is the need for a different account altogether, which I will take up in the next chapter.

(1) Harré agrees that 'as the metaphysical owner of my body, my person-hood is partly created by the individuating powers of that body's thing-like status. Without just *that* body I wouldn't be me.'[72] Now, the question becomes whether this 'thing' merely supplies a locational base or whether it contributes much more generously to our *sense of self* and to the differentiation between our selves and others? In fact, Harré runs the two together, which should be a source of difficulty with his theory, when he says that our embodiment creates an 'asymmetry between one's experi-ence of one's own identity and one's experience of the identity of other people (which) *emerges naturally*. One's sense of one's uniqueness as a person comes from the fact that one has a continuous point of view as a thing among things.'[73] Although location is stressed, naturalistic differentiation is also entertained. This goes further, for Harré proceeds to agree that the difference between knowing myself and others comes through the contrast between how I experience my body and the way I experience the limits of yours. Thus he admits physiological signifiers in defining our sensory reach. 'I know the "rim of felt embodiment" for my body *by how something feels*, but I know the rim of felt embodiment by your physiognomic reaction.'[74] So, it is sensory and not linguistic devices which enable us to differentiate between the 'inner' and the 'outer', and thus between myself and others.

Is this sensation either equivalent to or the precursor of a sense of self? This he does seem to concede when discussing the sense of touch in relation to one's own body, because in 'touching oneself perceiver and perceived are simultaneously given to consciousness'.[75] At the same time, the asymmetry involved in touching a table or any non-sentient thing reveals that 'it is neither *part of myself*, nor can I analogise to its feelings from my own, as I might if it were appresented as animate. *But in touching myself I have set up the outline form of a "self/other" dialectic in which, so to say, I have verified or founded my general intentional stance to experience, in particular to sensory*

---

[72] Rom Harré, *Physical Being*, Blackwell, Oxford, 1991, p. 28.
[73] *Physical Being*, p. 22. (My italics).   [74] Ibid., p. 20.   [75] Ibid., p. 96.

experience.[76] Thus, it is in the haptic sense that Harré has conceded that the consciousness of self, and differentiation from things inanimate, and from animate beings, have their origins. Equally crucially, he has accepted fully in the last quotation that we are pre-linguistic dialectical theorisers, so all our theories do not come from social appropriation alone, upon which he based the developmental model. Finally, as a transition to the next incongruity, Harré also accepts that these sensory discoveries, which are theoretical in nature, occur in the private realm and not the social arena, for 'touch permits the establishment of a distinction between perceiver and perceived that is wholly within the experiential content of *one perceiver*'.[77]

(2) Bodily feelings play an ambiguous role in the developmental theory. Harré certainly does not deny their existence, but he does question the status of these bodily states – public action or private feeling? His pre-ferred conclusion is that the 'bodily feeling is often the somatic expression to oneself of taking a moral standpoint'.[78] In other words, it is socially derivative and thus congruent with the overall theory. At the most, without moral authorisation of expression, 'private feelings played an unattended second fiddle'.[79] Is this consistently so?

To begin with, in discussing the origins of talk itself, bodily feelings and their physiognomic signifiers are admitted to be prior to and foundational of language about them. Thus in his discussion of pain and pain-talk, private expression precedes public articulation. Hence, pains 'may even be differentiated in relation to the discriminated type of pain that is pri-vately experienced. One rubs oneself for one sort of pain and groans for another, and so on. *Pain talk appears first as an alternative expression of pain, a substitute for a groan or a rub.*'[80] If this is the case for his key element, language, it raises questions about what other zones of behaviour are in fact derivative from the private realm.

For example, self-knowledge had been presented as coming to see oneself in relation to the moral order. However, through sensations, identifiable as one's own, a different scenario opens up in which one can ask, why should not the recognition of some of one's powers and liabilities be privately realised in interaction with the natural order? There are things one can learn to grasp experimentally (by drawing up the blanket to get the teddy from the bottom of the bed), things that are beyond one's reach, bodily sensations one learns to avoid and ones to court (throwing off the duvet and later learning how to retrieve it). Similarly, in phylogenetic history, why should (how can) initial self-mastery be a reflection of cultural discourses of command? The quality of patience can be learned through

---

[76] Ibid.   [77] Ibid. (my italics).   [78] *Physical Being*, p. 143.   [79] Ibid.
[80] Ibid., p. 99 (my italics).

theoretical trial and error in nature – remain in hiding from large animals (even before we discriminate the dangerous ones: approach small animals slowly and quietly when hunting etc.). Unless we try the ice before walking on it, we are liable to a bodily unpleasant dunking. Our species will have accumulated a substantial corpus of private knowledge in this way before it has uttered its first word. What this suggests, is that ontogenetically we continue this bodily learning in relation to our 'natural' environment, for though it has changed in some respects, our species being is continuous. What this threatens, is a revised developmental sequence which works not clockwise from public to private, but anti-clockwise from private practice to public demonstration and social accretion.

(3) Finally, the above leads on to the fact that the acquisition of practical knowledge (non-linguistically mediated and therefore not public) continues to grow throughout life. It is not something (as in 2) which might be held to give way with language acquisition. This again Harré largely concedes, and only partially claws back into the public domain. Thus he accepts that 'while "knowing that" is conceptually tied to consciousness and the discursive production of propositional knowledge, "knowing how" is conceptually tied to agency and the manipulation of skilled performance'.[81] Indeed when considering skilled bodily activities (he gives the social example of tennis, but riding would do better from my point of view), then the felt practical rightness of our movements is given equivalent importance to our bodily sensed location – 'the experience of the rightness of bodily activity is as central to our sense of "being-in-the-world" as such matters as one's sense of location at a certain point of view in space and time'.[82]

This is a surprising admission, but not a random one, for he continues to state that practical action is inscribed in the body itself. So too is his agreement that what is involved is trial and error learning: here however there is a caveat. He proposes that 'one's sense of embodiment in action comes only when a kind of random, inept fumbling is gradually succeeded by skilled performance'.[83] Nevertheless, and this is the caveat, efficiency of execution entails a social judgement which means that 'ways of acting . . . are excluded by what is seen to be done. The characteristics of the executive path require something else, namely some idea on the part of the onlooker as to what it is that is being done; what the end is intended to be.'[84] This may well be the case for tennis, as a rule-governed social game which gives shots their objectives, but it can often be irrelevant to riding *per se*. As someone who taught herself to ride, that was the end in itself, basically accomplished when I stopped falling off (a skill which had been bodily mastered and mercifully without an onlooker). As

---

[81] Ibid., p. 29.   [82] Ibid., p. 107.   [83] Ibid.   [84] Ibid., p. 108.

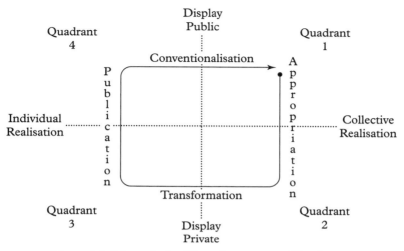

Figure 3.3 The orthodox Vygotskyan square (Harré)

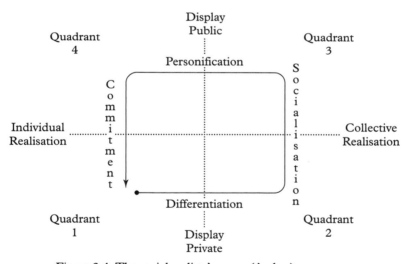

Figure 3.4 The social realists' square (Archer)

Harré concurs, when proficiency increases, 'the skilled actor does have a sense of the body's engagement in the action, but it is a very general feeling of aesthetic "rightness"'.[85] This feeling lies in the private domain and it comes every time that some skill becomes 'second nature'.

Although the books subsequent to *Physical Being* have become progressively more discursively oriented and socially constructionist, this early study represents something of a challenge to them which will not go away. At the time, Harré seemed to have appreciated the claims to primacy of the body-in-practice. Thus it was he who approvingly quoted Merleau-Ponty to the effect that 'Our bodily experience of movement is not a particular case of [theoretical] knowledge; it provides us with a way of access of the world and of the object, with a *'praktognosia', which has to be recognised as original and perhaps as primary'*.[86] It is on the basis of the primacy of 'praktognosia' that I present the reverse sequence of development in the next chapter and succeeding ones.

Since I am explicitly counterposing the social realist approach in this critique of Harré, just presented, the contrast will be clearer if I adhere to the same structure which he employed. In other words I will stick to the four Quadrants described by the 'Vygotskyan square' and will seek to demonstrate the primacy of practice within it – in contradistinction of our selfhood being society's gift alone. The divergent trajectories traced through the square by Harré and me are summarised in figures 3.3 and 3.4. Basically a realist approach to the primacy of practice, which must also give due importance to everyone's societal encounter, is one which accentuates emergent properties and powers at every stage. Since realists believe that there are a good many more powerful particulars, other than 'persons' alone, existing between 'molecules and meanings', the account is necessarily more complex than the derivation, by appropriation, of a secondary sector from a primary sector. With reference to Figure 3.4, five major differences from Harré can be highlighted and these constitute the principal themes which will be developed throughout the book.

(i) The realist account starts in 'privacy', in human exchanges with the natural world, rather than in the public domain of social relations.

(ii) The primacy of practice implies an anti-clockwise trajectory (unlike Harré's clockwise progression), as well as starting in a different place because we bring the effects of our natural encounters to our social ones.

(iii) What the human self does encounter in the social domain is not simply 'society's conversation', as a flat discursive medium, for in

---

[85] Ibid.   [86] Ibid., p. 109.

society the cultural realm is deeply stratified (containing emergent ideational properties – CEPs). Moreover, structural properties (SEPs) do not need to be discursive at all, in order for their powers to be causally efficacious.

(iv) The human arc is also a trajectory during which stratified personal powers emerge in every Quadrant, as a human being sequentially becomes a self, then a primary agent and has the possibility of next developing into a corporate agent and finally into a personalised actor.

(v) Personal identity and social identity are distinct on the realist account, whereas there is only the social identity of persons in Harré's version.

Part II

The emergence of self-consciousness

4   The primacy of practice

To assert the primacy of practice is a refusal to accord primacy to language, and this is what is maintained in relation to the emergence of self-consciousness. The effect of asserting it is to make the embodied practices of human beings in the world more important than their social relations for the emergence of selfhood, meaning a continuous sense of self, and for the development of its properties and powers, meaning reflexivity, which only exists *in potentia* for every neonate. The primacy of practice refers both to its logical and substantive *priority* in human development. This is not simply a matter of it coming before anything else, though temporally it does just that; it is also a question of viewing language itself as a practical activity, which means taking seriously that our words are quite literally deeds, and ones which do not enjoy hegemony over our other doings in the emergence of our sense of self.

Pointers to the primacy of practice

In *Realist Social Theory*[1] I presented three arguments for maintaining that our sense of self, as part of our humanity, is prior and primitive to our sociality.

(1) The first, which it is particularly important to accentuate here, concerns our human embodiment. Harré's argument that, as embodied animals, we have to wait until fairly late upon society for the linguistic appropriation of a theory of the self, involves a completely radical break between *homo sapiens* and other animal species. Even Durkheim, who also wanted to conceive of the 'self' as 'indeterminate material', awaiting the social impress, conceded that all animals, ourselves included, have the capacity to make 'rudimentary distinctions in the flux of experience',[2] otherwise they could not navigate around in their natural environment.

---

[1] Margaret S. Archer, *Realist Social Theory*, Cambridge University Press, 1995, pp. 280–93.

[2] Emile Durkheim, *Les Formes Elémentaires de la Vie Religieuse*, Presses Universitaires de France, Paris, 1968, p. 147.

This appears to be grudging minimalism. After all, any animal has to know a great deal to do so. Successful navigation entails notions of the animal's own shape and boundary, of its principal liabilities *qua* body, and of the principal properties of other entities, such as solidarity/penetrability, as well as relational properties between them like proximity/distance. Navigation is predicated upon a sense of the embodied self, and a differentiation between self and other things environmental. Moreover, to be navigating implies not only such consciousness but also intentionality. To withhold this from the stalking animal, the hovering buzzard, or the domestic cat, patiently staking out the mouse hole, is to render their behaviour inexplicable. Even if the burden of explanation is transferred to the so-called 'instincts', an instinct still has to be intentionally specified before it can be realised in the world: the dog has to be aware it must circumnavigate the tree to get at the rabbit. Bodily self-consciousness and intentional causal action are matters we share with all the higher animal species, and therefore they cannot be social gifts.

(2) Secondly, and deriving directly from the liabilities of our species-being, is that fact that we must all have transactions with an *undifferentiated reality* from our first day of life. At first we cannot know reality as subdivided into the inanimate and animate, animate and human etc. *before* we begin our practical dealings with it. Hunger, thirst and discomfort are our initial physiological prompts to such exchanges, but their imperiousness serves to reinforce Marx's important insight that we are committed to *continuous practical activity in a material world*, where subsistence is dependent upon the working relationship between us and things, which cannot be reduced to the relations 'between the ideas of men'. Our practical work in the world does not and cannot await social instruction, but depends upon a learning process through which the continuous sense of self emerges.

Yet this is exactly what Harré denies: that this self-consciousness can be learned from environmental praxis, rather than being taught by social appropriation. Considering the issue he asked, 'Might it not be that by a process of biological maturation an individual develops in such a way that it can discover empirically, by a certain kind of observation . . . that there are some states of affairs (and so a world) which are independent of any of his/her plans and best attempts to realise them and some that are not; that by and large, human sensibility extends roughly as far as the bodily envelope, and so on.'[3] His two arguments against this hinge on Husserl's failure to find the self as an *entity*, at the centre of experience, and Hume's

[3] Rom Harré, *Personal Being*, Basil Blackwell, Oxford, 1983, pp. 93–4.

similar failure to find a 'self', which can ever be present in experience. Harré is right, there is no *entity* or *substance* to find, but that only means he is looking for the wrong 'thing' when looking for the 'self'. What I am arguing for, is the self as an emergent relational property whose realisation comes about through the necessary relations between embodied practice and the non-discursive environment.

Such practice may have an autonomic component, as in suckling, but such action always has a theoretical element. Thus, Bhaskar correctly maintains that, 'in so far as practice is quasi-propositional, it will depend (analytically) upon some anterior theoretical reasoning, e.g. about the nature of the world that the practice is designed to change. But this depends upon practice, which also encompasses both theoretical and practical reasoning.'[4] Through the dialectic of presences and absences in practice (e.g. the realisation that I cannot nourish myself: only an exterior source can do this), the theory of the self and theories of otherness emerge. Harré is quite correct to be looking for a theory (of the 'self') rather than an entity, but he is seeking the wrong kind of theory in the wrong place, in society rather than in our embodied practices and environmental relations. It is creatively learned, at the price of non-survival, not didactically instilled. Unless I learn very early on to draw a line between myself and the world, I am literally incapable of any practical action, and it is in this practice that I learn to theorise in this way, one which is simultaneously a theory of self and of otherness. This is what we invoke in every practical deed. Thus, very early in life, to move away from the pressure of a cot bar implies practical referential detachment and a rudimentary theory about transfactual efficacy; the bar is fixed and cannot come after you. Although Harré does not deny that there is private knowledge, he makes a great play of it being distributed throughout the collective, so that a team is required to complete the activity successfully.[5] Thus, much of what seems to be singular action has had first to draw upon the 'primary structure' of the public/collective Quadrant. What his derivative model of socialisation cannot encompass, are shared properties of the species which emerge because each and every surviving member has realised one potential of their species-being, viz to know the difference between 'self' and 'otherness'. It does this because our species' survival cannot delay practical action in the environment until the linguistic concept of self (as 'I') has been acquired, by the semantic displacement of 'I' from the concept of the 'person'. The *sense* of self does not await linguistic encoding

---

[4] Roy Bhaskar, *Dialectic: The Pulse of Freedom*, Verso, London, 1993, pp. 67 and 69.
[5] Rom Harré, *Personal Being*, p. 48.

any more than our Kantian synthetic unity has to wait until we have read Kant. In short there never were, nor could have been, 'tribes without selves'.

(3) Thirdly, because *homo sapiens* represents a natural kind, our particular species-being endows us with various potentials, whose full development is indeed socially contingent, but whose pre-existence allows us to judge whether social conditions are dehumanising or not. Without this reference point in basic human needs (that which because of our nature, we must have in order to flourish – as distinct from induced wants, compliance or other appetitive states), then justification could be found for any and all political arrangements, including ones which place some groups beyond the pale of 'humanity'. (Where crimes against humanity are concerned, it seems that these are never perpetrated because the initial move is to withdraw the claim to human status from the victims in question.) It is politically and morally significant that Harré's position on the social derivation of selfhood commits him, on his own admission, to the position where other groups have to struggle to articulate a moral/human status for the inarticulate.[6] There can be no inalienable rights to human status where humanity itself is held to be a derivative social gift.

Natural relations as the source of the sense of self

(Quadrant 1– realist sequence: the private/individual)

Here the differentiation of a *sense* of the self is taken to define 'self-consciousness'. Since this sensing will be seen to be wordless, and necessarily so because it is both prelinguistic and alinguistic, then it cannot rest upon any concept appropriated from society. This does not make it unconceptual: the sense of self, like all other knowledge is conceptually formed. What it does mean, is that the theoretical work involved is performed and recorded in ways which are non-linguistic. The modality is practice and the medium of inscription is the body. Importantly this retains our continuity with the animal kingdom, whose higher forms are also held to manifest this embodied sense of self, and it is what unites all members into the community of humanity (for this sense is a necessary part of our developed species-being).

Thus a major distinction is being made between evolving *concepts* of the self, which are indeed social, and the universal *sense* of self, which is not, being naturally grounded. As Marcel Mauss maintained – 'the self (Moi)

[6] Ibid., p. 62.

is everywhere present' and this constant element or universal sense consists in the fact that 'there has never existed a human being who has not been aware, not only of his body but also of his individuality, both spiritual and physical'.[7] There is a persistent tendency, especially prevalent amongst sociological imperialists, to absorb the *sense* into the *concept*, and thus to credit a human universal to the effects of culture. Imperialism is probably assisted in these manoeuvres by the correct belief that conceptualisation is indeed indispensable, but this is coupled with the erroneous conviction that concepts have to be linguistic. Consequently, to imperialistic thinkers, the acquisition of concepts is held to be essentially dialogical in form. The *sense* of self advanced here is conceptually formed (it cannot be otherwise), therefore what I have to vindicate is not its atheoretical character, but rather its monological form of emergence from our embodied practices. (To avoid confusion the term '*concept* of self' will always refer to its varying social usages, whereas the '*sense* of self' will be reserved for our practical concepts forged in our environmental relations.)

Development of the sense of self takes place in the Individual/Private Quadrant (realist sequence), where privacy of course does not mean the absence of relations, but only that social relations do not feature as significant here. This is for the simple reason that what is encountered is an undifferentiated environment of objects – including the human, animate and inanimate. Differentiation of the social comes later on, and is itself predicated upon the distinction between the self and other things having already been established. Equally, there is no primordial individual born into this Quadrant, but only those with a potential for singularity, which itself has to be realised from embodied practice as an emergent property.

To defend this fundamental proposition about the origins of the sense of self, three distinct but interlinked arguments will be drawn upon about the sources and content of our sense of self or of singularity as a human being.

(A) Merleau-Ponty's discussion of our incarnation in the world, and how each is differentiated as a singular being by sensing itself to be such through the exercise of its bodily powers in nature. Here, differentiation emerges from the use and development of sensory-motor skills in the surrounding environment, where intrinsic to this relationship is an emergent awareness of difference between the two.

[7] Marcel Mauss, 'A Category of the Human Mind: the Notion of Person; the Notion of Self', in M. Carrithers, S. Collins and S. Lukes (eds.), *The Category of the Person*, Cambridge University Press, Cambridge, 1989, p. 3.

(B) The second source is the modern neuroscience of memory, where the acquisition of procedural (bodily) skills reveals their independence from, and greater durability than, declarative (verbal) skills. This will be particularly important for defending a neo-Lockean definition of self-hood. The 'embodied memory' will be used to buttress a naturalistic version of Locke's definition of selfhood, as the body plus sufficient continuity of consciousness – criticism of which has usually rested upon deficiencies in declarative recall (imperfect or grossly damaged memory).

(C) The third source is the rather underdeveloped realist argument about the embedding of reasoning in natural praxis. Here the quasi-propositional nature of practice will be used, in conjunction with the embodied memory (performative), to account for our practical referential detachment (our sense of the existential intransitivity of ourselves and of other things), and our emergent awareness of the transfactually efficacious laws of nature (that things drop or roll independently of agential intervention). From these, the two basic principles of the logical canon, those of identity and non-contradiction, will be seen as emergent from embodied practice and the case completed for our reasoning powers not being a gift of society.

Socialisation, which takes place in the next Quadrant in the realist sequence, is itself only possible because it builds upon the three arguments advanced above. It is dependent (a) upon the fact that each and every member has already realised one potential of their species-being, namely to make the primary distinction between the self and otherness, on which learning the subsequent distinctions between social and non-social depend. Socialisation (b) requires human beings with performative capacity and memory in order that they are the kind of beings whose repertoire can be socially extended to incorporate such activities as handling a spoon, becoming toilet trained or learning to speak. Finally, (c) the very possibility of communication, whether gestural or verbal, is ultimately dependent upon beings who are already obedient to the law of non-contradiction, otherwise no verbal information can be conveyed, including natural language itself, as distinct from mimetic babbling. The basic laws of logic are learned through relations with natural objects: they cannot be taught in social relations, since the linguistic medium of socialisation presupposes them. The two most important words in language, 'I' and 'no', batten on to a pre-linguistic sensing which is the scaffolding of socialisation.

A   Incarnation: self and otherness

'the whole of nature is the setting of our own life, or our interlocutor in a sort of dialogue' (Merleau-Ponty, *Phenomenology of Perception*)

The primacy of practice in conceptualising our experience is what allies realism with phenomenology. Contra empiricism, experience is not passively imprinted on the senses by nature as if on a blank page. For both realism and phenomenology, we are thrown into the real world and make what we can of situations, of which we have no prior understanding, through exercising our species' endowments in praxis. Thus, the opening statement to Merleau-Ponty's *The Structure of Behaviour*,[8] is quite compatible with realism: 'Our goal is to understand the relations of consciousness and nature: organic, psychological or even social. By nature we understand here a multiplicity of events external to each other and bound together by relations of causality.' In his phenomenology, objects in nature are self-sufficient, but their 'plenitude' defeats the finitude of human consciousness. Consequently, the lived consciousness (perception to Merleau-Ponty) is necessarily perspectival, since it always comes from a point of view (our constitution prevents us from having a universal view of a cube, for example, which would imply an unlocated consciousness). It is the body which constitutes the anchorage of our perceptual limitations and affordances. Thus it is from the body that the 'perceiving subject must, without relinquishing his place and his point of view, and in the opacity of sensation, reach out towards things to which he has, in advance no key, and for which he nevertheless carries within himself the project, and open himself to an absolute Other which he is making ready in the depths of his being.'[9]

In each perceptual situation, the organism is not free to take up a factual state of affairs in an arbitrary and uncontrolled manner. Fact is imperious in the normal visual situation, for we cannot take the gaps between the trees as figures and the trees themselves as background. In general, meaning optical illusions apart, the perceiver and her perceiving share in the constitution of the situation. Whilst ever these two, perceiver and perceived, are fully distinguished, as in their following characterisation, there is no quarrel in principle with realism and considerable congruity between them. 'The natural world is the horizon of all horizons . . . which guarantees for my experience a given, not a willed, unity

---

[8] M. Merleau-Ponty, *The Structure of Behaviour*, Beacon Press, Boston, 1963, p. 3.
[9] M. Merleau-Ponty, *The Phenomenology of Perception*, Routledge and Kegan Paul, London, 1962, p. 326.

underlying all the disruptions of my personal and historic life. Its counter-part within me is the given, general and pre-personal existence of my sensory functions.'[10] The disjunction with realism comes when perceiver and perceived are eventually elided in a subjectivism which constitutes one of the more blatant versions of the epistemic fallacy.[11] Nevertheless, up to this point, the question of how we confront the world through our practical action represents a concord which can be explored more fruit-fully than has yet been the case. Indeed, the two positions are fairly unique in their joint assertion of the primacy of nature and of practice within it, and in these relations according us our human sense of self. This, it must be admitted, is considerably more developed by Merleau-Ponty, who thus usefully supplements the argument at and on this point.

(1) Unquestionably, to Merleau-Ponty, our natural relations have priority over our social relations, both in the sense that they are prior to human development, but also in the sense that the former continuously grounds the latter and indeed obtrudes at every phase of our life course. Thus 'I never wholly live in varieties of human space, but am always rooted in natural and non-human space.' Personally and primordially, this natural world is not given to us by virtue of the disembodied Cartesian *cogito*, but through the body, its sensory reach and corresponding range of practical abilities. 'Everything I see is in principle within my reach, at least within reach of my sight, and is marked upon the map of "I can". Each of the two maps is complete. The visible world and the world of my motor projects are each total parts of the same Being.'[12]

What 'I can' do is co-determined by the nature of the body and that of the world, and is only established by their conjunction in practice. Without the body, we have no modality of presence in the world, and without its activity, none of the properties of reality can be disclosed. Merleau-Ponty is quite clear that this is a matter of individual incarnate discovery of nature, and not one of knowledge appropriated from society, because we could subtract socialisation (abstract ourselves from the

---

[10] Ibid., p. 330.

[11] In the following passage Merleau-Ponty gives priority to epistemology over ontology in a manner unacceptable to the realist. 'Things and instants can link up with one another to form a world only through the medium of that ambiguous being known as a subjectivity', *Phenomenology*, p. 333. While realists would contest little about the account of everyday experience, which does justice to its practical orientation and structured character (see Andrew Collier, *Critical Realism*, Verso, London, 1994, pp. 73–4), they would of course defend the differentiated and stratified nature of the world's ontology from subsumption under our perception of it. How things are in reality is always a different question to the realist from how people take them to be.

[12] M. Merleau-Ponty, 'Eye and Mind', in his *Phenomenology, Language and Society*, Heinemann, London 1974, p. 283.

social context) and yet would necessarily rediscover the natural world in Quadrant 1, of the realist sequence. Hence he maintains, 'Bodily existence which runs through me, yet does so independently of me, is only the barest raw material of a genuine presence in the world. Yet at least it provides the possibility of such presence, and establishes our first consonance with the world. I may very well take myself away from the human world and set aside personal existence, but only to rediscover in my body the same power, this time unnamed, by which I am condemned to being.'[13]

(2) The origins of the self/other distinction derive from our embodiment in the world, for our incarnation involves a theory of perception. As O'Neill puts it, the 'phenomenal body is the matrix of human existence. It is the centre around which the world is given as a correlate of its activities. Through the phenomenal body we are open to a world of objects as polarities of bodily action. The phenomenal body is a modality of being-in-the-world which is privileged because it is the archimedian point of action.'[14] It is the archimedian point, because the body image ineluctably gives us a scale against which to calibrate nature. Thus things are high or low in analogical relation with our head and feet (literally over our heads or at ground level). Similarly the 'thing is big if my gaze cannot fully take it in, small if it does so easily . . . circular if, all its sides being equally near to me, it imposes no deviation upon the regular curvature of my gaze . . .'[15] Yet these statements already presuppose that a differentiation between the self and the natural world has taken place, otherwise the body cannot act as the 'ruler' or 'setsquare' for things other than itself. The key to this differentiation lies in human powers of sight and movement (theory and practice), which we possess but nature does not. Thus, 'visible and mobile, my body is a thing among things; it is caught in the fabric of the world, and its cohesion is that of a thing. But because it moves itself and sees, it holds things in a circle around itself.'[16] So far, this has yielded an object/object distinction, certainly between objects with very different properties and powers, but nevertheless not a subject/object distinction which implies and requires self-consciousness on the part of the former. We need an account of its own provenance.

(3) This subject emerges from the 'impersonal self', or what is sometimes called the 'moi naturel', which constitutes my ineluctable 'primordial

---

[13] Merleau-Ponty, *Phenomenology*, pp. 165–6.
[14] John O'Neill, *Perception, Expression and History*, Northwestern University Press, Evanston, 1970, p. xxx.   [15] Merleau-Ponty, *Phenomenology*, p. 303.
[16] Merleau-Ponty, 'Eye and Mind', p. 284.

contact' with the world, given that my body cannot but find itself in some situation with its powers already at work. It is already at work because it cannot do or be otherwise. It gives its attention to some things rather than others and is incapable of *not* seeing the world as differentiated into figures and ground. Perhaps here, Merleau-Ponty is making the same point as Charles Taylor [17] about the 'significance feature' differentiating humanity, in which case the direction of our primary perception could be seen as our attention being grounded in and directed by our most basic human needs. However, the key point is that the body's powers are directed at itself as well as at the world, and it is in the asymmetries of these experiences that the subject/object distinction arises.

(4) The human body is unique, because of its dual role as the source of perception which is also able to sense itself. It is particularly in touching oneself, where there is only one sensation, unlike touching a table when toucher and touched are distinct, that the self-consciousness which constitutes me as subject, rather than object, arises. Touched objects are thus established as not being part of myself, whereas in touching my own body I have a sensory experience which demarcates me from the rest of the world. So too, in practice, we are sensibly aware of the difference between our own voluntary mobility and the quite independent movement of objects in the visual field. As Merleau-Ponty puts it, 'I say of a thing that it is moved; but my body moves itself, my movement deploys itself. It is not ignorant of itself; it is not blind for itself; it radiates from a self . . . The enigma is that my body simultaneously sees and is seen. That which looks at all other things can also look at itself and recognise, in what it sees, the "other side" of its power of looking. It sees itself seeing; it touches itself touching; it is visible and sensitive for itself. It is not a self through transparence, like thought, which only thinks its object by assimilating it, by constituting it, by transforming it into thought.'[18] Objects are before me in the world, but the body is constantly *with me*, and it is my self-manipulation, through mobility and change of point of view, which can disclose more of the object world to me. I can self-consciously manipulate the dialectic relationship between self and otherness and, in this very process, I reinforce the distinction between the two. Significantly, Harré admits that this is a Private/Individual experience, available to each and every lone perceiver. Hence his comment that, as 'a model, touch permits the establishment of a distinction between perceiver and perceived that is

---

[17] Charles Taylor, 'Consciousness', in Paul F. Secord (ed.), *Explaining Human Behaviour*, Sage, London and Beverly Hills, 1982.
[18] Merleau-Ponty, 'Eye and Mind', pp. 283–4.

wholly within the experiential content of *one perceiver*.[19] This is a crucial point at which *Physical Being* constitutes an auto-critique of the socialised theory of the self in Harré's later work.

(5) Having located the self in the sensed bodily envelope, Merleau-Ponty has drawn the line between self-consciousness and awareness of otherness. The former is described rather poetically as the achievement of an inner synthesis. 'The body's animation is not the assemblage or juxtaposition of its parts. Nor is it a question of a mind or spirit coming down from somewhere else into an automaton; this would still suppose that the body itself is without an inside and without a "self." There is a human body when, between the seeing and the seen, between touching and the touched, between one eye and the other, between hand and hand, a blending of some sort takes place – when the spark is lit between sensing and sensible, lighting the fire which will not stop burning.'[20] In turn the body is permanent, to the self, in contrast to objects which may disappear from the visual field, and the presence of the body is the condition for other objects presenting themselves at all. Furthermore, objects are *manipulanda* to the embodied self, which can change its point of view in order to see more of them or can sometimes (with smaller objects) literally grasp them whole. All of this is a matter of embodied praxis. Thus, 'I should not say that the unseen sides of objects are simple possible perceptions, nor that they are the necessary conclusions of a kind of analysis or geometrical reasoning. It is not through an intellectual synthesis which would freely posit the total object that I am led from what is given to what is not actually given; that I am given, together with the visible sides of the object, the non visible sides as well: I can touch the lamp, and not only the side turned toward me but also the other side; I have only to extend my hand to hold it.'[21] The realisation of self and otherness is a dialectical process, such that 'there is a world for me because I am not unaware of myself; I am not concealed from myself because I have a world'.

Consciousness is therefore essentially a lived involvement in a series of concrete situations. Progressive differentiation between the two entails practical action and such action always involves work, which is undertaken in the interests of our natural needs. Praxis is, as it were, a personal technology which transforms the world in conformity with anterior human needs. This is the Marxian side of Merleau-Ponty: our practical action is not wanton or directionless, it has a point to it which is

---

[19] Rom Harré, *Physical Being*, Blackwell, Oxford, 1991, p. 96 (my italics).
[20] Merleau-Ponty, 'Eye and Mind', p. 284.
[21] M. Merleau-Ponty, *The Primacy of Perception*, Northwestern University Press, Evanston, 1964, p. 14.

given by virtue of the way subjects are and the way in which the world is. It is also at this point in discussing the otherness of the natural world that we find Merleau-Ponty at his most realist – in allowing our human sensing of nature's self-sufficiency. 'When I say that I have senses and that they give me access to the world . . . I merely express this truth which forces itself upon reflection taken as a whole: that I am able, being conatural with the world, to discover a sense in certain aspects of being without having myself endowed them with it through any constituting operation.'[22]

(6) It should be highlighted that consciousness itself is not a series of articulate propositions of the form 'I think that', but is an inarticulate consciousness of the practical form 'I know how', which is in no way dependent upon language because it precedes it both phylogenetically and ontogenetically. Practical consciousness represents that inarticulate but fundamental attunement to things, which is our being-in-the-world. With experience and over time, we become accustomed to the 'habitual body', an inner map which resists contingencies like the loss of limbs, and which frees us from continuously having to decipher the immediate milieu because of what has become stably established in the subject. Here, memory, far from being some intellectualised representation, is the bodily sedimentation of accomplished acts: it is the 'habitual body' which gives us our past tense and enables us to contemplate a future, even though our embodied expectations have continuously to be reconciled with the dynamic nature of our existence in the world. The memory, as it were, sets us free and allows a reversal of the performative tasks, by virtue of which the body stands in its natural relationship to the environment. Thus 'to be in possession of my body independently of any urgent task to be performed; in order to enjoy the use of it as the mood takes me, in order to describe in the air a movement formulated only verbally or in terms of moral requirements, I must *reverse the natural relationship in which the body stands to its environment*'.[23] This is the gift of unimpaired memory lodged in the 'habitual body': it is what was damaged in the case of Schneider due to a shell splinter embedded in his brain, which restricted his performative abilities to those involving direct contact with the world of immediate practice. What he had lost was the 'habitual body' of familiar actions, which operates as the sedimented memory through which the body declares various manipulative possibilities to the consciousness. His case will be of particular interest when we turn to the findings of modern neurobiology.

---

[22] Merleau-Ponty, *Phenomenology*, p. 217.   [23] Ibid., p. 112 (my italics).

(7) So far we have remained within the Private/Individual Quadrant (realist sequence), where the human being confronts the primacy of the natural world, as we all must. Indeed Merleau-Ponty is emphatic that these natural relations always remain fundamental, even when we make the transition into the social domain. 'My body which through my habits ensures my insertion into the human world, only does so by projecting me in the first place into a natural world which can always be discerned underlying the other, as the canvas underlies the picture.' (Indeed it could be said that Schneider retained the (performative) canvas but had lost most of the (declarative) picture.) Thus, there is no sense in which privatised natural relations give way at some point to public social relations. The former enjoy primacy and also continue to play their part throughout the human life course.

(8) It is wholly consistent that Merleau-Ponty should approach inter-subjectivity via bodily sexual relations. Phylogenetically, in the 'state of nature', these would have represented our first social relationships. Phenomenologically, we are present to others and they to us through the medium of our bodies. Thus, 'in the preceding discussion where the relation of man with nature was the issue, incarnation meant the body's being a vehicle of one's presence to things and the natural world. Where the question of sexual relations brings into focus relations among persons, the body must be the vehicle of one's presence to other subjects and even the condition of their being for me.'[24]

Genealogically, our sociality begins in the practical expression of bodily desire. Eroticism supplies an intentional attunement to the other as sexually significant. Consummation means that body is linked with body in desire. Note that Merleau-Ponty is not yet speaking of people meeting (intersubjectivity), but only and initially of bodies coming together (inter-corporality). However, it is a direct result of this human relationship that, through the practice of sexuality, my body simultaneously becomes something different for me and for the other. Thus, we have here the genesis of a finer distinction between self and otherness, one which now discriminates between other things and other human bodies. Importantly this is a learned distinction, practically acquired under the promptings of the generalised libido. It emanates in both parties from private prompts in Quadrant 1 (realist sequence) and, although it takes two to tango, this precipitates them *towards* Quadrant 2, without placing them fully in it. This is because a genuine Collective realisation of action has to be based upon intersubjectivity, rather than bodily co-presence alone. At this point, we

[24] John F. Bannan, *The Philosophy of Merleau-Ponty*, Harcourt Brace, New York, 1967, p. 75.

have a bodily distinction which is a necessary stepping stone to sociality, but it requires the emergence of inter-subjectivity before we properly enter Quadrant 2 (realist sequence). Thus, we need an account of how we arrive, on this libidinal basis, at authentic inter-subjectivity.

(9) True inter-subjectivity ultimately arises from the relationship between two sets of embodied practices. To Merleau-Ponty, the problem of 'other minds' stems from the fact that the perception of one's own body is ahead of the recognition of the other.[25] Whilst in sexuality the body of another is present to one, how do we make the leap to this other being the possessor of a psyche? The problem is stated in incarnational terms, namely the impossibility of inter-embodiment. 'You cannot represent yourself in the same way in which I feel my own body; it is likewise impossible for me to represent to myself the way in which you feel your body. How, then, can I suppose that, in back of this appearance before me, there is someone who experiences his body as I experience mine?'[26] The answer is held to lie in common bodily comportment in the world. Thus, 'the problem comes close to being solved only on condition that certain classical prejudices are renounced. We must abandon the fundamental prejudice according to which the psyche is that which is accessible only to myself and cannot be seen from outside. My "psyche" is not a series of "states of conscious-ness" that are rigorously closed in on themselves and inaccessible to anyone but me. My consciousness is turned primarily toward the world, turned toward things; it is above all a relation to the world. The other's consciousness as well is chiefly a certain way of comporting himself toward the world. Thus it is in his conduct, in the manner in which the other deals with the world, that I will be able to discover his conscious-ness.'[27]

Hence, we define one another as 'conducts' at work in the world, where the other appears as the visible envelopment of another corporal schema. Sympathy, not empathy since I cannot occupy any other than my own

---

[25] Some have attempted to make this encounter with 'other minds' more primitive, because the child learns what a happy or an unhappy person looks like by seeing the mother's happy or unhappy face in response to the baby's own happy or unhappy feelings. (See D.Winnicott, 'Mirror-role of Mother and Family in Child Development', in Lomas, *The Predicament of the Family*, London, Hogarth, 1967.) There is no need to doubt that the baby does so respond, but not to *persons or to mother*. These are learned distinctions in what must first come to the child as a world undifferentiated into subjects and objects. Babies respond to lots of things, and are affected by them, *without knowing what kinds of things they are*. Winnicott seems to confuse being affected with knowing what it is that has that effect. Otherwise there would be a commitment to 'natural' or 'primordial' cate-gories in the newborn.

[26] M. Merleau-Ponty, 'The Child's Relations with Others', in his *The Primacy of Perception*, p. 114.   [27] Ibid., pp. 116–17.

enveloped point of view, is the spark which crosses the gap. It does so, without obliterating it, and allows the other to be credited with a similarity of psyche which alone can account for the similarities of embodied practice which the two share. Thus 'the adult *me* . . . is a *me* that knows its own limits yet possesses the power to cross them by a genuine sympathy . . . adult sympathy occurs between "other" and "other"; it does not abolish the differences between myself and the other.'[28] Sympathy thus springs up when I encounter another 'myself', who is also open to what I am, in the common situations which the natural world supplies to us equally.

(10) Language and speech are attended to last in the *Phenomenology of Perception*, precisely because they are the emergent terminus of the developmental trajectory. In the emergence of language, priority is given to gesture, thus maintaining the primacy of embodiment in speech itself. Merleau-Ponty cuts through the argument that gestures are natural (angry fist-shaking), whereas words are arbitrary, because of the consistent inter-penetration of the natural and social worlds, where relations with the former precede the latter. He insists, genetically, that 'we need, then, seek the first attempts at language in the emotional gesticulation whereby man superimposes on the given world the world according to man'. Gestures are practical activities by which our bodies mediate our responses to our immediate environment. The possibility of gestures leading to communication in words is based upon exactly the same argument as that which established primary intersubjectivity. Thus 'communication or comprehension of gestures comes about through the reciprocity of my intentions discernible in the conduct of other people. It is as if the other person's intention inhabited my body and mine his.' The word is earthed in the communality of embodied practice in the natural world. Accumulated and sedimented meanings never displace the word as activity: speaking is essentially practical action. The source of complex natural language is nothing other than 'productivity which is man's deepest essence and which is perhaps revealed nowhere so clearly among civilisation's creations as in the creation of language itself'.

Because of this insistence upon speech as a practical activity, it is not surprising that developed language is considered as a tool and that its acquisition is not due to some intellectual mastery of linguistic principles or syntax, but is of a piece with acquiring other kinds of practical conduct through habit. Hence, 'what is involved is a kind of *habituation*, a use of language as a tool or instrument' whose employment rests upon 'the child's assimilation of the linguistic system of his environment in a way

---

[28] Merleau-Ponty, 'The Child's Relations with Others', p. 120.

that is comparable to the acquisition of any habit whatever: the learning of a structure of conduct'.[29] Language is thus an emergent stratum of meaning, whose genesis comes from our natural relations, but it never severs its links with them, since both its acquisition and deployment remain matters of doing. Once language has emerged as a cultural property (CEP), it manifests its own powers of facilitation and constraint, such that the 'linguistic world figures in expression in the same way that the natural world serves as background for natural perception'.[30] Thus, it is the task of the philosopher of language, ultimately, to show how linguistic structures mirror and analogise the structure of perception. The two remain articulated by gesture and united in their practical orientation. Language shares intentionality with practice: they are both 'about' something. Thus Merleau-Ponty ends in accord with realism, for as Collier puts it, 'language can only be learnt by reference to reality. Not only is there no one privileged access to reality, language is not even the first runner. Linguistic interaction presupposes practical interaction, in which the pre-linguistic child engages, through play and the satisfaction of its physical and emotional needs.'[31] Together practice and language, and then genetically language-as-practice, bring us to Quadrant 2 (realist sequence). At rock bottom, what language is fundamentally 'about' there are our public and collective references to natural reality and to (the new) social reality.

Thus, we have an account which *ends* with language itself as practical action, and also one in which language is emergent from natural praxis. It is an emergent property which is predicated upon a lengthy sequence of practical actions in the natural environment, which I have schematised as points 1–10. Fundamentally, this whole sequence derives from what we humans are as a natural kind and how our species-being interacts with the way in which the world is, independently from us. Each one of us has to follow the same personal trajectory of discovering, through private practice and by virtue of our common human embodiment, the distinction between self and otherness and then that between subject and object, before finally arriving at the distinction between the self and other people – which only then can begin to be expressed in language. These discoveries are made by each and every human being and their disclosure is independent of our sociality: on the contrary, our becoming social beings depends upon these discoveries having been made. Thus Merleau-Ponty's great contribution is that he has given us an *account* of the primacy of practice – one which relies upon nothing

---

[29] Ibid., p. 99.   [30] John F. Bannan, *The Philosophy of Merleau-Ponty*, p. 81.
[31] Andrew Collier, 'Language, Practice and Realism', in Ian Parker (ed.), *Social Constructionism, Discourse and Realism*, Sage, London and Beverly Hills, 1998, p. 48.

more than our ineluctable embodiment and our inescapable relations with our environment.

B *Praxis, the embodied memory and neuroscience*

The argument in the last section dealt with the emergence of our *sense* of self: this section now turns to the *continuous* nature of this sense, or to what is usually called the 'continuity of consciousness'. In the neo-Lockean tradition, self identity is defined as the body plus such a continuity of consciousness. It is a definition which makes self identity distinct from our social identities, since it does not depend upon our relations in society. Now, necessarily, our continuous sense of being the same self over time makes appeal to our memories. Memory is central to the notion of selfhood which I am defending here, as primitive to any socialised conceptions. Without it I would lack the Lockean 'continuity of consciousness' which, together with my embodiment, makes me a particular human being. Without my *own* distinctive and recalled past, I would indeed reduce to the passage of an organic parcel through time, which would lack anything other than strict DNA identity. In theory I would become socially interchangeable with, or indistinguishable from, others subjected to the same momentary socialisation, though in practice I would become non-functioning, as would society, if today I behave as a skilled worker and mother whereas yesterday I acted as unskilled and childless. There are facts of the matter: either I have children and skills or I do not, and it matters greatly to my continuity and that of society that I, and all others like me, are continuously aware of which is the case.[32] However, much of the criticism which the Lockean notion has attracted boils down to noting gaps in our continuity of consciousness (and sometimes glaring ones in amnesiacs and the brain-damaged). In other words, the counter-argument goes, our self identity cannot rest on 'the body plus continuity of consciousness', given that the fact of imperfect recall in all of us means that none of us enjoys complete continuity over time.[33] However, Locke's definition rests upon sufficient rather than perfect

---

[32] See Margaret S. Archer, *Realist Social Theory*, pp. 283f.

[33] Locke put forward a definition which has considerable intuitive appeal, such that a person was 'a thinking intelligent being, that has reason and reflection, and can consider itself as itself, the same thinking thing in different times and places' (*Essay* II, xxvii,2). From Bishop Butler onwards, critics have construed such continuity of consciousness exclusively in terms of memory (recall) and then tried to show that memory alone fails to secure strict personal identity. See, for example, Bernard Williams, *Problems of the Self*, Cambridge University Press, Cambridge, 1973. A defence of a modified neo-Lockean definition is provided by David Wiggins, 'Locke, Butler and the Stream of Consciousness: and Men as a Natural Kind', *Philosophy*, 51,1976, which preserves the original insight.

continuity, and modern neurobiology shows that no philosopher can demand perfection.

Now, there seems no need to be detained in this discussion of the contribution of memory to self identity by those philosophical specula-tions about fictional 'look-alikes' (products of bodily fission or fusion who share the same memories) or functional 'do-alikes' (robots and automata with perfect memories), because these could not be candidates for human self-consciousness. They could not be registered as humans, since they fail to qualify as animals. Nevertheless, the question remains, what kind of appeal to memory has to be made to secure the continuity of our self-con-sciousness?

In this section, I want to argue that too much has been made to ride on the declarative, and therefore linguistically dependent, memory. On the contrary, the point will be to show that there are two non-verbal forms of memorising that anchor our sense of self over time and which prevent the title to humanity from being withdrawn from those who never attain speech or who lose it (the autistic and aphasic). These are our eidetic (visual image) memories, which supply seemingly boundless powers of *recognition*, as distinct from the universal deficiencies in our *recall*. Secondly, there are the procedural skills, which survive damage to the declarative memory, and secure the self identity of those who continue to 'know how', even when their 'knowing that' is discontinuous or damaged. Both of these are embodied phenomena, and the findings of modern neuroscience literally flesh out Merleau-Ponty's insight that the 'habitual body' gives us our past tense. They also, I maintain, provide criteria which answer the question posed by Locke's definition, namely what does represent a *sufficient* continuity of consciousness for self iden-tity to be deemed continuous. What neurobiology shows is that memory is a dynamic process of selection, where practice makes any notion of perfect recall non-adaptive. Our definition of continuity cannot turn on the kind of memory which is counterfactual in human development, and would be counterproductive to it. What is of significance here for my general argument, is that both the eidetic and procedural memories, which supply sufficient continuity, are located in the Private/Individual domain.

Probably most people would agree with the last statement, for our intu-itive reaction is indeed that the locus of memory is found in the Private/Individual Quadrant; after all, in some sense our memories are singular to each one of us. However, neuroscientists will be found agree-ing that certain memories are prompted, and perhaps not just triggered but actually created by social cues of the 'but surely you remember . . .' type, and also that recall involves constant refurbishment (it is not like pulling out and replacing a filing card).[34] This seems to open the door to discursive psychology, and to allow the Public/Collective domain to operate as much more than a screening device, but rather to play a major role in the social construction of memory. This is the path that we have seen Harré take, such that the conversational reconstruction and validation of memories are public and collective processes. Thus, for discursive psychology in general, 'as far as memory is concerned, the aim is not to specify how putative mental models might represent knowledge and experience, but rather how people represent their past, how they construct versions of events when talking about them'.[35]

What I want to show in this section, by taking a closer look at neuroscience, are four things: (a) that the social construction of memory is not implicit in the abandonment of the 'card-index' or engram model of remembering; (b) that recall is a practical action on the part of active subjects or species adapting to their environments; (c) that embodied memories are the most resilient and function much as Merleau-Ponty described them, that is as the body remembering without any linguistic intervention, and (d) that the emergence of textual storage (derivative from writing) is a real emergent phenomenon, which comes late in both phylogenetic and ontogenetic development, and thus cannot serve to buttress any account which seeks to give primacy to the social in retrieval processing. In other words, I am again counterposing the primacy of Private/Individual practice in memory-activity to the priority accorded to conversation, and hence to the Public/Collective domain by Harré.

To forestall the worries of those who are concerned with the reductionism of some neurobiology, let me begin this discussion with memory clearly defined as 'being an emergent property of the brain as a dynamic system rather than a fixed and localised engram',[36] before attempting to present its workings as a *genus* of practical activity. To view memory as a dynamic system is quite different from viewing it as an organic mode of information-processing, with storage and retrieval facilities analogous to the Library of Congress. What is different, and what is dynamic, is quite basically that a 'biological memory system differs from a mere physical information-storage device by virtue of the system's inherent capability of using the information in the interests of its own survival', such that 'anyone who is interested in memory, but looks only at the storage side of things, is essentially ignoring the fundamental distinction between dead and living

[34] Steven Rose, *The Making of Memory*, Bantam Press, London, 1992, pp. 34–5.
[35] D. Middleton and D. Edwards, *Collective Remembering*, Sage, London and Beverly Hills, 1990, ch. 2. This aim is quoted approvingly by Rom Harré, *The Singular Self*, Sage, London and Beverly Hills, 1998, p. 144.
[36] Steven Rose, *The Making of Memory*, p. 318.

storage systems, that is ignoring the essence of *biological* memory'.[37] As Edelman has argued, the nervous system is plastic to experience and is in continuous dynamic selection *vis-à-vis* challenge or constraint from the environment.[38] Obviously, a flexible memory with the ability to remember or not, according to environing circumstances, would be of considerable service to adaptation. Clearly it is not in our adaptive interests to remember everything: it is useful to recall phone numbers of family and friends, but not to do so by the equivalent of riffling through a mental telephone directory. These selective rememberings seem to be involved when we pick out our child from the mass in the playground, reach for the chopping knife 'unthinkingly' in the kitchen, or make the familiar drive to work on 'auto-pilot'. A living storage system will be selective rather than perfect, therefore 'total recall' is not what should be required of or for a neo-Lockean concept of the 'continuity of consciousness'.

One of the most interesting findings, in the present connection, concerns a significant difference between childhood and adult memorising. Children, until puberty, have a much more marked tendency towards a visual or eidetic (from the Greek 'image') memory than do adults, and this appears to be independent of gender, ethnicity, class or school achievement.[39] Thus, they can recall things like the number of stripes on the Cheshire cat's tail, having been shown an illustration. The interest of this finding is two-fold. Firstly, it confirms Merleau-Ponty's presumption about the primacy of perception and indicates that the acquisition of language does not represent a crucial break or a primary vehicle in early memorising. Secondly, what we are confronted with here is a non-linguistic process, but one which can readily be interpreted as adaptive practice, or the part played by visual practice in adaptation.

Most of us can detect this biographical shift, because our childhood memories come back to us as snapshots or short film clips which are often vivid, coloured and interestingly 'atmospheric', even sometimes being accompanied by smells and feelings of warmth or cold. Still, today, when I catch the smell of new cut hay, I am back in the field at three years old, sitting under a stook, feeling warm damp prickles through my socks and knowing that all was very well with the world. Yet, when I try to visualise the route to the library from the front door of the London School of Economics, which I must have traversed hundreds of times during my six years as a student, I simply cannot do it. What accounts for this eidetic phenomenon and its virtual demise in the adult?

[37] 'Interview with Endel Tulving', *Journal of Cognitive Neuroscience*, 3:89, 1991. See also E. Tulving, *Elements of Episodic Memory*, Oxford, 1983.
[38] G. Edelman, *Neural Darwinism: The Theory of Neuronal Group Selection*, Basic Books, 1987.   [39] N. R. Haber, 'Eidetic Images', *Scientific American*, 220, 36–40, 1969.

Speculatively, the answer seems to lie in memorising as active practice. As we saw in the previous examples, what is salient to us is perceptually filtered. We commit to memory on a need-to-know basis, blocking out and preventing de-selected material from burdening our memories. Thus on the familiar drive to work I do not know the other turnings which the signposts indicate: all I have retained is which way to go in order to get there. The point is that young children lack such criteria of relevance and hence selectivity. 'At birth, we may guess, all types of input may seem to be of about equal relevance; within only the widest possible classification rules, everything must be registered and ordered so as to enable each individual to build up his or her own criteria of significance. At this time eidetic memory, which doesn't prejudice the importance of inputs, is vital, because it gives the greatest possible range over which inputs can be analysed. But as we grow up we learn to select from key features of our environment.'[40]

Such key features will vary with the environment itself. As a once rural child, I do not see cows, I see breeds, and I do not catch a glimpse of a horse, but register a bay 16.2 hunter – practices which would be of utility in an agricultural setting. One can then speculate that Inuit children were making perceptual discriminations between different types of snow, long before they learned to name them, and that their desert Arab counterparts could pick out different kinds of camels, well before acquiring their large camel vocabulary. Through practice we sift for relevance. When, until very recently, the lifetimes of most people were spent within the same environment, the early eidetic maps remained serviceable and could be smoothly edited at puberty to include some more detailed occupational features, or extended in linear form to incorporate the new places visited. *Larkrise to Candleford* gives us the young Flora Thompson doing just that. The transition at puberty remains adaptive, even for the migratory: the old snapshots are not of utility, so become relegated to the mental 'shoebox', whilst the non-eidetic memories of adulthood can be tailored to grown-up criteria of practical relevance. Either way, the biological mechanism remains of survival value, but it is practice which determines in which way it will serve.

At a more macro level, practice shapes neurological development through the process of 'activity-dependent self-organisation', such that the properties of brain cells adapt to environmental circumstances. Held and Hein's [41] experiments with kittens, showed that those reared in darkness have visual systems whose inadequate development do not allow

[40] Steven Rose, *The Making of Memory*, p. 105.
[41] R. Held and R. Hein, *Journal of Comparative Psychology*, 56, 1963.

them to navigate obstacles when walking. Rearing kittens with large paper collars obscuring their bodies, had similar if less dramatic consequences for navigation than their growing up in darkness – which is highly congruent with Merleau-Ponty's argument about the importance of our body images and their acquisition through touch and sight. Following on, Blakemore's experiments of rearing kittens in environments featuring only vertical stripes, found them subsequently unresponsive to horizontal cues. The conclusion was that the visual system, in its developmental phase, had expanded the proportion of cells which responded to frequently met stimuli and decreased those devoted to infrequent stimuli. These, and variations on this experimental theme, are highly persuasive that (laboratory induced) deficiencies or peculiarities in the physical environment in which bodily activity takes place, have correlative effects upon brain cell development and specification. The bodily emergence of our senses thus seems to be just as dependent upon properties of the physical environment, as the whole normal development of our sociality was held to be upon our nurturing environment, in the Harlow-to-Bowlby argument. What we have at birth are potential bodily powers, but their realisation depends upon environmental circumstances: generative mechanisms can be diverted or immobilised, but their expression is always specified. As a process, specification is neither reducible to nor mediated through our sociality; it is a feature of us as human beings living in the natural environment.

So far, in this discussion of memory, language has remained rather conspicuous by its absence, and it largely remains so where visual recognition (rather than recall) is concerned. In the seventies, Standing demonstrated that if subjects were simply asked to judge whether they had seen pictures or words on a previous trial, the accuracy of their judgements exceeded ten thousand such items, leading him to conclude that 'there is no upper bound to memory capacity'.[42] Although words have been shown to aid in colour recognition tests, particularly by teaching new names for unfamiliar colours, they seem of little assistance in providing visual descriptions, whereas the same witness can usually build up an Identikit picture. Certainly a name from the past can summon up memories, but so can other senses. Chanel No. 5 brings back my mother preparing for a dance, and the taste of a madeleine cake triggered the fifteen volumes of Proust's *A la Recherche du Temps Perdu*. The conclusion here is that all our sensings seem to play a part in remembering and to be effective despite being wordless.

[42] L. Standing, 'Remembering Ten Thousand Pictures', *Quarterly Journal of Experimental Psychology*, 25, 1973.

However, we can become rather more precise by considering the findings about the distinctively human verbal, or 'declarative' memory, compared with our 'procedural' memory of skills like swimming or bicycle riding, which, as the adage goes, 'you never forget'. This distinction is the psychologists' version of Gilbert Ryle's 'knowing that' as opposed to 'knowing how', and it distinguishes activities involving 'naming' from those entailing 'doing'. That these are distinct, seems clear from brain-damaged subjects who cannot recall the word 'bike', but still do know how to ride one, and from those suffering from amnesia who can acquire skills, like doing jigsaws, but do not remember the experience of learning. More specifically, in patients in whom areas of the brain involving damage to the hippocampus are concerned, it is declarative rather than procedural memory which is affected – there is no resulting loss in learned motor skills. One subject studied by Milner steadily improved his game skill without any memory that he had encountered the particular game, even when a practice had taken place the previous day.[43] 'Procedural memories, unlike declarative, do not seem to be forgotten in the same way, suggesting that they are both learned and remembered by a very different mechanism from declarative ones. Perhaps this is because memories that involve pro-cedural rather than declarative modes – such as riding a bicycle – are not confined simply to the brain but involve whole sets of other bodily mem-ories, encoded in muscles and sinews.'[44] Of course, all memory is embod-ied, but the resilience of skills and habits implies a bodily remembering which we can call embodied practical knowledge or know-how. Unlike the eidetic memory, which seems to attenuate in the post-pubescent period, procedural knowledge is there for life and operative throughout it. This will prove to be of considerable importance when it comes to examining the dynamics of knowledge in Quadrant 2 (realist sequence), for in it we have a permanent non-linguistic component in skilled practical action.

As a species, the uniqueness of our memorising processes lies much less at the socio-cultural level (speech), than in the emergence of the Cultural System. With the development of writing and cultural artifacts, from wax tablets to the internet, memorising becomes collective. In oral declarative memory, the 'richness of our linguistic recall may be biolog-ically no more mysterious than the capacity of a homing pigeon to navigate precisely over hundreds of kilometres or a dog to distinguish and remember thousands of different odours at almost infinitesimally low concentration'.[45] Biologists have their differences with certain

---

[43] B. Milner, S. Corkin and H. I. Teuber, 'Further Analysis of the Hippocampal Amnesic Syndrome: 14 Year Follow-Up Study of H.M.', *Neuropsychologia*, 6, 1968.

[44] Steven Rose, *The Making of Memory*, p. 320.

[45] Steven Rose, *The Making of Memory*, p. 326.

linguisticians here,[46] but what is incontrovertible is that with extra-somatic sources of recording, memory breaks free of biology and from the individual, to become a collective phenomenon. (This does not pre-clude its working back upon biology, as the brain capacity thus freed-up may be diverted to other purposes.) The fluidity of oral traditions gives way to the fixed linear form of catechism and textbook,[47] which stabilises collective memory through codification – and is ultimately distinctive of the human species.[48]

Our artificial memory is lodged in the Cultural System: access to it depends upon a new level of skill in accessing artifacts, from books to computers, and control of it is a collective power shaped by corporate rather than primary agents. Knowledge becomes a new steeply inegalitar-ian distribution, which delineates interest groups in a similar manner to other unequal distributions. Simultaneously, the Cultural System, seen as the Universal Library, displays the three features of any emergent stratum, temporal priority to individuals, relative autonomy from them and causal efficacy over them. A major cultural emergent property has been elaborated (CEP), and its new internal relationships, especially the public codification of contradictory and complementary items, exert new powers of facilitation and constraint upon different collectivities of agents by defining the ideational situations which they confront (see *Culture and Agency*, chapter 6).[49]

Thus in Quadrant 2 (realist sequence), the Private/Collective, primary agents, which means all of us, do not meet socialisation as some flat, uni-versal process, but as a highly differentiated one, whose effect is to divide us socio-culturally according to the cultural capital we receive, depending upon the privileged/underprivileged positions into which we are involun-tarily born. In Quadrant 3, the Public/Collective, these differentiated interests then meet the full brunt of the Cultural System which imposes its situational logic upon all groups depending upon which ideas they seek to hold or to challenge. These concepts will be clarified in greater detail in the next chapter. For the moment the key point is that once memorising becomes detached from the individual artifactually, then what agents confront is not some innocent level playing field of meanings,

---

[46] See D. Bickerton's strong case for our human distinctiveness on linguistic grounds, *Language and Human Behaviour*, UCL Press, London, 1995 and *Roots of Language*, Karoma Publishers, Ann Arbor, 1981.

[47] W. Ong, *Orality and Literacy*, Methuen, London, 1982.

[48] The following comment is significant for my current argument: 'The transition from an oral culture to a literate culture is a transition from incorporating practices to inscribing practices', Paul Connerton, *How Societies Remember*, Cambridge University Press, 1989, p. 75.

[49] Margaret S. Archer, *Culture and Agency*, Cambridge University Press, Cambridge, 1989.

but the differentiated and stratified properties of the emergent Cultural System. For human agents, a good many properties and powers lie between their individual brain's molecules and society's corpus of meanings. For primary agents, the notion of their free and equal induction into 'society's conversation' is as ideological as viewing their entry into the market as a matter of consumer sovereignty. Only a commitment to individualism can support such a mis-representation of both social and cultural reality alike.

C   Practice: the wordless source of reason

Practice has never been given primacy in the philosophy of modernity. On the contrary, this starts from the essentially *unpractical* notion of consciousness in the Cartesian *cogito*. Since mind is divorced from practical experience, Descartes then concludes that his thoughts are those of an incorporeal substance. Yet, it is only as embodied human beings that we experience the world and ourselves: our thought is an aspect of the practice of such beings, and thus can never be set apart from the way the world is and the way we are. Both of the latter elements are crucial. Those who only accentuate *us* in our necessarily limited, because embodied, nature then endorse anthropocentricism – a world made in our image and thus bounded by our human limitations, as in pragmatism or the critical empiricism examined at the end of chapter 1. Yet, the affordances of human experience describe our point of contact with reality; but they neither exhaust reality itself, nor what can be discovered about it. Our 'Copernican' discoveries exceed and often run counter to the information supplied by our embodied senses. Our practical observations and the theories to which they give rise are umpired by reality itself, which, as Lakatos puts it,[50] pronounces a 'verdict of inconsistency' on the relationship between our observational theories and our explanatory theories. One or the other has to be adjusted, but no privilege is conferred on either side: we may simply be wrong, however compelling our experience is felt to be subjectively. However, it is only by venturing these first experiential thoughts that we hold them up for corroboration or disconfirmation (lengthy and frequently indecisive as this process often turns out to be). We thus recognise both our fallibility, but also the productivity of fallibilism in the generation of knowledge. Being what we are, we cannot but start from the experiential, but the world being as it is, means that the (pro tem) finishing point will be at some considerable distance from the

---

[50] Imre Lakatos, 'Falsification and the Methodology of Scientific Research Programmes', in I. Lakatos and A. Musgrave (eds.), *Criticism and the Growth of Knowledge*, Cambridge University Press, Cambridge, 1970, pp. 130f.

experience of any generation. The bridge between them is thought or reasoning.

Now, I want to take the next step, and to maintain that it is through the activities of embodied practice that we develop the powers of thought at all. To do so it is necessary to demonstrate that practical action is also the source, (i) of our thinking about distinct objects, distinct that is from both us and from one another, and, (ii) how they are subject to transfactual laws of nature which belong to them, but do not emanate from us. These are the first foundations of nonanthropocentric thought and, it is also maintained, of the logical canon. They occur very early on, well before the acquisition of language, and are thus fundamental to our being-in-the-world. As Bhaskar argues, 'all actions – even so-called basic ones – utilise or consist in the exercise of skills – practical knowledge or know-how, whether learned or innate. And the motivating belief or reason that prompts the action may be regarded as setting an initial condition for the exercise of the ability displayed in action. But of course, just as it is not a condition for an intentional action that the action does in fact possess the property for the sake of which it was performed, so it is not necessarily, and indeed will perhaps only exceptionally be the case that what is exercised in action can be expressed in speech.'[51] Here, in the neonate, we are dealing with quasi-beliefs, which are pre-verbal and depend upon the embodied memory rather than the linguistic code for their elaboration and retention.

What sorts of practical activities are involved, and what kinds of quasi-beliefs do they entail? It is necessary to answer these questions clearly before being in a position to show that they ground our very powers of reasoning. I will do so by unpacking an example given by Bhaskar, which could occur before the age of two. As he puts it, in 'order to pass a football we have to *practically referentially detach it*; and in order to understand our passing of it we have to believe that it is not only referentially detachable, i.e. existentially intransitive, but subject to *transfactually efficacious* laws of nature'.[52] Now, difficult as the terminology sounds, I argued earlier that the child lying prone in its cot, who moves away from the uncomfortable pressure of the cot bars is displaying mastery of both principles: she believes that the pressures come from without and that she can detach her body from the source of discomfort by rolling over and, moreover, that the bars are stationary in nature and will not come after her.

The work of Piaget is important here, because he draws a direct link between the emergence of the detachability of objects, as the child learns

[51] Roy Bhaskar, 'Emergence, Explanation and Emancipation', p. 291.
[52] Roy Bhaskar, *Dialectic*, p. 228.

to differentiate these from the self, and its concurrence with the dawning notion of causality. Neither emerge through the passive registration of environmental events, but depend upon interpretations which are formed in the context of practical action. In asserting that the beginnings of true objectification are inseparable from appreciation of external cause and effect relationships, Piaget sets out to demonstrate that once we detach objects from ourselves, we simultaneously accept that they are governed by powers which are independent from our own. Thus, 'it is only by achieving belief in the object's permanence that the child succeeds in organising space, time and causality' and therefore 'we must begin our analysis by trying to explain the behaviour patterns which tend to construct the object as such'.[53]

What is significant here, is that Piaget locates the development of referential detachment in the pre-verbal under twos, and attributes it to sensory-motor processes through which practical actions the child interprets the otherness of her environment. Thus he traces the six stages involved in young children's elaboration of an 'object concept'. Through the visual and auditory tracking of objects, through manipulative activities like reaching/grasping and throwing/dropping, to the point where she seeks for hidden objects, the child gradually shows in action that she attributes permanence to objects which are conceived of as possessing autonomy and independence from her own subjective state. Physical groping to find objects, under things like the coverlet, are involved in learning the fact of object displacement, that is that they remain the same object but may have been transferred from A to B, and then concealed. 'Such gropings in fact sufficiently demonstrate the necessity of active experience in order to build up sequential perceptions; that is for the child to understand that the object constitutes an independent body in motion which is capable of multiple displacements.'[54]

With the onset of true objectification, the child also abandons her anthropocentricism, accepts that her properties and powers are only one set amongst those of the world's, and makes the step from unconscious ego-centricism to the admission of external causality. Hence, to 'the extent that things are detached from action and that action is placed among the totality of the series of surrounding events, the subject has power to construct a system of relations to understand these series and to understand himself in relation to them. To organise such series is to form simultaneously a spatio-temporal network and a system consisting of substances and of relations of cause to effect. *Hence the construction of the*

[53] Jean Piaget, *The Construction of Reality in the Child*, Routledge and Kegan Paul, London, 1955, p. 93.   [54] Ibid.

object is inseparable from that of space, time and causality. An object is a system of perceptual images endowed with a constant spatial form throughout its sequential displacements and *constituting an item which can be isolated in the causal series unfolding in time. Consequently the elaboration of the object is bound up with that of the universe as a whole.*'[55]

Thus through doing, the child accedes to thinking and thought itself is conceptual; it is not conducted in empiricist terms derived from immediate sense data. For objectification, as the process of referential detachment, means conceiving of objects as possessing their own permanent properties and being subject to causal powers of their own kind. The non-empiricist nature of the 'object concept' is central to the conjoint emergence of core logical principles – firstly that of identity. Much of Piaget's experimental work was devoted to the emergent understanding of 'conservation' in the child: that is how things, like a given quantity of liquid, may appear to change (if poured into a squat container or a tall thin one), whilst really remaining constant. Objectification is the generic form of 'conservation', for the object may look different from different angles (e.g. when held or dropped), and in terms of sense data, it has no looks at all when hidden or concealed, so the concept of its permanence (that is its existential intransitivity) is not an empirical but a theoretical one. The theory consists in subscribing to intransitivity which is the basis of identity. 'In short, object conservation, *which is the first of the forms of conservation*, results like all the others in the close union of a rational or deductive element and an empirical element, indicating that deduction is constantly at work in close relation to things or at their suggestion.'[56]

It is as if the empirical realm of appearance confronts the child with a series of visual puzzles, that is, appearances that are inconsistent with what is known about an identical amount of liquid having been poured into differently shaped containers. The power to appreciate conservation (intransitivity) is crucially linked in Piaget's thought with both the logical principles of identity and of non-contradiction. The child needs to employ both principles to be capable of conservation. She has to master the *identity* argument, that it is the same liquid with nothing added and nothing subtracted, so that what has changed is not the quantity of coloured water, but its visual appearance when poured into tall or squat vessels. Equally, she has to acquire mastery of the *negation* argument, such that when the liquid is returned to the original container, the height of the column of liquid returns to its starting point, despite its having appeared differently in the tall and squat vessels. The negative argument shows that intransitivity is understood to persist through these visual transforma-

---

[55] Ibid., pp. 92–3 (my italics).   [56] Ibid., p. 96.

tions. This negative argument of reversibility thus provides experimental confirmation of the positive argument ('it's the same water'), and is therefore the practical demonstration that inconsistencies (literally, apparent contradictions) are not tolerated – these puzzles must be eradicated if sense is to be made of the world.

It can now be shown that practical action is indispensable for arriving at articulation of both the identity and the negative arguments. As has been seen, the primary process of objectification is activity-dependent, and through it the identities of self and otherness become progressively specified. To Piaget, 'the distinction between the internal or psychic world and the external and physical world is far from innate. It arises from action, which, engendered in a reality, of itself undifferentiated, comes little by little to group images about one or other of these two poles, round which two intercorresponding systems are built up.'[57] However, at the sensory-motor stage, the negative principle of reversibility (or return to initial state) is harder to master because it means tenaciously holding on to a starting point and not allowing it to be overridden by affirmations of apparent difference, which are inconsistent with it. Piaget noted that these apparent contradictions dogged his young sensory-motor group more than children at any other stage of development. Since this was the first stage, on whose supersession more complex mental processes depended, he was obviously fascinated by how the principle of non-contradiction was acquired and devoted a whole volume of experiments to this subject, *Experiments in Contradiction*.

What is of particular importance from the present point of view, is the role which the child's own practical action (engaged experimentally) played in the abolition of apparent contradictions, through reinforcing the connection between starting and finishing points and thus encouraging the development of the negative argument (reversibility). One experiment was especially significant for the current argument. Children placed beads simultaneously with their own right and left hands into two transparent tubes and then concurred that there was the same quantity in each. This was the case even if they had first failed a table-top conservation test, by denying that a widely spaced line contained the same quantity of beads as a more densely spaced line. They were then invited to decant the contents of their containers into similar tubes, again agreeing upon conservation, which this part of the experiment was designed to underscore. Then, each child was asked to take out a bead from each container with the right and the left hand simultaneously, and to place the

---

[57] Jean Piaget, *The Child's Conception of the World*, Routledge and Kegan Paul, London, 1967, p. 34.

pairs in two trays with indentations, one of which was widely spaced, the other densely so, such that the latter terminated one third of the distance short of the former. Obviously, to transcend visual appearances at the end of the experiment, the child had to remain aware of the initial state of equality in the original containers. One general experimental observation is relevant, before we come to the overall finding, namely that even those who 'succumbed' to the final visual impression of non-conservation were not acting atheoretically. In the conservation of liquids, one five-year-old subject who had predicted equality in the second vessels (squat and thin), when confronted with the visual 'appearance' of inequality, replied that *either* some of the liquid must have been spilled (in transferring it to the squat jar) or, when different coloured water was used, red tends to shrink and green to expand in pouring.[58] Thus there is evidence that those at the sensory-motor stage do not just live with contradictions but actively come up with (defective) theories to overcome them.[59]

Mastering the logic of non-contradiction demanded that visual stimuli of one kind could not empirically be allowed to override what was known to the subject about the totality of the situation. Totalisation was precisely what the experiment was designed to encourage. Significantly, it was *practical action* by the child (the fact that she had done all the initial placing of beads and subsequent displacement of them by hand), which was being tested for its power to instil the negative argument. Because many more of his subjects displayed mastery of conservation in this context, specifically planned to intensify active participation, Piaget felt justified in having confirmed his initial hypothesis, namely that 'it is the child's own action that encourages the acquisition of conservation'.[60] The theoretical resolution of apparent contradictions thus turns out to be highly dependent upon practical action. Most generally, the understanding of the conservation of matter is an endorsement of the law of non-contradiction, in thought as in reality. It is the acceptance that something cannot simultaneously be p and not-p, including the fact that this is a counter-intuitive belief whose mastery is reliant upon not succumbing to the empiricism engendered by visual appearances.

However, logical thought need not fully display its intricacies in linguistic practice, even when the child has acquired language proficiency, and this is particularly the case in language use itself. Thus to Bhaskar, 'We need not be able to say how we do what we very well know how to do (and sometimes we are not even able to say what it is that we do) – even, as Chomsky has made abundantly clear, when the first order

[58] Jean Piaget, *Experiments in Contradiction*, University of Chicago Press, Chicago, 1974, p. 190.   [59] Ibid., p. 194.
[60] Ibid., p. 195. This experiment is reported in ch. 11, pp. 185–201.

skills are verbal, discursive ones.'[61] This is confirmed by Piaget, who regards his *Language and Thought* as an attempt to show that 'the child neither spontaneously seeks nor is able to communicate the whole of his thought'.[62] What this serves to underscore is that *language is not the 'great divide', for there is a genuine primacy of practice which yields reasoned knowledge non-discursively and which also underlies practical proficiency in the linguistic domain.*

It should be noted that this defence of the primacy of practice sees it as the source of differentiation (of the self, subject/object, subject/subject), then the source of thought (the basic principles of logic, namely identity and non-contradiction), and thus makes practice the *fons et origo* of language and the discursive domain in general. As such, it is diametrically opposed to Bourdieu's treatment of practice, which is completely severed from theoretical discourse. Thus he can accord no primacy *in* the development of thought to our ineluctable practical relations with the world. On the contrary, he regards practice as issuing in its own logic – one of immediacy, urgency, contextual embeddedness and pragmatic common sense – which stands opposed to, and can only be misconstrued by, applications of the logical canon. Hence he maintains that, 'practice has a logic which is not that of the logician'[63] and thus that he is discussing 'the logic of practice which flouts logical logic'.[64]

This 'different logic', he argues, has to be understood in its own terms. These are ones of the 'logic of associations' and the 'logic of annexations and fusions',[65] which are governed by the 'practical principle of pertinence'.[66] Now it is perfectly possible to acknowledge associative thought and to accept that thought revolves around pressing concerns, is contextually embedded etc., without breaching the logical canon: on the contrary, it is necessary to understanding such thoughts. Yet Bourdieu maintains the obverse, namely that the logic of practice violates the principle of identity in its referential 'fuzziness' and breaks with the principle of non-contradiction in its nullification of transitivity. This position is simply regarded as untenable here, because without obedience to the principle of non-contradiction – whose abrogation would allow the simultaneous assertion of p and non-p, or that the cup is simultaneously full and empty – we can communicate nothing at all. And this includes being unable to answer the pressing practical concern about whether a drink is available or not. Indeed, without obedience to the law of non-contradiction it becomes very questionable whether we are even able to think at all.

[61] Roy Bhaskar, 'Emergence, Explanation and Emancipation', p. 291.
[62] Jean Piaget, *The Child's Conception of the World*, p. 6.
[63] Pierre Bourdieu, *The Logic of Practice*, Oxford, Polity Press, 1990, p. 86.   [64] Ibid., p. 91.
[65] Ibid, pp. 84–5.   [66] Ibid., p. 90.

There is a further antinomy between our positions. I am not only defending the *primacy* of practice here, a primacy which Bourdieu must deny precisely because he has made practical thought radically discontinuous with discursive thought, and therefore the question of primacy is struck out by definition: but also, in the next chapter, I want to defend the proposition that practice is *pivotal* to all of our knowledge. This proposition obviously rests upon interchanges between different forms of knowledge and implies a significant degree of 'translatability' between them. This, in turn, Bourdieu refuses because he holds that practices 'can only generate systematic products, but with an approximate, fuzzy coherence that cannot withstand the test of logical criticism'.[67] Thus, for all his vaunting defence of the logic of practice and *le sens pratique*, Bourdieu is advancing much less bold claims about the place of practice in thought and knowledge than those defended here.

Conclusion

In this chapter I have not left the Private/Individual realm (Quadrant 1: realist sequence) except occasionally to gesture towards later implications. However, this Private/Individual domain has turned out to be a busy place to which we owe our sense of self, its continuous nature and our reasoning since it is there that:

(a) The self emerges, meaning someone with a sense of self formed through our embodied relations with the natural world. This sense of self and its distinction from otherness and from others is not dependent upon joining in society's conversation.

(b) The *continuous* sense of self is embedded in our eidetic memories and embodied in our procedural memories. The latter are more resilient than our declarative memories and are also operative throughout the lifecourse. Together these two, the eidetic and the procedural, supply a continual resort for defining our selfhood, above and beyond our bodily identity. They are thus the modern ways of specifying what a neo-Lockean means by the 'continuity of consciousness', which is something distinct from perfect recall.

(c) Pre-verbal practical action is the source of basic principles of logical reasoning which are *prior to and necessary for discursive socialisation*. There is no reason to believe that such practical activity ceases with the acquisi-

---

[67] Ibid., p. 87.

tion of language. The primacy of practice has therefore been defended as prior to participation in society's conversation, and also necessary to our acquisition of the logical canon which is quintessential to our rationality. This primacy of practice is thus equally damaging to 'Society's Being' as it is to 'Modernity's Man'.

Together points (a) to (c) made a strong case for the primacy of practice, *within* the domain of private action, as the start of the whole developmental sequence of being human in the world. Succeeding chapters will explore the remaining three Quadrants of the reversed 'Vygotskyan square' with the aim of demonstrating two propositions. Firstly, that what we become at any subsequent stage *never* makes us into society's animal, for we continue with Private/Individual activities, alongside Public/Collective ones, and the former thus helps to make us the kind of unique *persons* we become. Secondly, as we do indeed become social beings, we do much more than simply joining in society's conversation. Necessarily, given the nature of social reality, we confront emergent properties which, in addition to our status as human beings (those with a continuous sense of self rooted in the Private/Individual realm), also makes us into very different kinds of *agents* and very different *actors*. As adult human beings, we are three-in-one – *persons, agents* and *actors* – but we never lose our genesis in the continuous sense of self which is formed non-discursively through our practical action in the world.

5   The practical order as pivotal

'Men, while living in society, do not thereby cease to live in nature, and to receive from it occasion and material for their curiosity and imagination.'   (A.Labriola)[1]

Realism insists that none of the properties and powers of subjects are understandable in isolation from reality. Deprived of this reference to, or regulation by, reality, then self-referentiality immediately sets in – consciousness becomes to be conscious of our own ideas (generic idealism), experience equates knowledge with the experienced (pragmatism and empiricism), and language becomes the internal relationship between linguistic signs (textualism). Instead, consciousness is always to be conscious of something. Even if its referent is to an internal bodily state, this has an ontological status independent of the ideas we hold about it: experience is necessarily an experience of something, for the verb cannot be intransitive. Thus the experiencer is someone who encounters something prior to it, relatively autonomous from it and causally efficacious upon it. Even if I engender my own experience, as in calling something to mind, what I re-experience in memory has the same three properties, otherwise we are dealing with a different element, namely fantasy. Language, too, has this same quality of 'aboutness',[2] for a purely self-referential language says literally nothing, including being mute about us, since our inner states are themselves about some state of affairs. These entail objective referents, as in appendicitis or bereavement, just as our emotions are also intentional, that is about some feature of reality. These can be fallible, of course (mice are not really dangerous), but we can only know this by consulting reality itself – that is by examining its causal powers.

---

[1] A. Labriola, *Essays in the Materialistic Conception of History*, Monthly Review Press, New York, 1966, p. 217.
[2] Andrew Collier, 'Language, Practice and Realism', in Ian Parker (ed.), *Social Constructionism, Discourse and Realism*, Sage, London, 1998, p. 48.

Language as practice

Realism 'is implied by our deeds, whatever our words, and then of course by our words, once we understand them as deeds' (Roy Bhaskar).[3]

If the 'aboutness' feature of language invokes reality, even when it treats of our most subjective inner conditions, it is impossible that language in general can be confined to purely social referents. A broken limb is something over which we can fume because of its direct restriction upon our mobility *per se*, that is regardless of it preventing us joining socially organised events. A convincing social constructionist account of a broken leg has never been encountered. However, we can be equally frustrated by a broken lock on a door and say so for the same reasons. The 'aboutness' feature characterises not only language-use but also language acquisition. As Collier puts it, 'The learning of language would . . . be miraculous if that interaction were not *about* independently existing entities in a public world, which language too is necessarily partly about.'[4] This being the case, then language can only be learnt by reference to reality and it gains its meaning from its relation to this same independent reality. It follows that there must be some non-linguistic access to reality, which is prior to language acquisition, if it is learnt referentially. In other words, practical interaction is presupposed as prior and involves the use of sensory-motor skills in the world which, as Piaget argued, determine the emergence of the 'object concept'. As was seen in chapter 1, even Saussure, who has often been held to maintain that words gain their meaning from their relationship to other words, was assuming the practical stance of the passenger when designating an object as the 'Paris-Geneva' train. The different practical stance of the engineer would not lead him to deem it the same object if it had a new engine.

But the priority of practice is not restricted to our dealings with manipulanda. If the expressive uses of language are also 'about' things in, or states of, the world, then there must be some worldly emotional practice which necessarily precedes our ability to learn to voice our feelings. There must be practices like the raw emotionality of the involuntary 'ooch' when the toe is stubbed on something hard, the 'argh' of fear when predators attack, and the 'oo's' of surprise or pleasure at a cool drink or a warm fire. Physiologically, the way we are made and the way the world is, together regulate these practices without verbal intermediaries. When cold, we extend our hands towards the fire, but excessive heat leads us to withdraw them, and it is upon these prior physiological signifiers that our language of feelings is built and our emotional expressiveness is born.

---

[3] Roy Bhaskar, *A Realist Theory of Science*, Verso, London, 1997, p. 33.
[4] Andrew Collier, 'Language, Practice and Realism', p. 48.

The same informational 'aboutness', which is grounded in prior practical activity with the world, is equally characteristic of our less literal uses of language. This is particularly clear with the simile, where the likeness has to be cashed in propositionally. Thus, when Burns says that his 'love is like a red, red rose', then to tell us something about his love he needs both a practical acquaintance with her and with roses. We are not meant to cash it in literally, meaning that the woman in question has every property which roses possess, such as being prone to black spot or benefiting from mulching, for these do not inspire love. Instead, he is signalling shared qualities like 'smells as sweet as', 'has the texture of' or 'shares the colouring', and thus he must practically have exercised his senses of smell, touch and sight on both in order to establish these points of positive analogy. This is less obvious with metaphors and their abstractions which do not lend themselves to cashing in (e.g. 'the messenger came flying'). Nevertheless, they are still grounded in practical knowledge of concrete things. Thus Collier cites the following examples: 'such abstract ideas as rest, dependence, expectation, obedience, virtue, wicked, heavy, round, bear on the face of them the marks of their concrete origin: to rest is to resist movement, to depend is to hang on, to expect is to watch out for, to obey is to listen to, virtue is manliness, wicked is bewitched, heavy is hard to lift, round is wheel-like'.[5] The use of metaphor in poetry and throughout science has its moorings in our practical activities. Thus Gerard Hopkins' employment of the adjective in 'whorlèd ear', like the use of 'wave', 'spring' and 'black hole' in theoretical physics, depends upon our previously having come across whorls and waves in nature.

Language use, like all other actions, entails the exercise of skills, but linguistic skills are tacit, and knowledge of them cannot be necessary, because it is rare for such skills to be expressed in speech. We have a low level of discursive mastery of the syntax we employ when speaking. On this Giddens is in agreement with Bhaskar. 'To speak a language, an individual needs to know an enormously complicated range of rules, strategies and tactics involved in language use. However, if that individual were asked to give a discursive account of what it is that he or she knows in knowing these rules etc., he or she would normally find it very difficult indeed.'[6] The reason why it is so difficult, at least in our mother tongues (for most of us are more grammatically proficient in our second languages, whether living or dead), is that our corpus of shared meanings was not constituted solely by speech acts but by other types of bodily action. As Merleau-Ponty argued, our desks and chairs do not only

---

[5] George Q. Thomson cited in Andrew Collier, 'Language, Practice and Realism', p. 50.
[6] Anthony Giddens, *Social Theory and Modern Sociology*, Polity Press, Oxford, 1987, p. 63.

become meaningful through being named in speech. Instead, they gain their meaning from the fact that in practical action we sit in them and write at them, that is we use them and are seen to use them meaningfully. Ontogenetically, we do things with objects (such as differentiating ourselves from them, as in Merleau-Ponty's account) and assigning them identity and transfactual powers (as in Piaget's experiments), before we are able to assign names to them or associate a name with a particular power. Phylogenetically, Popper may well be right that language evolved as an unintended by-product of actions directed at other aims.[7] If so, it was grounded in a practical action whose meanings it could only later reflect upon both argumentatively and critically, but it was only very far down the evolutionary track that ideas could themselves become objects of our reflection, such that we could allow them to die for us, instead of our killing one another for our cherished beliefs and practices.

However that may be, once language has been acquired in the species or by the individual, a new form of practice has been instigated. It is crucial to the force of my argument that speech acts be understood as deeds – as asserted in the quotation heading this section. On the truistic level this is obvious, for to voice an utterance is to do something. Rather more revealing are the verbs associated with certain types of utterances because these are all 'doing' words. Thus, we 'deliver' a lecture, 'send' our congratulations, 'give' talks, 'convey' greetings or condolences, 'explain' theories, 'present' papers, 'preach' sermons, 'defend' arguments and so on. These are not truistic uses but rather, as with all 'doing' words, they gesture towards the causal efficacy of the deeds, or at least to our intentions when engaging in them. Our words have the causal power to affect things in the world of matter. Language then is an emergent property because it is a causally efficacious practice.

Consider the simple defence of this view provided by Bhaskar: 'suppose B says to A "Pass the condiments" at tea and A does so, that is, performs action Xa. We must now suppose *either* (1) that Xa is uniquely determined by some set of physiological states N1 . . . Nn such that Xa would have been performed without B's speech actions; *or* (2) that B's speech action as interpreted by A was causally efficacious in bringing about Xa.'[8] To defend (1) would entail that Xa is determined by an antecedent set of physiological states, such that A would have passed the condiments even if B had not asked for them. This argument then reduces 'to a form of Leibnizian pre-established harmony of monads, in which each person's neurophysiology is so synchronised with every

---

[7] Karl Popper, *Objective Knowledge: An Evolutionary Approach*, Oxford University Press, Oxford, 1992, p. 117.

[8] Roy Bhaskar, *The Possibility of Naturalism*, Harvester, Hemel Hempstead, 1989, p. 105.

other's that it appears *as if* they were talking and laughing, smiling and winking'.[9] The sheer ludicrousness of this theory of parallelism is a good reason for accepting (2) which grants language causal efficacy and commits us to allowing that 'in the case of interpersonal communication, mind affects matter'.[10]

In this simple example, the conversational link between agents is not neuro-physiological but psychological and interpretative. If language did not possess this causal power of getting things done in practice, we can venture that there would be a good deal less of it around. All the illustrations given above of utterances as 'doings', entailed agential intention to have an effect on their interlocutors – to inform them, console them, uplift them etc. These are practical effects, and even the utterances which explain Pythagoras's theorem enjoin doings, for they take the form of 'were you to put a square on the hypotenuse then you would find it to be equal to the squares you have placed on the other two sides'. Practically, some such doings may be beyond the abilities of most of the audience, who lack the equipment for scientific experiments or the finance for anthropological field-work, but they cannot be beyond the practical actions of all. In any case, one of the doings which can be accomplished is the causal effect of mind upon mind by getting others mentally to entertain a hypothetical example, extrapolation or counter-factual. Similarly, expressive language, including the involuntary, has the practical effect of eliciting sympathy from fellow beings.

Can the argument be pressed further to maintain that all conversation, however stilted or fanciful, is causally efficacious in some sense? Perhaps we could abolish the category of 'idle talk' altogether, if we were content to match every type of utterance with some practical outcome in others (or the self). Thus, 'gossip' informs and blackens, 'polite enquiries' cement relationships, 'surrealistic poetry' puzzles and 'fanciful' academic exchanges impress, distract or entertain. The reason why this line of thought is resisted, is that many of these effects, though real, are unintended and therefore could only be attributed to the speakers' intentions by an unwarranted use of teleology. The practical uses of language are better restricted to cases where the reason for speaking is the cause of the ensuing action, in self or others. In other words, there does seem to be an important distinction, which is worth maintaining, between repeating a mantra to induce a meditative state and involuntarily humming a tune or lyrics which one cannot 'get out of one's head'. The latter may have a causal consequence, namely to infuriate others, but it is unintended.

Thus, there can be 'idle talk' where, as Wittgenstein puts it, 'language

---

[9] Ibid., p. 106.   [10] Ibid., p. 105.

goes on holiday' and we 'talk for the sake of talking' or just 'enjoy the sound of our own voices'. In the process we can talk about things we know nothing about, we can fantasise, cutting links with reality or suspending laws of nature when telling outrageous tales or speculating wildly. The significant point is that we cannot do this in practice, for a holidaying practice, as in thinking we can wield a garden fork anywhere with impunity, has its vacation swiftly terminated by reality. Practice is a workaday child which can never sever its relationship with reality. The distinction is that whilst language is practice, agential practices are not co-extensive with language but extend beyond them. There is a practical order which is more extensive than the linguistic.

This can readily be seen when it is recognised that in the argument about the power of mind over matter, it was not strictly necessary to introduce other people (if this had been what the argument was about, rather than being used to demonstrate the causal efficacy of speech). Bhaskar agrees with this lack of necessity of others, just as examples were given above of persons talking to themselves, but importantly he extends this power to our natural relations. Thus others need not be introduced, 'provided that the socialised individual is set in the context of the natural world which is open. For, literally, if it rains, and A opens his/her umbrella or takes any other form of protective or evasive action, the deterministic chain of neuro-physiological states is broken!' [11] Issue could be taken with the insertion of the word 'socialised' in this formulation, unless it merely covers the use of umbrellas, for it is next argued that there is an *important field of non-linguistic practices which are conducted in the context of non-social relations.* These are intrinsic to our particular powers as people, or to our agency when the term is used generically. Here it seems that Bhaskar was indeed preoccupied by umbrellas, for his ultimate defence of agential powers over matter turns upon our natural relations – 'to deny the phenomenon of agency becomes impossible when we recall that the normal setting for the exercise of our bodily powers is in interaction with, and transformation of, nature'.[12] Let us now move on to these non-linguistic practices in the world of things, and to the thesis that practice there can disclose forms of knowledge which are intrinsically independent from language.

Non-linguistic practice

Reality, be it natural or artifactual, has properties and powers which do not depend upon knowing subjects; nature never does, artifacts which persist unchanged through time once did, but, like the persistence of the

[11] Ibid. [12] Ibid.

Rosetta stone or the Dead Sea scrolls, they do not in the present tense. Both the natural and the artifactual are open systems because contingencies can intervene to suspend or transform their generative powers. We humans are the most powerful of those contingencies. Yet, we too are open systems, for, as has been argued, all of our human powers only exist *in potentia* and which of them do develop depends upon the contingent intervention of the world of things. We cannot deal with the world on our own terms, thus the natural attitude of human kind cannot be that of an agnostic or a manichaean.

Thus what emerges, at least initially, as non-linguistic knowledge, i.e. tacit information, skills, know-how, depends upon the practical interaction between us and nature – upon the confluence of the two sets of properties and powers. Here it may seem as if we are the leading part, for after all it is only people who intentionally intervene in nature to ride horses or to use tools. On the contrary, I want to maintain two things: firstly that many of our embodied powers and liabilities are causally efficacious in conjunction with the constraints and enablements of things, without any intentionality on our part, for we can learn without intending to do so. Secondly, both nature and artifacts encode information about possible practices, given the way that the world is and the way in which we are constituted. If the latter notion seems implausible, consider that in relation to water, our bodies are part of the category of 'floatables'. Water not only allows us to float but 'indicates' that we will do so more effortlessly if we relax, and only if we cooperate can the practice of swimming then evolve.

There are various propositions to defend in relation to practical knowledge acquired through tentative participation in nature. The first of these is that such practical knowledge is intrinsically non-linguistic, contrary to Giddens, who regards practical consciousness, like discursive consciousness and the unconscious, as being structured 'like language'.[13] Instead, it is maintained that the form and structure of practical knowledge are entirely different, that it comes in chunks or stocks rather than in linear sequences such as sentences, that it is stored by being embodied in the seat of our pants rather than in the declarative memory, and that it may be accessed by all of our senses, not just by one part – the auditory system. Thus we hear music, move in a dance, smell wine or cooking, see a painting or touch a sculpture (or their natural equivalents), without using some counterpart to the alphabet or sentence string. Secondly, it is also maintained that much of this practical knowledge cannot be easily or fully expressed in words; that much is lost, the circumlocutions are clumsy, and that the usual resort is to metaphor when verbal explication takes

---

[13] Anthony Giddens, *New Rules of Sociological Method*, Hutchinson, London, 1976, p. 127.

place. This is not to go in for the dualistic thinking of those like Bloch [14] and Langer,[15] who subscribe to radical 'non-translatability', but it is *firmly to maintain that our ability to describe things in words does not mean that practical knowledge is linguistic in kind.* Third, and most importantly, it is necessary to defend the claim that practical knowledge authentically discloses part of reality which is beyond the limits of language. Here Wittgenstein's adage that 'what we cannot speak about we must pass over in silence',[16] is both literally true and programmatically false. We cannot pass over non-linguistic knowledge as if it did not exist, and this is partly because there is an actual interchange between it and discursive knowledge in human life. Finally, it is maintained that our human relations with things (animate and inanimate, natural and artifactual), helps to make us what we are as persons. Not only do these supply that part of us which is not a gift of society, but also they predispose us towards those *social* practices which we will seek and shun. They are influential structurally in conditioning the roles, careers, sports or relationships in which people engage voluntarily, and equally so culturally, since practical knowledge serves to sieve the propositional knowledge which we willingly acquire or dismiss.

Thus far, things natural and artifactual have simply been grouped together because of the argument that they interact with us in much the same way, but differently from the ways in which discursive knowledge engages us. However, it is now essential to clarify the three orders of reality with which we interact for the duration of our lives. It is then necessary to visit these orders in turn to show how knowledge does emanate from each and to justify the argument that such knowledge is of three distinct kinds. Lastly, to show that practice is pivotal for the entirety of knowledge, the connections between the three forms of knowledge will need to be examined. These relationships are mapped in figure 5.1.

Nature, natural relations and embodied knowledge

Embodied knowledge is something which every human being possesses: what was distinctive about primitive humans was simply that this was the only form of knowledge which they had. Nor is there a firm dividing line between the embodied knowledge of humans and of animals. What distinguishes us from them is precisely our tendency to enhance or extend our embodied knowledge by the invention and use of artifacts, i.e. the development of material culture which is simultaneously the deposition

---

[14] M. Bloch, 'Language, Anthropology and Cognitive Science', *Man*, 26, 1990.
[15] S. K. Langer, *Philosophy in a New Key*, Harvard University Press, Harvard, 1967.
[16] L. Wittgenstein, *Tractatus Logico-Philosophicus*, Routledge, London, 1988, p. 74.

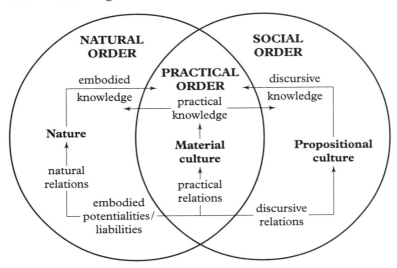

Figure 5.1 Three orders of reality and their respective forms of knowledge.

of the practical order. Embodied knowledge, as such, has three distinguishing characteristics; it is based upon sensory-motor interactions with nature (both animate and inanimate); it is possessed in unawareness of its cognitive content, which is not disentangled from physical operations; it can only be exercised in direct contact with nature, and is never detached from it in the form of abstract and decontextualised propositions. Its *object*, its *unawareness* and its *embeddedness* all serve to distinguish it from knowledge in the practical order, as does the mode of acquisition, which always entails an element of personal bodily discovery, which may be helped by initiation or induction, but which in an important sense has to be self-realised.[17]

Embodied knowledge is a know-how about nature which has literally become 'second nature'. It is a 'knowing how' when doing, rather than a 'knowing that' in thought. Because it has to be realised by each individual in their natural relations, it is unsurprising that our ontogenetic development recapitulates phylogenetic developments. Thus, it is significant that many of the physical skills which children evolve in free play – their

[17] This section owes much to discussions with Dr Tim Holt in relation to his thesis *Material Culture: An Inquiry into the Meaning of Artefacts*, University of Warwick, 1996. However he did not introduce the natural order into his discussion of material culture nor treat discursive knowledge as part of the Cultural System as I developed it in *Culture and Agency*. My debt to him is great for prompting me to link the primacy of practice to these other two orders. Direct use is made of his work over the next few pages.

throwing, swinging, sliding, building, hiding, chasing, jumping, climbing, hammering, gathering and making – are personal realisations of our species-powers which have to be recreated in every generation. In what follows, I will stick to purely naturalistic examples, because one of the effects of the intercommunication between practical and embodied knowledge is that material artifacts (baby-walkers, playgrounds and toys like the Fischer-Price activity board) are now inserted into the child's environment to speed-up embodied learning.

Generic to our natural relations is the (non-anthropomorphic) notion that 'nature sets us problems'. Of course it only does so in the form of 'if we want to do X then . . . we have to solve Y', but such human intentionality has to be assumed for acquiring knowledge in any of the three orders. Thus the practical order is only efficacious in yielding practical knowledge if we wish to do things like making flints, driving cars or working computers, and the social order only predisposes to new discursive elaborations if we want to go on holding an idea, vindicating a belief or defending a theory. In the natural order, I want to maintain that nature encodes information about possible practice, given the way it is and the way we are, which is disclosed in our relations. At the extremes, nature resists some of our actions (climbing a precipice) and facilitates others (floating down river). It operates on us through physical discouragement (falling, being poisoned) and conversely, by positive and negative feedback: nature 'tells' us how we are doing by physical prompts (the more we relax in still water, the closer we are to swimming and the more we thrash about, the closer to drowning). Between these extremes are various forms of accommodation in our natural relations, which most people work out for themselves and use as unthinking embodied knowledge. Most of us were never taught to lean into the wind or incline our body-weight forward when climbing a hill, and backwards when descending, nor do we do it cerebrally – which is not to deny intentionality.

To give an example of nature's prompts and our physical accommodation, consider the gaits of the horse and their implications for proficient riding. The horse has four gaits: walk and gallop are four-time, meaning that each hoof touches the ground sequentially; the canter is three-time and only the trot is two-time, as horses spring from one diagonal pair of legs to the other pair after a moment of suspension. Because of the springing action, the suspended moment is literally a punch in the rump for the rider, which leaves novices bumping along in the trot like a sack of potatoes. However, as the once Director of the Spanish Riding School puts it, naturally, the 'regular hoof beats of the diagonal legs, interrupted by the moment of suspension, give the rhythm of the movement, as it were, the music of riding'.[18] The solution is the 'rising trot', where the rider lifts herself off the horse's back for the moment of suspension and sits as a diagonal hits the ground. The problem is how to explain this music to the equestrian deaf. I have tried it many times, shouting 'one' and 'two', 'up' and 'down', which is of no avail until the novice rider somehow 'catches on' and begins rising and sitting in rhythm. The British Horse Society's manual gives an excellent explanation of the prompting and accommodation involved. 'The *body should be placed in such a position that the pony is made to do all the work of throwing the body up* . . . If the rider tries to rise without stirrups, with his body in the correct position, he will find that it is very little extra effort.'[19] Thus the postural skill does not depend upon the practical introduction of stirrup or saddle; nor will the skill be acquired through perusing this classic discursive manual.

Natural relations prompt all sorts of postures, but above all it is through them that we learn the human posture in the world of nature. Thus embodied knowledge acquired through throwing instils the difference between 'within-reach' and 'out of reach'; chasing inculcates relative speeds, approaching or evading animals teaches timing and distances, pulling and swinging give lessons in weight and tensile strength, banging teaches that one substance is harder than another, and digging and squeezing inform about different textures. This knowledge itself is almost, if not completely, impossible to verbalise: we know that some things are possible, that others are 'not on', but a texture feels like a texture feels and there is no explaining why the particular *feel* of impactable snow means that we can build from it.

Yet it is clear that embodied knowledge is real knowledge because misuse is regulative. There is an incorrect way of doing things which indicates that there are such things as embodied rules. We have all had the experience of banging our teeth when we wrongly take an empty vessel to be full and raise it to take a drink – the arm seems to tell us we are wrong in mid-air, but it is too late to arrest the gesture. Similarly our legs get jarred when we jump into shallow water with the bodily 'assumption' that it is deep. Again, we all know what a shock it is to the body when we wrongly take an 'extra step' at the top of a familiar staircase. What is significant about these examples of every day embodied knowledge is not simply that they are carried in the body, but that errors are bodily registered as bangs, jars or stumbles: we know that something has gone wrong *from* our bodies' reactions, and not vice-versa by the mind telling it so – the latter happens after the event when we wonder 'why our bodies let us

[18] Alois Podhajsky, *The Complete Training of Horse and Rider*, Harrap, London, 1981, pp. 32–3.   [19] British Horse Society, *Horsemanship*, London, 1954, pp. 8–9.

down'. Here, there can be disjunction between the natural order and the practical order with its innovations in material culture. Thus my book-seller husband, a man physically well acquainted with parcels, reports his experiences with modern polystyrene packaging as follows. Embodied experience had inculcated a principle which in words roughly means 'big equals heavy'; thus he heaved up a bulky but feather-light box, which encased one book in chippings, and then over-balanced. In short, we do become aware of this embodied rule-following when we make mistakes. Indeed we can speculate that the mess very young children make with their drinks is at least partly due to the fact that they have not yet acquired an embodied sense of 'full' and 'empty'.

Misuse in nature is regulative in another way, for our natural relations not only supply feedback on error, they spur us to improvement and reward our improvements. Better eye-hand co-ordination brings the reward of more fish caught or more food gathered: developing a better swimming style gets us to safety more certainly and enables us to traverse greater distances. Out of the bodily experimentation which constitutes our natural relations, the embodied theoretical attitude is born. If the ice cracks and we get dunked, or the liana breaks and we take a fall, this does not foster a simple association of aversion (stimulus-response), but rather an accentuated environmental awareness that there is ice and ice and fibre and fibre (just as there are parcels and parcels). This fosters the theoret-ical attitude of tapping-and-testing or hanging-and-feeling. It is, as Popper argued, the start of evolutionary trial and error learning. Yet, it remains embodied rather than being the primitive exemplar of the cogni-tive hypothetico-deductive method, for what is felt through the foot and fingers is known by them and translates into words badly, because incom-pletely. We can tell someone to 'tap and test', but have difficulty in con-veying the *feel* of the tap which indicates that it is safe to cross the ice.

Nevertheless, it seems reasonable to conjecture that as the theoretical attitude develops through embodied knowledge, then the next step involves a reflexivity towards it which is the midwife of material culture. After all, the higher primates can and will use sticks to obtain things that are beyond their reach. Thus, from using floatables came canoes, from buildables, shelters, from swingables, knots and plaits, from hammering, flints and from murmuring came singing. On this argument then, second-generation material culture would involve items like sand shoes, snow skis, sledges, stirrups and bridles. The key point is that the sensory-motor skills involved in all of these practices can *themselves* become embodied as second nature. The good rider 'feels the horse's mouth' and always retains 'contact through the reins', constantly communicating without words and with implicit cognitive intent. What this shows is that there is an interface between the natural and practical orders and their respective forms of knowledge (for we all once had to be shown how to hold the reins, just as we first needed instruction in dressing ourselves). However, let us first examine the practical order before discussing the 'translatability' of the different knowledge forms.

The practical order, material culture and practical knowledge

Just as the embodied knowledge emerging from our natural relations was not anthropocentric, subjective, nor pragmatist, because it is regulated by how the natural order is, so practical knowledge is none of these either, because it is regulated by the objective properties of material culture, which deny idealism by preventing us putting any construction we please upon them. It is acquired through our practical relations with material culture, which is what distinguishes it from knowledge in the natural order, and has four defining characteristics which differentiate practical from discursive knowledge (i.e. from 'knowing that' or from 'connaissances').

Firstly, practical knowledge involves an active process of doing since it is performative in relation to material culture. It is therefore *procedural* rather than declarative in kind, and we have already seen the important role that the procedural memory plays in securing self identity. Secondly, it is *implicit*, being encoded in the body as skills. Thus because it is still embodied, it is knowledge from somewhere rather than being part of detached scientific observation.[20] Thus the active body interrogates the object from a particular point of view, such that action, perception and understanding intertwine, as in Merleau-Ponty's example of the footballer seeing 'openings', 'passes' and 'opportunities', unlike the overview of the football commentator. Thirdly, practical knowledge is *tacit* because it is reality understood through activity, not through the manipulation of symbols but of artifacts. Its cognitive element entails non-verbal theorising, an active questioning of how things work, of their practical potentials and limitations whose answer is the development of a skill, not the enunciation of a proposition. However, in discussing 'hexis', or bodily skills as permanent dispositions, Bourdieu goes too far in arguing that 'The principles embodied in this way are placed beyond the grasp of consciousness, and hence cannot be touched by voluntary, deliberate transformation, cannot even be made explicit',[21] for I maintain that the

---

[20] See Aurora Paloma, *Phenomenology, Geometry and Vision*, Avebury, London, 1991.
[21] Pierre Bourdieu, *Outline of a Theory of Practice*, Cambridge University Press, 1993, pp. 93–4.

tacit lends itself to the public, and thus explicit, codification of practice over time – what else are maps, knitting patterns or sheet music?

Fourthly, the development of practical knowledge is *extensive* of the body and of our bodily powers, which is possible because we humans are open systems whose properties and powers can be amplified by the contingencies of material culture. This extension was readily realised by Merleau-Ponty in his discussion of the blind man's stick as a prosthetic which extended the range of his body, whilst coming to feel or work as part of its activities. It is familiar too in Heidegger's discussion of the hammer as ready-to-hand. Of the four defining features, extension has the furthest reaching effects, since the artifacts involved eventually encompass productive machinery, modes of transport, science laboratories, television and so on, and thus lead to a progressive elaboration of the skills which constitute practical knowledge over time.

Taken in conjunction, these four characteristics mean that if the mode of acquiring embodied knowledge was quintessentially that of self-discovery, the means of gaining practical knowledge is apprenticeship (whereas propositional knowledge is obtained through scholarship). These different modes have considerable implications for the socio-cultural relations associated with them – those of co-action, interaction and transaction respectively, for the natural, practical and propositional orders. However, for the moment, what is of concern are not these relations at the socio-cultural (S-C) level, but now that we are dealing with artifacts, then relationships with the cultural system (CS) come into play for the first time. There are causal properties between things (or parts of things) which cannot be reduced to the ideas maintaining between people. With material culture we are treating of emergent properties which stem from the engineered and engineering relations which constitute artifacts. These powers which are most obvious with machinery, are universal to the practical order, as simple objects like the drinking gourd or spoon illustrate. However, these are built into their shape and form, their juxtapositioning and interlinkages, their cogs and wheels, strings and windholes; into the powers of a recipe, a flint, a medicine, a tune – and as such they are non-discursive. This is why they were not included in *Culture and Agency*, which confined itself to the propositional part of the Cultural System.

Thus although such meanings were inscribed in material objects by their original artificer, they become embodied in the artifact itself. When we discover how to use one, we learn how objects work, we do not learn the mind of their designers. Artifacts enshrine their intention to make them work, but artifacts tell us nothing further about those often anonymous minds, including the motives which prompted the designs or the exact uses to which they were initially envisaged as being put. In a very serious causal sense, material culture 'escapes' its makers. Artifacts become independent of their makers, because practical meanings are carried by the objects themselves and their causal powers are built into them and may have been unrealised, or only partially realised, by their first inventor.

In other words, artifacts have a dispositional character for being understood, in and of themselves. Certainly, we have the capacity for misunderstanding them, for all our knowledge is fallible, and there are many instances of archaeologists assigning unknown workaday objects to the category of 'object of ritual significance'. However, the functions of material culture limit the constructions which can be placed upon it. An artifact by its nature cannot be purely symbolic, for even a symbolic object, such as a thurible or a ciborium has distinct functions in religious practice. They can set us puzzles as to what each should contain and ones whose solutions do not depend upon resort to the Socio-Cultural level which implies extant practitioners, but can be disclosed by other artifacts like paintings, icons, stained glass and engravings. Unless material culture had this quality of knowledge without a knowing subject, the domain and discoveries of archaeology would be non-existent. By corollary, today's artifacts possess the same property. Thus we often find it is easier to 'fiddle around' to make a new gadget work, than to pore over the book of instructions. How then can inert objects communicate their meaning to us, which is another way of asking what is involved in practical relations?

Practical knowledge, like any other, is engendered by constraints and enablements – this is how objects 'tell' us how to behave towards them. Donald Norman's book[22] is full of examples of how the combination of affordances and constraints guides our practical relations with them. Thus when 'we approach a door, we have to find both the side that opens and the part to be manipulated; in other words, we need to figure out what to do and where to do it. We expect to find some visible signal for the correct operation: a plate, an extension, a hollow, an indentation – something that allows the hand to touch, grasp, turn or fit into. This tells us where to act. The next step is to figure out how: we must determine what operations are permitted, in part using the affordances, in part guided by the constraints.' Thus, as far as the hardware of an unlocked door is concerned, it 'need not have any moving parts: it can be a fixed knob, plate, handle, or groove. Not only will the proper hardware operate the door smoothly, but it will also indicate just how the door is to be operated: it will exhibit the proper affordances. Suppose the door opens by being

---

[22] Donald Norman, *The Psychology of Everyday Things*, Harper Collins, New York, 1988.

pushed. The easiest way to indicate this is to have a plate at the spot where the pushing should be done. A plate, if large enough for the hand, clearly and unambiguously marks the proper action. Moreover, the plate constrains the possible actions: there is little else that one can do with a plate except push.'[23] Norman readily admits that people can muddle affairs by cluttering their doors with useless furniture, but this does not detract from the fact that some of these must constitute working parts. Since all artifacts are human products, there is always the task of separating the decorative from the functional – *homo faber* is also an embellisher and some of his utilitarian objects are also some of the most beautiful, like Copernicus's astrolabe or a pair of engraved duelling pistols.

The very physicality of material culture 'informs' by resisting certain practical actions: a normal corkscrew can only be made to work in a clockwise direction. Moreover artifacts discriminate among their legitimate users: blisters ensue when a right-handed person tries using left-handed scissors, and safety tops on pill containers deter children. Furthermore, like nature, artifacts give us cues and clues as to how we are doing. Tim Holt, who works out a long example of our driving practice, points out how the gears crash, the engine whines or coughs and the car eventually stalls for the learner-driver. He also maintains that whilst an instructor can say 'change now', the proficient motorist hears and feels when to change gears.[24] Such drivers will talk anthropomorphically of the engine 'straining', 'screaming', or running 'sweetly', again indicating the discursive difficulty of practical knowledge. This is a kind of talk common to all means of transport and most games and sports. Thus, misuse is again regulative, though it may take some time to acquire the good practice of, for example, not cutting paper with one's best sewing scissors.

The enablements of material culture not only 'instruct' in a given usage, they also encourage practical knowledge through the extensiveness they accord to the human body. These operate in relation to each one of our senses. Ability to touch is extended by the new reach supplied by saddles, bikes and cars; hearing by musical instruments, aides and radio; taste by cuisine, viticulture and distilleries; smell by perfume and aromatherapy and sight by spectacles, telescopes, microscopes and remote sensing. Their cumulative effect is to carry our practical knowledge further and further away from the natural order, as our extended bodily powers are increasingly turned towards canalising and dominating nature. Nevertheless the limits of our practical knowledge, at any given time, condition how far this may go, just as early map-makers

---

[23] Ibid., pp. 87–8.
[24] Tim Holt, *Material Culture: An Inquiry into the Meaning of Artefacts*, chapters 7 and 8.

were fundamentally constrained by the extent of possible exploration. Simultaneously our practical knowledge takes us collectively into a different realm from the self-knowledge and self-mastery emerging from our natural relations. None of this is to deny that today the practical order is on collision course with the natural order: indeed this is the negative consequence of the interchange between them.

The acquisition of practical knowledge is rather different from the repetition involved in gaining embodied knowledge, because of the higher cognitive content. Piaget's two-fold assimilation and accommodation scheme seems apposite here. On the one hand, the external environment has to be assimilated to the cognitive structure, particularly where unfamiliar artifacts are concerned. These are the head-scratchers where much discursive information only goes a little way, as with learning to ride a bike where the key break is in 'catching on': the remainder is practice in handling, and the accomplishment is an embodied practice. On the other hand, there is the accommodation of the existing cognitive structure to novelty in the artifactual environment. Garage mechanics show extraordinary adroitness in jumping into unknown vehicles and manoeuvring them accurately around the forecourt. Most of us ordinary motorists take time and tentativeness to get the 'feel' of a different car and have the greatest difficulties forcing ourselves into the counter-intuitive turns of the wheel needed to back a trailer. The articulated-lorry driver has done a great deal of accommodation to his wide, long, jack-knifing body before effortlessly turning a corner. Yet, once a performative skill has been acquired, then clumsiness ensues if it is *not* employed as second nature. Thus Polyani notes that: 'If a pianist shifts his attention from the piece he is playing to the observation of what he is doing with his fingers while playing it, he gets confused and may have to stop.'[25] The same seems to be true of touch-typists, who do not think of the keyboard in alphabetic terms, and are thrown when asked to do so; they work in terms of finger-reach.

What all of this points to is that acquiring practical knowledge is learning a skilled trade; it is a matter of apprenticeship. Thus the key figures who assist in learning are the Mastercraftsman, Instructor and Professional who teach by example, demonstrating good practice and some postural correction, practical criticism and evaluation. What they seek to convey is practical virtuosity, where the 'feel' for the task is virtually incommunicable and thus can only be examined in practice itself. Michael Luntley is worth quoting on the habits that mark out the successful jazz musician and which testify to mastery of a 'feel for music'.

---

[25] M. Polyani, *Personal Knowledge: Towards a Post-Critical Philosophy*, Routledge and Kegan Paul, London, 1973, p. 56.

The idea of a feel for music does service on two fronts. First it captures the notion of involvement with a practice and tradition which makes one's belief about which note or chord to play next distanced from a sentential model of belief that is subject only to a cool engagement of pure reason. Believing that the chord to play next is a C major seventh is not a belief that appears as a sentence before the mind's eye of the experienced pianist. It is a belief that appears as a sense of what they must do, in their sense of appropriateness of responding in just that manner.

Second, the concept of a feel for music gives some content to the notion of immanence in the world by which the world can impose a sense of things to be done or said, or played or sung . . . For players with a developed feel for the music, the music is read in such a way that their embeddedness in the flow of music means that they are left in no doubt about what has to be done next. Determining the course of the next chord is not a matter of ratiocination, indeed it is not really a 'determining' at all if we stick with the sentential model of reason. It is the kind of creative response that comes from having precisely that embedding in a situation that is captured by the phrase 'feel for the music'. When we are playing a piece and improvising successfully we live in the music; it is at our fingertips.[26]

Moreover, it is significant that Luntley defines mastery and creativity in terms of the stages of an apprenticeship, such that musicians of ability have learnt 'most of what is available in terms of (a) the underlying components of play – the scales, arpeggios, snapshots of standard melodies and standard melodic developments; (b) current good habits of play, that is predominant styles of harmonic and melodic structure; and then, (c) in the light of a critical assessment of these habits they devise novel strategies of musical expression'.[27] Now Luntley's aim here was not to inform us about jazz, but about criteria of truth and judgement in non-discursive knowledge. What it seems important to acknowledge is the range of practical knowledge and that the scope of apprenticeship extends from the tennis player to the young scientist being inducted into Kuhnian 'normal science'. Contrary to what some believe (and without denying contrived industrial deskilling), the explosion of material culture has vastly extended the global practical order and its attendant forms of practical knowledge.

Despite the deep embeddedness of subjects in their practical activities, and their absorption in a particular artifact, we must nevertheless avoid conflating subject and object in mutually constitutive activities like bike-riding, singing or sailing. Practice does not transcend the subject/object distinction as Giddens[28] and Bourdieu maintain. In the following quotation

[26] Michael Luntley, *Reason, Truth and Self*, Routledge, London, 1995, pp. 211–12.
[27] Ibid., p. 213.
[28] Anthony Giddens, *Central Problems in Social Theory*, Macmillan, London, 1979.

Bourdieu seeks to avoid both subjective idealism and objective material-ism, only to end up in the 'central conflation' of subject and object. 'The construction of the world of objects is clearly not the sovereign operation of consciousness which the neo-Kantian tradition conceives of; mental structures which construct the world of objects are constructed in the practice of a world of objects constructed according to the same struc-tures. The mind born of the world of objects does not rise as a subjectivity confronting an objectivity: the objective universe is made up of objects which are a product of objectifying operations structured according to the very structures which the mind applies to it. *The mind is a metaphor of the world of objects which is itself but an endless circle of mutually reflecting meta-phors.*'[29] What goes awry here is that their compaction precludes our examining the interplay between subject and object, which constitutes their practice and the nature of whose combination determines good practice.

On the contrary, analytical dualism[30] insists that there are independent properties of subject and object, some of which are entirely irrelevant to the activity and others which are conditions of the very possibility of prac-tice. Thus the colour of a singer and that of her songsheet are inde-pendent of one another and irrelevant to the practice of singing. On the other hand, a baritone cannot tackle an alto tenor's part and vice versa. Examining the interplay is crucial for explaining the outcome and its virtuosity. Everyday actors appreciate the distinction, or craftsmen would not have their 'faithful' tools, hairdressers would not be attached to their own brushes, and cooks would not cherish their battered paring knives. Similarly professional musicians or sports players would not search out the best instruments and equipment, nor try out technical innovations, nor expensively insure their choice of object at a particular time. Humans as practical actors are highly reflective about the objects of their skills and upon their contribution to good performance. Last year I listened to the harpist Eleanor Bennett giving her first recital on the electronic harp and explaining that it was the limited volume of sound produced by the tradi-tional harp which had restricted its orchestral repertoire and thus the scope of practice, which she now hoped would be extended thanks to the newly adapted instrument.

One reason why this is important is that it conditions the communica-tive interface between practical and discursive knowledge. Certainly there are attempts to codify good practice in written manuals through-out the practical order. What these cannot encompass are how to gain a

---

[29] Pierre Bourdieu, *The Logic of Practice*, Polity Press, Oxford, 1990, p. 91 (my italics).
[30] See Margaret S. Archer, *Realist Social Theory*, Cambridge University Press, 1995, ch. 6.

'feel' for music or for a car. Thus it is interesting that these guides tend to break down into 'tips' for the subject (how to improve your backhand or golf swing) and, usually in part 2, lengthier details on the constitution, varieties, workings and maintenance of the object of material culture itself. Where of necessity these manuals remain mute or become metaphoric is where the practical 'feel', constitutive of virtuosity, comes into play. Here descriptive language witnesses to this ineluctable hiatus by formulations of the kind, 'whereas the beginner commonly does . . . the skilled player will. . .' To adapt Wittgenstein's adage, that which cannot be formulated propositionally is passed over in virtual silence.

The social order, propositional culture and discursive knowledge

Where the social order is concerned, it is even more important to adhere strictly to analytical dualism between the corpus, which constitutes the propositional culture, and the discursive relations between its human users, because it is their interplay which brings about elaboration of discursive knowledge itself. Thus in *Culture and Agency* which was devoted to these issues,[31] the Cultural System (CS)and the *logical* relations pertaining between its components was clearly distinguished from the *causal* relations maintaining Socio-Culturally (S-C) between different groups of thinkers. As an emergent entity, propositional culture, that is the CS at any given time, has an objective existence and autonomous logical relations amongst its component items (theories, beliefs, values, arguments, or more strictly between the propositional formulations of them), in the sense that these are independent of anyone's claim to know, to believe, to assert or to assent to them. At any moment the CS is the product of historical Socio-Cultural interaction, but having emerged (emergence being a continuous process) then *qua* product, it has properties of its own which influence discursive relations with S-C actors. In other words, there are causal influences exerted by the CS on the S-C level. Cultural encounters are thus far removed from joining in some flat activity portrayed as 'society's conversation' (chapter 3). Instead, subject and object relations have to be distinguished throughout and their interplay examined – just as was the case in nature between our subject constitution and nature's prompts, and in practice between our skills and the constraints and affordances of material culture.

---

[31] See Margaret S. Archer, *Culture and Agency*, Cambridge University Press, 1989, chapters 5,6,7 and 8 for a full exposition.

Thus when groups maintain ideas which stand in manifest logical contradiction or complementarity to others, this places their holders in different ideational positions. The logical properties of their theories or beliefs create entirely different situational logics for them. These effects mould the context of discursive relations and in turn condition different patterns of ideational development. Consequently, Socio-Cultural relations are marked in completely different ways by these differences in situational logic, as are the eventual modifications of propositional culture which are generated at the CS level. Let us now look at two contrasting influences which stem from different relationships within propositional culture or which characterise different parts of it – the 'constraining contradiction' and the 'concomitant complementarity' – to see how these condition ideational action through the usual process, of placing agents in different situations.

The 'constraining contradiction' is a property of the CS (propositions A and B are logically inconsistent): it exerts a constraint upon the S-C level if any actor(s) wish to maintain A (whether a theory or a belief). Assuming that protagonists of A exist, the key point with a constraining contradiction is that their action in invoking A also ineluctably evokes B, and with it the logical contradiction between them ('concomitant complementarities' share exactly the same features, the crucial difference being that they evoke logical consistency). The reason for this is some necessary connection between A and B, that is the dependence of A on part of the general preserve of B such as Durkheim analysed between Christianity and classicism. This confronted the Church with a 'contradiction against which it has fought for centuries without ever achieving a resolution. For the fact was that in the literary and artistic monuments of Antiquity there lived and breathed the very same pagan spirit which the Church had set itself the task of destroying.'[32] Yet the Church's origins were entangled with Graeco-Latin and it could not repudiate these languages. B thus constitutes the hostile environment in which A is embedded and from which it cannot be removed. For A cannot stand alone, it is compelled to work in terms of B and to call upon B in order to work at all. This is part and parcel of the propositional constitution of A: but part of the parcel that is B constitutes a threat to A because it simultaneously contravenes it.

What the 'constraining contradiction' does in practice is to confront those committed to A who also have no option but to live with B, with a

---

[32] Emile Durkheim, *The Evolution of Educational Thought*, London, Routledge and Kegan Paul, 1977, p. 22.

particular *situational logic*. According to this logic, and presuming their continued commitment to A, they are driven to engage with something both antithetical but also indispensable to it – which therefore they can neither embrace as it stands nor reject out of hand. Instead the inconsistency has to be tackled and repaired by *syncretic* redefinitions correcting the A/B relationship and the correction to them then must be taken up. Syncretism is the task that the situational logic enforces on all those who neither make their exit nor change sides in the context of a 'constraining contradiction'.

In contrast, the situational logic generated by the 'concomitant complementarity' is problem-free for the actors involved. The consistency of its components makes exploring B rewarding for the protagonists of A – the source of ideational bonuses like the corroboration of theories, the confirmation of beliefs and the extension of their conspectus. Yet because their 'truths' are not challenged but only reinforced from the proximate environment, then actors confront no ideational problems, are propelled to no daring feats of propositional elaboration, but work according to a situational logic fostering the protection of consistency and generically resulting in ideational *systematisation* at the CS level. Examples of such clusters were supplied by Weber's studies of other-worldly religions, especially Hinduism.

What happens in propositional systematisation is a phase of intensive discursive preoccupation with working out the inclusive linkages and tying them into the original core to form a comprehensive conspectus of high logical consistency. It does produce a distinctive end-product, namely a substantial increase in 'cultural density', by which this sector of the CS becomes particularly rich in fine and subtle distinctions, possesses an elaborate and often technical vocabulary to describe them and a complex body of concepts to manipulate or capture them. The intricacies of caste rights and prohibitions and bulging libraries of exegetical literature are the products of the discursive relations generated by this situational logic.

These are not the only discursive relations through which propositional culture is elaborated and discursive knowledge expands accordingly. Human beings can never put aside the fact that they have material interests as well as ideational involvements in the propositional culture of the day. Such material interests are generally rooted in our embodiment, in what we need to survive, thrive or excel. Consequently at any given time there may be groups at the S-C level who feel their interests to be ill-served by a given hegemonic CS and who are concerned to advance ideas more conducive to improving their material conditions through their discursive relations. Yet, these too cannot be immune from the existing propositional culture for this is the ideological source of their perceived oppression. On the contrary they must challenge its legitimacy or validity with a counterposed set of ideas. Here the accentuation of an independent contradiction is a supremely social matter. Accentuation of a 'competitive contradiction' depends upon groups, actuated by interests, *making* a contradiction competitive, by taking sides over it and trying to make other people take their side. In short these oppositional interest groups *cause* the contradiction to impinge upon the (relevant) population: it does not obtrude itself, as is the case with the 'constraining contradiction' the moment anyone asserts A.

Because of this, its operative effect is quite distinct for it confronts people with *choice* in their discursive relations. It is a logic which induces people to make choices, by accentuating differences, by undermining indifference and by making the question of alignment problematic. As many have pointed out, the traditionalist ceases to be one from the moment he realises that he is one, and similarly the rug is pulled from underneath unthinking habitualism and conventionalism. As far as the active opponents are concerned, that is those already aligned in discursive antagonism, the situational logic here conduces towards *elimination*.

Since these partisans of A and B are unconstrained by any dependence between these items, there is nothing which restrains their combativeness, for each has everything to gain from inflicting maximum damage on the other's ideas. Victory consists in so damaging and discrediting oppositional view(s) that they lose all social salience, leaving their antitheses in unchallenged supremacy. However, although the aim is to eliminate inconsistency by annihilating the incongruent viewpoint, because both competing groups have the same goal, their confrontation generically results in an unintended consequence, totally at variance with the desires of the rivals, namely ideational *pluralism*. The archetypal product of the 'competitive contradiction' is thus a sustained differentiation of ideas from one another at the propositional CS level, which is associated with a polarisation of the relevant population through these discursive relations. This is exemplified equally by competitive research programmes in natural science and by the dynamics of ideological debate.

Finally propositional culture possesses an unknown number of potential compatibilities, just as it does contradictions. What is made of these is purely a matter of ideational opportunism by social groups, usually the marginal, who have the opportunity and an interest in seeking out complements for their present endeavours. Because the components making up the 'contingent complementarity' are unconstrained by logical dependence and are not trapped into the logic of either/or competition, then there is nothing about their constitution which restrains what is made of their congruence. The situational logic is a loose one of *opportunity*, for the components can be combined in any pattern and it is specialist S-C interests which determine the actual patternings to take shape. This interweaving of novel strands of thought generically results in discursive synthesis, that is the building-up of separate elements – concepts, propositions, data, into a new connected theory. The result at the propositional level is the sustained generation of new *variety* in propositional culture (such as biochemistry, psychometrics, biotechnology, genetic food modification etc.), leading to a process of progressive diversification. Its direct counterpart at the S-C level is increasing specialisation (of discursive knowledge itself and its allied skills, terminology, methodology etc.) among the relevant population, which is reflected in social re-grouping along specialist lines. The clearest examples of this process are the proliferating specialisations and hybridisation of academic disciplines.

All knowledge entails an *interplay* between properties and powers of the subject and properties and powers of the object – be this what we can learn to do in nature (embodied knowledge), the skills we can acquire in practice (practical knowledge), or the propositional elaborations we can make in the Cultural System (discursive knowledge). Any form of knowledge thus results from a confluence between our human powers (PEPs) and the powers of reality – natural, practical and social. Thus what have been discussed sequentially are the physical powers of the natural order, the material affordances and constraints of material culture, and, lastly, the logical constraining powers of the Cultural System. However, for the three orders equally, the way in which they affect the subject is by shaping the situations in which he or she find themselves, and there supplying constraints or enablements in relation to the subjects' projects. What has been accentuated here are the similarities between the three orders in this respect. What has also been underlined, however, is the difference between the three kinds of knowledge to which they give issue (embodied, practical and propositional). The next stage of the argument, which is a continuation of the 'Primacy of Practice' in the last chapter, is to ask whether practical knowledge is simply *primus inter pares*, or whether it has some special pivotal role in relation to the other forms of knowledge?

Relations between embodied, practical and discursive knowledge

Intercommunication is continuous between the knowledge generated in the three different orders because of the manifest advantages which each form of creativity offers to the others. Simultaneously, we are not talking

about a simple process of appropriation but about an elaborative synthesis where value is added at each juncture. Such interchanges are realised not only due to the fact that all three forms of knowledge have a
cognitive content, but also by virtue of all three being obedient to the
logical canon, which, as was seen in the last chapter, is itself emergent
from practice in the world. However, although in this way they are
commensurable, their substantive differences as three kinds of very
different work on a non-transparent world mean that transition from
form to form is a disjunctive process.

'Translation' is both constrained and enabled by the different human
interests which are vested in the three knowledge forms. Thus, (i)
Embodied and Practical knowledge are embedded in an instrumental
concern ('does it work?'), that is both challenged and extended by discursive knowledge which abstractly explicates the causal powers involved
('this is how it really works in principle'). The hiatus is more than the
psychological resistance of agents who will not trade well-tried practice
for new tentative (and fallible) theorising. Rather the onus is upon the discursive order to prove itself by enhancing practice. Science has to show its
applications in the practical order before it can uproot established practice and underpin the elaboration of better practice. Similarly, (ii)
working in the opposite direction, the new possibilities opened up by discursively informed/applied practice confront agents with a new phenomenal domain, which, with every technical advance, sets a new challenge to
embodied incorporation. Working from the middle, (iii) innovations in
practical knowledge set the same problem of whether it can be mastered
in an embodied fashion by naturalising an artifactual process (like knitting), and equally (iv) whether the new skilled 'feel for' doing something
can be metaphorically conveyed in a manner sufficient for eventual discursive illumination ('what we are doing when we have a sense of. . .')

These relationships are summarised in figure 5.2. This diagram also
helps to show what is meant by the 'primacy of practice', as other than a
political slogan. Practice is called a 'lever' or 'fulcrum' in order to underscore that it is itself only a midpoint in total action.[33] Nevertheless, practice is truly pivotal because of the role that material culture plays as a
'translation medium' which, through 'technology', enables theory to be
the growing point of practice, and which, by virtue of 'instrumentation',
enables the codified diffusion of future embodied knowledge. Each arrow
will now be taken in turn to show the possibility of knowledge transmis-
sion from order to order, but also to vindicate the pivotal role of practice

---

[33] E. Scarry, *The Body in Pain: the Making and Unmaking of the World*, Oxford University
Press, Oxford, 1987, p. 310.

Figure 5.2 Relations between embodied, practical and discursive knowledge.

in this process. This, of course, should be contrasted with the growth in knowledge on the 'Hamlet model' which stems from those who endorse the primacy of language.

It is worth noting that this is another parting of the ways between the present argument and that of Bourdieu. At the end of chapter 4 attention was drawn to the opposition he posited between 'totalising' scientific knowledge and 'the logic of practice which understands only in order to act'.[34] The radical disjunction between the two was held by Bourdieu to be based on *logical* grounds – that the two domains operated in terms of different 'logics'. This is quite different from the distinctions made here between embodied, practical and discursive knowledge in relation to the different orders of reality (natural, practical and social) in which they emerge. Whereas Bourdieu endorses an epistemological break between forms of knowledge, I only insist upon their different ontological origins. Consequently, Bourdieu's position then precludes 'translatability' between knowledge domains: mine does not, which is precisely why I can venture the thesis that practice is pivotal to knowledge in general, whereas he cannot.

Bourdieu denies 'translatability' because of his epistemological argument that practice follows its own autonomous logic, i.e. 'practice has a logic which is not that of the logician',[35] which thus precludes inter-communication with the discursive domain. Therefore, it follows for him, where any practitioner is concerned, that 'Simply because he is questioned, and questions himself, about the reasons and the *raison d'être* of his practice, he cannot communicate the essential point, which is that the very nature of his practice is that it excludes this question.'[36] It is, as it were, as if practical knowledge were hermetically sealed, which is precisely what I will seek to deny in the remainder of this chapter.

[34] Pierre Bourdieu, *The Logic of Practice*, Oxford, Polity, 1990, p. 91.   [35] Ibid., p. 86.
[36] Ibid., p. 91.

If my argument succeeds, it will show practice to be pivotal for knowledge in general, and that it is therefore accorded pride of place. Bourdieu, on the contrary, wants practical knowledge to be respected in its place. Yet ultimately, this is because he derogates it and this derogation is the real source of 'untranslatability'. Thus to him, practices 'obey a "poor" and economical logic';[37] practical efforts to deal with events like death and misfortune through ritual, apply a practical logic which entails category mistakes, for they are 'forlorn attempts to act on the natural world as one acts on the social world'.[38] He gives a humane interpretation of why this is the case: 'Rites take place because, and only because, they find their *raison d'être* in the conditions of existence and the dispositions of agents who cannot afford the luxury of logical speculation.'[39] Yet this is misplaced if, as I have maintained, practice and especially its generic expression in work, is the lot of everyone. In no sense is it only the powerless who encounter practical reality, for we could not be human without doing so. It is also misleading to give practical knowledge an inferiority complex, such that discursive knowledge can only intrude upon it by domination. The following pages reject Bourdieu's epistemological break and his sociological explication of it, and seek instead to vindicate the pivotal role of practice, the democracy of practices, and the integral nature of knowledge.

The 'demonstration' of embodied knowledge

Embodied knowledge has two 'eurekas' to it, the first at the initial performative feat of the practitioner, who may be a child accomplishing its first handstand, but the second is external and depends upon an audience wanting to give a performance a permanent encore. That it will be prolonged rather than permanent is largely due to the intervention of the discursive order. Why the audience wants this encore is because it perceives a surprising utility in the embodied performance, which it seeks to capture and disseminate further. It is the capturing which involves material culture, that is the elaboration of suitable artifacts, which in turn are the tools for the distillation and dissemination of skills to a wider population. However, manifest utility first requires convincing demonstration.

Let us take the example here of how informal navigation within the natural order led Polynesians to develop embodied navigation systems which enabled them to explore and settle the islands of the Pacific Ocean, some 3,500 years ago. Eurocentric history usually begins the story only 200 years ago, with Captain Cook's exploits in an era of developing

---

[37] Ibid., p. 86.   [38] Ibid., p. 95.   [39] Ibid., p. 96.

instrumentation coming from applications of propositional scientific culture: which is to start the story towards the end. Oatley roots this extraordinary accomplishment of Polynesian flat-earthers, navigating over 2,000 miles, in the human ability to retain a sense of direction (which can be demonstrated experimentally by blindfolding subjects and asking them to walk the other two sides of an isosceles triangle, having led them along the hypotenuse). Thus, the basis is an endowed human ability, realised in conjunction with relational prompts from nature. 'This intuitive sense of direction is a basis for most navigational systems. Elaborations whether by instruments or cues from the outside world, are typically made to supplement the ability to keep travelling in a straight line.'[40]

For the Polynesians, this was non-instrumental navigation, involving 'dead reckoning' which entails both a concept of 'here', which is thought of as the fixed centre of two moving frames of reference, one the islands which 'move past' the craft, and the other the pattern of stars wheeling overhead from east to west, by which the navigator keeps an account of the ship's position. Although it is a complex task involving knowing the positions of 50–100 islands, the rising and setting positions of 32 stars which constitutes a natural compass system, plus an appreciation of distances calculated in terms of time taken to make the voyage, Oatley insists that this is what I have termed embodied knowledge, obtained through natural relations. Thus, 'navigation in Oceania emphasised the deliberate refinement of people's intuitive sense of direction and the learning of direct perceptual cues from the natural environment'.[41]

In addition, whilst voyaging on, further cues from nature are combined so that the boat is sailed with a constant orientation to wind and waves, both of which are felt bodily and can be equally useful at night. Moreover, the system of back triangulation to one island passed,

allows the navigator to gauge when he has arrived in the vicinity of his landfall, where a new set of clues become important, namely those for detecting the presence of land. The visual sighting range of atolls is about 10 miles, but this is reliably extended to about 20 miles by the predictable behaviour of certain birds which fly off the islands at dawn to go and fish, and fly straight back again at dusk. So a voyager, thinking himself to be within a 20 mile range, might have to heave to until dawn or dusk to look for these birds. Other indications of land are reflections on the underside of clouds, a slight slowing in the drift of a cloud as it passes over the convection current above an island, reflections and refractions of wave patterns around islands, and patterns of phosphorescence seen deep in the water at night. These and other cues which extend the visual sighting range clearly both expand the landfall target, and allow of course to be altered when land is near.[42]

---

[40] Keith G. Oatley, 'Inference, Navigation and Cognitive Maps', in P. N. Johnson-Laird and P. C. Watson (eds.), *Thinking: Readings in Cognitive Science*, Cambridge University Press, Cambridge, 1977.   [41] Ibid., p. 542.   [42] Ibid., p. 546.

Although extraordinarily sophisticated, similar navigational systems, cued by natural phenomena, have been found among desert nomads, American Indians, and Australian Aboriginals. That this particular embodied know-how did not spread is due to the Polynesians only reaching unsettled lands, but its self-evident utility was sufficient for it to spread through the islands and make its first steps into apprenticeship through artifactual codification. Instructional charts were made with pebbles in the sand, and in the Marshall Islands they were made out of sticks and fixed by mnemonics. These were not taken to sea (as static objects), for the two frames of reference of the navigational system were in motion, and the system itself dynamic. Tupaia, the exiled navigator-chief whom Cook took on aboard the *Endeavour* in his 1769 voyage to Tahiti, had a geographical knowledge spanning 2,600 miles and most significantly the two collaborated on the production of a durable artifact, a map which included seventy-four islands. Thus there is no need to speculate about embodied demonstrations being seized upon and translated into the material culture of the practical order. What we need to do now is to reverse the perspective and examine how propositional knowledge can penetrate and refine the practical order. To pursue the same example, how can it help make for better methods of navigation?

The 'application' of discursive knowledge in practice

The impact of (new) discursive knowledge in practice is both indirect and delayed. The initial effect of a new theory is to undermine the old theoretical bases underpinning established practices. What it does is to show that the premises of practice are ill-founded. However, although the theoretical import is that the practice should be abandoned, because the new theory does not tell us what to do instead, it is a poor pragmatic reason for jettisoning an established practice whose practical utility remains unassailed. Thus, for discursive theory to act as the growing point of practice, a second stage is involved, where new theories enter the practical order, but only through their application as successful additions to material culture. This pays their admission fee. Applied science and technology are the artifactual modes of transition from discursive to practical knowledge.

Thus, if we think of formal celestial navigation, at least two of its necessary theoretical components pre-existed it for a considerable time. Firstly, the notion of a spherical earth set in a Copernican planetary system challenged the 'flat earth' basis of Polynesian-type 'dead reckoning', but this certainly told no one of a better way to navigate a boat. Interestingly, the second component, the development of an elaborate theory of spherical trigonometry, appeared purely propositional and of little interest to the practical explorer. It was only when these two elements of discursive knowledge were combined into accurate instruments, such as chronometers and sextants, plus additional artifacts such as carefully combined tables of the position of celestial bodies, that the superiority of a navigational practice, enabling the ship's position to be established anywhere on the earth's surface to an accuracy of about a mile, encouraged its adoption. In other words, applied discursive knowledge, like pure theory, is only considered to be an advance when it can accomplish everything that previous practices enabled, plus some additional practices. Yet before it becomes a new *established* practice, a new body of proficients have to assume mastery in the practical order, becoming skilled in the elaborate formulae for how the position lines drawn on the chart can be inferred from sextant sights, chronometer and table readings.

Underlying challenge and supersession of traditional practices, is the need for the inventor(s) of the new artifact not only to understand the implications of the novel discursive theory but also to diagnose the practical deficiencies of the relevant item of material culture which supported old instrumental practices. That is to say, they had to understand a previous practical theory from within the framework of a new discursive one, in order to supersede it in practice. This then raises all the old problems about incommensurable frameworks, non-translatability and consequential relativism. Now it is perfectly possible to protect against relativism by adducing methods for getting translation going, assuming only a bridgehead which is established in simple perceptual situations, and I have done so myself.[43] Nevertheless, a better defence is presented by Doyal and Harris. This is based on getting translation securely off the ground by literally earthing it in shared practices (of shelter building).

Thus it is when something practically turns on using words that translators acquire a cutting edge concerning ostensive ambiguity. Since relevant practical activities will be constitutive in character and joining it can occur without the use of language, it will be possible from the beginning of the translation exercise to agree – to some extent at least – with the aliens about what needs to be done and about how they use language to do it. This has to be seen as a very different kind of activity from merely pointing things out and naming them.[44]

Why this is a better defence is itself practical; we do it much of the time and particularly when teaching our children to become language users and in acquiring new languages ourselves. Few of us, on the other hand, have ever had the experience of getting our hypothetical bridgeheads

[43] Margaret S. Archer, 'Resisting the Revival of Relativism', *International Sociology*, 3, 1987.
[44] L. Doyal and R. Harris, *Empiricism, Explanation and Rationality*, Routledge and Kegan Paul, London, 1986.

going. In other words, practical action in the real world, made up of all three orders, is the practical bridgehead of intelligibility between embodied, practical and discursive forms of knowledge. Thus, in this crucial sense, practice is once again found to be pivotal.

The practical order as pivotal

Our final consideration (the lower line of figure 5.2) has to do with that knowledge which originates in the practical order itself and which then communicates sideways with the natural order, on the one hand, and the discursive social order, on the other. Now it is important in concluding this chapter to correct the false impression which may have been engendered, through the examples offered, that the practical order and its material culture are preoccupied by matters of 'applied science'. This has been offset by frequent remarks that material culture is considerably broader than its (important) subset of 'technological artifacts', because the category also includes embellishment, paintings, sculpture, buildings, objects of non-scientific design and application, and, crucially, the codification of practice itself – the choreography of the dance, liturgical ritual, or musical repertoire, along with their costumes, vestments, accessories and accoutrements. Thus in turning to knowledge which *originates* in the practical order, let us consider religion, as a codification of practice, and how it translates into the other two orders.

Knowledge in the religious realm entails experience, illumination and ecstasy rather than explanation, and though it too is fallible like all our knowledge, what is corrigible are distorted relationships rather than defective theories. Like all practical knowledge, it entails a 'feel for' the sacred, rather than propositional knowledge about it: it is quintessentially a matter of doing, of spiritual 'know how'. The consolidation of 'a religion' is the codification of practice, and thus there is no such thing as a non-liturgical religion. Significantly, new religious movements immediately codify their practices liturgically, although they know them under their own particular descriptions. In prophetic religions, the prophet's own practices and practical injunctions constitute the exemplary, ascetic, regulative and normative model of the good life, whose impetus in the practical order is to generate rites whose quintessential purpose is that of *anamnesis*, a symbolic remembering which sustains the vibrancy and salience of the prophetic life-practice. Religious practice elaborates upon material culture to inscribe its memories, encode its ritual means of continuity and enduring contact, and to express its lasting illumination. At the level of the Cultural System this means the generic elaboration of liturgy, which gains expression through a variety of artifactural forms, painting, sculpture, buildings, sacred objects, music, dance and vestments, which are part of the progressive codification of practices, which span initiation, celebration, and the marking of spiritual proficiency. At the Socio-Cultural level, the institutionalisation of a 'Church' is usually intimately connected with the development of its 'priesthood', as custodians of codified practice, often with the privilege of sole use of certain artifacts, and as teachers of the lived tradition.

As such, the practical religious order cannot and does not remain self-contained. On the one hand, its catechetical impulse impacts upon the *natural order* because its very aim is ineluctably tied to the transcendence of the incarnational – formalised as *metanoia*, the change of mind-set in the Christian tradition, or as *kenosis*, the self-emptying of Buddhism, or the *karma* of Hinduism. The very notions of prayer, contemplation or meditation imply new embodied relations, which in turn involve bodily discipline, as, of course, do 'totemism and taboo'. On the other hand, liturgical codification fosters discursive commentary and exegesis resulting in a 'theology', which shares an interface with *propositional culture*. Whether this results from proficients striving to communicate their religious experience to a wider audience, or from secular thinkers seeking to render practical religious experiences intelligible, dialogue is inescapable. However, we must not lose sight of the fact that it is a 'Church' which creates 'scripture', and not vice versa.

Embodied 'incorporation'

Here religious practice is one of embodied veneration and imitation. The process entails practical discipleship, but it is impossible to explicate the incarnational involvement, which is essential to incorporation, unless we reject the Enlightenment's *logocentric* view of human beings. There, truth was defined in terms of formal logical deductions performed on symbolic strings; this model was incapable of explaining a normativity which is not fully propositional but is rather aimed at lived practice. We fare rather differently in understanding embodied religious experience if we cut through this distinction between reason and the emotions. Let us start by accepting the force of the point that unless we were already affective beings, then no amount of knowledge could move us to anything.[45] So let

---

[45] St Augustine makes this assumption when he talks about the incompatibility between apathy and morality 'if apethia is the the name of the state in which the mind cannot be touched by any emotion whatsoever, who would not judge this insensitivity to be the worst of moral defects', *City of God* (trans. Henry Bettenson), Harmondsworth, Penguin, 1972, pp. 564–5.

us grant that emotions are the basis for moving us, but now qualify this such that the passions are not blind urges, but involve knowledge (contra-Hume). This means that feelings are not just felt, they relate to the nature of their object and what makes an emotion appropriate or inappropriate is nothing self-referential, but the nature of the emotion's object. Hence, the appropriate response to divinity is love, but love of the Transcendent itself, and not because of its value to us. Love certainly moves one to action and it does so in the sense that the loving practice is a moral end in itself, thus cutting through the modernist idea that ends must be abstract entities like propositions, desirable states of affairs, facts or events. It means that the quality of goodness must inhere in the sacred (this is the cognitive element), but that what it evokes is an emotional commitment to a discipleship of lived practice.

Thus, for example, in the Christian tradition, the centrality of the 'imitation of Christ' is an embodied commitment of the whole person, which is distorted if fragmented into a cognitive-propositional 'grammar of assent' and a modern decalogue of prescribed behaviour. Instead, the goal of unity with the transcendental involves a bodily remembering which is clearly inscribed in the Western monastic tradition, in the discipline of fasting and scourging, and perhaps even more clearly in the Eastern orthodox pattern of repetitive prayer, with the aim of the pilgrim incorporating the prayer into his or her bloodstream, so that it reverberated to the pattern of breathing, to the heartbeat, to the pace of walking.[46] These modes of harnessing the body to praying constantly were not exclusive to a small group of proficients, and the Christian Church's calendar of fast days, Lenten self-denial, Friday observance and feast days, extended and inscribed them in the body of the faithful. The semantics of the Church as Christ's body on earth are literal rather than metaphorical – an active and practical force for good, not a passive traditionalistic exemplar. Indeed it is of the highest significance that the central mystery of the faith is constituted by embodied knowledge, for the sacrifice of the Mass extends beyond symbolic *anamnesis*, beyond a shared congregational meal, to the corporeal reception of the body of Christ. Precisely because this action is itself deemed a 'mystery' by the faithful, and thus eschews propositional formulation, we encounter the difficulty of how faith, rooted in practice, and incorporated as embodied knowledge, can ever stretch over to the other side and explain itself to the discursive order? Yet, it has been maintained that discipleship, however much its attraction is inarticulate and its practices are embodied, never severs its links with cognitive evaluation; as in the Augustinian dictum 'fides quaer-

---

[46] Simon Barrington-Ward, *The Jesus Prayer*, Bible Reading Fellowship, 1996.

ens intellectum'. Does this make the communication of wordless experience possible?

'Metaphoric' communication

Communication within a religion can be as difficult as that with unbelievers, because doxastic experience does not come sententially. Hence, there is a tendency, within any tradition, to remain within the practical order with midrash, allegory and parable, with testifying, homily and exegesis.

Nevertheless, the need to communicate *experience* comes as much from inside the faith as from outside, and in both the western mystical tradition and the orthodox hesychastic tradition the classic works were produced at the request of co-religionists. Some of their titles alone are supremely revealing of the metaphorical mode of communication – *The Cloud of Unknowing, The Interior Castle (Las Moradas), The Ascent of Mount Carmel, Dark Night of the Soul* and so forth. Indeed St Teresa's autobiography is a record of her struggle with prose, frustration with its inadequacies, attempts at sustained simile (such as four stages of prayer likened to four means of watering a garden) which leave her puzzled as to whether she has conveyed anything. She is both right and wrong in her concerns: wrong for those who share her own practical experience of living in love, and who thus have the bridgehead for following her discourse; but right for those who do not, and who shed what animates it and only extract secular moral injunctions from it. Discursive impoverishment is a characteristic of translation from the practical to the propositional domain.

For instance, apparently the majority of Americans believe that the 'golden rule' epitomises Jesus' ethical practice, namely 'do unto others as you would have them do unto you'. Now this is morally active because it involves seeking the good of others. Nevertheless, it is hardly the highest standard in ethics, since (i) our desires themselves may not be morally commendable, (ii) it is quite compatible with self-fulfilment on our own terms, or, (iii) it can become merely an ethic of conventional reciprocity designed, like Utilitarianism, to bring about the smooth running of everyday life. It does not call us to any kind of extraordinary goodness. All the same, it is more demanding than the earlier 'silver rule', which can be formulated as, 'that which you would not want others to do to you, do not do unto them'. This is more morally passive, for it largely places negative constraints on our behaviour, but this very refraining from harming others could be based on purely prudential grounds of self-interest. Although there is no positive admonition to virtue here, the silver standard is still higher than the 'tinsel rule', 'treat others as they deserve', which requires that they have to earn moral treatment, they have to gain respect, and even win their place in the 'kingdom of ends'.[47]

The three rules are a hierarchical structural of increasingly demanding injunctions, but simultaneously they disclose the limitations of that which can be expressed sententially. What they miss is the 'platinum standard', the radical demand of one *life* on the lived practice of others, summed up in Jesus' new commandment to 'love one another as I have loved you'. This is a call beyond convention into supererogation; a call to perfection in a love which includes enemies as well as friends. As such, it is a call to model ourselves on love, which cannot be interpreted in terms of mere procedural ethics, unlike the other three rules. What has to be emulated is a life in its fullness, and the urge to do so engages all our personal sensibilities in a moral vision of 'discipleship', something defying codification into stateable rules because it retains its identification with apprenticeship in the practical order and thus enjoins developing 'a feel for' living rather than a sentential formulation of detached tenets.

What can be communicated to the propositional order is not nothing, but in so far as it makes a mark, it bids its auditors to return to the practical order, to 'come and see' – the experiential substance rather than the discursive shadow. Thus practical knowledge both remains pivotal and retains its primacy.

Conclusion

What is the significance of having argued for the 'primacy of practice' in our self-consciousness, and as that which supplies strict identity to the self as a human being? Equally, if the argument has been sustained that 'Practice is Pivotal', in the development of humans and of their knowledge, what hangs upon it? In other words, what are the implications of the two chapters which made up the last section? Basically, four conclusions are drawn, which link back to earlier chapters and forward to later ones.

(1) Firstly, to emphasise the centrality of practice in our constitution as self-conscious human beings, and in the forms of knowledge generated by them, is a radical challenge to 'Society's Being' (chapter 3) and to 'Modernity's Man' (chapter 2). The former regards all of our non-biological human powers as gifts of society. This is summed up in Harré's dictum that there is 'nothing in the mind that was not first in the conversation'[48] of society: therefore, the very notion of a self is derivative from a

---

[47] See Douglas V. Porpora, *Landscapes of the Soul*, forthcoming.
[48] Rom Harré, *Personal Being*, Basil Blackwell, Oxford, 1983, p. 116.

social theory, which is appropriated by people, and our knowledge is also socially mediated, as permutations upon the societal depository of meanings. What has been shown, *par contre*, is that our undoubted sociality does not make us into society's creatures. There is plenty in our minds, crucially including our very self-consciousness, which hinges on our human relations with the natural and practical orders of reality. Thus, the incontestable fact that we are social beings does not make us into 'Society's Being', because, equally incontestably, we are also natural and practical beings. In opposition to 'Modernity's Man', which stresses an atomistic being, pre-endowed with the properties and powers which make us recognisably human, it has been countered that all of these only exist *in potentia*. The realisation of every human property and power depends upon our relations with the natural, practical and social orders, without which these tendential developments will be suspended. What we are, and our continuous awareness that we are the same being, are emergent from humanity's relations with reality, which thus undercuts atomistic independence.

(2) Secondly, the argument that 'practice is pivotal' has, as its basic implication, that what is central to human beings are not 'meanings', but 'doings'. This is a fundamental challenge to the hegemony of language, because language itself has been presented as one doing among other non-linguistically dependent doings. The fact that our embodied and our practical knowledge develop in direct interplay with nature and material culture, respectively, entails that many of the things that humans know have not been filtered through meanings belonging to the discursive order. To reinforce the point, much of our practical knowledge cannot even be fully translated into propositional meanings, but can only be conveyed linguistically in the form of metaphor. This is of considerable importance in resisting those who see the entirety of human life as rule-governed, by the social meanings attaching to *any* of our doings. Such popular views, in the Wittgensteinian tradition, necessarily make epistemology prior to ontology. Social realism reverses this relationship, and can do so because it sees practice as pivotal. It is our doings in the world which secure meanings, and not vice versa.

(3) The third implication is, therefore, that there is much more to the human being than a biological bundle of molecules plus society's conversational meanings. In fact, between the two, and reducible to neither, emerge our most crucial human properties and powers – self-consciousness, reflexivity and a goodly knowledge of the world, which is indispensable to thriving in it. Thus it is in and through practice that

many of our human *potentia* are realised, potentials whose realisation are themselves indispensable to the subsequent emergence of those 'higher' strata, the individual with strict personal identity, who is also a social Agent and Actor. Because so much happens, in practice, between the 'molecules' and the 'meanings', analysis of the human being cannot just be a simple division of labour between those (partial) *explanations*, furnished by the neurobiologist, which are then completed by the *interpretative* understandings of sociologists, and immediately transform an organic parcel into a socialised being. Indeed, it has been argued here that a human being who is *capable of hermeneutics* has first to learn a good deal about himself or herself, about the world, and about the relations between them, all of which is accomplished through praxis. In short, the *human being* is both logically and ontologically prior to the *social being*, whose subsequent properties and powers need to build upon human ones. There is therefore no direct interface between molecules and meanings, for between them stretches this hugely important middle ground of practical life in which our emerging properties and powers distance us from our biological origins and prepare us for our social becoming.

(4) Nor are we finished with the middle ground and its doings. So far what has been disengaged is a human being with a continuous sense of self, which anchors strict human identity through the eidetic memory and procedural knowledge. This is morally vital, because it does not make the title to humanity dependent upon socio-linguistic accomplishments, nor threaten its withdrawal if they fail, through accident, illness or mal-development. However, strict human identity, which makes each of us a unique being, is not the same as strict personal identity, which makes each of us a unique particular person. The emergence of persons from selves is also the work of this middle ground, where we uniquely define ourselves by virtue of our constellations of concerns about the world. Yet, to arrive at a definition of such concerns entails considerable experience of the natural, practical and social orders of reality, in which none has any automatic precedence. To prioritise our ultimate concerns, which define our own personal identities, depends upon the activity of the reflective human being, whom, it has just been seen, bears no relation to that preformed entity, 'Modernity's Man', nor to that social product, 'Society's Being'. Thus the next section is concerned with the emergence of personal identity, and only at that point can our undoubted sociality be given its proper due, but without succumbing to sociological imperialism.

Part III

The emergence of personal identity

6   Humanity and reality: emotions as commentaries on human concerns

---

One of the major concerns of this book is with those properties of people which are intertwined with their sociality, yet are irreducible to it. These properties make for personal identity and their emergence is the subject of this chapter and the next. Introspectively, we are all constantly aware of the main property upon which this emergent process depends. As human beings we know that we live a rich inner life: that we are in continuous communion with ourselves and that we engage in a continual running commentary with the events going on around us. We are aware of how our inner lives monitor our responses to external situations in which we find ourselves and indeed modify some of the circumstances to which we willingly expose ourselves, be these natural, practical or social. For example, it is doubtful if there is a (normal) human being who is unaware of an internal dialogue which silently voices sentiments like, 'Isn't he ever going to stop talking?', 'Careful, that truck's pulling out', or, 'I can't face that again.' Moreover, we all also know that these are not just idle commentaries.

They are more than *sotto voce* asides as daily life goes by, passed by some unengaged spectator. Rather, the commentary is interwoven with our responses themselves: they are part of the action. Certainly we may wish that his interminable speech was over, but we also monitor ourselves to conceal our irritation and even to simulate a politely attentive demeanour. Life is always a predicament and never a spectacle, because we cannot shed our status as participants, as all good research methodology acknowledges. The inner life enjoys its own relative autonomy, temporal priority and causal efficacy, as a player in the drama and not as some disinterested 'voice off'. Sometimes we would like to turn it off and to confront life directly without the accompaniment of this cynical, prudential, censorious, apprehensive, assertive, smarting and forbearing inner commentator, who is all of these things. Yet even when we come closest to doing so, when we are fully absorbed in action, the commentary only becomes discontinuous but does not disappear: the mountaineer interrogates and instructs herself on hand-holds, the lover internally begs that this may not stop, and the lazing holiday-maker or the jump-jockey, in their different ways, think 'this is the life'.

Since this experience is so universal and continuous to human beings, and also one of which they are acutely if not infallibly aware, one wonders why it has suffered such considerable neglect within sociology.[1] Because it is part of the action (obviously including interaction), it cannot be relegated to the domain of personal psychology as if separate from sociological concerns. Thus, over the present chapter and the next, this rich inner life will be explored as an emergent property of persons (a PEP), which generates their *personal identity*. It intertwines with their sociality, but exists *sui generis* and cannot be reduced to it. The focus will be upon the emergence and elaboration of this personal property and power, whilst it will only be in the last chapter that personal identity is considered in conjunction with structural and cultural properties (the relationship between PEPs and SEPs and CEPs), that is with *social identity*.

The central assumption made here is that our emotions are among the main constituents of our inner lives. They are the fuel of our internal conversation and this is why they matter. Thus there is no difficulty in going along with Elster (at least the Elster of *Alchemies of the Mind*[2]) and arguing that quite 'simply, emotions matter because if we did not have them nothing else would matter. Creatures without emotion would have no reason for living nor, for that matter, for committing suicide. Emotions are the stuff of life.'[3] In exactly the same vein, St Augustine asked rhetorically if we would not consider a general *apatheia* to be the worst of human and moral defects. The importance of the emotions is central to the things we care about and to the act of caring itself.

On the one hand, such a view is fundamentally opposed to 'Modernity's Man', discussed in chapter 2, and to all those subsequent exertions to take the passions out of his or her preferences. Quite the reverse: the aim here is to reunite human *pathos* with human *logos* and to show their inter-linkage within the internal conversation. On the other hand, the present approach is equally opposed to 'Society's Man', discussed in chapter 3, where everything that we are, and this includes our full emo-

[1] The scattered insights of Charles Peirce into self-talk will be used in this chapter and especially the next. Freud's analysis of these dynamics could not issue in the internal conversation because of his stress upon the unconscious and the dynamics of repression and projection.

[2] This, as the following quotation indicates, seems to be a very different Elster from the author of *Strong Feelings*, published later in the same year, who pursues his sympathetic dialogue with Rational Choice Theory by presenting his analysis of emotions as 'Studies in the Subversion of Rationality'. See chapter 2 for a critical discussion of the 'other Elster'.

[3] Jon Elster, *Alchemies of the Mind: Rationality and the Emotions*, Cambridge University Press, 1999, p. 403.

tionality, is itself a gift of society. Again the object is the reverse: namely to show how irreducible properties of our human selves interact with our sociality and that their interplay is significant *by virtue of the inner dialogue* and its outcomes.

However, there is a lot of ground to trace between the first emergence of our emotions and the full elaboration of the internal conversation. Thus the discussion is divided into these two parts, spanning the two chapters. This is more than a matter of convenience, because my claim is that we are dealing with first and second-order phenomena respectively. Where (first-order) emotional emergence is concerned, there is a massive literature outside sociology that requires sifting for its sociological significance. However, emotionality's (second-order) contribution to the internal management of our concerns is precisely where sociology could be of significance. The following is a broad over-view, using everyday language, of the argument that will be put forward in this chapter and the next:

(i)   different clusters of emotions represent commentaries upon our concerns and are emergent from our human relationships with the natural, practical and discursive orders of reality respectively. Matters do not finish here.

(ii) because of our reflexivity, we review these emotional commentaries, articulate them, monitor them, and transmute them; thus elaborating further upon our emotionality itself.

(iii) this occurs through the inner conversation which is a ceaseless discussion about the satisfaction of our ultimate concerns and a monitoring of the self and its commitments in relation to the commentaries received.

The definition of emotions as 'commentaries upon our concerns', calls for its own commentary. It is, of course, a straightforwardly realist definition which presumes that emotions are about something in the world (they are intentional or, as some would prefer, intensional in nature). Thus as Charles Taylor puts it, we speak of 'emotions as essentially involving a sense of our situation. They are affective modes of awareness of situation.'[4] They are thus relational to something, which is what gives them their emergent character, and that something is our own concerns which make a situation a matter of non-indifference to a person. Taylor himself calls these 'imports' and rightly maintains that in 'identifying the import of a given situation we are picking out what in the situation gives the grounds or basis of our feelings . . . *We are not just stating that we experience a certain feeling in this situation*'[5] (my ital.). This sets the

---

[4] Charles Taylor, *Human Agency and Language*, Cambridge University Press, 1985, p. 48.
[5] Ibid., p. 49.

definition apart from subjectivism and emotivism which reduce the judgemental element involved to a series of grunts and groans. Equally, it sets it apart from emotional irrationalism because we are not free to make what we will of a state of affairs, independently of how things are. (Indeed some of the inner dialogue is precisely about the relationship between our epistemology and our ontology, and to miss this is to condemn our emotionality to a living-out of the epistemic fallacy.)

Simultaneously, the present approach is equally far removed from emotional cognitivism which reduces the emotions to mere expressions of a full-blown commitment system and thus denies the active role that a commentary plays towards a concern. This properly includes the modification of concerns themselves – within the framework of the internal conversation – which any cognitive theory rules out by definition in favour of expressive monologue.[6] Thus those cognitivists who maintain that our emotions derive from our cognitive interpretations, imposed upon reality, rather than from reality itself, have the problems, (a) of explaining where any commitment (such as 'become a concert pianist') comes from if emotions provide no shoving-power,[7] (b) how they can be maintained without (in this case) positive feedback from practical reality signalling (some) performative achievement, and, (c) how, since negative feedback in the form of incompetence would lead to modified career aspirations, we can disregard encounters with reality and view all of them as sieved through some pre-existent and utterly resilient cognitive focus. Instead, emotions are like any emergent property in that one of their powers *qua* emergents is to modify those of its constituents – in this case the cognitive goal itself, the desired career. Here the commentary does so as part of the conversation, which it is insisted does not function like the sporting commentator's 'voice-over', but rather plays an active part in the second-order inner deliberations – perhaps in the reduction of career aspirations from concert pianist to music teacher.

Finally, in defining emotions as relational, that is as emerging from situations to signal their import for our concerns, there is less preoccupa-

[6] See Andrew Ortony, Gerald L. Clore and Andew Collins, *The Cognitive Structure of Emotions*, Cambridge University Press, 1988. 'The emotions are very real and very intense, but they still issue from cognitive interpretations imposed on external reality, rather than directly from reality itself', p. 4. Thus, the example is given of a person's goal structure, pre-eminent amongst which is to 'become a concert pianist', which acts as a cognitive focus for all relevant emotions.

[7] Although we need reasons for our commitments (see Roger Trigg, *Reason and Commitment*, Cambridge University Press, 1973), I doubt that these are ever all we need, or, in other words, that there can be such a thing as a purely cognitive commitment. Even such matters as 'honouring a contract' are not just about cognitively seeking a state of affairs, but also entail notions of 'honour' and 'honourability' which cannot be dissociated from our feelings.

tion here than usual with the occurrence of 'an' emotion, its nomenclature or classification. Because of their situational and relational character as imports, our emotionality is regarded as a continuous running commentary (that is something we are never without) and therefore it is only in sudden or urgent contexts that we are aware of a specific emotion. This tallies extremely well with Frijda's conclusion: 'Emotions in this paradigmatic sense, however, are but crystallisations in a stream of emotional response, of readiness and tendency, that faithfully follows the continuous bed of concern-relevant events and that overflows that bed in intentional activities and passions; but which stream of relevance appraisals goes on incessantly, mostly only felt by the person herself or himself.'[8] Thus, there is no need to compile complex lists of named emotions and accommodate them on this account, for, as Greenwood[9] argues, there is no necessary correlation between the richness of emotional experience and the existence of an equivalent subtlety of available linguistic labels in any given culture.

Instead, in dealing with the emergence and progressive elaboration of (first-order) emotions, the task will be to delineate clusters of emotions whose emergence is rooted in the different orders of reality – the natural, practical and discursive. In other words, distinct tracts of our emotionality are internally linked to equally distinct kinds of real world objects, whose three different kinds of imports register themselves as commentaries on three correspondingly different kinds of concerns. Prototypical examples can and will be given of each cluster, but it is not part of the aim here to accommodate the four hundred or so emotions discriminated in the English language to the three clusters, because of the naive nominalism which would be entailed. Since synonyms can proliferate and the narcissism of small differences may flourish, we should be duly cautious in assuming that each appellation connotes a different experience, just as we should beware of thinking that the absence of a name in certain cultures implies a corresponding absence of a feeling.

The emergence of three different emotional clusters

Persons necessarily interact with three different orders of reality – the natural, the practical and the discursive, which were defined and discussed in the last chapter. Exactly the same will be argued here for the emergence of our human emotionality (first-order). In other words, the natural order, the practical order and the discursive order are the

---

[8] Nico Frijda, *The Emotions*, Cambridge University Press, 1993, p. 479.
[9] John Greenwood, *Realism, Identity and Emotion*, Sage, London, 1994, pp. 162f.

intentional objects to which three different clusters of emotions are related. Because emotions have been defined as 'commentaries upon our concerns', a distinct type of concern has plausibly to be identified with each of these three orders. This can be established for each, and it seems preferable as a procedure to the search for some portmanteau concept which covers the eliciting conditions for the full gamut of emotions. The problems with these portmanteaux, such as 'appraisal', 'arousal', 'approach', 'avoidance', is basically that their very generality verges on vacuity: they can indeed be made to cover all emotions precisely because, with very little ingenuity, there is very little human behaviour that they cannot embrace. Thus they tell us correspondingly little about emotionality as opposed to other forms of behaviour which are emotionally neutral (catching a bus entails some form of 'appraisal' of timing and destination, enough 'arousal' to get aboard, and obviously the 'approach' of some places and 'avoidance' of others, but our mundane trip to the supermarket may be entirely free of affect).

Instead, our concerns have to be sufficiently specific for the situations that we confront to carry equally specific imports for them. Firstly, it is maintained that all persons have to confront the natural world and that their embodiment ineluctably confers on them concerns about their physical well-being as they encounter the hard knocks, pleasures and dangers of their environments. This concern itself is embodied in our physical constitution and, although the imports of nature can be over-ridden (at the second-order), they cannot avoid being viscerally registered and resulting (indirectly, as we will see) in the emergence of first-order emotions.

Secondly, all persons are constrained to live and work, in one way or another, in the practical world: necessary labour is the lot of *homo faber*. Performative concerns are unavoidably part of our inevitable practical engagement with the world of material culture. The precise objects of performative concerns are historically, cross-culturally and socially varied, but the import of our competence in dealing with the practical realm is universal. In other words, the annoyance of primitive man about breaking a good spear belongs to the same emotional family as the feelings of the playboy of the western world when he prangs his best Lamborghini. The import of the situation is to the subject and has nothing to do with where our sympathies may lie as hypothetical observers.

Thirdly, sociality is also necessarily the lot of human beings, who would be less than what we understand by human without their social engagements. Participation in the social realm entails concerns about self-worth which cannot be evaded in this discursive environment. We cannot avoid becoming a subject among subjects and with it come 'subject-referring properties' (such as admirable or shameful) which convey the import of

OBJECT OF EMOTIONS	CONCERNS	IMPORTS	EMERGENCE FROM
Natural order	physical well-being	visceral	body-environment relations
Practical order	performative achievement	competence	subject/object relations
Discursive order	self-worth	normative	subject/subject relations

Figure 6.1 The emergence of (first-order) emotions

normativity to our concerns about our social standing. These may be very different concerns since we can choose (second-order) to stand in very different places (our self-worth is crucially dependent upon the nature of our commitments), but these of course are all equally social and cannot obviate the (first-order) impact of social norms which inflict evaluations on our comportment.

Thus the argument to be developed can be broadly summarised in figure 6.1.

What follows is an analytical account. Nevertheless, it is impossible to present it other than sequentially. In so doing it will be hard to avoid conveying the impression that the first is more basic than succeeding clusters of emotions, especially since more and more variety will be introduced consecutively. However, there is a particular theoretical reason for resisting the notion of 'basic emotions', over and above the disputes arising from how to designate what is basic and the divergent classifications to which they give rise. (Thus Ekman and Frisen[10] and Izard,[11] both defining as basic those emotions manifested by unambiguously different facial expressions, register six and eleven respectively, whereas Plutchik,[12] classifying in terms of elementary action tendencies, registers eight, with overlap between them all being confined to the following six – happiness, fear, sadness, surprise, anger and disgust.[13]) This discord seems to be ineradicable[14] and the designation of what is basic will necessarily remain

[10] P. Ekman (ed.), *Emotions in the Human Face*, Cambridge University Press, New York, 1982.   [11] C. E. Izard, *Human Emotions*, Plenum, New York, 1977.
[12] R. Plutchik and H. Kellerman (eds.), *Emotion:Theory, Research and Experience*, vol. 1 *Theories of Emotion*, Academic Press, New York, 1980.
[13] For a selection of lists of 'basic emotions', see A. Ortony, G. L. Clore and A. Collins, *The Cognitive Structure of the Emotions*, p. 27.
[14] 'Classical writers on the emotions, from Descartes on, are fond of making lists of primitive emotions, then going on to show how the more complex are built out of those. The diversity in the resulting lists is warning enough that this is an unpromising strategy'. Ronald de Souza, 'The Rationality of Emotions' in Amélie Oksenberg Rorty (ed.), *Explaining Emotions*, University of California Press, Berkeley, 1980, p. 142.

contested while ever the bases of classification remain as varied as the above.

My own reason for avoiding the designation of 'basic' emotions is tightly allied to the arguments in the next chapter about the importance of the 'internal conversation' which can monitor, displace and re-order the priorities accorded to the different emotions through the relative importance assigned to the commentaries which they supply. In other words, the first-order of emotional emergence has no authoritative role in relation to the second-order prioritisation of emotions. There is a second supportive consideration, of a substantive nature, which reinforces the refusal to designate any given cluster as 'basic', and this is the simple fact that for most of our lives we confront the three orders of reality simultaneously.

There are two arguments that it is not necessary to resist, which, however, have no bearing upon the present analysis. The first might maintain that phylogenetically the human species confronted the three orders successively, thus making those emotions emergent from body/environmental relations in the natural order the most basic in historical terms. This may well be correct, it may well coincide with that measure of agreement on the six emotions listed above, and it may even coincide with evidence supportive of hard-wiring, but none of this obviates the fact that the time of living (predominantly) in the natural order is long gone and that the historicity of emergence says nothing about the contemporary salience of the three clusters. Secondly, and ontogenetically, it may well be the case, as certain developmental psychologists maintain,[15] that during the short period of our maturation the three orders of imports and concerns do emerge in the sequence in which they are presented in figure 6.1. However, this again becomes irrelevant once the inner dialogue engages because, since this is conducted through language, it is predicated upon our engagement with all three orders of reality and the emotions emergent from them.

In other words, these perfectly valid preoccupations of the anthropologist or child psychologist are entirely different from the analytical concerns of the sociologist which are developed here. Were the two above arguments to be extended to deny according any primacy or priority to language, again there would be no quarrel: just because the inner conversation uses a linguistic medium, this does nothing to stack the cards in favour of emotions emerging from the discursive order, because we are sufficiently proficient in articulating what it is about our environ-

---

[15] See Michael Lewis, 'The Emergence of Human Emotions' in Michael Lewis and Jeanette M. Haviland (eds.), *Handbook of Emotions*, Guildford Press, New York, 1993.

mental and object relationships which result in their associated forms of affect. Indeed it may be a good deal easier to convey verbally why we fear a heavy fall than why we dread downward social mobility. Nevertheless, the key argument against considering any of the three clusters to be more basic than the others remains that we are dealing with first-order emergents which literally undergo a second-ordering. Let us now turn to the emergence of the three clusters themselves.

1   The emergence of emotions in the natural order

The aim here is to show that emotions convey the import of natural situations to us. Such emotions are emergent from the relationship between nature's properties and our bodily properties – this of course being a necessary relationship given the way the world is constituted, the way we are made and the fact that we have to interact ceaselessly. What ensures that the import of the environment is conveyed to us is our very self-consciousness (that continuous sense of self which was defended in chapter 4). By definition, self-consciousness means that we are necessarily reflexive beings [16] and this enables us to respond to circumstances which adversely or beneficially affect our bodily concerns – themselves given by our organic constitution. It is reflexivity too, which enables us to act purposively 'to avoid or to ameliorate circumstances of this kind where there is a conflict between the interests of a creature and forces which are endangering or undermining them'.[17] However, in themselves, these relationships between a body and its physical environment do not explain where the affect comes from which is the signature-tune of emotion. After all, a sunflower makes reflexive adjustments to its circumstances when it turns towards the sun, but we would not feel it correct to impute emotionality to this plant in the same way that we might to sunning animals, including human animals.

Whilst emotions depend upon the causal ability of visceral occurrences to give us pleasure and pain, they cannot be identified with them: for the body to feel pain, it does not necessarily feel anything other than being in

---

[16] '. . . being conscious in the everyday sense does (unlike unconsciousness) entail reflexivity: It necessarily involves a secondary awareness of a primary response. An instance of exclusively primary and unreflexive consciousness would not be an instance of what we ordinarily think of as consciousness at all. For what would it be like to be conscious of something without being aware of this consciousness? It would mean having an experience with no awareness whatsoever of its occurrence. This would be, precisely, a sense of unconscious experience. It appears, then, that being conscious is identical with being self-conscious. Consciousness is self-consciousness', Harry G. Frankfurt, 'Identification and Wholeheartedness', in his *The Importance of What We Care About*, Cambridge University Press, 1988, pp. 161–2.   [17] Ibid., p. 163.

pain. The crucial link which casts visceral factors into their proper role as imports, is that the body 'remembers' pains and pleasures. Although this is meant quite literally (despite being unable to specify what it means neuro-physiologically), and though most people would agree that they internally recognise the type of headache whose onset threatens, there is a less contentious way of putting the matter. Human beings (and many animals) have the power to *anticipate* what the import of environmental occurrences will be for their bodies. Anticipation is the key to affect. We know what the bodily consequences of fire or icy water will be, and somatically this is projected as fear: if we did not anticipate it there would be nothing other than the pain of the event. Hence our capacity to die a hundred deaths in advance, but also to report that something 'was not as bad as expected'. Often it is not, for anticipation dwells on future events, whereas when they happen we are actively engaged in them. Similarly the somatic commentary can come after the event, when the shaking body projects forward what could have happened and how nearly it did happen. As Pascal put it, 'we almost never think of the present, and when we do, it is only to see what light it throws on our plans for the future'.[18] But this light does not play randomly over the field of possibilities, it is elicited by a determinate horizon of incipient occurrences (or ones felt to be so), whose import is understood to bode well or ill for the body. In short, our emotions go out before us to meet the future.

This means that emotions do not just happen as internal events (which may be true of moods). Instead, '(e)motions are elicited. The eliciting events appear to fulfil a special role; they are not just stimuli. They appear to act through their significance, their meaning, their rewarding or aversive nature.'[19] They are not matters of stimulus and response because they entail cognition about the intentional object. Like all human cognitions these are fallible and can lead to the wrong expectations. As Hume argued, we must 'make a distinction betwixt the cause and the object of these passions; betwixt that idea, which excites them, and that to which they direct their views, when excited'.[20] This is the distinction between the branch scratching on the window and the human panic about a midnight invasion. Equally we can be wrong the other way round and read imports far too complacently for physical well-being. Our emotional commentaries, being cognitive in part, are always corrigible. This is one of the things which makes some accentuate the irrationality of our emotions – after all there is no good reason to be scared about mice – but the

---

[18] Blaise Pascal, *Pensées* (1670), Mercure de France, Paris, 1976, p. 165, section 80.
[19] Nico Frijda, *The Emotions*, p. 4.
[20] David Hume, *A Treatise on Human Nature* (Selby-Bigg ed.), Oxford University Press, p. 278.

same fallibility characterises all our knowledge, which not so long ago thought there was nothing to fear in sunbathing, double cream and cigarettes.

It is this cognitive element which is found crucially lacking from Damasio's 'somatic-marker' hypothesis, which otherwise might seem to sit quite well with bodily commentaries in the natural order. Thus he argues that somatic markers function as 'gut feelings' in a given context which have 'been connected, by learning, to predicted future outcomes of certain scenarios. When a negative somatic marker is juxtaposed to a particular future outcome the combination functions as an alarm bell. When a positive somatic marker is juxtaposed instead, it becomes a beacon of incentive.'[21] This he then links to rational decision-making, arguing that the automatic signal protects against future losses, reduces the choice to one amongst fewer alternatives, thus contributing to better, more focused decisions (rather than just to quicker ones). This unabashed association-ism[22] is incurably actualist. Cognitively it is restricted to learning Humean constant conjunctures, and therefore our emotional commentaries can never be informed by knowledge of underlying generative mechanisms. Yet often they are, and feelings are appropriate to them. Thus we know that birds have a tendency to fly into windows, central heating systems to develop air-locks, and people to lose their tempers when under pressure: their occurrence may surprise us, but our knowledge of the generative mechanism stops this from becoming alarm. Hence, it is maintained that our emotional commentaries are more sophisticated than associationism allows and that were our 'gut feelings' to be only matters of reinforcement, we would make some terrible decisions (like the gambler who believes in his winning-streak) and could not make a single creative one.

The issue of cognitive fallibility apart, what the simple associationism of the 'somatic-marker hypothesis' also misses is the emergent nature of emotions from the relationship between an event's imports and our concerns. It is this which leads Damasio to believe that somatic-markers operate in the same fashion throughout the natural, practical and discursive orders. Instead, they seem to work best within the natural order, where bodily concerns are laid down in the organism's constitution and the whole emergence of commentary *appears* more like association because our concerns are constant for the species (and beyond it). This produces far more observable similarities in our hopes and fears in the natural world than would be true of our species' concerns about classical music or the stock exchange. Associationism will not do, firstly because it

---

[21] Antonio R. Damasio, *Descartes' Error*, Macmillan, London, 1996.   [22] See p. 180.

denies any theoretical attitude at first-order level, and secondly, because it neglects entirely our second-order capacity to reflect upon, and through that transform our emotionality, actively promoting or demoting our bodily concerns in a process which is far too deliberative to reduce to the play of 'gut feelings'.

It is crucial to stress that in the natural order we are dealing with emotional properties which are emergent from the relationship between the import of situations and our bodily concerns. Undoubtedly there are standards of acceptability which are laid down in the organism and constitute its parameters of tolerance, prior to any actual or anticipated environmental change. Thus, we could say that bodily concerns are pre-defined and to a large extent pre-given. However, in seeking to answer the question, 'where does affect come from?', the solution is one which is only forthcoming in relational terms. It is from the interaction between environmental circumstances and embodied concerns that, because we are conscious beings, we can anticipate their conjunction and supply this to ourselves as an emotional commentary. Thus Frijda's formulation correctly stresses both intentionality and emergence: 'Emotions are elicited by significant events. Events are significant when they touch upon one or more concerns of the subject. Emotions thus result from the interaction of an event's actual or anticipated consequences and the subject's concerns.'[23]

What then is the point of these emergent emotions, or do they indeed have one? So far this account of affect as an anticipatory commentary would be quite compatible with regarding these emergents as redundant. They could be seen as playing the same role in our lives as the sporting commentator has towards a game – one which can in no way influence the outcome. Yet emergent properties are known by their powers and these include the power to modify the constituents of the relationship as well as things outside it.[24] This modification of the relationship is precisely what is happening here, for the emotion functions to modify the relation between body and environment. Since the body is under (more of) the subject's control than is the environment, it removes itself and severs

---

[23] Nico Frijda, *The Emotions*, p. 6.
[24] One of the external effects of emotions in the natural order may be to communicate their commentaries to parties other than the self. For such a communicative theory, see Keith Oatley, *Best Laid Schemes: The Psychology of the Emotions*, Cambridge University Press, 1992. On the contrary, I would agree with Frijda that the emotional process is one 'serving to implement or modify the subject's relationship to the environment. Obviously, expressive behaviour does serve communication. It permits others to make inferences concerning the subject's state of mind, and these inferences are often correct. However, it does not exist for that purpose. It is not produced for that purpose nor, we may assume, did evolution maintain or develop it for its communicative value', *The Emotions*, p. 60.

Environmental import to the body	Emotion	Tendential effect towards the environment
harm	fear	flight/shrinking
assault	anger	resistance
startle	wonder	arrest/attention
loss	sadness	withdrawal
gain	joy	encounter
revolt	disgust	emission
enrich	hope	awaiting
abreact	relief	relaxation

Figure 6.2 Emotional emergence in the natural order

contact or prepares itself and inspects, establishes or even abandons itself to closer contact. Thus modified relational activity is one of the powers emergent from the body/environment relations which generated the emotions. 'Relational activity establishes or modifies relationships; and it does so mainly not by modifying the environment, but by modifying the location, accessibility, and sensory and locomotor readiness of the subject. It does so by endeavouring to achieve certain useful effects: hiding and crouching diminish chances of being hurt or seen, flight increases distance to danger, disgust movement ejects distasteful substances, and so forth.'[25]

To put flesh on the bones of this argument, let us briefly inspect those clusters of emotions which emerge in the natural order from relationships between the body and the environment. These are clusters in the plural and in the singular. On the one hand, a single emotion like 'fear' denotes the range of its manifestations which represent variations in intensity – e.g. caution, timidity, apprehension, fear, dread, terror and panic. On the other hand, the cluster as a whole shares the single property that each emotion mentioned can emerge purely within the natural order. Thus, although all can also be manifest in both the practical order (fear of riding a bike) or in the social order (fear of disapproval), what differentiates this cluster from other emotions is that their emergence can be naturalistic because such commentaries need make no reference to either material culture or language. The relationship between properties of the environment and of our embodiment are sufficient for their emergence. (See figure 6.2)

Emergent properties are generative mechanisms and, although their expression may be suspended by intervening contingencies in the open system which is our environment, the last column lists their tendential

---

[25] Ibid., p. 13.

outcomes. Here, the effect of each emotional commentary will be seen to be an action tendency. This is emphatically not to assert that all emotions issue in a tendency to act. It would not, for example, be the case for disappointment, regret or nostalgia, and, as Hume maintained, 'pride and humility are pure emotions in the soul, unattended with any desire, and not immediately exciting us to action'.[26] In this context, Elster demonstrates persuasively that none of the properties which various authors have striven to attach to the full range of our emotional lives (with the exception of 'quality feel') holds without exception, and this specifically includes 'action tendency'.[27] However, no such general claim is being made: the very point of associating the emergence of different clusters of emotional commentaries with the natural, practical and discursive orders is precisely because they have properties particular to the respective orders. Yet it is claimed that the particular property of emotions emergent in the natural order is an action tendency towards the environment.

For this cluster then, though not beyond it, Frijda's definition works well, although his analysis makes only oblique and brief reference to the notion of commentaries, which is the one communality detected here between emotionality in the three different orders. 'Emotions, then, can be defined as modes of relational action readiness, either in the form of tendencies to establish, maintain, or disrupt a relationship with the environment or in the form or mode of relational readiness as such.'[28] Emotional action tendencies in the natural order are thus like plans or programmes *vis-à-vis* our environmental relations. They have this programme-like quality because our bodies as organisms are very similar and it is this organic likeness which makes this cluster closer to that which we share with the higher animals than are the other two. Frijda's definition is also an impeccably realist one, for he does not state that action tendencies will ensue, but only that they have a tendency to do so which 'may consist only of being set to achieve a given end by whatever programme may turn out to be feasible and appropriate, when action turns out to be feasible and appropriate. Such emotions merely consist of the urgent desire to have the situation change, the object attained, or the intrusion removed.'[29] Moreover, his discussion of bodily-environmental mismatch (or potential match) which gives rise to embodied signals (rooted in feelings of pain and pleasure),[30] calling for action to remove the discrepancy, becomes very similar indeed to the notion of emotions as commentaries about how the body is faring in its natural order.

This notion of mismatch, in turn, can serve to explain variations in the

---

[26] David Hume, *Treatise on Human Nature*, p. 367.
[27] Jon Elster, *Strong Feelings*, MIT press, Cambridge, Mass., 1999, p. 40.
[28] Nico Frijda, *The Emotions*, p. 71.   [29] Ibid., p. 75.   [30] Ibid., pp. 77f.

embodied (liabilities/enablements)
conditioning   anticipation
T1   T2
           environmental interaction
                    T3
              emotional elaboration
                         T4

Figure 6.3 Emotional morphogenesis in the natural order

intensity with which any given emotion is felt. At this point the argument can be linked-up with Jonathan Turner's theory of the progressive elaboration of emotional responses as a product of the degree of congruity between embodied expectations and environmental experiences.[31] As an account of the intensity or of the progressive specification of the strength of emotional commentary, it fits rather nicely in explaining why we feel, say, 'apprehension' rather than 'terror'. Thus he argues that, as 'a basic hypothesis, I would argue that when expectations and experience are congruent, whether activating positive or negative emotions, the low intensity state is the most likely mode of activation – that is satisfaction, mild aversion, mild assertiveness, disappointment or startlement. Conversely, as the incongruence between expectations and experience increases . . . the high intensity end of the emotions is activated.'[32] This could then lend itself to an account of (first order) emotional morphogenesis in the natural order, which can be depicted as in Figure 6.3 using the basic morphogenetic diagram.[33]

Why is it then, or how is it then, that if our naturalistic emotional commentaries are regarded as what seem to be eminently reasonable outcomes of our bodily concerns in relation to our environmental situations, that one of the most common characteristics of our emotional life is often held to be its capacity to overwhelm us in an irrational manner or with irrational effects?[34] Above all, this is *itself* because emotions are commentaries on our concerns: they are anthropocentric perspectives on the situations in which we find ourselves and not dispassionate reviews. As many have stressed, there is both urgency and emergency attached to

[31] I would not, however, endorse this as a theory of emotional 'arousal', and neither it seems would Frijda, since both of us see our environmental encounters as generating a constant stream of emotionality.

[32] Jonathan Turner, 'Towards a General Sociological Theory of Emotions', *Journal for the Theory of Social Behaviour*, 29:2, 1999, p. 149.

[33] See Margaret S. Archer, *Realist Social Theory: The Morphogenetic Approach*, Cambridge University Press, 1995, especially chapter 6.

[34] John Sabini and Maury Silver, 'The Not Altogether Social Construction of Emotions: A Critique of Harré and Gillett', *Journal for the Theory of Social Behaviour*, 28:3, 1998.

protecting our bodies from their liabilities or granting them exercise of their enablements in desire fulfilment. This is what this emotional cluster does, particularly at high intensity. It comments imperiously on the need to attend to our proximate bodily concerns. As for the commentaries themselves, this implies neither their *infallibility*, nor their *functionality*, nor their *uncontrollability*.

Firstly, then, the commentary may simply get things wrong (mice do not warrant flight and open spaces do not warrant the reaction of agoraphobia): these are simply cognitively wrong in their diagnosis of environmental threats to our physical well-being. Moreover, if it can mis-diagnose the cause, the commentary can also disregard the consequences of the recommended action tendency – just as a liking for certain foods may foster over-indulgence with painful effects. Emotional commentaries are felt now, in the present, as urges to bring about some immediate adjustment in our environmental relations which may be heedless and reckless about our future well-being. Flight is an urge to get away from some source of harm: it entails no flight-plan to arrive at safety. Avoiding pursuit is one reason why so many animals end up under car wheels. Thus Elster seems correct in his belief that 'the lack of regard for consequences – including the lack of concern for more information – is the most important mechanism by which emotion can subvert rationality'.[35]

Secondly, the sheer anthropocentricism of these commentaries may be counter-functional for the organism. Pre-occupied with sadness over some recent loss, we may fail to perceive the environmental availability of a potential gain, but also to detect the onset of potentially harmful circumstances. Because we only seem to be capable of feeling one (high intensity) emotion at a time, then our emotional commentaries may cut off our noses to spite our faces. Emotions are relative to our concerns, but their commentaries can do nothing about mis-placed concerns or over-limited concern. Hence Frijda's conclusion appears to be correct: emotions 'cannot be said to ensure concern satisfaction: They are plans and readiness for ensuring satisfaction. What they do, though, is reflect and "express" what the individual is concerned with.'[36] What they cannot do is to protect us against the dysfunctional concerns and their consequences.

Yet the effects of cognitively defective commentaries and those of dysfunctional concerns are corrigible in principle. This is not by converting a Humean creature of the 'passions' into one who heeds the stern

---

[35] Jon Elster, *Alchemies of the Mind*, Cambridge University Press, 1999, p. 287.
[36] Nico Frijda, *The Emotions*, p. 487.

Kantian voice of duty and external reasons. Instead, we are dealing with a reflexive being who not only has (first-order) concerns but who also has the (second-order) capacity to evaluate her concerns and to arrive at her ultimate concerns. If this were not the case we would not find agoraphobics who sought to extend their freedom of movement through therapy, rather than living with their primary commentary, nor would we encounter those dieting, using nicotine patches or taking vows of celibacy. What the next chapter will try to show is that these are not just acts of willpower (though overcoming *akrasia* may be involved), but rather they are generated through the 'inner conversation' where the self corrects and prioritises her concerns – a process which would be wrongly viewed as rationalisation and much better seen as the emergence of her life's 'super-commentary' as guided by her ultimate concerns.

2   Emotional emergence in the practical order

Emotions do not form a natural kind, which is the main reason why general theories of emotionality have proved so unsuccessful. Just because our feelings are almost continuous, this does not mean that they share a common denominator. Instead, different clusters of emotions constitute different individual kinds. These are emergent from distinctive types of concerns in relation to equally distinctive contexts. Thus each emotional cluster represents a different type of commentary on human preoccupations in different tracts of our existence. So far, what have been examined are those emotions emergent from our bodily/environmental relationships in the natural order, where the standards for commentary are inscribed physiologically in our organic make-up and its capacity to feel pain and pleasure, which we, as conscious beings, have the ability to anticipate. As such, at the first-order level, emotionality tends to be rather similar for the entire species (and likely beyond it). Differences do arise even amongst first-order emotions because of cognitive variations in interpretations of the natural environment (as was seen for mice and open spaces). Yet far more human variability towards the natural order is in fact a second-order phenomenon, because persons debate with themselves what importance they will attach to a given import: asking and answering how much they are prepared to suffer physically in relation to their ultimate concerns.

When we turn to the practical order, and deal with *subject/object relations*, there is no sense in which our concerns are laid down biologically under those two mentors, physical pleasure and pain. On the other hand, confronting the practical order is no more optional than was confrontation with the natural order: indeed our dealings with all three orders are ineluctable. *Homo faber* has to thrive in the practical domain, which involves that cluster of emotions specifically linked to human praxis. Thus, we are dealing with those emotions emergent from people's necessary labour, from performative relations, from practical imitation and curiosity, from involvement in all doings which entail material culture, and this includes those of the spectator.

Since the material imperatives of survival can be met in an increasing number of different ways, and are generally easier and less time consuming to meet in the developed world, then we are dealing with a much wider group of potential imports than was the case in the natural order. Because practical orders vary so greatly throughout the world and its history, the substantive nature of our concerns will vary accordingly. Thus the key question here is whether there is any communality of concern which characterises the practical order as a whole and stands in the same relationship to it as did bodily pleasure and pain to the natural order?

Here it is maintained that *performative achievement* is the generic concern of *homo faber*. The source of a new cluster of emotions, emergent from our subject/object relations, develops through the commentary which our competence supplies on our doings. Care should be taken here because the commentary is what emerges between the subject and in its relationship with the object; it is, as it were, the object's judgement of competence or incompetence upon the subject's dealings with it. The widget can be made to work or it cannot. Of course it is the subject who passes the judgement, but he or she does so upon an objective performance. Certainly people can deceive themselves, thinking they are better than they are at a given activity, for this commentary too has a cognitive element and as ever we can err. However, we err in relation to an objective standard, otherwise our responses could not be called self-deception nor be corrected, usually through further practice itself. Furthermore, at the second-order level someone may also conclude that 'if a job's worth doing, it's worth doing badly', but here the import of competence has been taken into account. Just as in making the decision about how much bodily suffering our ultimate concerns entail, so too a person can deliberate upon how much practical frustration or boredom they should tolerate. Yet under no circumstances is the practical import of competence to be elided with something entirely different, namely social judgements (of praise or contempt) on our performative achievements.

Social comments may be attracted by or accorded to our performances – as in the report card reading 'not a great sporting contribution to the school', sayings like 'he's all thumbs' or work dismissed as that of a 'Sunday painter'. It is not denied that these may be extremely hurtful, even to the point where they serve as a deterrent to the activity in question. Nevertheless, if they are taken to heart, this is to do with our self-worth in the social order. As such, this is no different from the equivalent second-order judgement that the physical costs to be paid for some performative achievement are, on balance, too high. Michelangelo could have decided that the ceiling of the Sistine Chapel did not warrant back-problems. Yet neither of these undermine the fact that there are first-order emotions which are intrinsic to our subject/object relations. These are occurrent even if they are overlaid, as is the case for the other two clusters of emotions as well.

In the practical order, emotions are emergent from the relationship between the practical task and the human undertaker. The crucial feature here is that action and urge do not correspond (as they frequently do in the natural order), which is why these practical emotional commentaries cannot be construed as direct action tendencies. Where practice is concerned, it is never enough simply to want to do something because there is always the stumbling block of skill. Practical actions are performative achievements – hence the perverse truth of the sayings 'he's a natural' or 'she's a born x', which testify that some very difficult skills seem to come rather easily to rare individuals.

Physical tension witnesses to our concern about practical mastery. There is enhanced attention, readiness and self-control which is manifestly associated with delicate tasks. Many tongues protrude when threading a needle; children sub-vocalise on their first maths problems; and only the exceedingly well practised can open a champagne bottle without holding it at arm's length and grimacing in anticipation. Such tension reduces reaction times and is recorded to increase in motorists when overtaking or in pilots upon take-off and landing.[37] Tension, of course, is not an emotion itself, it is merely a sign of our involvement in situations which place a demand upon our skills. It is interesting that it is also characteristic of spectators, who hold their breath, bite their knuckles and physically 'will' some sporting skill to come off or other feat to be achieved. Thus, Frijda comments that '(t)enseness, it is true, is intimately related to emotion. It is somewhat in the nature of emotions to emerge when the situation cannot be resolved as smoothly and effectively as seems called for.'[38] Although this may apply to the other two orders of reality, its particular home is in relation to concerns about performative achievement in the practical order.

The claim made is broader than this. It is that there is a distinct cluster of emotions which are emergent here and which thus extends our overall

[37] Ibid., p. 40.   [38] Ibid., p. 41.

emotional repertoire. Those in question are the two strings made up of frustration, boredom and depression, on the one hand, and satisfaction, joy, exhilaration and euphoria, on the other. Certainly, these can be found in the other orders, for we can know both frustration and exhilaration in nature and society. However, there is something special about their emergence in the practical order. The task/undertaker relationship is quintessentially that of subject confronting object and what exactly goes on between them is known to the subject alone. Each task makes its own demand upon the undertaker if a skilled performance is to be produced. It thus carries its own standards which give the undertaker either positive or negative feedback. If performative achievement is a strong concern of the subject, then emotions 'occur at junctures where pre-formed plans and expectations have not worked. If, at such a point, a new piece of action can be made from available resources and skills, we make the necessary modification, carry on with the plan, and tend to experience the juncture joyfully. If, on the other hand, a problem has arisen that cannot be solved with current resources, we experience the juncture as dysphoric.'[39]

If we consistently fall short on a particular task, meaning that we cannot match up to objective standards of performative achievement, then frustration, boredom and depression ensue as emotional commentaries, leading *ceteris paribus* to its abandonment. The same is the case for tasks which are insufficiently demanding. Of course other things may not be equal: at school we are forced to continue with sport, art and music for quite a time, whatever our performance, meaning that many of us are condemned to the frustration of our own incompetence. Alternatively, in working life, a task may be so monotonously unchallenging that protracted application yields no intrinsic satisfaction, such that prolonged boredom and stultification is the outcome if this is inescapable work.[40] If, on the contrary, we perform well in relation to a challenging task, 'catching on' quickly, then the feelings of satisfaction, joy or even euphoria, themselves encourage further activity for the enhancement of competence. This is central to prowess in music, sport and art: it is what gets the competitive swimmer up at four in the morning for training and keeps the

---

[39] Keith Oatley, *Best Laid Schemes*, p. 399.
[40] A good example is provided by Adam Smith's discussion of work under conditions of an extreme division of labour: 'The man whose whole life is spent in performing a few simple operations, of which the effects are, perhaps, always the same, or very nearly the same, has no occasion to extend his understanding, or to exercise his invention in finding out expedients for removing difficulties which never occur. He naturally loses, therefore, the habit of such exertion, and generally becomes as stupid and ignorant as it is possible for a human creature to become', *An Inquiry into the Nature and Causes of the Wealth of Nations* (Cannon edn), London, 1904. vol. 2, bk. 5, ch. 1, p. 267.

musician to hours of daily practice. Equally, it is what sets the 'green fingered' at their winter gardening tasks, gets knitted garments finished and keeps people sitting under green umbrellas on river banks.

In other words, the sense of failure and sense of achievement are reflected emotionally. These emotions are commentaries upon our doings and, in the privacy of the subject–object relationship, they embody the standards of the inanimate object which cannot lie: golfers who discard sliced strokes can take little satisfaction in their faked scores. Certainly, we can continue to take pleasure in activities at which we know we will never excel, but we recognise this by withdrawing our involvement and calling these 'leisure pursuits' or perhaps by becoming avid spectators. This self-monitoring, in accordance with the emotional commentary received, is the key contribution of subject/object relations. The emergent first-order emotions affect and direct our continuation or cessation of the task in question, but their internal power is at least as important as this external causal influence. We learn to monitor ourselves in the practical order, to determine which achievements are important to us and this is a necessary step towards becoming second-order monitors of our ultimate concerns. In a crucial sense, it is in the privacy of our truth-telling object relations that we become a subject who is neither under the dictatorship of the body nor is the broken reed of society. In our dealings with the practical world, we not only learn something about our relations to it via our emotions, but we also learn something about ourselves and our powers to order our priorities in relation to emotional commentary. In this acquisition of standards, which are not physiologically inscribed, the practical order is again pivotal.

Thus the four features of knowledge characteristic of the practical order are very closely paralleled by the type of emotionality emerging there: (i) knowledge was procedural and not declarative, and here a 'feel for' is very closely allied to having a 'feeling for' which is also independent of language; (ii) knowledge was implicit and encoded through bodily skills and so too are feelings that stem from competence/incompetence and which register themselves in the same way; (iii) knowledge was a tacit and known in activity just as these emotions are also activity-dependent; (vi) knowledge was extensive of our bodily powers and so too it has been argued that our emotional repertoire is extended into a distinctive cluster of emotions. Where knowledge was concerned, this extension was held to be the key contribution made by the practical order and the same was maintained for the practical order in our emotionality through its introducing the capacity for emotional self-monitoring.

However, it is equally important to stress the extension of this cluster of emotions to include the spectator, who in a real sense is also a practical participant. Spectating is far from being a passive activity, as is evident at football matches, but is equally the case at music concerts, art exhibitions and chess tournaments. It demands its own tacit knowledge (often vocally shared with all and sundry), and its own emotional involvement. Spectating is itself a skilled achievement, involving an appreciation of what the task requires in terms of competence. The spectator reverberates, as does the player, to the emotional commentary on performative success or failure (together with gradations between them). Audiences display bodily tension, alongside players and conductors, as they anticipate crucial movements or moments and express their emotional satisfaction/dissatisfaction in applause and booing. In the same way too, dissatisfaction is related to cessation (either by walking out after the 'first half' or by progressively declining attendance) and satisfaction is related to increasing competence (through appreciation classes, buying specialist magazines, private practice with CDs, videos and the Internet, as well as through increasing attendance itself).

Since to be a good spectator or member of the audience involves an apprenticeship and a performative concern whose personal importance should not be underestimated, it is impossible to agree with Elster that musical emotions lack cognitive antecedents[41] and that in 'the case of music, we seem to experience emotion in something like a pure state, a qualitatively unique experience similar to the unique shade of red'.[42] Firstly, this disallows the fact that music (or art or sport) do not have blanket emotional effects upon people: a great (or for that matter mediocre) performance will leave the uninvolved completely unmoved. Testing this proposition would be simple; try swapping the audiences for a top football match with those attending a really good concert. Secondly, it disallows that audiences have served their tacit apprenticeship and only when they are both concerned about the performative achievement involved, and are able to assess the competence entailed, can they reverberate emotionally to performances in the practical order. Audiences require a lot of tacit skill before they can get caught up in virtuosity – of whatever kind. Thirdly, since audiences have both to care and to understand, they are self-selected by the self-same process that makes or breaks performers: the emotional feedback of boredom leads to cessation of the practice whilst enhanced satisfaction is what makes for the buff. Only by allowing for the engaged spectator as well as the active participant, can we appreciate the full role of the practical order in extending this cluster of emotions to all persons, through both their voluntary and their involuntary engagements with praxis.

[41] Jon Elster, *Alchemies of the Mind*, p. 270.   [42] Ibid., p. 405.

3   Emotional emergence in the social order

Once again it should be stressed that emotions are not a natural kind and that this section is addressed to those particular types of emotion which are essentially social in that they arise from people's relations to the social order. As such, they are emergent from *subject/subject relations*, but since the realist acknowledges that society cannot simply be reduced to 'other people', but entails emergent structural and cultural properties, then the key relationship here is between the individual subject and society's normative order. In all three orders it was maintained that standards were involved in the eliciting of emotions. These were the environmental threat or benefit in relation to the body in the natural order, and the task's ease or difficulty in relation to the undertaker in the practical order. The equivalent in the discursive order are judgements of approbation/disapproval that are rooted in social norms and which have an impact upon the social subject.

Thus, such emotions are defined as those which emerge from subjects' concerns in relation to society's moral order. As Greenwood puts it, 'it is an objective fact about many human emotions that they are socially constituted: that they are intrinsically social'.[43] That is the status claimed for the cluster examined here, which includes shame, remorse, pride, envy, jealousy and guilt. These are not socially *constructed* by the social imposition and individual appropriation of emotional labelling, but rather are socially *constituted* properties which are emergent from the internal relationship between the subject's concerns and society's normativity. Their emergence is thus dependent upon three factors: our subject status in society, the receipt of moral evaluations from the social order, and the conjunction between our personal concerns and the nature of society's norms.

Firstly, then, our subject status: it is just as ineluctable that we have subject/subject relationships in the social realm as that we had subject/object relations in the practical world and bodily/environmental relations in nature. The three together make up the human condition; they stem from our human nature and we would not be recognisably human in the absence of any of them. Yet, there is something distinctive about our lives in society which concerns our very status as subjects. In nature and in practice we could speak ontologically about factors which impinged objectively upon the human person. Thus the environment at any time was either dangerous or it was not, and this was a matter of objectivity for it was gauged by whether it damaged our bodies or was

---

[43] John Greenwood, *Realism, Identity and Emotion*, p. 142.

benign towards them – something which could be ascertained medically, that is without resort to human subjectivity. Similarly, a practical task was either difficult or easy, which again could be assessed by objective observation of performative achievements. These could be termed 'self-referring' properties of the two orders, where the questions which were relevant to emotionality were respectively 'can it hurt me?' and 'can it be done?'

Crucially, these situations were as they were independently of human evaluations of them: something did not become less menacing or testing because we subjectively viewed it as such. Certainly it was argued that people could be in cognitive error about such situations, but also it was maintained that they would pay for their errors, this objective cost being the main inducement to correction. This is entirely different for situations which could be termed shameful, because their being so depends upon our subjectively acknowledging them to be such. Nevertheless, they retain a real ontological status. Charles Taylor reserves the term 'subject-referring properties' for those which involve our subjective compliance. 'For shameful is not a property which can hold of something quite independent of the experience subjects have of it. Rather, the very account of what shame means involves references to things – like our sense of dignity, of worth, of how we are seen by others – which are essentially bound up with the life of a subject of experience. I should like to call properties of which this is true, like shameful, "subject-referring" properties. These are properties which can only exist in a world in which there are subjects *qua* subjects.'[44] Depending upon the social norms in operation, only certain actions are those which merit this negative evaluation. We can err here too, for example, by feeling ashamed at being short which is not within the area of our moral responsibility, nor is something of which we can morally repent. Nevertheless, where it is socially appropriate to be ashamed in a given situation, shame has no efficacy without the subject's concordance. (This is not to deny that societies can sanction unwanted behaviour, but without any concordance, all the individual feels is the punishment not the shame. They may of course feel shame at being punished but this does not entail being ashamed of the action which precipitated it.)

Were there not beings capable of this experience, such as those lacking any aspiration to dignity or ones totally indifferent to the regard of all others, then the concept of 'shameful' could obtain no purchase. This is quite different from nature's menacing, to which we may show personal indifference (after second-order reflection) but which will wreak itself

---

[44] Charles Taylor, *Human Agency and Language*, p. 54.

upon our bodies quite regardless. Instead, there cannot be any sense of remorse without the personal acceptance that I have done something wrong. Thus Taylor continues that it 'is only through our feelings that we are capable of grasping imports of this range at all. The fact that we are sometimes dispassionately aware of an import should not induce us to think that we could always be so dispassionately aware. That supposition is absurd. This is a domain to which there is no dispassionate access.'[45] Although there is no quarrel with this as a generalisation, it is crucial to the account being given here to explicate the confluence itself between subjects and standards. Otherwise we cannot account for why the same situation is one of shame to some and not to others. Society holds out innumerable norms without these gaining universal take-up. It is perfectly possible to be wholly indifferent about school achievement, whilst dispassionately recognising the standards and expectations involved. Thus, in order to say something more precise about the emergence of social emotions we need to go further into the nature of society's normative evaluations and into what individuals themselves bring to the relevant situations – which together account for the emergence of emotionality in the social order. After all, if no importance is attached to a subject's concerns we end up with yet another 'oversocialised view' of the social subject, and would not be talking about emergence but about unilateral social causality.

The cluster of social emotions does not occur independently of social forms of evaluative representations of our actions and ultimately of us. This is a matter of fitting caps and it is quite distinct from whether the subject assents that the cap fits him or her. Both elements are necessary for the emergence of a social emotion, but for the moment we will concentrate upon the hatter rather than the wearer. Ultimately, however social emotions 'are constructed or created out of the *joint commitment* to certain arrangements, conventions, and agreements by those who are parties to them'.[46]

From the realist point of view, normative conventions are not like some version of the social contract which acquires powers from its signatories, having none prior to this notional compact. Instead, such conventions and agreements are themselves culturally emergent properties (CEPs) which derive from past chains of interaction, but which, in any contemporary context, are pre-existent to, have relative autonomy from,

---

[45] Ibid., p. 62.

[46] John Greenwood, *Realism, Identity and Emotion*, p. 149 (my italics). The quotation continues, 'This is not, however, what is standardly claimed by social constructionist theorists: they claim that emotions are social constructions in the sense that they are constituted by, or are nothing more than, socially constructed theories of emotion'.

and exercise causal efficacy over the present 'generation' of subjects. Individuals confront them, they do not create them, although they may transform them.

Such social norms are attempted regulators of behaviour in society, but we must be cautious not to conflate the attempt with a successful outcome. The difference can be sustained by being clear about how the normative order works. Well established norms can be seen as a template which is slid across the total array of actions exhibited by members of society at a given time. As such, they both categorise our actions and attach evaluative judgements to them. Certain behaviours or relationships are represented to the subjects in question as being offensive, morally reprehensible and normatively unacceptable, above and beyond their legality. (Thus despite the law, negative evaluations may still be forthcoming for homosexuality among consulting adults, and beyond the law it is often commented that paedophiles have the toughest time in jail from their fellow prisoners.) In short, there are evaluative standards, but their effect is dependent upon our feeling bad if we fall short of them and good if we live up to them. This is very different from the pragmatics of, say, traffic control, which regulates behaviour by penalties for contraventions. The fine operates as a simple deterrent which does not rely upon the internalisation of a normative evaluation. Pragmatic controls do not depend upon our feeling anything (and if we do it is more likely to be annoyance at enforcement than guilt about the offence) which is why they can be exerted universalistically upon a population: they are one-sidedly extra-punitive and their effectiveness is independent of any corresponding sense of intra-punitiveness.

Normative discourse is about the moral evaluation of our comportment as acceptable or unacceptable, praiseworthy or blameworthy, and is not about labelling emotional states or about subjects' appropriation of labels. The obverse of this is that when we do feel something, it is about the nature of our circumstances and our relationship to them and not about naming our state. 'Anxiety is constituted by our evaluative representation of situations as threatening, not by our representation of our emotional state as anxiety.'[47] Still the question remains, what makes this normative discourse apply to us? Of course, it is there to be learned, like chemistry, although probably more people are concerned that we acquire table manners than mastery of the chemical table. Indeed they may succeed pragmatically simply by nagging, but without our feeling anything about the matter. Furthermore, no developed society (at least) has only one homogeneous normative register, so why do some evaluations,

[47] Ibid., p. 158.

like whether your behaviour matches that of a good Catholic, affect some people but not others? It is not enough here to invoke baptism and upbringing, for many cradle Catholics fail to attend Mass without feeling badly about it.

All of these questions point to the fact that an emergent property (here social emotions) depend upon a relationship. In addition to there being a normative order, we the subjects have to care about it, or at least about some of it. For social evaluations to matter – and without mattering they are incapable of generating emotionality – they have to gel with our concerns: 'an import defines the way in which our situation is of relevance to our purposes, desires, aspirations'.[48] Such concerns are not asocial matters which we bring to society (for example, from the other orders). Instead they are socially forged out of subjects' reflections upon what is important to them in their ineluctably social lives. 'They incorporate a sense of what is important to us *qua* subjects, or to put it slightly differently, of what we value, or what matters to us in the life of the subject. We also value other things, for instance going on living, which pertain to us qua living organisms. But our feelings of shame, remorse, pride, dignity, moral obligations, aspirations to excel, just because the imports they involve are essentially those of a subject, all incorporate a sense of what is important to us in our lives as subjects.'[49]

Generically, the most important of our social concerns is our self-worth which is vested in certain projects (career, family, community, club or church) whose success or failure we take as vindicating our worth or damaging it. It is because we have invested ourselves in these social projects that we are susceptible of emotionality in relation to society's normative evaluation of our performance in these roles. Our behaviour is regulated by hopes and fears, that is anticipations of social approbation/disapprobation. Simply to be a role incumbent has no such emotional implications – pupils who vest none of their self-worth in their school performance are not downcast by examination failure, just as the Uncle playing cricket is concerned about giving his nephews and nieces a good time and not about his score, which he may deliberately downgrade, for his worth in this context is that of a good Uncle not a proficient cricketer. As Elster put it, '*amour-propre* is the engine of Alchemies of the mind'[50] and, in its first meaning of legitimate self-respect, this feeling of worth is what is in the social balance. However, it is our own definitions of what constitutes our self-worth that determines which normative evaluations matter enough for us to be emotional about them. In strict parallel, what we are

[48] Charles Taylor, *Human Agency and Language*, p. 54.   [49] Ibid., p. 60.
[50] Jon Elster, *Alchemies of the Mind*, p. 417.

emotional about also makes it possible to know what constitutes the good life in society for particular people.

Thus, for the emergence of social emotions, it is not sufficient that society has normative register and that its members continuously pass a stream of evaluations on the comportment of fellow subjects: in addition we have to be parties to these social norms. Nor 'is it sufficient that I recognise certain actions as satisfying conventional criteria for offensive actions according to the semantics of such forms of moral commentary. In order to be angry, I have to *take offence* at another's action. I have to treat the other's action as reflecting negatively upon my reputation and self-worth.'[51] As in the other two orders, our emotions are commentaries upon our concerns and what they basically tell us is how we are doing in pursuing them in the social environment of which they are part.

Conclusion

This chapter ends by confronting all people with a dilemma. It arises because, as has been seen, every person receives three kinds of emotional commentaries on their concerns, originating from each of the orders of reality – natural, practical and social. Because they have to live and attempt to thrive in the three orders simultaneously, they must necessarily in some way and to some degree attend to all three clusters of commentaries. This is their problem. Nothing guarantees that the three sets of first-order emotions dovetail harmoniously, and therefore it follows that the concerns to which they relate cannot all be promoted without conflict arising between them. Hence, an evasive response to the promptings of physical fear can threaten social self-worth by producing cowardly acts; cessation of an activity in response to boredom in the practical domain can threaten physical well-being; and withdrawal as a response to social shaming may entail a loss of livelihood. In other words, momentary attention to pressing commentaries may literally produce instant gratification of concerns in one order, but it is a recipe for disaster since we have no alternative but to inhabit the three orders simultaneously, and none of their concerns can be bracketed-away for long. It is only on rather rare occasions that a particular commentary has semi-automatic priority – escaping a fire, undertaking a test or getting married. Most of the time, each person has to work out their own *modus vivendi* within the three orders.

In this context, it is not that 'the unexamined life is not worth living', but rather that it is unliveable. The human subject cannot live with a welter of contradictory first-order emotional commentaries, that is, ones

51 John Greenwood, *Realism, Identity and Emotion*, p. 167.

whose heeding would damage other concerns. It is this dilemma which provides the push towards second-order emotionality among all normal human beings (those who are not addicted, fixated by trauma or otherwise incapable of reflection).

What it entails is striking a liveable balance within our trinity of inescapable concerns. This *modus vivendi* can prioritise one of the three orders of reality, as with someone who is said to 'live for their art', but what it cannot do is entirely to neglect the other orders. Thus it is significant that enclosed congregations of religious, who are said 'to have renounced the world', all had Constitutions which minutely proscribed bodily relations (food, sleep, clothing, bathing, walking, custody of the eyes etc.) and closely regulated social relations (recreation, friendships, family contact, visiting etc.). Most of us have to work it out for ourselves, and the difficulties we experience probably account for public curiosity about how prominent personalities have done it – how long does the Prime Minister sleep, how hard does the Princess work-out, or even how does the President care for his dog? We know what questions to ask because, as fellow human beings, we know the problems that have to be resolved.

Yet, which precise balance we strike between our concerns, and what precisely figures amongst an individual's concerns is what gives us our strict identity as *particular persons*. Because these concerns can never be exclusively social, and since the *modus vivendi* is worked out by an active and reflective agent, *personal identity* cannot be the gift of society – except for those who believe that socialisation also regulates our extra-social relations and supplies a template of harmoniously integrated concerns which are internalised by passive agents. To subscribe to that view is to endorse the natural, practical and social orders as closed systems, where contingency can never challenge convention, where convention is never without an appropriate repertoire, and where a creative reflective response to unscripted circumstances is never required. Those of us who hold the world, including the social world, to be an intrinsically open system, can never accept with Rorty that socialisation is capable of going ' all the way down' and will therefore uphold the distinction between personal and social identity.

How a particular *modus vivendi* is forged by any particular person is the subject of the next chapter, which deals with the 'inner conversation' through which personal identity is shaped. What connects the two chapters is the argument that it is also through this internal dialogue that first-order emotionality is reflexively transformed into second-order emotional commentary.

7   Personal identity: the inner conversation and emotional elaboration

So far, three clusters of emotions have been discussed as emergent commentaries, relating to our physical well-being, performative achievement and self-worth in the natural, practical and discursive orders respectively. Matters do not end there with a series of immutable first-order emotions, ranked as it were, simply by their relative intensity. They do not because of our human powers of reflexivity; our capacity to reflect upon our emotionality itself, to transform it and consequently to re-order priorities within our emotional sets. That *there is some second-ordering process involved* commands broad agreement.[1] Thus Elster refers to it as 'transmutation', Greenwood as 'transformation' and Taylor as 'transvaluation', amongst those who have systematically dealt with second-order emotions. There the agreement ends, for two very different accounts are advanced about what the process of emotional revision entails. They turn out to have equal but opposite defects: one tends to rationalism (or rationalisation), whilst the other tends towards intuitivism.

On the one hand, there are (a) those who present this as a matter of *cognitive reflection* in which reason is brought to bear upon the beliefs underpinning first-order emotions, whose revision then leads to emotional re-direction (second-order). A typical illustration would be a person who goes into therapy to combat their agoraphobia, with the aim of strengthening their (partial) belief that open spaces are not really physically threatening and thus modifying their emotional response to their environment. Cognitive reflection thus arbitrates among our first-order emotions, re-directing them, such that only those with good reason to survive into the second-order do so, whilst those failing to obtain this *imprimatur* become weeded out. It should be noted here that the old head and heart dualism has thus been reinstated between first and second-order emotionality.

On the other hand, (b) there are those who decline this re-instatement

---

[1] This statement holds much better in the philosophy of the emotions and those discussed all tend towards a philosophical approach. Acknowledgement and analysis of a second-order is much less characteristic of the psychology of the emotions.

and who picture the process of emotional revisionism as *evaluative reflection,* in which the subject asks, if emotions are affective commentaries upon our situations, which of these have the greatest import for our greatest concerns? Since our highest concerns are about what we value most, then reflection is about which commentaries are the best guides to what matters most to us. Rather than trying to rationalise our first-order emotions, we evaluate them as guides to the life we wish to lead, and thus end up embracing some and subordinating others. A typical example would be the athlete who says to herself, 'no pain no gain': in no way modifying her belief about the painful feelings involved, but determining that this commentary will not govern her sporting life. It is not a process of rational optimisation in which the desired life is selected according to reason and then emotions are assessed for their goodness of fit. Instead, it is evaluative through and through, but *pathos* and *logos* work hand in hand at the second-order level.

(a) The first path, that of cognitive reflection, is taken by Elster and Greenwood in their accounts of second-order emotionality. The statements they advance are very similar as far as transformability is concerned. Thus Elster maintains that if 'emotions do not act like charms or enchantments but depend on beliefs, they are amenable to rational argument designed to change the beliefs'.[2] In exactly the same vein, Greenwood states that 'emotions can be rationally and morally appraised in terms of the beliefs upon which they are based, and the appropriateness of the emotion given such beliefs. In consequence many emotions are modifiable – at least in principle – by rational persuasion.'[3] Thus first-order emotionality is seen as an immediate affective response to present-tense circumstances, whilst rational reflection modifies the second-order emotions which survive into the future-tense. Greenwood's version is very much in accord with Francis Bacon's dictum: 'affection beholds principally the good which is present; reason looks beyond and beholds likewise the future and sum of all'.[4]

To Elster this 'transmutation' operates either to make emotions more acceptable to agents themselves, that is better serving of their *amour propre,* or to make them more acceptable to others. In other words, reason works in an ingeniously 'Humean' manner to generate second-order emotions which are more tolerable to the self and its social context. Thus he argues that the 'first-order pain of envy can induce behaviour to

---

[2] Jon Elster, *Alchemies of the Mind,* Cambridge University Press, 1999, p. 56.
[3] John D. Greenwood, *Realism, Identity and the Emotions,* Sage, London, 1994, p. 156.
[4] Francis Bacon, 'On the Dignity and Advance of Learning', *The Works of Francis Bacon* (1875), Longman, London, vol. IV, p. 457.

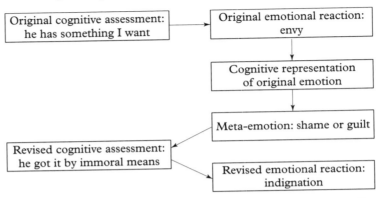

Figure 7.1 Elster's cognitive transmutation of emotion. Source: Jon Elster, *Alchemies of the Mind*, p. 99 and *Strong Feelings*, p. 109

destroy the envied object or its possessor; alternatively . . . it can trigger cognitive adjustments so as to enhance the perceived flaws of the other and thereby make him less enviable. The second-order pain can also induce a rewriting of the script . . . I can tell myself a story in which the other obtained the envied object by illegitimate and immoral means, and perhaps at my expense, thus transmuting the envy into indignation or anger.'[5] Elster's diagram (figure 7.1) highlights the cognitive nature of this process of reflection.

In *Strong Feelings*, however, Elster makes it clear that transmutation involves the ability of emotion to subvert rationality because reflection 'turns on the capacity to modify and distort cognition.'[6] Greenwood, as can be seen above, follows the 'Kantian path', for whilst no less cognitive, his account sees the transformation of the first-order into the second-order as a process of 'rational persuasion'. Although their second-orders end up in different places, being more rational (Greenwood) and more rationalised (Elster), in relation to their first-orders, the process of transformation itself is a uniquely cognitive one. This purely cognitive process, which works solely on the belief component of first-order emotions, is rejected here because of its reinstatement of the dualism between knowing and feeling, whichever is held to predominate.

(b) Instead, Taylor takes the evaluative path, and interprets the emergence of the second-order as a process of 'transvaluation' of the first-order. Thus he begins by rejecting the dualism endorsed above and notes

---

[5] Jon Elster, *Alchemies of the Mind*, p. 98.
[6] Jon Elster, *Strong Feelings*, The MIT Press, Cambridge, Mass., 1999, p.108.

that we 'often say "I know that X, but I feel that Y", or "I know that X, but I don't feel it". But it would be wrong to conclude that knowing can be simply opposed to feeling. What I know is also grounded in certain feelings. It is just that I understand these feelings to incorporate a deeper, more adequate sense of our moral predicament. If feeling is an affective awareness of a situation, I see these feelings as reflecting my moral situation as it truly is; the imports they attribute truly apply.'[7] Here the account starts to wobble, for how can (first-order) feelings 'truly' reflect our moral situation when, apart from anything else, Taylor does not regard our first-order emotions as having the last word? Indeed he cannot because the very process of 'transvaluation' is held to improve emotionality as a moral guide.

Taylor goes directly on to maintain that 'we can feel entitled to say on the strength of certain feelings, or inferences from what we sense through certain feelings, that we know that X is right, or good, or worthy, or valuable; and this even when other feelings or reactions fail to concur, or even have an opposing purport! "I know that X, but I feel that Y" does not oppose knowing to feeling, but rather reflects our conviction that what we sense through certain feelings is valid or adequate, whilst it devalues others as shallow, blind, distorting or perverse.'[8] But what is the process which allows 'certain feelings' to preponderate over others which do not concur, and by which some are valued as 'deep' and others are demoted for their 'shallowness'? This is where the evaluative account is least satisfactory for it then succumbs to an ethical intuitivism which confers morality directly upon our emotions, as can be seen from the following quotation. 'Our emotions make it possible for us to have a sense of what the good life is for a subject; and this sense involves in turn our making qualitative discriminations between our desires and goals, whereby we see some as higher and others as lower, some as good and others as discreditable, still others as evil, some as truly vital and others as trivial, and so on.'[9]

Its basic error is to conflate our concerns with our emotional commentaries upon them. Concerns are judgements of worth and cannot be reduced to our human reactions towards them. Conflating worth with being can only result in anthropocentrism[10] because it elevates our epistemic judgements over the ontological worth of their objects. Although emotions are undoubtedly of moral significance because they provide the shoving power to achieve any ends at all, their goals (intensional objects) may be completely unethical: doubtless the Nazis regarded their sense of

---

[7] Charles Taylor, *Human Agency and Language*, Cambridge University Press, 1985, p. 61.
[8] Ibid., p. 62.   [9] Ibid., p. 65.
[10] Andrew Collier, *Being and Worth*, Routledge, London, 1999.

the good life as 'higher', 'good' and 'truly vital'. Blasi[11] seems quite correct in discounting the notion of 'moral emotions' and maintaining the distinction between the two terms by arguing that the moral significance of emotionality rests upon it being harnessed to ends justified by other means as moral. However, it would be wrong to see this criticism of moral intuitivism as leading us straight back to cognitive revisionism. The evaluative approach can be shorn of this intuitive element if the objects of the emotions are given a more robust and realist role.

The morphogenesis of second-order emotions

There is much that can usefully be gleaned from Taylor's discussion of transvaluation *per se* to contribute towards an account of the emergence of second-order emotionality. (This is particularly the case because transvaluation paradoxically dwells upon our emotional fallibility rather than upon the intuitive acuity of emotions.) Transvaluation entails *progressive articulations* of our first-order emotions. To begin with many initial feelings may remain fairly inarticulate, such as a diffuse feeling of guilt about our relations with an elderly parent. In such cases we may seek further understanding, by interrogation of self and of circumstances, and through this the feeling may be transformed one way or another. It might dissipate upon further inspection; it may intensify as we appreciate the significance of neglect; or it could diminish if we find that to do more would be to the detriment of other duties. 'Hence we can see that our feelings incorporate a certain articulation of our situation, that is, they presuppose that we characterise our situation in certain terms. But at the same time they admit of – and very often we feel that they call for – further articulation, the elaboration of finer terms permitting more penetrating characterisation. *And this further articulation can in turn transform the feelings.*'[12] (my ital.)

There is real emotional elaboration going on here which is very different from the action-replay which Frijda describes: 'If relevant event features generated emotion in the first place, recurrence in thought of these features may be expected again to be responded to in a somewhat similar fashion.'[13] This would be a case where inner experimentation yielded reconfirmation, but since evaluation is involved this is not the necessary outcome. Suppose we felt trepidation about giving an after-dinner speech and on the action replay the same emotion surfaced. Upon its reoccurrence we might well remind ourselves that we give plenty of other

---

[11] Augusto Blasi, 'Emotions and Moral Motivation', *Journal for the Theory of Social Behaviour*, 29:1, 1999.   [12] Charles Taylor, *Human Agency and Language*, pp. 63–4.
[13] Nico. H. Frijda, *The Emotions*, Cambridge University Press, 1993, p. 256.

talks without apprehension, and tell ourselves that next time we will simply pretend it is another routine lecture.

Moreover, first-order articulations may simply be wrong about the import which something has for us; we can be afraid of things that are not fearful, be disturbed about a performance which is not disturbing and be ashamed of what is not shameful. There is a getting it right and getting it wrong which is similar in the natural, practical and social orders, for things are as they are and not just as we take them to be. The very act of offering oneself a second-order articulation serves to 'open the question whether this characterisation is adequate, whether it is not incomplete or distortive. And so from the very fact of their being articulated, the question cannot but arise whether we have properly articulated our feelings, that is whether we have properly explicated what the feeling gives us a sense of.'[14] Second-order revision can thus be indefinitely elaborated as we analyse further our understanding of imports and discard previous interpretations, both of which are transformative movements in this process. From feeling rejected by our teenage children's obvious preference for the company of their peers, we can reflect upon the restrictiveness of our own dependence and then take pleasure in their new independence, new things to talk about and new social skills.

Thus the movement from first-order to second-order emotionality entails a shift from the inarticulate to the articulate, from the less adequate to the more adequate characterisation and from initial evaluation to transvaluation. The process can thus be represented as the morphogenesis of the emotions and expressed on the usual diagram[15] which incorporates prior conditioning, interaction and elaboration as occurring over time:

Prior experience conditions first-order emotions
T1

               Articulation and re-articulation
          T2   T3
                         Elaboration of second-order emotions
                                T4

Now the middle element (T2 to T3) of the morphogenetic cycle is always made up of interaction, which is conditioned by prior factors but is never determined by them. Exactly the same is maintained for second-order emotionality, only the form of interaction is unique. It is internal and takes the basic form of 'I says to myself says I', which is the popular characterisation of the interior conversation.

[14] Charles Taylor, *Human Agency and Language*, p. 64.
[15] Margaret S. Archer, *Realist Social Theory: The Morphogenetic Approach*, Cambridge University Press, 1995, especially ch. 6.

The two crucial questions here are 'Who is talking to whom?' and 'About what?' Both need to be answered if an account is to be given of the *process* of emotional morphogenesis, rather than just noting the emergent effects. The internal conversation, as analysed by the American pragmatists, and particularly by Charles Peirce,[16] can be employed unslavishly to gain purchase on those inner deliberations whose outcome is emotional emergence. Such deliberations are of particular importance here, because three clusters of (first-order) emotions have been disengaged in association with the natural, practical and social orders. Yet, as has been repeatedly stressed, most of the time most of us live in the three orders simultaneously. Therefore, one of the tasks which falls to everyone is to determine how to deal with the affective commentaries coming in from the three orders to inform very different kinds of human concerns – in physical well-being, performative achievement and self-worth. *These concerns are real: not to heed the relevant commentaries may be deleterious to them, and yet nothing guarantees their compatibility.* On the contrary, to heed our physical fears could well lead to performative incompetence or to behaviour of which we are ashamed in many different contexts. It is maintained that this major problem can only be overcome if each human being arrives at some relationship between their ineluctable concerns with which they can live. This will entail disengaging ultimate concerns from subordinate ones.

But this ultimate affirmation can only be made after evaluating the consequences for self, taking account of the positive and negative costs to be borne and establishing how much we care. It is this that we do, fumblingly and fallibly through the internal conversation. Basically we 'test' our potential or ongoing commitments against our emotional commentaries which tell us whether we are up to the enterprise of living this rather than that committed life. Since the commentaries will not be unanimous, the conversation also involves evaluating them, promoting some and subordinating others, such that the ultimate concerns which we affirm are also those with which we feel we can live. We may of course be wrong, or circumstances may change, which is why the conversation is ongoing and why the second-order will be progressively revised and elaborated over the life-span of everyone.

Let us look more closely at the interlocutors in this inner conversation which Peirce sees as 'a dialogue between different phases of the ego'.[17] His basic conversational partner to whom thoughts are addressed is the 'You', one's future self as a second person. Thus a person's 'thoughts are

---

[16] For an interesting extension of this work see Norbert Wiley, *The Semiotic Self*, Polity Press, Oxford, 1994.

[17] Charles Peirce, *Collected Papers of Charles Sanders Peirce*, vol. 4, para. 6.

what he is "saying to himself", that is saying to that other self that is just coming into life in the flow of time'.[18] Since the current 'I', the agent of all action, is spontaneous and free, because 'I' can define any situation regardless of habit or precedent, 'I' am nevertheless trammelled for 'I' must know that my future self consents – otherwise there is inaction because the 'You' will soon move down the line and become the 'I'. Hence 'your self of one instant appeals to your deeper self for assent'.[19] At this point, Peirce makes the 'You' in the future, who is thus both ontologically and logically distinct, very committed to the rules of the community. This is not endorsed here for it seems that precisely one of the things that the 'I' and the 'You' have to sort out between them is the nature and degree of their affiliation to the community, versus other concerns. Nevertheless, he seems substantially correct that the assent of the 'You' has to be sought and that this takes place in a dialogue (iso-morphic with interpersonal conversations), in which the grammatical 'You' is a second person direct object, much as another person might be such an object. The 'I' can address instructions to the future self – 'I will never let You do that again' – but intra-personally as interpersonally, assent is still needed and sought, even though it may later be withheld or withdrawn.

Conversely, the 'You' can also address the 'I', for like the conversational other, it can see the 'I' more clearly than it sees itself and can be highly critical of it – as in 'when will you stop' or 'can't you be quiet', where the grammatical 'You' in this case is nominative and subjective. Here the 'You' anticipates the time at which it will become the 'I' and indicates the self it seeks to become.

There is one adaptation which is introduced, since the Peircean conversation involves only the 'I' and the 'You', and this is the historical (non-Meadean)[20] 'Me'. Since the 'Me' is all the former 'I's' who have moved down the time-line of future, present to past, it functions as the known to both 'I' and 'You' as knowers. As such it serves as a memory bank of all the past emotional commentaries which have been run past it. Having had its moment of choice, it is now inactive, but it serves as a con-stant reference point in the dialogue, providing data for both other selves – thus the 'I', referring to the 'Me', can say 'I know that was awful', or the future 'You' referring to the 'Me's' experience might say to the 'I', 'You

[18] Ibid., vol. 5, para. 421.   [19] Ibid., vol. 6, para 338.
[20] George Herbert Mead's 'Me' is too overburdened with social normativity because of its association with the 'generalized other'. This prejudges precisely what is at issue here, namely the relative importance attached to the discursive order versus that of the natural and practical orders. See also J. Habermas, 'Individuation through Socialization: on George Herbert Mead's Theory of Subjectivity', *Postmetaphysical Thinking*, Polity Press, Oxford, 1992, which shares the same tendency.

know you couldn't go through that again.' Thus reflexively, the object 'myself' serves as a store of all first-order emotional commentaries on past concerns. These will be activated by both 'I' and 'You' in their dialogue, for much of their joint deliberations about our deepest concerns will have to review these commentaries and negotiate their transvaluation.

The conversation: ultimate concerns and emotional commentary

The dialogue is a dialectic between our human concerns and our emotional commentaries upon them. Its outcome at any time is the designation of certain concerns as ultimate ones to us, but also ones with which we can live. The dialogical process is one which aligns our predominant concerns with our pre-eminent emotions, but in this process both elements will undergo modification because of the interplay between them. Yet although they are interrelated, both retain relative autonomy and therefore one does not become the dependent variable of the other. As was seen for the three sources of concern, these are not derived from our emotions towards them. Thus our unavoidable concerns with our physical well-being, performative achievement and self-worth derive from our necessary relationships with the environment, with the inevitability of practical work and with the ineluctability of occupying some positions in society. Emotional commentaries were thus upon something independent from emotionality itself.

Where they are decisive is in determining *how much* we are concerned about these various matters, which cannot but be of some concern to us as human beings. Our ultimate concerns retain their relative independence because, to a significant extent, they represent a 'ranking' of the three primary sources of concern. Yet precisely because these can be ranked differently, they exercise no dictatorship over humanity's emotional attitudes towards them. Conversely, emotional commentaries do not possess hegemony either: that about which we are most deeply concerned is not simply that to which we are most emotionally attracted, otherwise there would be no dialogue or deliberation but only a monologue from the passions. The emotions stand neither in the role of the Freudian Superego nor of the Id: they retain their part as commentaries upon something other than themselves. In other words, at the second-order level, they do not lose their property of intentionality: they are about states of affairs (or potential ones) which are not emotionally self-referential.

Thus, the dialogue cannot be construed as driven either by *logos* or by *pathos*: instead they intertwine within the conversation. In form, this dialogue is more like internal experimentation between thought and feeling. The interplay between them is an interior examination of future scenarios to discover if and how the two can fit together and live together in alignment, were certain concerns to become designated as a person's ultimate ones. Nor do the 'I' and 'You' represent one or the other (thoughts or feelings), for although in the conversation *logos* poses questions and *pathos* gives its commentary, both the present and the future self make use of each of them. The conversation is passionate and cognitive through and through. And this is how it must be, for the whole purpose of the dialogue is to define what we care about most and to which we believe we can dedicate ourselves.

Procedurally too, just because the conversation takes place using words (the private use of the public linguistic medium), care must be taken not to stack the cards in favour of *logos*. Firstly, words themselves can be infused with passion; they do not condemn us internally, any more than in our interpersonal exchanges, to being dispassionate conversationalists. Secondly, words themselves depend upon the non-verbal images they summon-up and often need supplementing with pictures of future reality. So too, part of the conversation will be wordless, as the various parts of the self jointly contemplate their past, present and future emotional reactions by reviewing, reliving or imagining the quality of their feelings. The 'agenda' of the 'I' and the 'You' is to produce a joint articulation of their ultimate concerns, as ones to which the self can be wholeheartedly attached: but since this is about caring, which entails both an external 'object' and a subjective commitment, the outcome itself will be a blend of *logos* and *pathos*.

The start of the dialogue (meaning wherever it is taken up again in time, since it is life-long), presumes no solidarity between the 'I' and the 'You': if the opposite were the case, their consensus would make the conversation redundant. Hence, whatever 'I' now think to be of great worth can be questioned by the future self – 'So what will happen when you're past your athletic peak?' Similarly the 'You' may propose enhancing some commitment in future time, to which the 'I' replies, 'I can't live like that: this is hard enough.' What the conversation is about is exploring the terms of a workable degree of solidarity, which is what we mean by personal integrity or wholeheartedness.

There are three significant moments which can be distinguished in every phase of the conversation: these have been termed Discernment, Deliberation and Dedication. The DDD scheme is what occupies the middle stage of each morphogenetic cycle and generates second-order emotionality as its elaborated outcome.

1   Discernment

Here the subject and object, the 'I' and the 'You', work together to review the projects in which they might invest their caring. Emotionality, as a commentator, indicates clearly that to which we are drawn. Thus 'emotions can be thought of as involving a certain manner of apprehending or viewing the world, our emotions create interests and purposes for us in the world, and our interests and purposes are clearly important for determining who we are and how we see ourselves'.[21] Certainly it is the case that no project could move or motivate us unless it were anchored in such feelings.[22] Nevertheless, however strongly we are drawn to a particular project, there are other concerns which have to command our attention, such as the state of our health, the need to earn a living and other people's views of our relationships, actual and potential. This is not to oppose our emotional inclinations to some 'reality principle', because we can become very emotional indeed about these other considerations; at the prospect of ill-health, unemployment or a broken engagement. It is merely to say that many things have to go into the 'balance' which cannot be tipped simply by that about which we feel most strongly at any moment: and many of these are counterbalancing concerns which emanate from the other two domains of reality. Momentarily I may be consumed with fury about the motorist who has just cut-in, but my future self would not sanction that I decide my future life on this basis.

Because concerns are not reducible to emotions, then it is important not to turn the commentary into some sort of moral direction finder, which was the tendency found unacceptable in Taylor. Certainly our 'emotions make it possible for us to have a sense of what the good life is for a subject'.[23] But our sense may be mistaken and that to which we are drawn can be morally vicious, for people are emotionally drawn to apartheid and paedophilia. Emotions are morally significant, because without their shoving-power we would get little done, but they are not always morally good or right and therefore the notion of 'moral emotions' should be resisted.

Whatever projects are reviewed for shaping our lives, such as staying in good shape, improving our skills, having children or writing books, the basic question which the 'I' and the 'You' have to thrash out between them is 'Do I care enough to live with it?' This involves a judgement of *worth* about the project and a judgement of our emotional *attraction* to

---

[21] Justin Oakley, *Morality and the Emotions*, Routledge, London, 1992, p. 64.
[22] However, we should beware of taking Oakley too literally in the above quotation. Emotions do not 'create interests and purposes', but rather highlight these by means of their commentaries.   [23] Charles Taylor, *Human Agency and Language*, p. 65.

it.[24] Discernment is a preliminary review of those projects we have reasons to deem worthwhile. As they are mentally paraded, the 'I' and the 'You' register their emotional commentaries about self adoption of them. Thus, the 'I' may single out the worth of becoming a doctor, but the 'You', consulting the 'Me's' experiences, responds 'you couldn't do it – you've always been too squeamish'. Matters can work the other way around. Some project is highlighted for its immediate attractions, but in solidarity the self cannot endorse its worth: 'yes, he's great company, but he wouldn't make a good husband', or, 'Sure it's pleasurable, but "You" can't spend your whole life knocking a little white ball around.' We can go wrong on both counts, about our estimates of what is worthwhile and how strongly we are drawn to it, but this is what the conversation is about, and since we can revise both judgements this is why it recurs. Such was the case with Dorothea in *Middlemarch*. She is dazzled by the seeming worth of Casaubon's intellectual project and is so attracted by becoming associated with it that she marries him, subordinating all other concerns to being his amanuensis, only later to admit herself mistaken about its worth. Conversely, in *Jude the Obscure*, it is not the worth of his academic project which is doubted, hence his pursuit of it; but in the end he brutally acknowledges his inability to see it through, given his circumstances.

Moreover, the 'I' and the 'You' are making a judgement on one project in relation to others which may already have their conjoint approval – we might want to succeed in all the projects listed at the start of the last paragraph. This is one reason why it seems preferable to talk about our ultimate concerns in the plural, rather than of a 'moral career' which is implicitly (though not necessarily) in the singular. For the 'I' and the 'You' have to determine 'Do I care enough to live with it?' *given* their other actual and potential commitments. Their enterprise is to establish an overall *modus vivendi*. We can often watch our younger colleagues as they struggle to juggle family and academic aspirations, both of which they discern to be worthwhile and desirable. Yet, sustaining their *modus vivendi* often finds them deciding that having a second child is simply not on.

At any time a life entails the things we are doing, the things we have done and the things we could do, which relate to the 'I', the 'Me' and the 'You' respectively. Discernment is basically about putting together the reflective, retrospective and prospective through a dialogue which compares and contrasts them. The 'I' is never free of some concerns because it is living in all three orders of reality: those to which it ministers are partly involuntary due to physiological, practical, structural and cultural factors

---

[24] For a full discussion of the relationship in terms of a realist theory of ethics, see Andrew Collier, *Being and Worth*, Routledge, London, 1999.

and are attributable to decisions which the self has made about them in the past. For example, this is what determines the house in which we now live. The 'I' is constantly engaged in a review of its current concerns, though this is rarely how people think of it themselves, but it becomes more recognisable if we put it in terms of the constant stream of internal awareness about our satisfactions and discontents – which are our emotional commentaries upon our present position. When living in any particular house, we continuously register its inconveniences and attractions which crystallise into decisions about home improvements or *ceteris paribus* into a decision to move.

During this moment the self is no practitioner of resignation (that may come later as an outcome of the reflective sequence), but *pro tem* the unsatisfying can always become better and the good can become best. The 'I' expresses its condition through *appeals* ('I can't go on like this') and *aspirations* (the 'I wishes' and 'if onlys') which are addressed to the 'You', since change can only occur in future time. It buttresses its judgements with contrasting retrospective reflections by drawing upon the memory store of the 'Me'. In other words it summons up past commentaries upon variations in its condition and this itself is a sifting process. On the one hand, the 'I' may recall, 'Wasn't it good when – I only weighed 8 stones – used to go backpacking – when I was single.' This review may be sufficient to convince the 'You' to go on a diet or to regard its family size as complete, thus, heeding the aspiration 'I wish I were slim and fit again', or the appeal 'I can't go through another pregnancy.' On the other hand, the 'I', being a learner, also counts its blessings retrospectively; 'Thank goodness I never have to sit another examination – that the children now sleep through the night – that I learned a trade', and these serve to reinforce his or her commitments.

But the assessment of concerns is wider than a past/present contrast because both the 'I', and especially the 'You', are aware of other possibilities that such a framework forecloses. Specifically, the 'You' is a source of commentary on current and potential concerns and it persuasively unreels hypothetical future scenarios with their associated emotional charges. Fundamentally the 'You' is concerned with conservation and change and it works through *reproaches* and *challenges*. Where a valued concern is at stake, the 'You' reproaches the 'I' for endangering it. It says, 'How could you . . .' and runs through a scenario in which continued recriminations or jealousy break up a partnership; it pleads, 'You can't do that again' as the ex-smoker longs for a cigarette and it projects the image of rapidly being back up to 40 a day; it chides, 'You must stop it' as we turn into workaholics or heavy drinkers and it imagines our burn-out or the atrophication of our skills. But the 'You' also challenges the 'I' by bringing up an agenda where good is turned into best and new possibilities are explored: 'If you care so much about x, then why don't you . . .'; 'So what's stopping you from . . .'; 'You've never even tried . . .' Again scenarios are unreeled of a life which changes in response to taking certain concerns more seriously.

Discernment is an inconclusive moment of review. At the most it begins to clarify our relationship to reigning concerns by bringing to the surface our predominant satisfactions and dissatisfactions. As a conversation it is restricted to opening gambits, to one line appeals, aspirations, reproaches and challenges. The 'I' and the 'You' are invited to consider statements, evaluations and proposals, but during this moment, the respondent is a recipient: not a passive one for they will mull over and play over the scenarios which have been put to them and be receptive to the commentaries their emotions supply. Nevertheless there is no dialogue backwards and forwards between them: this is what pushes reflection forward in the next moment.

2   Deliberation

The moment of Discernment served to highlight our concerns without discriminating between them. It can be seen as a logging process in which actual and potential items of worth are registered for consideration. Sifting of a negative kind is involved, because out of the plenitude of possible concerns available to a human being, the various aspects of the self review a restricted set. Only those which have been logged-in constitute topics for further deliberation. Both moments are ones of non-solidarity for the self. In the first we have seen the 'I' appealing and presenting its aspirations to the 'You', and the 'You' issuing its reproaches and challenges to the 'I'. In the second moment the 'I' and the 'You' engage in a dialogue which begins with non-solidarity but whose purpose is the achievement of the solidarity, as they thrash out the concerns with which the self can live.

For example, someone may feel so committed to their unrequited love, that for a time their physical languishing and the fact that their self-worth has plummeted to zero are uncomfortably accepted. Eventually they have to ask themselves whether they can live this way – 'alone and palely loitering'. This means questioning both 'is she really worth this?' and also ' do I care so much for her despite becoming ill, unemployed and a laughing-stock?' The expression 'calf love' implies that the solidarity of the self re-emerges as concerns are re-negotiated, either by discerning that she lacks sufficient worth to merit such misery or that the misery itself is intolerable. In Victorian novels, this is when the character takes himself off to

deepest Africa for a bachelor life as a stiff-upper-lipped colonial adminis-
trator.

Deliberation is a matter of question and answer, of re-questioning and
following-up, of amended questions and modified responses. The basic
question, which can be posed by either the 'I' or the 'You' is 'How much
do you care about. . .?' and the answer eventually has to be in terms of
'How far will You go?' There are many opening couplets. The basic question may gain the response 'Well, it's not as important as it once was',
which is followed by, 'Is it really worth You keeping it up?' – 'Not if I could
φ instead.' In an uncomplicated dialogue, this is how concerns are dis-
carded – a skill falls into disuse, a practice is discontinued, a friendship
lapses or a commitment is transformed. Alternatively, the initial response
may be 'Does it really matter?' – 'Of course it matters. You don't have any
alternative' – 'But I do, You just won't consider . . .' – 'I have, but it's too
risky' – 'But you know it needn't be if . . .' Here the challenge, which may
be over changing jobs, is inconclusive. Both the 'I' and the 'You' project
rival scenarios (which is the importance of day-dreaming) and the dialogue continues over a contested concern. Finally, consider the string
where the first response is 'I do care very much', followed by 'Then You
ought to be doing more . . .' – 'I would like to do more, but x' – 'You've
done without x before' – 'Well, it would be great if I could . . .' Here the
two appear to be negotiating their way to accepting a challenge.

These dialogues go from the extreme of discarding projects, through
contesting concerns, to the opposite pole of preliminary determination.
In themselves these represent a very provisional ranking of the concerns
with which the self can live, or more precisely feels they can live. In the
process concerns have been progressively compared and clarified and the
relative worth of various projects has emerged. Yet the self still needs to
know, as best it can, whether it really has the emotional shoving power to
see these through. Take a short-term example. Just before the Millennium
I walked through central London, so appalled at the number of homeless
people that paying £1 for the *Big Issue* seemed a totally inadequate
response. 'How far will You go?' Well, since the street party of the century
lacked appeal, the project surfaced of volunteering to work in a Shelter for
that week. However, the self needs to test the determination much further
and does so through a continuing conversation which is an exploration of
costs.

Here the 'I' and the 'You' seek to pin one another down by extracting
an explicit emotional commentary on what could be called 'terms and
conditions' of the concern, whose worth is now no longer under dispute.
As far as working in the Shelter was concerned, the 'I' appealed that it
had just finished a book and doubted that it could summon up the nec-

essary energy, which the 'You' reproached as pusillanimous. But the 'I' rejoined with a list of costs that would fall on others who represented on-going commitments: 'the boys will want to come home' and 'I've promised to give my husband a hand with x'. When Mother-in-Law became ill, the Shelter project was decisively sidelined: other costs had prevailed. The aim is always to ascertain how costly the enterprise would be, given that discussion has not already ruled it out as too costly. To make headway with their negotiations, questions come from both the 'I' and the 'You' and are of the kind, 'Could you do without x?', 'Can you keep it up?', 'Is it worth it?', 'Could you do it again?' etc. The 'You' reflects upon the 'I's' experiences of itself, the 'Me', and the 'I' assesses the strength of the 'You's' inclinations. Together they re-prioritise their concerns, demoting and promoting, cutting the coat as the emotional cloth allows.

3   Dedication

This represents the emergent moment to which the previous two moments of dialogical interaction have been leading intra-personally. Analytically it entails a 'ranking' of the three orders, by virtue of the concerns belonging to them, which means that the subject has to arrive at a personal judgement of worth and one with which he or she can live emotionally. The expectation is not that subjects themselves will see their internal conversation in terms of a debate about objective worth for this would be illegitimately to impose the way the world is upon our knowledge about it and deliberations towards it. It would be one version of the 'ontic fallacy' which subordinates our epistemology to being a reflection of ontology and entails equal and opposite defects from the 'epistemic fallacy': we are no more compelled to see and to know things as they are than we are free to make what we will of any state of affairs.[25] Both fallacies fundamentally make either reality or knowledge the epiphenomenon of the other, withholding real autonomy from ontology or epistemology respectively, and thus denying the interaction between them. Nevertheless, although the existence of the three orders of reality does nothing which constrains people to think of them *as such*, and indeed it cannot because these themselves are only particular (epistemic) descriptions under which reality is known, nevertheless these aspects of reality, however they are known, exert a claim upon our concerns. This is necessarily the case because such is the nature of the world and of our

---

[25] See Roy Bhaskar, *Reclaiming Reality*, Verso, London, 1989, pp. 157–8, on the 'ontic fallacy' and Andrew Collier, *Critical Realism*, Verso, London, 1994, pp. 76–85 on the 'epistemic fallacy'.

constitution in relation to it that we are ineluctably and thus involuntarily embroiled in these three kinds of relationships, whether they are perceived as such, interpreted under other descriptions, or not even articulated at all.

Because *some* relationship is necessarily the case, then under their own descriptions people have to come to terms with them, with all of them.[26] What they *may* see themselves as doing at the moment of dedication is vowing themselves to a single concern which guides their lives. They are not mistaken if they think this: merely relatively unaware that this is actually a predominant concern which is so strong that it has adjusted the other two types of concerns unproblematically to it. Yet, adjusted them it necessarily has. However, it seems very rare indeed for such a process to take place in complete discursive unawareness: fanaticism is the closest we come to it, but it is hard to see even the fanatic as being *wholly* undeliberative or totally unaware of the accommodations which have necessarily been made with the other orders. For example, any kind of religious, military, political or ideational fanaticism always has implications for bodily comportment, restraint, discipline, or a studied cultivation of neglect. These are known even if they are not deemed to be of much importance as part of the 'terms and conditions'.

In general this is what the conversation is about when we come to the moment of dedication. Analytically it entails the *prioritisation* of the three orders, via an evaluation of concerns pertaining to them, and an *accommodation* of the concerns belonging to the other two orders, in such a manner that the subject believes this to be a working balance – one with which he or she can live as their individual *modus vivendi*. This is done in their own conversational terms (i.e. under their own descriptions) and it is intrinsically fallible, yet corrigible. Constellations which are unstable because they are internally contradictory will be considered shortly. It is because the moment of dedication is one of prioritisation, that the very activity of accentuating our prime concerns is simultaneously one of counting the costs of relegating others. Thus dedication is a moment of conversational struggle, for the completion (*pro tem*) of the dialogue has to achieve both prioritisation and alignment.

It is quite common to find commentators who emphasise the role of our emotionality in fostering our commitments (not determining them for, as has been seen, the reasons for our judgements of worth have been considered during the deliberation phase). Thus Oakley asserts that

---

26 Someone may decide to go on a hunger-strike, risking death, but in so doing he or she also has to decide that they have no 'unfinished business' which cannot do without them, that their parents will not be intolerably harmed, that their dependants have some alternative form of provision etc.

we cannot give a rich and deep account of *attachment* without involving emotions. In support of this claim, consider initially people's impersonally conceived projects or objects. For example, could a person really be regarded as *committed* to fighting for multi-lateral nuclear disarmament unless they were taken up by care, concern, and interest for that cause, such that they respond with disappointment to breakdowns in arms talks between the major powers, and with hope and encouragement to the groundswell of support for what they believe in? Or, could we adequately describe Gauguin as single-mindedly *devoted* to his art unless we saw this in terms of a passionate attachment?[27]

He is quite correct because alternative accounts of the above actions which reduced commitment to activities alone, such as attending rallies or spending many hours painting, would be lacking precisely because they do not show any attachment to these projects. Indeed such actions could be performed for other purposes, perhaps as part of a sociological study or as occupational therapy. Nevertheless this is only to tell part of the story, the one which deals with accentuation, whereas the full story is in three parts, since it also entails accommodation and subordination, which is why there is a struggle. Importantly, it is also why emotional elaboration is involved because this is also the moment of the trans-valuation of our emotional commentaries.

To leave matters there would imply a very simple account of dedication (attachment, commitment, devotion etc.) in which the only question about the emotions, or about which the subject consults their commentaries, merely boils down to 'which is the strongest?' Now we saw at the end of 'deliberation', that the subject has not only to deem a concern worthy and to ascertain that they would feel a real sense of loss (grief, wistfulness, failure, unworthiness) were they not to prioritise it, but also that they have to consider its 'terms and conditions'. The rich young man of St Mark's gospel does so consider and goes away downcast because he cannot internally summon-up the financial price of discipleship, cannot sell all to obtain the pearl of great price. Sometimes the costs are found too high, and there is no commitment without cost. It is part of the human condition that, because of our ineluctable concerns *with* the three orders, we are condemned to struggle towards their alignment in dedicating ourselves to those things about which we are most concerned.

Here the internal conversation finds the 'I' and the 'You' conducting their final review which proceeds from a conjoint agreement upon 'That's what it takes', to a final consideration of 'Is it worth it to me?' and 'Can I see it through?' The dialogue now is about the costs of aligning other concerns and subordinating inner emotional advocacy for them, so the debate revolves around 'doing without' or 'doing with much less', and whether

[27] Justin Oakley, *Morality and the Emotions*, p. 65.

the two active aspects of the self can reach solidarity on the matter. Thus the dedication of the athlete to a commitment in the *natural order* has to take account of and accept costs in the practical order, as other skills and interests take a back seat and training requirements entail such things as taking the part-time work which fits in, giving up on late evening entertainment and ceding to the dictates of the timetable – the cost which *Chariots of Fire* was all about. Similarly, in the social order there are sacrifices which have to be made, whether or not social acclaim partially offsets these for the successful few, who nonetheless have to accommodate their friendships and family lives, often accepting such things as the postponement of having children. If such cases seem to involve only a very small minority of professionals, is the conversation so very different for those who wish to establish a different relationship with the natural order, such as vegetarians, greens or organic farmers? After all, even the commitment of keeping a dog entails trade-offs in the other orders – the places to which one cannot go and the people one cannot visit.

In parallel, the prioritisation of concerns falling in the *practical order* have their own sacrificial iconography: from artists various starving in garrets and Gauguin leaving his family in Paris to paint in Tahiti, to the archetypical ascetic monk. But this category also includes all of those intriguing sub-groups who organise their lives around canal restoration, ballroom dancing, vintage motors etc. and who 'make' their social life around this practical passion. It is this willingness to 'organise around' which is the hallmark of alignment at work. For example, the Catholic church's teaching in the encyclical *Humanae Vitae* (whose implications are satirised in David Lodge's aptly entitled *How Far Can You Go*) has left succeeding generations reaching accommodations between their religious dedication and their relationships to the body and to their interpersonal relations.

The trade-offs involved when priorities are vested in the *social order* also have their stock figure in the workaholic and his peripheral concerns for other things, but similarly a real commitment to raising children involves realigning other concerns, as well as precluding workaholia. This is so well understood by everyone that 'wishing to spend more time with the family' has become the stock excuse when politicians wish or have to step down.

The dialogue concludes when internal solidarity is achieved about prioritisation, accommodation and subordination. These elements are often expressed internally and represent a final check that we can live with them. Thus the affirmation, made by the 'I' in the present that 'It's too important not to ϕ', means the 'I' pauses to ascertain that 'You', who will be the executor, fully assents. Absence of solidarity indicates that the process of dialogue is unfinished and nothing can issue from it but shilly-shallying, rather like Groucho Marx's 'I'm an expert on quitting smoking; I do it all the time.' Similarly the 'I' checks out the terms of accommodation – 'So x is going to have to take a back seat', again waiting for a last minute appeal for a stay of this execution. Finally sacrificial harmony needs sealing between the two on matters of subordination: 'So it hurts, so what?' requires joint acknowledgement.

Why does the dialogue finish here: after all the subject may be making an unwarranted judgement about the worth of her concerns or a mistaken one about her emotional ability to live with them. She may indeed, for this is always possible with any judgement, but there is still no arbitrariness in deciding to end a sequence of potentially endless evaluations which could never conclude with certainty. 'Terminating the sequence at that point – the point at which there is no conflict or doubt – is not arbitrary. For the only reason to continue the sequence would be to cope with an actual conflict or with the possibility that a conflict might occur. Given that the person does not have this reason to continue, it is hardly arbitrary for him to stop.'[28]

The internal conversation is fundamentally a process of forging *personal identity*. The subjects, meaning the different aspects of the self do not hold themselves apart from their concerns: potential sources of commitment only remain at arm's length whilst they are being inspected and alternative commentaries vie for a hearing during the moments of discernment and deliberation. Instead and in solidarity, the self comes to identify with her ultimate concerns. As the successive moments of the conversation culminate, 'It is these acts of ordering and of rejection – integration and separation – that create a self out of the raw materials of inner life.'[29] It does not matter in the least that these concerns do indeed originate outside ourselves in our ineluctable relationship with the natural, practical and social orders, for in dedication we have taken responsibility for them and made them our own. We have constituted ourselves by identifying the self as the being-with-these-concerns. The self and its reflexive awareness have been continuous throughout the conversation, but on its completion *the self has attained a strict personal identity through its unique pattern of commitments*.

The emergence of second-order emotions

By this act of personal-constitution, *a new source of imports has come into being*. This is what proves crucial for the subsequent transvaluation of our second-order emotions. It is what leads to emotional elaboration – to the

---

[28] Harry G. Frankfurt, 'Identification and Wholeheartedness', in his *The Importance of What we Care About*, Cambridge University Press, 1988, p. 169.   [29] Ibid., p. 170.

emergence of second-order emotionality. Because of our identification with our ultimate concerns, it is the import of our emotionality upon them which counts henceforth. Because this is our personal identity we articulate imports in the light of our commitments which define us, and this brings with it a transformation of emotional commentary. Thus if one of our ultimate concerns is wife and family, the emotional commentary arising from an attractive occasion for infidelity will not just be the first-order desire for the liaison, but emotionally we will also feel it as a threat, as a potential betrayal of something which we value more. Its emotional import is literally that of a *liaison dangereuse*. In an important sense, we are no longer *capable* of the simplicity of a purely first-order response: reactions to relevant events are emotionally transmuted by our ultimate concerns. Think, for example, of the commitment to writing a book and of how this filters our responses to otherwise pleasurable activities. We tend to feel irritability at the telephone ringing, even whilst acknowledging that it is a wanted caller; we can feel resentment in having to respond to what we simultaneously accept are other quite legitimate calls upon us; and disinclination to break up a weekend with what we know would be pleasant company. These events can no longer be taken 'straight', they come to us coloured as distractions and our responses to them are generally distracted.

Our commitments represent a new sounding board for the emotions. They both mean that we see things differently and feel them differently. Devoted parents see objects and events from the child's perspective, feeling alarm for them at what will alarm them (rather than what is alarming to the adult, such as a big wave) and experiencing enjoyment through their child's enjoyment, for they can 'enter-into' fairgrounds, flumes or pantomimes through the door of their commitments. Sometimes we are very aware of the transvaluation, particularly at times when mentally we can contrast the same event 'with or without' the commitment involved. Imagine driving along a lonely coast road with the light falling and having difficulties finding a B and B; we are not perturbed for we can drive on to the next seaside town for accommodation. Now put two young children in the back seat and, as the light fades and the cafés close, finding that vacancy becomes a matter of urgency; we can feel real trepidation, even whilst knowing quite well that if alone spending the night in the car would be at worst uncomfortable.

Since transvaluation is literally changing our feelings because the emotional commentary is now directed to our constellation of committed concerns, it is not surprising that we have some awareness of the difference in the commentaries received. After all we only have to be determinedly dieting for a few days to have feelings of temptation towards the forbidden list. The meaning of temptation itself implies a degree of commitment, otherwise the attitude is simply can one get away with an infringement, but an internal commitment means that it is ourselves we let down and even self-deception has an intrusively objective reference point. The awareness coming from transvaluation may appear imbalanced and 'overdone' to observers, for example the self-righteousness of some new ex-smokers or the enthusiasm of the 'born again', but it is probably an unintended externalisation of a new and deep internal satisfaction. Equally, some transvalued feelings appear perverse and surprising, such as very work-oriented people who feel resentment and anger at being ill, or those parents who, given a break from the children, spend it worrying about them. There can indeed be over-investment in transvalued feelings, as with people who are said to 'live for' their families or careers, to the extent that others wonder whether they need such concerns more than the object of concern needs them.

The committed person can never be fully care-free (in excess of those first-order concerns which are part of the human condition), because they have acquired a prism on the world which refracts their first-order emotions. Their responses are sieved through their caring and little is untinged by it. Certainly they can give themselves short holidays – a cup of coffee and the crossword before the day starts, a railway novel, or a trip without the children, but for the real carer, these are registered as time-out. This makes caring sound like strenuous puritanical business. It is not because it brings its own rewards and ones which do not entail deferred gratification. Nevertheless, it is true that maintaining the ultimate concerns arrived at by the end of an internal dialogue requires cultivation. There appear to be both retrospective and prospective mechanisms which serve to reinforce dedication. These relate to reinforcing transvalued feelings themselves and to developing an environment in which they can flourish.

Retrospectively, the dedicated life takes up an increasingly distanced stance from his or her previous first-order emotions and their commentaries, *for the past itself becomes transvalued*. The person may actually view this in 'before and after' terms and wonder at its past doings, with a variety of feelings – wry amusement, indulgence or profound guilt. The past 'Me' can seem like someone else, and the present 'I' may devoutly wish that such was the case. Graham Green's whisky priest in *The Power and the Glory* progressively embraces his loss of self-worth and endorses his love of God as his ultimate concern, which will lead him to martyrdom. During this transmutation, he initially treasures his old photograph of the well-fed and well respected Father of his immaculate flock, at a time when his vocation had seemed to entail little sacrificial subordination of physical or social well-being. As his ultimate concern becomes ultimately demanding, his feelings towards the photograph are transformed into non-recognition, and its eventual loss is simply to be separated from a reproachful irrelevancy. This process of transvaluing one's past life is closely linked to the 'terms and conditions' negotiated in the internal conversation and especially to those activities, interests or attractions which were assigned to subordination. The autobiographical confessions of many of the Saints are often suspected of exaggerating their past transgressions, just as the evangelical 'testimony' seems to revel in blackening the person's past. This is very much the outsider's view: the insider reverberates much more closely to John Henry Newman's words adjusted for domain. 'The truest penitence no more comes at first, than perfect conformity to any other part of God's law. It is gained by long practice – it will come at length. The dying Christian will fulfil the part of the returning prodigal more exactly than he ever did in his former years.'[30] The Catholic practice of making a periodic 'general confession' (a life review) is a sacramental recognition that feelings of contrition will spread and deepen, precisely the greater the distance which separates present commitment from past attitudes and actions. Growing penitence is the growth of transvaluation, a realisation of how very contrary past behaviour was to what now concerns us most, and this is deeply affective in itself.

Penitence is not a preserve of the religious: self-reproach goes hand in hand with caring and takes a variety of affective forms. Ex-smokers can feel disgust at their previous dependency and also accentuate the degradingness of past searching for a stub when the packet was finished; political activists feel contempt for years of apolitical unconcern; vegetarians talk of physical revulsion from the self who once savoured a rare steak; greens shudder at once having worn a fur coat. The list is endless, because for every concern there is the transvalued condemnation of manifestations of unconcern, which is harshest upon the concerned person.

There are lighter forms of affect which are nevertheless isomorphic. A feeling of regret may attach to what are seen as wasted years or missed opportunities, such as not having bothered at school, not having had enough time for the children when young, or never having expressed love or appreciation to someone now dead. Such feelings mirror our commitments because they are reflections upon their antitheses. Someone who never came to care about education would not come to regret their early school-leaving. Alternatively, where the internal conversation led to the 'successful' displacement of an activity or the downgrading of a pre-

---

[30] Owen Chadwick, *The Mind of the Oxford Movement*, Adam and Charles Black, London, 1960, p. 153.

occupation, looking back upon them may simply bring a feeling of nostalgia. In sport, for example, there is a fairly common sequence of letting-go: competitor – player – spectator – follower, until the involvement may become past-tense. We can look back quite fondly on the days before we hung up our boots and allowed some skill to atrophy, since it presents no challenge to our current concerns. Finally, the commentary can include inner feelings of pride or superiority about dedication itself, where the 'I' and the 'You' congratulate one another on how well they are doing, or less vaingloriously, there may just be relief or thankfulness that it is proving possible to stay the course.

The effect of these retrospective feelings provides positive feedback reinforcing our commitments. Unintentionally they supply a transvalued commentary which strengthens our resolves. However, the same kind of reinforcement develops prospectively, as an unintended consequence of living out these same commitments, for the simple reason that our lives become organised around them. Every involvement has its own liturgical year, its open and closed seasons and its festivals. One of their explicit functions is to bring the like-minded together in celebration, but this often exceeds expectations in ways which have been intentionally harnessed by old religious sects and new religious movements alike, as well as by corporate organisations. Book fairs are not meant to be dating agencies, canal restoration is not intended to circumscribe friendships, political protests are not film guides, nor are pop festivals planned to influence our child-rearing practices. Yet a concern is the source of ripple-effects, spreading out over our way of life and insulating it as they go. The concerned need one another for it is only together that they can be themselves (expressing their full personal identities), sharing spontaneously, without self-editing. The most significant transvalued feeling here is that of discomfort. It is felt by political activists when in mixed ideological company and reported by feminists when in predominantly male gatherings struggling for political correctitude. The mechanism which circumscribes a way of life is bilateral. We know the edginess about entertaining those with other commitments than ours: the artificiality of censoring our language and opinions to avoid giving offence; the apprehension that the guests will start to 'go on' in proselitising vein, or the sheer boredom when they never stop talking about their children, football, local environmental planning etc. The concerned are drawn to one another but also thrown together, and this accentuation and protection of commitments is significantly regulated by the transvalued feelings themselves.

None of the above discussion of retrospective and prospective mechanisms implies that living out the conclusion of the internal conversation will be unproblematic: poignant regrets and powerful temptations often recur. However, when such a confrontation takes place, 'What the person's commitment to the one eliminates is not the conflict between it and the other. It eliminates the conflict *within the person* as to which of these desires he prefers to be his motive. The conflict between the *desires* in this way is transformed into a conflict between *one* of them and the *person* who has identified himself with its rival. That person is no longer uncertain which side he is on, in the conflict between the two desires, and the persistence of this conflict need not subvert or diminish the wholeheartedness of his commitment to the desire with which he identifies.'[31] Nevertheless breakdown and re-negotiation must be considered.

Instabilities of the second-order

To begin with, durable and effective transvaluation is an achievement: not one which can be accomplished straight away and not one which can necessarily be sustained. Not everyone attains to second-order emotionality: some remain confined, at least for long periods, to the first-order. For children and young people, the establishment of a stable second-order is a virtual impossibility because they know insufficient about themselves, the world and the relations between them. Certainly they have an internal conversation, but it is exploratory in nature, confined as it were to the moment of discernment. First-order commentaries vie for precedence amongst one another and often achieve it. Thus minors often go through a succession of short-lived enthusiasms; in parental vocabulary, 'it's only a phase'. Since what we are is what we love, nothing guarantees that we love in due order of worth. Young people often conclude just that: that there are limits to the full investment of self in ponies or pop, but it can only be concluded by trying it. These are like dry-runs at a second-order which are inherently unstable because new encounters drive proto-deliberations back to re-discernment. Schooling allows for a progressive exploration of our practical skills, a pinpointing of internal satisfactions (which are often institutionally pre-judged and over-directed because of formal achievements), but the school years are the same ones in which we are also exploring the social relations which give us self-worth, and the two processes rarely run in synch. The first serious love affair can have such first-order precedence, just as can the first essay into a social movement, that any nascent *modus vivendi* is overturned.

Nor is there any inevitability or maturational certainty about graduation to the second-order. Some can remain at the mercy of their first-order pushes and pulls, drifting from job to job, place to place and

---

[31] Harry Frankfurt, 'Identification and Wholeheartedness', p. 172.

relationship to relationship. Drift means an absence of personal identity and the accumulation of circumstances which make it harder to form one. Its obverse is not some kind of generalised conformity: its real opposite is the personal adoption of a distinctive lifestyle. The downward spiral of homelessness and addiction, is downward precisely because it condemns people to being pre-occupied with the satisfaction of first-order commentaries – the next night and the next fix. There is no inevitability here either, because reversal is possible, but it seems that it entails subduing the primacy of first-order concerns (literally a detoxification), before the internal conversation can truly begin to engage since it cannot be conducted in the present-tense alone.

Secondly, there are destabilised commitments resulting from an external change of circumstances, some of which are predictable, others being due to the contingencies of life in an open system. The most obvious and universal are those associated with the life-cycle, where for many people milestones consist in children going to school, leaving home, retirement, bereavement and ageing, which may preclude certain activities and, finally, entail entering care. Common contingencies include involuntary redundancy, chronic illness, bereavement, changes of political regime, economic recession, enforced migration, scientific transformations and so forth. In all of these cases a commitment may be unsustainable because its object has somehow changed or gone. These are nodal points which prompt a re-opening of the internal conversation. Sometimes there is resistance, rejection and disorientation associated with a new phase of discernment, as the person hankers after the *status quo ante*, often experiencing not just grief but anger and recrimination towards the cause of its disruption. Thus the bereaved are counselled not to make major decisions immediately. Those made redundant often go through a period of intensive job applications which, if unsuccessful, can lead to a radical disorientation in which there is no reason to get up in the morning, to dress or not to turn day into night. Things can become so dark that we cannot see there is a drawing board to which to return.

For those who can, and this again is circumstantial and sometimes driven by the need to keep faith with other ongoing commitments, the dialogue recommences and reaches a revised conclusion. Thus it was found that the majority of our mature Access students, entering as Sociology undergraduates at Warwick, were those whose circumstances had changed in the immediately preceding period, with the two most common precipitating conditions being children starting school or involuntary redundancy.[32] One of the consequences noted in this group is

[32] John Alford, *Journeys: Personal Morphogenesis*, Warwick University PhD, 1995.

transvaluation itself, as the new commitment acts as a new sounding board against which old concerns can reverberate incongruously (as is reflected in their high divorce rates). The fortunate ones have discovered a new best: the tragedy for the enforced migrant is the feeling that they have been forced to settle for second-best.

Where predictable changes are concerned, we are all given good advice about 'planning for retirement', but for some the promises on the back of the cereal packet of transvalued concerns for conservatories and cruises is not on. Academics are privileged in their ability to refuse it: some of us can live on our ongoing contributions, collegiality and conferences, though a generous dose of citations helps. Perhaps for most, age and infirmity are the real threats to destabilisation, because of the perceived futility of restarting the internal conversation. I once interviewed a group of frail elderly nuns who were scathing about the general assumption that they were serenely contemplating their beatific vision. Their complaint was the common agony of 'being useless' – and not seeing how this could be otherwise.

Finally, there are of course unstable commitments because everything in the internal conversation is *pro-tem*. We may simply have got it wrong in our assessments of concerns and costs, as we are mundanely reminded by those stickers reading 'a puppy is not just for Christmas'. Moreover, the dialogue is ceaseless and references above to it 're-starting' only indicate discriminable new cycles. In particular, the frustration of our first-order concerns may rebel against the terms of the second-order settlement: we can all miscalculate what it takes and know this as we succumb. Dialogically we can chivvy ourselves back onto the rails and perhaps the safest form of commitment is that which knows its own fragility, which the 'You' confides to the 'I', if it confesses it to no one else and looks impregnable. This is quite distinct from the waning or wearing out of commitment, as signalled by attenuating transvaluation and a questioning of the worth of our concerns. It is the well-trodden site of the mid-life crisis, in which the subject, perhaps with others, but necessarily through internal dialogue, manages to negotiate 'renewal' or to re-negotiate her re-partnering, re-employment and re-orientation. The noon-day sun is a busy place for the internal conversation: it would be a pity if this remained the domain of the counsellors rather than becoming of interest to the sociologist.

This chapter has been concerned with the vivid inner life of the subject and the emergent properties and powers of our personhood. It has emphasised our activities of self-making and the crucial role played by our emotionality in shaping our commitments which define our identities as persons. Yet in all of this it must not be forgotten that the account began with our ineluctable human involvement in the natural, practical and social orders, as the basic sources of our first-order emotions. The focus has been upon the voluntary element in this chapter, because every version of the 'oversocialised view of man', including 'his' post-modernist dissolution, grossly traduces our personal powers of living meaningful lives. Their conjoint denial of human autonomy and authenticity dismisses the power of personal identity to shape our lives around what we care about and commit ourselves to.

Nevertheless, we do not ever make our personal identities under the circumstances of our choosing, since our embeddedness in nature, practice and society is part of what being human means. From here three separate but interrelated accounts could be given of how involuntary placement in the three different orders intertwines with the voluntary human response. Since this is a work of social theory, the last section is concerned with the third order. Specifically it deals with our involuntary placement as *social agents* and how this affects the *social actors* whom some of us can voluntarily become. This is how we acquire a *social* identity which is part of our destiny, given human sociality. What will be insisted upon to the end, is that where the social person is concerned, due recognition is given to both terms, and what will be resisted to the end is that all that we are is a gift of society. Another way of putting this is that the internal conversation is never stifled: we remain active subjects in our own lives and do not become passive objects to which things happen – this is our human power of personal integrity.

Part IV

The emergence of social identity

8   Agents: active and passive

It is doubtful if anyone would dispute the fact that human beings are intrinsically social animals. Logically, however, nothing can be deduced from that concerning the role which society plays in making us what we are. Sociologically, this book represents an extended critique of two approaches which are diametrically opposed to one another about the part played by sociality in our constitution. On the one hand, protagonists of 'Modernity's Man' would basically answer that society contributed 'nothing' to our making: on the contrary, it is that pre-formed and atom-istic being who, along with others like him, generates the entirety of the social structure from his built-in disposition to be a rational actor.[1] On the other hand, advocates of 'Society's Being' would basically answer that society contributed 'everything' to our making: since this view contains no human beings as such but only social agents, formed from 'inde-terminate material', who energise the social system after appropriate socialisation. Equally basically, the position taken here is that society does indeed contribute 'something' rather than 'nothing' to making us what we are, but that this 'something' falls a good deal short of that 'everything', which would make all that we are a gift of society.

The last two sections of this book, which dealt with the emergence of *self-consciousness* and of *personal identity*, can be read as attacks upon the overly-social nature of 'Society's Being' and the overly-individual nature of 'Modernity's Man'. These critiques were symmetrical because in both cases it was maintained that their deficiencies sprang from the failure to acknowledge the impact of all three orders of reality upon our human development. Thus, the sociological imperialism which would present us as nothing but the gift of society was held to fail twice over. Firstly, its account of the self, which hinged on the charter 'nothing in the mind that was not first in the conversation',[2] was criticised because there was a great deal in the mind which derived from our natural and practical relations

---

[1] See Chapter 2 for progressive modifications of 'Rational Man' or *homo economicus*, to incorporate our normativity and emotionality.
[2] Rom Harré, *Personal Being*, Basil Blackwell, Oxford, 1983, p. 116.

rather than deriving from our discursive relations alone. Furthermore, contra the prime role assigned to socialisation in 'Society's Being', it was maintained that practice had primacy in the emergence of our *self-consciousness* – that *continuous sense of self*, which is crucial to our human properties and powers (the PEP which is the most fundamental of all PEPs). Secondly, this downward conflationary account of personal identity, founded upon tenets like a 'person is not a natural object, but is a cultural artefact',[3] was criticised because it made no allowance for our ineluctable human involvement in all three orders of reality – natural, practical and social – but confined our reflexivity to the social domain alone (thus conflating personal and social identity within this PEP).

Similarly, sociological individualism also failed twice over, but in different ways. In so far as it proffered an account of the *self*, this PEP was held to be innate and therefore none of our natural, practical or social relations contributed anything to its emergence. The main criticism was that those vital distinctions between subject and environment, subject and object and subject and subject, have to be viewed as pre-inscribed in the nature of 'Modernity's Man'. This is manifestly not the case with the neonate, and it was argued in chapters 4 and 5 that these vital distinctions took considerable learning. Attempts to rescue the case, by holding the ability to make such distinctions to be matters of maturational unfolding, were argued to come to grief because the activity-dependent nature of learning them could be experimentally demonstrated. Secondly, there are major difficulties in explaining from where an atomistic individual acquires the properties and powers which define strict *personal identity*. 'Preferences' were held to be our defining characteristics, but the key question remains as to where these come from, if reflexive monitoring of how the world is found to be is held to play no role in their formation? The latter-day suggestion that we choose our preferences only means the problem deepens, for on what grounds can we make this choice if not on the basis of our inescapable concerns with the natural, practical and social orders?

In contradistinction to both 'Society's Being' and 'Modernity's Man', social realism introduces a *stratified view* of 'the subject' whose different properties and powers (PEPs) emerge at each level. To anticipate, the four strata involved are the *self*, the *person*, the *agent* and the *actor*. The latter two are undoubtedly our 'social selves' which emerge respectively through our involuntary embroilment in society's distribution of resources and our voluntary involvement in society's role-array. However, they are themselves dependent upon the prior emergence of a *continuous*

---

[3] Ibid., p. 20.

sense of self and are co-dependent with the emergence of *personal identity*, which reflectively balances its social concerns with those embedded in the natural and practical orders of reality.

The emergence of our 'social selves' is something which occurs at the interface of 'structure and agency'. It is therefore necessarily relational, and for it to be properly so, then independent properties and powers have to be granted to both 'structures' and to 'agents'. This is what is distinctive about the social realist approach. It grants the existence of people's emergent properties (PEPs) and also the reality of structural and cultural emergent properties (SEPs and CEPs), and sees the development of agents and actors as relational developments occurring between them. Conversely, 'Society's Being' is a downward conflationary view in which 'agency' becomes an epiphenomenon of 'structure', whilst 'Modernity's Man' is a version of upwards conflation in which it is 'structure' which is the epiphenomenon of 'agency'.

To recapitulate, the human powers (PEPs) upon which structural (SEPs) and cultural (CEPs) powers impact, leading to the elaboration of 'agents' and 'actors', are those of the *self* and of *personal identity*. The *self*, that continuous sense of being one and the same subject, emerges *early in life* and is the source of reflexive self-consciousness which lasts throughout life – continually informing us that the things which happen to us ourselves and the things that we make happen, all pertain to the self-same being. Since practice rather than nature or discourse was accorded primacy in the emergence of the *self*, then this cannot be construed as a social process. Thus, to the social realist there is always a crucial distinction to be sustained between the evolving *concept of self* (which is indeed social) and the universal *sense of self* (which is not). Thus Mauss could trace the slow historical development of more individualised concepts of persons from the Pueblo's assumption of ancestral roles, through classical legal conceptions, to the fully individuated soul which became central in Christianity. Yet, at the same time as allowing for such progressive (and unfinished) *conceptual* individuation as a supremely social process, Mauss juxtaposed this with the *universal sense of self* – 'the "self" (Moi) is everywhere present'.[4] This constant element consists in the fact that 'there has never existed a human being who has not been aware, not only of his body but also of his individuality, both spiritual and physical'.[5] There is a

[4] Marcel Mauss, 'A Category of the Human Mind: the Notion of a Person; the Notion of Self', in M. Carrithers, S. Collins and S. Lukes (eds.), *The Category of the Person*, Cambridge University Press, Cambridge, 1989, pp.3f.

[5] Locke put forward a definition which has considerable intuitive appeal, such that a person was 'a thinking intelligent being, that has reason and reflection, and can consider itself as itself, the same thinking thing in different times and places' (*Essay* II, xxvii, 2). From Bishop Butler onwards, critics have construed such continuity of consciousness

persistent danger (or temptation to those who see sociology as a colonial enterprise – of the civilising mission variety) to try to absorb the sense into the concept and thus to turn human universals into cultural variables.

The best way of showing that the distinction should be maintained is a demonstration of its necessity – that is a sense of self must be distinct from social variations in concepts of subjects, individuals and so on because they could not work without it. Thus for anyone to appropriate social expectations, it is necessary for them to have a sense of self upon which these impinge such that they recognise what is expected of them (otherwise obligations cannot be internalised). Hence, for example, the individual Zuni has to sense that his two given names, one for Summer and one for Winter, apply to the *same self,* which is also the rightful successor of the ancestor who is held to live again in the body of each who bears his names. Correct appropriation (by the proper man for all seasons) is dependent upon a continuity of consciousness which is an integral part of what we mean by a human being. No generalised social belief in ancestral reincarnation will suffice; for unless there is a self which (pro)claims *I* am *that* ancestor, then the belief which is held to be general turns out to be one which has no actual takers! Nor is this situation improved by vague talk of 'social pressures' to enact roles or assume genealogical responsibilities. On the contrary, this is incoherent for it boils down to meaning that everyone knows what roles should be filled, but no one has enough of a sense of self to feel that these expectations apply to them. The implication for society is that nothing is done, for without selves, who sense that responsibilities are their own and who also own expectations, then the latter have all the force of the complaint that 'someone ought to do something about it'. Thus the strongest versions of socialisation theory (and in particular those 'oversocialised views of the men' proffered by downwards conflationists), ultimately cannot work with completely 'indeterminate material': it has to be determinate in this one way at least, that of acknowledging itself to be the same being over time.

Moreover, it is worth pointing out that the staple material of social change for this school of thought, namely role clash, also falls to the above argument. Unless a human being has a sufficiently continuous sense of self to recognise that both roles are theirs and that performing the two will

Footnote 5 (*cont.*)
exclusively in terms of memory and have then shown that memory alone fails to secure strict personal identity. See, for example, Bernard Williams, *Problems of the Self,* Cambridge University Press, Cambridge, 1973. A defence of a modified neo-Lockean definition is provided by David Wiggins, 'Locke, Butler and the Stream of Consciousness: and Men as a Natural Kind', *Philosophy,* 51, 1976, which preserves the original insight.

mean confronting their incompatibility sooner or later, then there is neither an individual dilemma nor any social impetus to avoid the impasse (by resigning, re-interpreting etc.). If Antigone did not know that she herself was both Kreon's niece and subject and also Polynices' sister, then she could have no dilemma about whether to comply with the family duty to bury her brother or to obey the royal prohibition on the burial of traitors. Given no continuity of consciousness, she might still lose her life through a fleeting act of compassion, but without dying a thousand deaths in anticipation. With no continuous sense of self, she could act in a way which saved her life, but would be incapable of knowing it, just as 'she' would not keep it *as* either a loyal subject or a disloyal sister, because both roles imply a continuous awareness of their on-going obligations. In other words, Greek tragedy relies upon a sense of self, even though ancient Greek concepts of persons are unlike modern ones.

So far, what has been emphasised is the indispensable contribution which our humanity makes to our whole lives, including our social lives, which are premised upon it, through furnishing this *continuous sense of self*. It is the necessary anchorage for the *person, agent* and *actor* alike, necessary that it is in order to unite a variety of life experiences, reflective evaluations, structural conditionings and normative expectations in one human being. But if this sense of self occurs close to the beginning of life, it was argued that *personal identity* could only emerge at maturity, once the reflective self had surveyed the full three orders of reality (natural, practical and social) and then determined where their ultimate concerns lay and how others were to be accommodated to them. On the one hand then, *personal identity* is obviously a property which depends upon the prior emergence of the self, because the latter has to secure the fact that the three orders of reality are all impinging upon the same subject. On the other hand, because one of the orders which impinges on each human being, and thus helps to foster their emergence as a person, is the social order, then persons, unlike selves, are not prior and primitive to our sociality. Nevertheless *personal identity*, which has been seen to result from the subject's considered response to its encounters with nature, practice and society, via the internal conversation, must not be confounded with *social identity*. Although the two are intertwined, and indeed their emergence will be presented as a dialectical process, personal identity is always broader than social identity because it is the former which both animates the latter and defines its standing relative to other concerns, which social concerns do not necessarily outweigh. Social identity is only assumed in society: personal identity regulates the subject's relations with reality as a whole. Therefore, of the two emergent human properties, the *self* stands as the alpha of social life itself, whilst the *person* represents its omega.

Hence society now needs to be introduced systematically into the middle of this account, to give it its proper due, and in order to answer three major questions. How do we become the kind of social beings that we are both collectively and individually, i.e. what are the social origins of 'agents' and 'actors'? How do we acquire social identities in the process? What is the relationship between our personal and social identities? The answers to all three questions will turn upon the interplay between three sets of emergent properties, those pertaining to people, to structures and to cultures respectively (PEPs, SEPs and CEPs), none of which are reducible to the others. In other words, these answers all relate to the 'structure and agency problem' and to the distinctive way of tackling it through the morphogenetic approach. If the preceding volume, *Realist Social Theory*, examined how the stratified self influenced society, bringing about reproduction (morphostasis) or transformation (morphogenesis), the present task is the reverse. However, it was insisted that these are two faces of the same process. A 'double morphogenesis' is involved: agency leads to structural and cultural elaboration, but is itself elaborated in the process. One can focus upon the actions responsible for remodelling structure and culture but it is equally important to recognise that the self-same sequence of interaction, which brings about social and cultural transformation, is simultaneously responsible for the systematic transforming of 'agency' itself. It is this latter which the present chapter and the next will seek to unpack in much greater detail in order to answer the three key questions posed about our sociality. To do so, it will have to be very precise about the referents of 'agency' itself, which is not just a pretentious way of referring to people, and to show equal precision in differentiating between 'agents' and 'actors', who are frequently treated as interchangeable in the literature. Only in this way can the resultants of our sociality – our emergent powers as 'agents' and 'actors' – be articulated with our human powers as 'selves' and our singular powers as the bearers of a 'personal identity'. Since our emergence as 'social selves' is inextricably related to the emergent properties of the social structures and cultures in which we find ourselves, and which we both reproduce and transform, then the processes involved have nothing in common with that misleading metaphor of 'becoming part of society's conversation'.

Little could be less true than the portrayal of becoming a social agent as being a matter of 'joining in society's conversation'. This is a misrepresentation in three important respects. Firstly, the notion of 'joining', unlike being conscripted, has distinctly voluntaristic connotations, whereas I will maintain that this involuntary process is in fact much closer to conscription. Secondly, the concept of 'society's conversation' implies a flattened field which is merely extrapolated from interpersonal dialogue to involve large numbers conversing at a distance. This is misleading for it implies that culture is not structured,[6] with the erroneous corollaries that, (a) any part of it is equally accessible to all, meaning that cultural capital is equally distributed, (b) that the beliefs and theories held in the sector which one 'joins' have no constraining or enabling effects because of their logical relationships with other theoretical and belief systems, and finally, (c) that different socio-cultural groups are simply alternative dialogical partners, rather than being those with vested ideational interests in the promotion of certain ideas and the demotion of others, through the generic process of ideological manipulation.

Thirdly, the representation of society as fundamentally 'conversational' misleads by neglecting all those structural properties whose influence is not mediated through discourse and whose effects are quite independent of whatever discursive conceptions may be entertained about them. This is witnessed by their causal efficacy being undiminished if no ideas happen to be held at all (just as inflation affects spending power regardless of how it is conceptualised, or if indeed it is conceptualised). In short, 'society's conversation' is pre-structured in terms of its access, its deliberations and its non-discursive context. It is a catchy metaphor which runs every risk of catching us out.

To illuminate the emergent relations between persons, agents and actors, I will return to complete the discussion of the reverse sequence around the Vygotskyan Square, whose first quadrant alone was examined in chapter 3 and which was then put on hold, whilst we examined the primacy of practice in the formation of the human self and the import of all three orders of reality in the subsequent emergence of the person. The full diagram is presented in figure 8.1 and much of this chapter will be devoted to elaborating a notion of the 'social self' which pays due respect to both parts of the term. This social self is viewed as an emergent identity and, moreover, one which does not emerge in a single movement. This is therefore unlike any form of conflationary theorising which basically pictures one move – simple aggregation in upwards conflation – socialisation in downwards conflation – or progressive specification in central conflation, of a sociality which is antenatally pre-inscribed and neonatally given precise definition.[7]

In fact, several moves are involved in order to give a full account of the emergence of the stratified social subject. What is meant by a full account

---

[6] That culture is indeed structured was the main argument of *Culture and Agency*.

[7] See Margaret S. Archer, *Realist Social Theory*, chapter 4, for a detailed critique of central conflation in this respect, as exemplified by Structuration Theory.

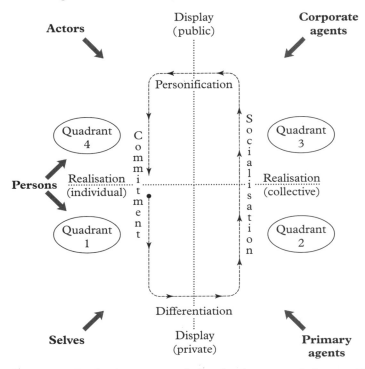

Figure 8.1 Realism's account of the development of the stratified human being

is one which is developmental, and traces the progressive elaboration of the stages by which the human self, whose own emergence has already been discussed, gradually comes to acquire a *social identity*, at maturity. There are three phases involved, which will be examined sequentially, but can be summarised as follows:

(i)   How society impinges upon the human self, i.e. the development of *Primary Agency*.

(ii) How Primary agents collectively transform themselves in seeking to transform society, i.e. the development of *Corporate Agency*.

(iii) How social reproduction or transformation affects the extant role array and thus the potential social identities available, i.e. the development of *Social Actors*.

In addition to this *developmental* account, which only takes us up to maturity, a *lifelong* account then has to deal with the dialectical relations between social identity and personal identity, which serve to monitor our subsequent commitments to, and doings within society.

The stratified social subject

Agents are defined as *collectivities* sharing the same *life-chances*. Because of this, (i) everyone is necessarily an Agent, since being an Agent is simply to occupy a position on society's distribution of scarce resources. However, (ii) simply to be part of a collectivity which is similarly placed *vis à vis* resource distributions cannot give strict identity, because it only makes one part of a group of those who are equally privileged or under-privileged. Agency is therefore a term which is always and only employed *in the plural*. (Usage in the singular, that is reference to a single Agent, thus denotes a collectivity or group.) By contrast, it is only social Actors who properly exist in the singular and who alone meet the strict criteria for possessing unique identity.

Actors, as will be seen in the next chapter, acquire their social identities from the way in which they personify the roles they choose to occupy. However, what array of roles is open to them at any given time, strongly conditions who may become an Actor at that time and thus who may acquire a social identity. Unlike Agency, which is universal to members of society, not everyone can succeed in becoming an Actor – that is in finding a role(s) in which they feel they can invest them-selves, such that the accompanying social identity is expressive of who they are as persons in society. Yet to explain any extant role array, it is necessary to backtrack to the collective interaction of Agents which were responsible for shaping it in that particular way. Over time, the Agent (plural) is therefore the parent of the Actor (singular) and facilitates their obtaining a social identity, which may have eluded Agents themselves.

Primary Agents: involuntary agency
(Quadrants 1–2) – differentiation

Thus far, a considerable amount of time has been devoted to the emer-gence of human beings who are self-aware and thus capable of reflecting upon themselves and their environment, which they understand to be something other than the self. The continuous sense of self was presented as developing through practice (chapters 4 and 5) and thus this emergent power (PEP) did not depend upon society.

Crucially important as this is, it is nevertheless also the case that, at the start of life (within Quadrant 1), the human subject simultaneously becomes enmeshed in society's structural and cultural properties. This occurs involuntarily, unconsciously, but inexorably. It happens because, at birth, we are all assigned to positions on society's distributions of scarce resources and it is through this involuntary assignment that we all become Primary Agents.

Agents, from the morphogenetic perspective, are agents of something. Baldly, they are agents of the socio-cultural system into which they are born (groups or collectivities in the same position or situations) and equally they are agents of the systemic features they transform, since groups and collectivities are modified in the process. Fundamentally this is a shorthand account of the morphogenesis of agency: the drama of interaction may be centuries long, but the storyline is a simple one of pre-grouping and re-grouping. In many respects, it is much the same story as the one which is usually called 'social stratification' and deals with the distribution of different 'life chances' to different collectivities.

Because of the *pre-existence* of those structures which shape the situations in which we find ourselves, they impinge upon us without our compliance, consent or complicity. The structures into which we are born and the cultures which we inherit mean that we are involuntarily situated beings. We have become English speakers before we can decide what language we would like to speak, and no other can then become our mother-tongue. We have become the beneficiaries of parental cultural capital or the victims of the poverty trap, prior to the development of our powers to monitor our situation. Because as humans we are 'late developers', compared with other species, the circumstances in which we remain involuntarily embedded throughout childhood condition what we project as possible, attainable and even desirable.

Thus, humanity enters society through the maternity ward doors and we immediately acquire the properties of Primary Agents through belonging to particular collectivities and sharing their privileges or lack of them – as males/females; blacks/whites; foreigners/indigenous; middle class/working class. In short, we are always born into a system of social stratification and it is crucial to my argument that 'privilege' and 'under-privilege' are regarded as properties that people acquire involuntarily and not as roles that they occupy through choice. It is defensible, I submit, to view these as positions rather than roles because of the impossibility of specifying any but the fuzziest and most highly contested normative expectations associated with them. Whilst systems of social stratification, especially rigid and unidimensional ones, may generate roles associated with particular strata (such as Brahmin, Nobles or Literati), this is contingent to stratification rather than being a necessary and internal feature of it. The quintessential features of all stratification systems, namely "propertylessness", "powerlessness" and the lack of prestige (together with their opposites), are thus distributions determining life-chances, rather than an array of roles with clearly defined normative expectations.

Hence Primary Agents are defined as collectivities sharing the same life-chances. Internal and necessary relations exist between these two elements, for this concept is irreducible to 'people plus some statistical probability about their future income, influence etc.' On the contrary, the major distributions of resources upon which life-chances pivot are themselves dependent upon relations between the propertied and the propertyless, the powerful and the powerless, the discriminators and the subjects of discrimination: and these, of course, are relations *between* structured and social groups. (Further interdependencies are entailed with other SEPs, e.g. property forms or political organisation and CEPs, e.g. forms of instruction or ethnic categories.) Equally, it is their activity-dependence upon collectivities which secures the notion of life-chances against reification. They are neither statistical artifacts nor hypostatised entities. However, to recognise them as emergents is to acknowledge their internal and necessary relationship over time with structured social groups.

In the morphogenetic approach, when we talk about 'Primary Agents' we are of course referring to people, but *not* to everything about people *since it is always and only employed in the plural*. Usage in the singular (i.e. reference to a social Agent) therefore denotes a group or collectivity. Everyone is inescapably a Primary Agent in some of their doings, but many of the doings of human beings have nothing to do with being an Agent. Membership of a collectivity, and thus sharing its life-chances, hardly exhausts what we mean by our humanity. Yet, Primary Agents are real, agency involves real actions by real people, which is why we can legitimately talk about agents acting. For agency is not a construct, not another heuristic *homo sociologicus*, which tells us about Herr Schmidt's positions but nothing about those like Herr Schmidt. Here in telling about those like Herr Schmidt as agents, we tell something real about them and their doings, but we have not told all about them as real human beings.

One of the most important things to probe is how the self-conscious human being reflects upon his or her involuntary placement. This comes gradually throughout childhood, as 'I' realise *my* privileged or underprivileged position *vis-à-vis* him or her – the objects and opportunities which they have and 'I' do not, or vice versa. Because this is a completely involuntary placement, the Primary Agent is an object to herself: there are many things that 'I' can discover about 'my' objective position. This is only possible because there is a self-conscious 'I' which can make discoveries about 'Me' as a Primary Agent. This 'Me' is indeed an object; it can have no strict identity, because it is merely part of a pre-grouped collectivity with determinate life-chances. The 'Me' is thus the object of society (which delineated its positioning along with others like it) and is also an object to the 'I', who has the capacity to learn about it and reflect upon it.

What it reflects upon is clearly not her sociological status as a Primary Agent, but rather the day-to-day manifestations of objective and externally determined life-chances. The most basic of these reflections is an early recognition of constraints and enablements – as in the child who questions 'Why can't I have more to eat, or a bike?', versus the one who learns that its 'wants list' is always much better satisfied than those of its peers. Both understand that they have a place in the social world which is independent of (and oblivious to) their own exertions. Scarce resources do not become less so through clamouring. Probably the recognition is earlier and easier where constraints are concerned, because the ready satisfaction of wants can more readily be mistaken for the effects of our egocentric powers.

However, the notion of 'self-worth', that supremely social concern which is operative in the discursive order, begins to develop as 'I' discover that there are all sorts of things about 'Me' which are positively or negatively regarded, despite their being involuntary. These are qualities which are objective to the self, for they belong to a different category from those things which 'I' can change through acting differently (as in promises of 'good behaviour'). With these discoveries that the 'I' makes about the 'Me' come various forms of affect. 'I' have concerns about the things 'I' see (whether bikes or birthday parties) and the emotion is the commentary passed when 'I' realised that they are not for 'Me' – or conversely are 'mine for the asking'. Frustration and gratification are therefore the basic affective responses to constraints and enablements.

Reflectively, the 'I' makes all kinds of discoveries about the 'Me', which are every bit as much a discovery as those which it makes about self-standing objects in its world. Just as the 'I' learns that there are 'dangerous' and 'pleasant' objects, she also learns that she herself has 'desirable' and 'undesirable' characteristics: the difference being that whilst the 'dangerous' may be avoided, the 'undesirable' has to be lived with. Thus, the 'I' may be distressed to learn that its 'Me' is considered to speak with the wrong accent, to be of a disfavoured colour or gender, and that nothing 'I' can immediately do will change matters. Alternatively, 'I' may be gratified that there is something about 'Me' which has to be lived up to in order to keep my position ('live up to my good name'). In both cases, considerations of self-worth have dawned, along with the consideration that both sets of characteristics in question, and the evaluations they receive, are external in origins. As a reflexive monitor, the 'I' may squirm inwardly to distance itself from the disfavoured 'Me': whether it can eventually do so will depend upon intra-personal, inter-personal and societal factors. Inter-personally, it will be highly dependent on the early caretakers (whose personal and social identity formation is complete) and upon whether they reinforce the 'I' ('You can become anything you choose') or weigh in on behalf of the 'Me' ('Know your place'). Socially, it will depend upon what objective opportunities there are for social mobility and to what extent structured and encultured positions condition who may avail themselves of them. Intra-personally, effects will depend upon the emergence and efficacy of personal identity.

Social mobility of Primary Agents exists in every social formation, and we will see that it is of variable numerical significance over history, though there has never been a formation without its 'self-made men'. However, what individual mobility does not do is to transform the relationship between Primary and Corporate groups, whose inter-relationship sets life-chances for the population in general. Instead, it is merely a reassortment of individuals within these confines.

The alternative, which does have systemic consequences, is to overcome their aggregate status as Primary Agents by developing collective action. Organised interest groups represent the generation of a new emergent property amongst people (a PEP), whose power is the very special punch that they pack as far as systemic stability and change are concerned. Only those who are aware of what they want, can articulate it to themselves and to others, and have organised in order to obtain it, can engage in concerted action to reshape or retain the structural and/or cultural features in question. These are termed 'Corporate Agents': they include self-conscious vested interest groups, promotive interest groups, social movements and defensive associations.

Primary Agents are distinguished from Corporate Agents at any time by lacking a say in structural or cultural modelling. At that particular time they neither express interests nor organise for their strategic pursuit, either in society or in a given institutional sector. As against the American pluralists,[8] the conditions for a group to acquire the status of Corporate Agency and make itself heard in the decision-making arena are far from being met universally. On the contrary, as Lukes has argued,[9] many collectivities of Primary Agents, whose members are similarly positioned, are deprived of having a say, are denied an effective say since the use of non-decision-making keeps their concerns off the agenda, and denied any say at all when social organisation serves to repress potential issues and thus the possibility of stating related demands. Such Primary Agents will not and cannot be *strategically* involved in the modelling or re-modelling

---

[8] As typified by Robert A. Dahl, *Who Governs? Democracy and Power in an American City*, Yale University Press, New Haven and London, 1961.
[9] Steven Lukes, *Power: A Radical View*, Macmillan, London, 1974.

of structure or culture. Nevertheless, to lack a say in systemic organisation and re-organisation is not the same as to have no effect upon it, but the effects are unarticulated in both senses of the word – unco-ordinated in action and unstated in aim. Collectivities without a say, but similarly situated, still react and respond to their context as part and parcel of living within it. Similarities of response from those similarly placed can generate powerful, though unintended aggregate effects, which is what makes everyone an agent – but it does not give all the properties and powers of Corporate Agency.

As an emergent stratum, Corporate Agency has powers proper to itself. This is the other reason why this notion of Agents cannot be rendered by any formula of the sort 'individuals plus resources'. Its typical powers are capacities for articulating shared interests, organising for collective action, generating social movements and exercising corporate influence in decision-making. Corporate Agents act together and interact with other Agents and they do so strategically, that is in a manner which cannot be construed as the summation of individuals' self-interest. To talk of strategic action implies that Corporate Agents are 'active' rather than 'passive',[10] that is they are social subjects with reasons for attempting to bring about certain outcomes, rather than objects to whom things happen. This is the case for the Corporate Agent but it may well be queried whether Primary Agents (lacking collective organisation and objectives) are not indeed of 'passive' status. Certainly they behave in that way – as people to whom things happen and who respond to happenings which are not of their making – *and whilst ever they do so* it is valid to analyse their agential effects as aggregate responses. Equally, however, it is important that they are not deemed intrinsically passive (i.e. of a kind incapable of activity), for their passivity itself represents a suspension, often a deliberate suspension, of their agential powers on the part of those Corporate Agents whose interests this passivity serves.[11] In short, this passiveness can usually only be understood in terms of the relations between Primary and Corporate Agency. Moreover, unless it is understood in this way, it then becomes incomprehensible how Primary Agents frequently do form themselves into new social movements and eventually become new Corporate Agents. Yet they do so regularly and especially when Corporate groups change or step up their strategic pressures.

Corporate Agency thus shapes the context for all Agents (usually not in the way any particular agent wants but as the emergent consequence of Corporate interaction). Primary Agency inhabits this context, but in

---

[10] Martin Hollis, *Models of Man*, Cambridge University Press, 1977.
[11] This is an instance of the third dimension of power delineated by Steven Lukes, *Power: A Radical View*, Macmillan, London, 1974.

responding to it also reconstitutes the environment which Corporate Agency seeks to control. The former unleashes a stream of aggregate environmental pressures and problems which affect the attainment of the latter's promotive interests. Corporate Agency thus has two tasks, the pursuit of its self-declared goals, as defined in a prior social context, and their continued pursuit in an environment modified by the responses of Primary Agency to the context which the latter confront.

At the systemic level this may result in either morphostasis or morphogenesis, depending exclusively upon the outcome of interaction, but since social interaction is the sole mechanism governing stability or change, what goes on during it also determines the morphostasis or morphogenesis of Agency itself. This is the 'double morphogenesis' during which Agency, in its attempt to sustain or transform the social system, is inexorably drawn into sustaining or transforming the categories of Corporate and Primary Agents themselves.

The basic question therefore which arises in relation to Social Agency is 'What are the conditions for the morphostasis or the morphogenesis of Social Agency?' Morphostasis demands an account of the divide between Corporate and Primary Agents and how some given pre-grouping of both is maintained during interaction, and morphogenesis calls for a discussion of how Corporate and Primary Agents are re-grouped in the course of interaction. It is only when the morphogenetic scenario engages that 'involuntary agency' can be left behind, that collectively Primary Agents can cease to be the largely passive recipients of their positions in the social distribution of life-chances and can begin to play an active part in their shaping.

The morphogenetic scenario has the following consequences for the 'double morphogenesis' of Agency: the progressive expansion of the number of Corporate Agents, of those who are counted among them and of the divergent interests represented by them, which thus results in substantial conflict between them. Accompanying this process is a complementary shrinkage of Primary Agents, due in part to their mobilisation to join burgeoning promotive interest groups and in part to the formation of new social movements and defensive associations, as some of them combine to form novel types of Corporate Agency. This can be represented by figure 8.2, a variant on the basic morphogenetic diagram.

The implication, at this stage, is that the 'I' and the dissatisfactions it experiences as it discovers and reflects upon the involuntary 'Me', can only transform the socio-cultural conditions (SEPs and CEPs) which gave the 'Me' that particular object status by elaborating the 'We' of collective action. This will not accord it a strict social identity, because the 'We' of Corporate Agency is still only a group whose members share its goals and organisation. But it is a stepping stone towards social

Social-cultural conditioning
of groups
_____
T1
     (Corporate Agency and
     Primary Agency)

          Group interaction
          _____
          T2   T3
          (Between Corporate Agents
          and Primary Agents)

                    Group elaboration
                    _____
                                    T4
                    (increase of Corporate Agents)

Figure 8.2 The morphogenesis of corporate agency

transformation which will then create a greater array of roles in which the 'I' feels that it can invest itself. In short, the activities of Corporate agents are the linking mechanism which narrows the gap between the 'I' and the 'Me' for increasing sections of the total population.

Corporate Agents – collective action: the double morphogenesis
(Quadrants 2–3) socialisation

Agents transform themselves in the process of pursuing social change. Another way of putting this is that the lines between Primary Agency and Corporate Agency are redrawn. Their *pre-grouping* into the two categories within a prior socio-cultural context gives way to their *re-grouping* at the precise point at which agency succeeds in challenging and transforming this context itself. The absence of such a challenge means that Primary Agents remain as they are. In quantitative terms, whatever tract of the population could not articulate its interests or organise with others for their pursuit remains unchanged. In qualitative terms, these Primary Agents remain 'passive': they can play no part in the strategic guidance of society because they literally have no say. As has been seen, this does not mean that they have no effect, but their influence is that of unco-ordinated co-action of those similarly placed, rather than co-ordinated inter-action of promotive interests groups with clearly defined goals. Another way of expressing this is that these pre-grouped Primary Agents are confined to the 'Me', and seek to make-out *within* the confines of the existing socio-cultural structure, rather than being able to become part of an active 'We', which seeks strategically to transform this structure in order to make it a better place within which to live.

Now, agential powers are always conditioned, though not determined, by the socio-cultural context in which people live. This conditional influence is transmitted by structural and cultural factors (SEPs and CEPs) shaping the contexts in which agents find themselves. The efficacy of this mediatory mechanism is entirely activity-dependent; that is reliant upon what agents make of these contexts. However, collectivities of agents cannot make just what they will of the situations in which they involuntarily find themselves. This is because the shaping of their situations also includes the distribution of those resources – both material and ideational – which are available to them. In other words, collective action is an emergent property of agency (a PEP), and the power to realise it can either be suspended or fostered by the nature of the systemic context in which agents are placed. Primary Agents have a vested interest in acquiring the powers of collective action in order to ameliorate the subordinate position in which they find themselves and to improve upon the inferior life-chances assigned to them there. Only in this way can they aspire to become active participants in society's decision-making. Only if they do, can they hope to re-design the social array of roles, such that the positions available to them are ones in which they willingly invest themselves, and thus become the kinds of 'social selves' with whom they can voluntarily identify.

What therefore requires examination are the socio-cultural characteristics of social formations which are hostile to the collective re-grouping of Primary Agents, versus those which predispose towards the development of collective action by enabling more Corporate Agents to disengage themselves as active promotive groupings. Such conditions can be analysed at a variety of levels – societal, sectoral, institutional or organisational – depending upon the interests of the investigator. What follows works at the most macro-societal level and seeks to delineate, in broad brush-strokes, a succession of three historical social formations which have had completely different conditional effects upon the potential for Primary Agents to exercise their powers to re-group themselves into Corporate Agents. Since such re-grouping is explained as a 'double morphogenesis', in which agency is transformed in the course of social transformation itself, then these three phases are themselves part of the story of the historical shift from enduring morphostasis to the inception and then acceleration of morphogenesis. The three phases to be sketched are crude snapshots which neglect the wealth of substantive variations within them. The only justification for advancing them is that they do dramatically capture three different historical moments in which structural and cultural factors impacted quite distinctively to restrain or to facilitate Primary Agents from assuming the powers of collective action. As such, they represent a trajectory in which the stable reproduction of agential pre-grouping progressively gave way to an intensification of agential re-grouping – that is to a proliferation of Corporate Agents (organised for and articulate about their promotive goals) and a corresponding shrinkage in the proportion of the category of Primary Agents.

(1) The pre-modern scenario In a thoroughly morphostatic scenario, the two types of Agents, Corporate and Primary are starkly delineated from one another, the distinction between them is maintained through interaction and proves long-lasting. What are taken as typical here are those 'old and cold' social systems, such as ancient India and China in Max Weber's classic portrayal of them. These hierarchical systems were characterised by a small elite of Corporate Agents who successfully confined the rest of the population to Primary status for centuries. This static situation basically arose because there was a conjunction between structural morphostasis and cultural morphostasis, which reinforced one another and simultaneously reproduced the dividing line between Corporate and Primary agency.

Substantively this meant that in the cultural domain there was one set of hegemonic ideas and a culturally dominant group of proficients (Brahmin or Literati), who had not (yet) encountered ideational opposition, and were thus able to reproduce ideas among the collectivity of Primary Agents, hence maintaining a high level of cultural unification throughout society. In parallel, structural morphostasis pointed to a monolithic form of social organisation, with the superimposition of elites and a heavy concentration of material resources, which prevented the crystallisation of opposition – this subordination of Primary Agents thus allowing the structure to be perpetuated. The reciprocal influence between the structural and cultural domains (SEPs and CEPs), reinforced the *status quo* and in the process perpetuated the preliminary divide between Corporate and Primary Agents by precluding their re-grouping.

Since the articulation of ideas (expressing interests) and the acquisition of organisation (for their pursuit) are quintessential properties of Corporate Agents, it is clear why this morphostatic conjunction repressed their proliferation through its influences upon interaction itself. First, the fund of cultural ideas which are *available* to Primary Agents engaged in structural interaction is extremely homogeneous. There are no visible ideational alternatives with any social salience for those with inaudible

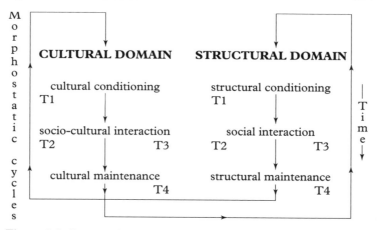

Figure 8.3 Structural and cultural configurations reproducing morphostasis in society and agency

social grievances to adopt and thus *articulate* the sources of their smoul-
dering discontent. Instead, by reproducing a stable corpus of ideas over
time, the cultural elite (the sole Corporate Agent in this domain) works to
produce a unified population. These Primary Agents may indeed be the
victims of perceptual power rather than voluntary adherents to consensual precepts, but in any case they are incapable of articulating dissident
views and of passing these over the intersection to stimulate structural
disruption.

In direct parallel, the social structure contains no developed marginal
groups or powerful malcontents with sufficient *organisation* to attract
the culturally disenchanted. Subordination means that there is no
differentiated interest group *available* to challenge the cultural conspectus, by exploiting its contradictions or developing diversified interpretations. Thus from neither side of the intersection between the
structural and cultural domains is the raw material forthcoming (i.e.
organised interest groups and articulated ideational alternatives) for
transforming Primary Agents into new forms of Corporate Agency.
Primary Actors can neither articulate projects nor mobilise for their
attainment. They cannot interact promotively but only re-act atomistically. Antipathetic reactions are restricted to the quiet cherishing of
grievances or doubts, the lone rebelliousness of sacrilege, insubordina-
tion, or personal withdrawal – geography and ecology permitting. The
major systematic effect of Primary Agency is purely demographic.
There are too many or too few (to feed or to fight), in the right or the
wrong places, which can create problems for the (morphostatic) goals

of Corporate Agents. In the long run, even this dumb numerical pressure of Primary Agents can be a big enough environmental problem to prompt Corporate policies intended to preserve stability, but ultimately inducing change. Slavery and conquest, as copybook solutions to demographic problems, also introduce group differentiation and cultural diversification.

This is not a necessary outcome and in any case the short run can last for centuries. So, the other question which arises is why do the Corporate Agents, the structural and cultural elites, whose composition was determined in a prior social context, tend to remain solidary, consensual and reinforcing, often to the point of merger? Of equal importance in this configuration is the fact that elites too are constrained by the absence of ideational or organisational alternatives, but each elite is simultaneously enabled by what the other is doing. Thus, the structural elite is trapped in the only kind of cultural discourse which is currently in social parlance; similarly the cultural elite is enmeshed by the monolithic power structure which is the only form of social organisation present. Given this conjunction, the two elites have no immediate alternative but to live together, but what is much more important is that they have every interest in continuing to do so. Here, cultural morphostasis (through the stable reproduction of ideas amongst a unified population of Primary Agents) generates an ideational environment which is highly conducive to structural maintenance. Structural morphostasis (through the control of marginality and the subordination of the mass of Primary Agents) in turn contributes greatly to cultural maintenance.

In whatever way the elites view one another (as out-and-out barbarians or jumped-up witch doctors), the opportunity costs of turning on one another to promote a different organisation or to stimulate new ideas is too high for this to become common practice. Quite the reverse. Because of mutual recognition of benefits received, the two domains often become progressively intertwined, with interlocking roles and interchangeable personnel – thus approximating to the superimposition of structure and culture which Weber described for Ancient India or China. Hence, where there is unopposed cultural traditionalism and unchallenged structural domination, Corporate Agency tends to congeal into one body, rather than developing fissiparous tendencies, and, as a single group is even more empowered to mould and manipulate Primary Agency by controlling its opportunities for and aspirations towards greater social participation. The exclusive position of those Corporate Agents which have been differentiated out becomes even more exclusive: meanwhile the mass of Primary Agents remains subordinate and powerless, because of their relational dependency, based upon their lack of resources.

The overall effect is to reinforce the stable composition of Primary Agency over time. Most of these systems appear to tolerate a certain amount of individual action, such as 'sanskritisation', where people manage to pass as members of higher castes through geographical mobility, but since this involves imitation of traditional lifestyles, it constitutes no threat to systematic stability. On the contrary, such individual mobility serves to reproduce the existing cultural conspectus. In so doing, those few Primary Agents who advance their individual positions do nothing to create a more diverse fund of ideas which furnishes Primary Agency as a whole with new cultural resources that would foster new forms of (transformatory) reflexivity.

(2) The scenario of Modernity *Grosso mondo*, the defining feature of Modernity is the progressive disruption of the morphostatic synchrony between structure (SEPs) and culture (CEPs). This can occur through the development of two types of disjunction: between cultural morphostasis and structural morphogenesis or vice versa, through cultural morphogenesis in the context of structural morphostasis. In both cases the net result is to increase the proportion of the population who number amongst Corporate Agents and to bring about a corresponding diminution of those who remain Primary Agents. However, the latter category remains large and embraces at least the vast majority of the rural population. *The distinctive agential feature of Modernity is not yet any version of pluralism, but rather that Corporate Agency becomes dichotomised into opposing groups, thus losing its unified character, which had been typical of premodernity.* On this scenario, it makes no difference in terms of outcomes for agency whether the disjunction is prompted by the onset of either structural or cultural morphogenesis. The two will briefly be taken in turn to illustrate this point.

In the structural domain, morphogenesis got underway for a variety of reasons (war, colonialism, mercantilism, political alliances, urbanisation) which were independent of any corresponding shift in the cultural domain, away from traditionalism. Whatever the cause, the key result for the middle element of the cycle, where the two domains intersect through social interaction, is a substantial growth in the differentiation of material interest groups. Depending on the types of structural development taking place, these groups are pre-occupied with self-definition, self-assertion and self-advancement through social interaction. But regardless of what kinds of structural change are being elaborated, the fact remains that all this activity initially takes place in a stable cultural context. *Culture provides no spur to the group differentiation of Corporate Agents which is the genetic motor of structural change, but rather acts as a drag upon it.*

The differentiation of new collectivities (for example the rise of the European leisured aristocracy), or more particularly their development into self-reflective, promotive interest groups, is itself restrained by cultural unification and reproduction. Indeed, cultural power will be deployed against them but this is most efficacious against weaker groups, lacking in both clout and confidence. However, when change concerns those with the opposite attributes, and simultaneously increases their ranks and augments their interests, the group which is already engaged in the 'brute' assertion of these interests also soon recognises that they do not gel with the prevailing form of cultural traditionalism.

These new Corporate Agents do indeed lack ideas to counterpose against the cultural hegemony which obstructs them. But they also have a structurally induced motive for acquiring them, in order to challenge the legitimacy claims of others and to establish their own. They are motivated to exploit cultural contradictions and to prevent these from being cloaked, just as the European aristocracy exploited the *renaissance* and prevented its recontainment by the counter-reformation. Similarly, where cultural systematisation was high, and had enjoyed unchallenged hegemony, it is the material interest groups most hindered by it who have the motive to diagnose the problems it cannot solve, the issues with which it cannot deal, and to produce interpretations which accentuate those of its elements which are more congruent to them[12] – as the French absolutist monarchs accentuated the Gallican rather than the Ultramontanist strand of Catholicism.

Once new material interest groups have unleashed novel ideas and providing that they continue to hold to them, then by definition the old cultural unification of the population has been undermined. Henceforth, the traditional reproduction of ideas has to contend with the new options on offer. Because the material interest groups seek to legitimise their advancement in the social structure, by appeal to the newly elaborated ideas, then they necessarily promote cleavage and sectionalism in the cultural domain. Those whose quietism had been the product of containment strategies and those whose conformity had been due to lack of alternatives may well now leap to competitive opposition or flock to the new opportunities, thus augmenting Socio-Cultural conflict well beyond its original structural impetus and issuing in dramatic Cultural Elaboration. Without the structural stimulus, rooted in the disjunction between the two domains, this elaborative sequence would not have been triggered, for agents with the power to promote it would have been lacking. Here,

---

[12] A. W. Gouldner, 'Reciprocity and Autonomy in Functional Theory', in N. J. Demerath and R. A. Peterson, *System, Change and Conflict*, Free Press, Collier Macmillan, New York, 1967.

then, structural elaboration exerts more of an influence upon cultural elaboration than vice versa, through the crystallisation of new Corporate Agents who are not only organised but have also become ideationally articulate.

Conversely, it may be cultural morphogenesis which precipitates agential change, as for example, the French Third Estate's progressive endorsement of Republicanism served its emergence as a new Corporate Agent. Structural stability and the forces maintaining it undoubtedly acted as a break at first on cultural change, by resisting the capacity of social agents to mobilise or re-group for, quintessentially, social control is directed against re-differentiation in society. Yet ideational diversification is totally dependent on differentiated groups who have enough power to introduce and then sustain divisive or specialised ideas. Structural restraints will delay their emergence. However, given the relative autonomy of the two domains, structural influences can constrain the emergence of new material interest groups but they can do no more than retard the development of new ideal interest groups.

Cultural morphogenesis not only means that ideational uniformity ceases to be produced, but that what takes its place is a new fund of divisive ideas (presenting competitive advantages or new opportunities to material interest groups) which now intrudes into the structural domain. When the story is told from the structural side of the intersection, this intrusion is pictured as some inexplicable 'rise of ideas', or what could be called the 'great-wave theory', in which the upsurge of the Renaissance, the Enlightenment or the scientific revolution, washes over and around social institutions, reducing them to crumbling sandcastles.

The 'great wave' is, of course, no 'theory' at all, but one can respect its imagery while deploring its lack of grounding in human interaction. Yet the mechanism is there and its influence is ineluctable – though it works on people and only through them on social institutions. For what cultural morphogenesis does is to change people (or at any rate some people), from unthinking traditionalists into evaluators of alternatives and from passive conformists into potential competitors. Although this occurs in the cultural domain, its effects do not stop there, because cultural actors are also structural agents. Thus, cultural change leads to the reconstitution of structural subjects. Here the 'great wave' image is pretty accurate, for the sandbags of social control cannot stem the flow of ideas.

Modernity thus witnesses an expansion in the number of Corporate Agents and an alteration in the nature of their internal relationships, changes which are due to disjunctions between morphostasis and morphogenesis in the structural and cultural domains. Let one enter a morphogenetic sequence and the newly differentiated groups or strata to emerge, or the new ideas made salient, serve to speed up the process of re-grouping, as ideas gain organised sponsors and nascent organisations gain powers of self-expression. What fundamentally changes during this period is that Corporate Agency ceases to be unitary. At least two groups have achieved this status: Church/State, Court/Parliament, Privileged Estates/Third Estate, Monarchy/lower Samurai or Nobility/Intelligentsia. Moreover, as vested interest groups, their relations are now oppositional rather than possessing the solidarity of the previous period. As their opposition intensifies, Primary Agents are not immune, since they become the targets of efforts to mobilise and to manipulate them in order to determine the outcomes of issues which were not of their making. However, they themselves largely remain the recipients of struggles over decision-making between Corporate Agents: it is not until the next period that the vast majority can shed their status as Primary Agents and begin the pursuit of their own interests.

(3) *The scenario of high Modernity* This is the prime configuration for the rapid shrinkage of the category of Primary Agents and their transformation into new, varied and more powerful promotive interest groups. Here the distributions of resources are much flatter. In this social formation, compared with all others, more and more groups acquire the characteristics of Corporate Agency – namely organisation and articulation. This final pure case deals with instances where morphogenesis is concurrent in the two domains. The two processes are mutually reinforcing, as can be seen in figure 8.4, and their consequences accelerate over time. *In sum, these are the proliferation of more and more Corporate Agents, whilst Primary Agency not only shrinks accordingly, but eventually becomes residual and disparate in composition.*

The basic feature of this configuration is a *mêlée* of competing and diverging Corporate Agents in both structural and cultural realms, in neither of which is domination unopposed or diversification unfamiliar. Given this high level of interaction between differentiated interest groups, seeking structural and cultural advancement respectively, the question is how material and ideal interests now intersect. Although the empirical alliances formed in reality are matters of historical contingency, this does not blur the generic reciprocity of their mutual influence across the intersection.

Let us abstract completely from history and simply picture an array of material interest groups surveying a variety of ideas, with the single thought of which will serve their structural designs best. Confronting them is a series of ideal interest groups which assesses the former purely in terms of their value as potential sponsors. It really does not matter who

M
o
r
p
h
o
s
t
a
t
i
c

c
y
c
l
e
s

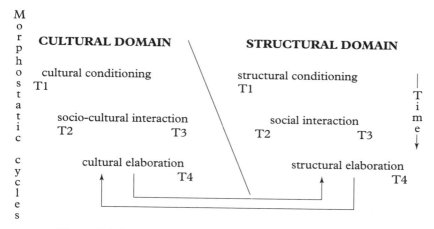

Figure 8.4 Structural and cultural configurations generating morphogenesis in society and agency

makes the first move or in which direction the first move is made. Whether some alliance is initiated from the cultural side (in quest of sponsorship) or from the structural side (seeking a legitimatory source), eventually all ideational options are taken up in social interaction, just as all interest groups become involved in cultural interaction. The only difference in real life is that the first move has probably already been taken or at least is practically predetermined by historical complicity.

To see how this intense and reciprocal set of influences works at the interface, let us consider the two sides separately. Supposing quite baldly that one set of cultural ideas gains the sponsorship of a powerful material interest group, then their cultural opponents too are irresistibly drawn towards the structural domain. For if one group alone makes headway in winning support there, all others will suffer from the augmented power and resources now brought to bear against them. Consequently, they must woo other material interest groups to acquire their support in order to ensure the survival or the salience of their own ideas. Thus, the pattern of cultural diversification aligns itself to the pattern of structural differentiation.

Alternatively, the intersection can be examined from the other side, although of course this is purely a matter of analytical convenience, since the mutual interpenetration of cultural and structural affairs is simultaneous. In the context of on-going morphogenesis, the outcome of social interaction is unresolved. However, the fact that it is underway means that differentiated interest groups have developed divergent material interests, which they now attempt to advance in the face of one another, including the opposition of any antecedent dominant group. Because interaction is intense but its outcome uncertain to participants, each attempts various ploys to gain an edge over its opponents. The one which is of concern here is the endorsement of ideas for the advancement of their cause.

Again, it matters little who makes the first move; this certainly is not the prerogative of dominant groups, since frequently domination develops no well-articulated form of justification until it comes under severe challenge or pressure. The group which is the first to go in for ideational endorsement introduces a cultural dimension to social interaction to legitimate the pursuit of its vested interests. What follows is the direct counterpart of the argument about embattled ideal interest groups; let one acquire a sponsor and the others have to seek sponsorship. So here, let one material interest group present its claims as legitimate and those opposing them have to take up ideas which undermine this legitimatory source and buttress their own counter-claims.

In sum, social interaction and socio-cultural interaction reinforce one another, and this, in turn, fosters intensified morphogenesis in both domains. Structural sponsorship means that oppositional and sectional ideas are assured of retaining salience in social life, which is a necessary though not sufficient condition for their victory. However, the very fact that ideational pluralism enjoys continuing social support is sufficient to prevent the re-establishment of old-style cultural morphostasis. Re-unification around an original syncretic formula or resumed reproduction of a traditional systematised conspectus are simply impossible in the face of divided or sectionalised socio-cultural groups. Similarly, the interaction of a variety of material interest groups, each of which has become articulate in its own defence and capable of detecting self-interest in the claims of others, is enough to preclude any drift back to unquestioned structural morphostasis. The groups have mobilised, ideas have helped them to do so, and assertion will not fade away because the material interests it seeks to advance do not evaporate.

In turn the co-existence of a plurality of Corporate Agents, seeking to push and pull the systemic or institutional structure in different directions, has profound effects on re-shaping the context for Primary Agents, who are also dragged into the ideological fray, mobilised for the convenience of Corporate opponents and usually let down by them. The fate of the people during the French Revolutionary Assemblies and of the English working class during the passage of the Great Reform Bill were typical in all these three respects. However, such Corporate raids on the slumbering giant of Primary agency prompt its awakening. With all the uncertainty displayed by the English Chartists over organisational strategy and ideological articulation, leadership of the lower classes sloughed

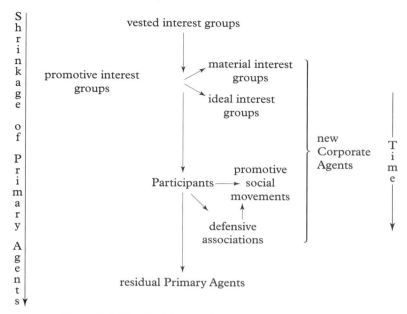

Figure 8.5 The double morphogenesis of agency

off its Primary status. It became a participant in the great age of ideolog-ical debate, generated its main organ of collective action in Unionisation and made its debut into Corporate decision-making when it gained the vote. The advent of representational class politics punctuated the end of Modernity's dichotomous form of Corporate Agency. Henceforth a plurality of political parties, in close or loose alliance with other organised interest groups – unions, professional associations, business confedera-tions, federations of peasant proprietors, religious denominations etc. – blurred the lines of the previous dichotomous opposition and did so because more and more Primary Agents realised their powers of organ-isation and articulation.

In the twentieth century, the lead given by the lower classes was passed like a baton to the other interest groupings who had remained confined to the status of Primary Agents. Class, followed by gender and ethnicity grounded the triad of new Corporate Agents throughout the developed world. Pursuant of their interests, each eventually made the political and institutional breakthroughs which spelt social incorporation – enfranchisement, civil rights, citizenship, social security, education and health services. This is illustrated in figure 8.5, which also shows this is not the end of the story.

Necessarily, morphogenetic scenarios have a strong tendency to accelerate. The mechanism involved is simple reinforcement. Cultural morphogenesis spawns more and more ideas, which, at the level of the Cultural System, represent increased ideational pluralism and specialisation, whose social effects are growing cleavage and sectionalism in the population.[13] In parallel, structural morphogenesis fosters increased competition and differentiation at the level of the Social System whose effects for social interaction are the polarization and the diversification of the population.[14] Since structure and culture continue to interact, their combined effect is to stimulate a profoundly new form of agential re-grouping – *one which for the first time enables the accentuation of difference* rather than constraining and confining Corporate Agency to those sharing narrow similarities (pre-modernity) or broad homogeneity (modernity). The final element accounting for the acceleration, and accentuating re-grouping by difference, is due to the contribution of PEPs to this tendency which cannot be attributed solely to the interplay of SEPs and CEPs. Minority interests, either materially or culturally based, reflexively seek the same influence for themselves that they have witnessed larger promotive groupings achieve. Since the social world is an open system, which has now become a global one, as a macroscopic consequence of the world traffic in ideas, in conjunction with structural multi-nationalism, a 'minority interest' can potentially attract larger numbers to its Corporate Agency than was ever the case even at the high-tide of Unionism.

Recombination based upon difference is operative at all levels, but the concern here is with its transformative effects upon Primary Agency, both quantitative and qualitative. New forms of Corporate participation mean a reassortment such that those whose material interests had not been prominently promoted by existing forms of collective action (such as women, gay and ethnic groups) generate new organisations, dedicated to giving their concerns maximum 'voice'. These can work as ginger-groups within existing Corporate Agencies (e.g. political parties, the Churches or Professional Associations) but generally they also meld with a broader and more diffuse cultural movement. Such new social movements, whose articulation primarily depends upon the media and whose organisation relies upon public demonstrations and direct action, attracting further media attention, focus upon single-issue ideational concerns which mobilise those differences which were again subordinated by existing Corporate Agents. Thus the form of promotive action spearheaded by the

---

[13] See chapters 6,7, and 8 of my *Culture and Agency*, which form the background to the discussion in this section.   [14] See my *Realist Social Theory*, pp. 303ff.

Campaign for Nuclear Disarmament and Anti-Apartheid has been globalised by Green Peace, Animal Rights, Amnesty, Oxfam etc. In the light of their successful mobilisation, defensive associations, again based upon difference, are spurred into being, such as the current British 'countryside' movement, which already blends a straightforward defence of field sports with a promotive concern to 'keep Britain farming' – coming from that 2 to 3 per cent of the population which is too small for its concerns to be prominent on any political party's agenda.

The impact upon Primary Agency is to leave it truly residual and disparate in composition. Its members are rightly termed the subjects of exclusion, which highlights the radical discontinuity in hierarchies of remuneration, representation and repute, thus replacing the old continuities of social stratification. However, the very diversity of contemporary Primary Agents – single mothers, immigrants, the homeless, non-working youth, the handicapped and isolated old – precludes collective organisation. Their social exclusion plus their diversity condemns them as a collectivity to the passivity of Primary Agency. Their reflexive response intensifies this, since various sections themselves seek to capitalise on the accentuation of difference rather than confronting the daunting task of mobilising the similarities of 'underclass' grievances into collective action. As has often been noted, the poor of high modernity are a disparate collectivity and one which is less and less synonymous with the working class. Though still structured by the complexities of late welfare capitalism, the members of this collectivity are more reflexively concerned with their differences than their similarities. Thus generational differences divide the young unemployed from the old-aged (two of the largest categories of the poor), ethnocentrism erects a 'racial' barrier to cohesion, whilst the handicapped, homeless and single-parent families increasingly pursue their interests through special interest groups rather than by more generalised forms of collaboration. Social affinities and antagonisms thus fuel fissiparousness: they do not preclude the development of relatively weak Corporate agents, but mean that these will be in the plural (addressing single-issues) rather than in the singular (confronting the plurality of vested grievances shared by the underprivileged).

Thus on the minus side of the balance-sheet of high Modernity is found a residual category of Primary Agents, which itself is partly a recombination (for the first time) of those who have ceded or lost prior insertion into forms of Corporate Agency (such as the involuntarily redundant, non-working single parents, or youngsters who have left home and education). The force of social exclusion strongly condemns them to agential passivity as a collectivity. On the plus side of the balance-sheet, the increasing differentiation and diversification of Corporate Agency means the realisation of more PEP powers of organisation and articulation by more people. This has two implications, both of which are propitious for the acquisition of social identity. On the one hand, through the growth of Corporate Agents, more involuntary 'Me's' (from Quadrant 2) have found a 'We' with whom they voluntarily associate (in Quadrant 3), since many more 'I's' believe their positions will be enhanced by so joining.

The strong probability is that their reflexive judgements are correct, but it is a necessary and not a sufficient condition for obtaining a social identity. Here I am in full agreement with Greenwood[15] that membership of or affiliation to, say, a feminist or ethnic group does not secure strict identity (except for the small minority who become some type of full-time officer) because it only makes one a member amongst others and undifferentiated from them. Talk of 'identity politics' is premature at this level. On the other hand, what the new plethora of interacting Corporate Agents do have as their combined consequence is a steady modification and amplification of society's extant role-array, such that more positions (and more positions of a new kind) are created in which more people feel they can invest themselves. In other words, the opportunities for Agents to become the kind of Social Actor with whom they can identify are increased and with this, the probability of acquiring a social identity also grows.

[15] John D. Greenwood, *Realism, Identity and Emotion*, Sage, London, 1994, pp. 130–2.

9   Actors and commitment

To view Social Agency in terms of interrelations (interactions between groups and collectivities which redefine both through re-grouping) obviously means that this concept of the Social Agency (always in the plural) is not synonymous with the notion of the Social Actor (in the singular). There is a good deal more to be said about the Social Actor, most especially how she or he acquires an identity as a social self. The next emergent stratum thus concerns the Social Actor who emerges through the 'triple morphogenesis' in which Agency conditions (not determines) who comes to occupy different social roles. Actors, then, are defined as role incumbents and roles themselves have emergent properties which cannot be reduced to the characteristics of their occupants. These can be demonstrated by the pre-existence of roles, their greater durability over time, a capacity to endure despite considerable changes in the personal features of their successive holders, and the relatively autonomous powers of constraint and enablement which are lodged in the role, not the occupant, and can be lost (or shed) with loss of occupancy.

Just as the concept of Social Agency is necessarily incomplete for dealing with Actors, since it is only concerned with action in, or as part of, a collectivity, equally, however, any attempt to conceptualise the Social Actor needs to be completed by reference to their properties as Agents, if we are finally to arrive at an adequate conception of social identity and how it is attained.

Social Actors – the triple morphogenesis
(Quadrants 3–4) 'personification'

Those who start out as 'strong actionists', with the laudable aim of defending 'Autonomous Man', a model of the Social Actor, who is neither the passive puppet of social forces, nor a pre-social self, whose adroitness at playing social games begs the question of how the individual became so endowed, hit two major snags. Both, I believe, could be avoided if, in the attempt to present Adam as his own 'sovereign artificer'[1] the part of Adam as Agent was fully recognised. By neglecting it, the best of such accounts ends up by having to endorse the social contract and to overplay social convention.

Such an account opens with Adam (or Eve) in the singular confronting the social stage, and seeks to conceptualise a *social self* for him or her which, whilst dependent on society, also meets the strict criteria of identity as a particular Actor. It proceeds by eschewing two notions: that of an actor undertaking a pre-scripted part (too much of society: too little of self), or one who merely dons and doffs masks, behind which his private business can be conducted (too much self: too little of the social). The proper balance is struck by a concept of the Social Actor who becomes such by choosing to identify himself or herself with a particular role and actively to personify it in a particularistic way. The Actor's real interests come with the role she or he has chosen to personify; the snag is of course that the Actor '*qua* atomic pre-social individual' has no reason to *adopt* one identity rather than another,[2] and he or she cannot have a reason on this account because he or she has no prior interests upon which reasons can work. Consequently, the initial choice of a position is contractarian, a contract which in prospect it is non-rational to enter but which can in retrospect be rational or rationally corrected. The trouble here is that the choice either remains inexplicable or is handed over to depth psychology.

In fact there are two difficulties here. The first does concern the 'missing account' of *how* an individual makes a choice of role, which is not simply a leap in the dark. This situation can be remedied if Adam (or Eve) *as Agent* is allowed on the scene. We become Agents *before* we become Actors. In other words, Agency is a springboard to positions in the total role array and the interests which we possess *qua* Agents serve to make the choice of role positions reasonable. The importance of Corporate Agency is dual. Through interaction with other collectivities it expands the array of available positions, as part of the primary morphogenesis of society which its organised interaction brings about. Simultaneously, through interacting with others in the same collectivity, Agents become more articulate about their interests and thus better able to reflect upon the role positions which will further their realisation. Because the *how* question is the more tractable and will be tackled first. However, attractive as the notion of 'personification' is for securing our strict social identity, the second problem gradually obtrudes, namely *who* is doing the personifying? The problem will grow in urgency, but it will

---

[1] Martin Hollis, *The Cunning of Reason*, Cambridge University Press, 1988.
[2] Martin Hollis, *Models of Man*, pp. 104ff.

be allowed to unfold in the course of dealing with the *how* issue, before being tackled head-on.

Infant Agents have a long way to go before they become mature Actors. Nevertheless, the kind of Agents that they start out being without any choice, due to parentage and social context, profoundly influences what type of Actor they can choose to become. Certain opportunities and information are open to the privileged and closed to the non-privileged. Options are not determined but the opportunity costs of attaining them are stacked very differently for the two groups. It is the fact that people heed such opportunity costs which produces the well-known regularities in differential attainment of top positions, according to class, gender and ethnicity. Such differential costings constitute good reasons for initially opting for different sections of the total role array. Initial choice of position is corrigible, but big corrections entail increased costs which are further reasons why not very many will undertake drastic remedial measures (why, for example, so few female, Asian home-workers ever find their way to university).

These initial interests with which Agents are endowed, through their life-chances, provide the leverage upon which reasons (otherwise known as constraints and enablements) for different courses of action operate. They do not determine the particular Social Actor an individual chooses to become, but they strongly condition what type of Social Actor the vast majority can and do become. The notion of Adam as Agent literally fostering Adam as Actor can be worked to eliminate the contractual leap in the dark, since the former supplies the latter with a rational interest in accepting a social position. Here, only choice of part of the role array has been made explicable, but further argument about the differential availability of information, role models and work experience to different Agents could bring the residual contractual element into the area of sensible choice – explaining why Johnny becomes a fireman and Tommy a policeman.

All of this is predicated upon not bundling all interests into roles (the *locus classicus* of the Social Actor) but allowing that some interests pertain to Social Agents (privileges being the broadest way of construing these). I now want to make further use of this assumption to mount a morphogenetic assault on the role-rule set, which 'strong actionism' both takes as given, but does not explain, and treats as all-encompassing, which condemns Actors to a normative conventionalism, thus severely limiting their innovativeness as 'artificers'. So far I have only introduced the pre-grouping aspect of Social Agency, now this needs to be linked to its promotive re-grouping aspect, in order to tackle this problem. For it is the latter which gives considerable purchase on how new positions/roles are constructed out of something other than role-clash and how the action involved is not restricted by rule-governed normative conventions. These are the lot of the Social Actor *qua* Actor, however much discretionary and strategic judgement she or he is allowed when pictured as an 'intelligent steward' rather than a mindless reader of the small print. Social Agents are not limited in this way.

Two things need to be stressed now. Firstly, that as Social Agents, groups and collectivities of people confront problems which are interest-related but not role-related. Secondly, that as Social Agents they engage in promotive activities, when tackling these problems, which are too innovative to be construed as 'games' – since they follow no regulative rules and embody no constitutive rules. Having refused to bundle all interests into roles, it is now possible to see how broader categories of Social Agents confront problem-ridden situations in relation to these wider interests (which are rooted in their life chances). To take an example from institutional morphogenesis, when educational control was exclusively in Church hands, this created exigencies for a number of groups and where such problems represented a clash of beliefs, an obstacle to a nascent social movement, or the exclusion of a particular category, these could only be interpreted as impinging upon roles by over-stretching that concept to turn 'believer', 'radical', or *'nouveau riche' into* roles.

Secondly, what such Corporate Agents then did in the face of these obstructions to their self-declared interests was to seek to eradicate the hindrance by transforming the nature of educational control.[3] Yet there was no 'game' called 'how to go about winning control of education', no regulative rules governing educational conflict, and the constitutive rules concerning governance of an educational system could only be *ex post*, since the elaboration of State Systems was an unintended consequence of interaction between Corporate Agents. Out of this undoubtedly came an array of new roles – teachers, inspectors, administrators and Ministers. Therefore the elaboration of roles and rules is part and parcel of the morphogenesis set in train by Corporate Agents, as they collaboratively transformed the structural context, for the very good reason that it presented them with too many environmental problems with which to live.

The argument can be broadened by considering that the 'under-privileged' confront plenty of daily exigencies, given their poor life chances, and thus have the best of reasons for struggling towards collective organisation (unionisation, franchise and civil rights movements, feminism), just as privileged Corporate Agents find good reason in the protection of their vested interests to try to contain or repress the former. In the struggle between them (and the privileged and non-privileged are not playing

[3] See Margaret S. Archer, *Social Origins of Educational Systems*, Sage, London, 1979.

some 'Us and Them' game), the extant role array undergoes considerable transformation. New positions get defined under the prompting of pro-motive interest groups, though they will bear the marks of compromise and concession in the course of interaction against opposition. Equally, the defence of vested interests may prompt role changes precisely in order to defend interests themselves. Kings will accept any form of constitu-tionalism in order to remain King – but a Constitutional Monarch is a very different role embedded in a much modified role-set.

In short, the re-grouping of Social Agents through the double morpho-genesis provides the motor which generates new role-rule sets as some of its unintended consequences, thus providing an account of their develop-ment in terms of non-rule governed action, which is not open to Social Actors as incumbents of roles hedged by normative conventions. Morphogenetically, Corporate agency invents new rules for new games which contain more roles in which Social Actors can be themselves. Another way of putting it is that Agency makes more room for the Actor, who is not condemned to a static array of available positions.

Thus, separating Social Agents from Social Actors ends up by destroy-ing some of Adam's illusions, but adding greatly to his powers as an artificer. What he loses on this account (because of the pre-grouping of Agents) is the spurious illusion of contractual freedom to become any social self he chooses to personify. What he gains (thanks to the re-grouping of Agents) is the collective capacity to refashion social positions, thus ultimately making society as well as himself.

Let us be clear, the Social Agent and the Social Actor are not different people – the distinction is only temporal and analytical. When we look at the Agent as parent of the Actor, we are examining Adam himself at different ages. Upon maturity, Adam becomes both Agent and Actor, but it remains analytically invaluable to distinguish between what he does in the problematic or beneficial situations he confronts *qua* Agent from what he does *qua* Actor in his particular roles with their rule requirements. After all, a great many of us belong to or support social movements *as well as* willingly occupying and personifying our chosen roles.

Therefore, Actors themselves, as role incumbents, cannot be under-stood without reference to Agency. So much for the *how* question, but the issue of *who* does the 'personification' and on the basis of *what*, is now becoming very pressing indeed. Generally, in sociological theory, if Actors are allowed to diminish to the point where they are nothing but the objects of roles (instead of being subjects who are active role-makers rather than passive role-takers), we not only endorse the pre-programmed executor but also exclude Actors themselves as a source of role change. This is inevitably the case because 'indeterminate material' lacks the wherewithal for all innovative reinterpretation, for testing the elasticity of role requirements or exercising 'intelligent stewardship' over resources. This is precisely *not* what the 'strong actionist' wishes to fall back upon, nor will it do for my own account because it collapses back into 'Society's Being' again: instead we both need people to be able to bring to any role they occupy the human qualities of reflexivity and creativity. Without these qualities, the Actor is not a subject who can reflect upon the stringency of role governed constraints and decide whether nothing can be done other than routine acts of reproduction, nor one who can bring his or her personal ingenuity to bear in order to exploit the degrees of freedom and thus attempt role transformation. From where do these personal powers (PEP) come – since the Actor cannot find them in the role, and the Agent's contribution finished with helping to make the position available and assisting certain categories of people to have access to it?

What we need is *personal identity* in order for any individual to be able to personify a role, rather than simply animating it. The trouble is that it seems we cannot have it! The difficulty arises because *personal identity* cannot be formed (even *pro tem*) until the 'first round' of the inner conversation has been finished. Yet, if it has been, then the people who have completed it have necessarily been in a position such that they could weight their social concerns against all others. This is where we left them at the end of chapter 7, and at the conclusion (again *pro tem*) of their internal dialogues, whose precise commitments gave them their uniqueness and hence strict identity as persons. It is an uncomfortable place to be: for it looks on this account as though *personal identity* cannot be attained before *social identity* is achieved, because how otherwise can people evaluate their social concerns against other kinds of concerns when ordering their ultimate concerns? Conversely, it also looks as if the achievement of *social identity* is dependent upon someone having sufficient *personal identity* to personify any role in their unique manner. These are the two horns of the dilemma.

It seems that the only way out of this dilemma is to accept the existence of a dialectical relationship between personal and social identities. Yet if this is to be more than fudging, then dialectics has to mean a good deal more than the fact that we believe there is a relationship, but cannot disentangle it. Thus I will venture three 'moments' of the interplay (PI ↔ SI) which culminate in *a synthesis such that both personal and social identities are emergent and distinct, although they contributed to one another's emergence and distinctiveness.*

(a) What do we have to account for in this first moment? Answer: why anyone is drawn to experiment with a social role and its requirements, above and beyond the fact that it is available to them (courtesy of Agential doings). Obviously, it is chosen roles which are being dealt with here, although the significance of involuntary roles (daughter, pupil, patient, baptised Christian etc.) will be introduced almost immediately. This moment is held to be one in which nascent *personal identity holds sway over nascent social identity* (PI → SI). Confronted with a choice, let us say the first real decision to be made about someone's occupational future, what resources do they have to draw upon? The answer has to be their experience, including that as spectators, of the three orders of reality, natural, practical and social. Now it was granted that minors could not complete an inner conversation (even *pro tem*), precisely because they lacked the experiential information to do so: but it was also maintained that they sustained interior dialogues which represented provisional (and highly corrigible) 'dry runs' at completion. This is what they have to contribute to the decision-making situation in which I have now placed them.

Firstly, their experience in the natural realm is not negligible, through play, sport, travel and outdoor activities. It is at least extensive enough to perform a regulatory function over what is sought or shunned when considering the array of occupational roles. My older son, a frustrated explorer, calls it 'life in a fleece', the younger one, who hated riding, will never be found applying for stable management. Natural relations are quite sufficient for completing significant sections of Vocational Guidance questionnaires, such as 'Indoors/Outdoors', 'Urban/Rural', 'Environmental concern' etc.

Secondly and similarly, constant interaction in the practical order has supplied positive and negative feedback about the kinds of activities from which satisfaction is derived. To an important extent, play functions as a self-regulated experience, however strongly others attempt to structure the play-environment with help from the early learning centre. As all parents discover, it is quite unpredictable which toys will prove absorbing for a long time and which will be neglected after first inspection: this is something which appears independent from the child's preliminary 'I want', which can be reflexively rescinded in short order, and from marketing pressures, which do what they were intended to do in terms of satisfying 'wants', but are quite indifferent to the rejection of the object in question with the dismissive, 'is that all it does?' Childhood self-regulation operates in an identical manner *vis-à-vis* practical activity, as was described in chapter 6, with competence reinforcing further practice and the frustrations of incompetence or boredom leading to abandonment of a toy or game.

Enforcement seems to be of little avail: Victorian novels give plenty of examples of girls who never finished their samplers, and plenty of boys today shuffle out of their music lessons with an unwanted Grade 1 certificate. Of course, they may later be grateful for the rudimentary competence which allows them to sew on a button or pick out a note, but this hardly determines their life course. Ironically, the most powerful effect of enforcement is negative: by withholding the materials for certain activities, or selectively withholding them according to gender, or their being withheld because of expense, then certain potential sources of satisfaction cannot be fully explored. However, in general, exposure to, and variable involvement, in a host of common activities such as painting, drawing, music, construction, sewing, mechanics, gardening, computing, religious practice, childcare, cooking and household maintenance allow further sections of the Vocational/Guidance questionnaire to be completed.

Thirdly, in their involuntary social roles children continue to be reflexive beings, and it is they who determine which of their available arenas is the locus of their own self-worth. Peers may be chosen over parents, and out of school activities can assume greater importance than teachers' encouragements and assessments. Evaluation works both ways, for the child and especially the teenager basically asks, 'do I want to be like that?', or, more searchingly, they interrogate themselves about which aspects of a role are worth having and which they would want to be different for themselves. In other words, they inspect not only their own involuntary roles but also the lifestyles of those who have put them there, which are sifted into elements worthy of replication versus others meriting rejection. 'I like studying x, but I don't want to teach' is a frequent verdict of many undergraduates.

These three sources of experience from the natural, practical and social orders of reality are the resources of nascent *personal identity*. It is not fixed, because the experiences are too limited and too little can be known about the terms and conditions of making any one concern predominate. However, the internal conversation has begun a dialogue about the kind of person an individual believes they want to be: that it will undergo revision in the light of further experience is precisely what makes this a dialectic process. However, there would be no process at all unless the nascent personal identity brought something to the task of role selection. Otherwise we would be dealing with an entirely passive procedure of role assignment through socialisation. What it brings is rather like the elements of an Identikit, constructed from the individual's reflective judgements on his or her knowledge of the three orders. It is a best-guess sketch of a potential future life. Indeed some Vocational Guidance tests work by synthesising the priorities and preferences supplied, and then presenting the subject with the resulting occupational possibilities. In short, our subjects can make an active and informed choice about their future occupations, but only because they have done considerable preliminary work on their environments and have internally conversed about the person they would like to become and the job which will best express this.

(b) Of course their choices are fallible because the crucial missing piece of information is the experience of having made the choice itself. But without taking the plunge, there is no other way in which it can be acquired; yet in its acquisition, the individual herself undergoes change. This is why it is legitimate to disengage a *second 'moment', where the nascent social identity impacts upon the nascent personal identity* (SI → PI). All 'first choices' are experiments, guided by the nascent personal identity, but once they have been made, then reasons are acquired along with the role. The question now is, will the individual choose to make them his or her own? The reasons themselves are various. Most jobs provide pay, a working environment, companionship of fellow workers, some training, an induction into why the task is worthwhile and what is expected of employees, and, above all, work experience. At this point, the 'terms and conditions' of investing oneself in the role, and choosing to identify with it to the minimum necessary degree to exercise incumbency, become manifest. Young girl grooms, predisposed to these posts by their prior love of horses, find they supply the lowest pay and worst hours on offer; stable-lads, wanting to race, discover that they have to begin the battle to keep their weight down; trainee teachers realise they will have to confront disruptive classrooms; supermarket check-out staff learn that they must politely handle irate customers for the entire shift etc.

What new employees have to do is to evaluate the up-side against the down-side, and come up with a positive balance if they are going to find cause to invest something of themselves in that role. Here, induction is an inducement: it presents a meta-rationale for why the new appointee should find the reasons embedded in the role sufficiently good to make them their own. The typical defining feature of the professions, their possession of an ethical standard, is not just a guide to professional conduct but also a moral *raison d'être* for the profession itself. Nor are modern commercial concerns immune from inducting 'business ethics', alongside a financial incentive structure, for those who throw their lot in with the firm. Trainees schemes of all kinds basically present a vista in which today's drawbacks will be more than compensated for by tomorrow's bonuses.

If ideological induction is one facet, then work experience is the other feature of this experiment. No job is as the neophyte sees it in prospect, and there can be unexpected satisfactions as well as dissatisfactions which are discovered. Many academics are not enamoured of administration, but a few do progressively absorb themselves in becoming university administrators. What appointees have to ask (internally) is whether they wish to invest any of themselves in their experimental enterprise. Reflectively their answer can be 'no' to endorsing this social identity, in which case their choice is corrigible; they can search for an alternative source for their social identity. However, in the process of experimentation, they will have undergone certain subjective and objective changes. Subjectively, they have acquired some new self-knowledge which will impact upon their personal identity: they are now people who *know* that they are bored by x, disillusioned by y and uneasy with z. Yet objectively they have changed too, because the opportunity costs have altered for their revised 'second choice'. They are now older, lack a clean sheet, may lack decent references, and can have a wasted and possibly inappropriate training. Corrected positions may be harder to come by, or the applicant may have to settle for them at a lower level, which may carry its own quota of discontents. Exactly the same is true of the failure of 'first relationships'. The re-partnering market is narrower for the man paying child-support or the woman living as a single-mother.

In neither case is re-employment or re-partnering on a satisfying basis precluded, but corrigibility seems to have its social limits. On the nth attempt at correction, positions or partners may very well become decreasingly available, at least in terms of representing any improvement over past experiments. At this point, the individual is in the unfortunate position where experimenting with social identities has unfitted him or her for attaining a satisfying social identity. Effectively, this throws the problem back onto personal identity and to the (re)discernment phase of the internal conversation. Having 'failed' to secure a social role or roles which are regarded as an important component of the person, then further inner dialogue is required to come up with some *modus vivendi* which is satisfyingly liveable, *without* the social identity aspired to in the first moment. This can either be accomplished by the promotion of non-social concerns, such as life revolving around some skilled activity which becomes increasingly absorbing, or by radically re-defining the type of social role which personal experience has *made* more acceptable and which remains socially accessible – perhaps voluntary work of some kind. Without one or the other, then strict identity itself is threatened and the process of 'drift' sets in, as discussed in chapter 7.

(c) What is perhaps less obvious, is that those whose experimentation with social roles has been 'successful', also have to return to the inner conversation. Once they have found a satisfying role, whether on the first or subsequent corrected attempts, they have a decision to make, namely, 'how much of myself am I prepared to invest in it?' *This is the moment of synthesis between personal and social identity, which takes to the PI ↔ SI form.*

Any social role makes its demands on time, energy, and commitment. Those who have experienced enough of it to wish to make some of its associated interests their own have also changed, to the degree that they now *know*, what they may have previously anticipated, namely that they do indeed find these things interesting. Quite literally they have lost their disinterested stance because they now see their self-worth as being constituted by role occupancy. Moreover, most roles are greedy consumers: there are never enough hours in the day to be the 'good' academic, billing lawyer, or company executive; a 'good' parent can be on the go around the clock; and the 'good' churchgoer is inveigled into becoming active in the parish. Does this mean that this crystallising social identity swamps personal identity?

This cannot be the case for three reasons. To begin with, most of us hold several social roles simultaneously – perhaps all three of the above, academic, parent and churchgoer. Now, if all of them are 'greedy', then who or what moderates between their demands? Were we to leave this as a matter which is simply arbitrated by the strength of these competing role demands, then we would again have reconciled ourselves to the passive actor. It is not then even her decision about where her self-worth lies which defines her social identity. But actors are not passive in the face of competing social demands. They strike their own balances, even if regretfully and even if observers find them imbalanced. People carve out quality time for their children, swap a holiday for a conference and make their Sunday Mass going sacrosanct. They go in for part-time work, job-sharing, homeworking and early retirement. In other words, they themselves are the active jugglers with their competing role requirements, for it is their own definition of what constitutes self-worth in society which is at stake.

Secondly, if they are granted this active capacity, then we have to ask who is exercising it? The answer can only be a person, otherwise we are back to passivity. However, if it is indeed the person who has these abilities, then we have to grant that if they have the capacity to 'weigh' one role against another, then they can also evaluate their social concerns against their other commitments. This is precisely what it was argued (in chapter 7) that the 'adult' internal conversation was about. Certainly, as a recent role incumbent, new and socially derived information is brought into the inner discussion, but *in relation* to the claims of other ongoing concerns. Only dialogically can their prioritisation and accommodation be worked out. The resultant is a personal identity *within which* the social identity has been assigned its place in the life of an individual. That place may be large ('she lives for her work') or small ('he's only in it for the money'), but there is nothing which automatically ensures that social concerns have top priority. It is the individual who prioritises, and even if conditions are constrainingly such that good reason is found for devoting many hours to, say, monotonous employment, nothing insists that subjects put their hearts into it. Plenty of people live for their time off from social role taking.

Thirdly, in determining *how much* of themselves anyone will put into their various ultimate concerns, they are simultaneously deciding *what* they will put in. This arises because in arriving at their concerns and deeming some ultimate and others as subordinate (and thus to be accommodated to the former), they define themselves as unique persons. It is this *overall* personal identity that they will bring to executing any particular component of their concerns. This means that we are at last in a position to answer that crucial question about *who* personifies a role in a particularistic way, such that they achieve strict social identity as an actor. The answer is that the person does this, and acts as he or she does in the role precisely because they are the particular person that they have become. Without allowing that it is the *person* who animates the *actor* we are left with a conundrum, which too easily gets solved by invoking socialisation and thus re-condemning the actor to passivity. By allowing that we need a person to do the active personifying, it finally has to be conceded that our personal identities are not reducible to being gifts of society. *Unless* personal identity is indeed allowed on these terms, then there is no way in which strict social identity can be achieved. Personification needs a person: without personification no social identity derives from any role. Certainly, I have agreed that the social positions we occupy do contribute to the person we become, which is why this is presented as a dialectical process: but the final synthesis is one which finally defines the person as someone with concerns in the natural and practical orders, as well as the social order. *In the process, our social identity also becomes defined, but necessarily as a sub-set of personal identity.*

We can now represent this acquisition of social identity in Quadrants 3–4 as a process of progressive individuation, which is underpinned by the self-conscious human being who emerges through the 'primacy of practice'. This is the 'I' whose continuous sense of self is needed throughout the sequence described in figure 9.1. The 'Me' is the self-as-object who, in the individual's past, was involuntarily placed within society's resource distribution as a Primary Agent. The 'We' represents the collective action in which the self engaged as part of Corporate Agency's attempt to bring about social transformation, which simultaneously transformed society's extant role array as well as transforming Corporate

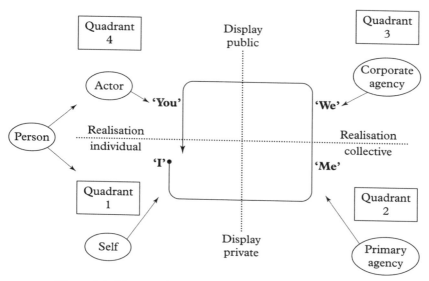

Figure 9.1 The acquisition of social identity

Agency itself. This then created the positions which the 'You' could acquire, accept and personify, thus becoming an Actor possessing strict social identity.

Persons: Quadrants (4–1) commitment

This is not the end of the story. So far what has been presented analytically has been a *developmental* sequence which takes the individual from birth to maturity, when he or she has then acquired the full range of personal powers (PEPs) – those of *self, agent, actor* and *particular person*. That leaves the *lifelong* story untold, because of course these human properties and powers do not stay frozen throughout life – they do not remain just as they were at the time of their emergence. As with all emergent powers, they modify their own internal constituents and also exert causal effects upon their environments. Only by signalling these subsequent influences upon a life and its environment can the significance of this account finally be differentiated from 'Modernity's Man' and 'Society's Being'. This has been the aim throughout the book, but the time has come to highlight the *point* of sustaining this distinction. In a nutshell, it will be maintained that the individual, as presented here in his or her concrete singularity, has powers of ongoing reflexive monitoring of both self and society, which enables this subject to make *commitments* in a genuine act of solidarity.

the conditioned 'Me' – Primary Agent
$$\frac{\text{the conditioned 'Me' – Primary Agent}}{\text{T1} \qquad\qquad\qquad\qquad \text{T2}}$$

$$\frac{\text{the interactive 'We' – Corporate Agent}}{\text{T3}}$$

$$\frac{\text{the elaborated 'You' – PI + SI}}{\text{T4}}$$

Figure 9.2 The emergence of personal and social identity

These are far outside the register of 'Modernity's Man', who remains shackled to his own individualistic preference schedule. In parallel, this subject is also capable of authentic *creativity* which can transform 'society's conversation' in a radical way, one which is foreign to 'Society's Being' who is condemned to making conventionally acceptable permutations upon it.

Perhaps the easiest way to pinpoint these lifelong properties of commitment and creativity is to illustrate how they arise from the morphogenesis of the 'successful' subject; that is everyone who has managed to attain to both social identity and personal identity. In effect, what has been traced through as the development sequence is also a morphogenetic cycle as is depicted in Figure 9.2. Thus the morphogenesis of personal and social identity (whose emergence has just been presented as a dialectical development) can be seen as the outcome of a process which is undergirded throughout by the continuous self-consciousness of the human being.

As always, the features elaborated at the end of a morphogenetic cycle by T4, then become the new T1, that is those features which condition subsequent interaction. Thus, at the end of the developmental sequence, we finished with subjects who had achieved strict social identity by finding a role(s) in which they found it worthwhile to invest themselves, and who also had the personal identity which enabled them to personify it in a unique manner, reflective of *who* they themselves were. Of course they go on doing this at the new T1. In living out the initial role(s), which they have found good reason to occupy, they bring to it or them their singular manner of personifying it or them and this, in turn, has consequences over time. What it does creatively, is to introduce a continuous stream of unscripted role performances, which also over time can cumulatively transform the role expectations. These creative acts are thus transformative of society's very normativity, which is often most clearly spelt out in the norms attaching to specific roles. For example, consider that distant and unapproachable figure of my own student days, the University Professor, who was always addressed as such and maintained this distance, in turn, by calling upon his students as 'Miss', 'Mrs', or 'Mr'. Here I would argue that, *inter alia*, it has been the cumulative effects of thirty years of very different personifications of this role which have led to a much more approachable and pastorally involved occupant of the 'same' role – to the point where students, at least, now consider those remaining as distant Professors to be 'no-good academics'. The same could be said of doctors who remain 'uninformative' to their patients, and of clergymen who hide behind their dog-collars. Of course, creativity need not accumulate in this way, but every unscripted performance creatively elasticates role expectations and prevents them from becoming set in concrete. The effectiveness of these ripples is at the mercy of a host of contingencies, but every time that someone thinks, 'if only there were more doctors like x', or 'if only there were other priests who shared rather than pontificating', then creative personification has begun to set a new role agenda by questioning established modes of execution.

Simultaneously, our personal identities continue their reflective work. The internal conversation is never suspended, it rarely sleeps, and what it is doing throughout the endless contingent circumstances it encounters is continuously monitoring its concerns. Inwardly, the subject is living a rich unseen life which is evaluative (rather than calculative, as is the case for 'Modernity's Man') and which is meditative (rather than appropriative, as is the lot of Society's Being). What this subject is doing is conducting an endless assessment of whether what it once devoted itself to as its ultimate concern(s) are still worthy of this devotion, and whether the price which was once paid for subordinating and accommodating other concerns is still one with which the subject can live. If the answer is affirmative, then we have a person who has *determined* to marshal his or her personal powers into a genuine act of commitment. Since social concerns need not be the predominant ones, this may spell enhanced commitment to an activity or a cause. However, if (as is likely) any social concern does figure among the constellation of his or her ultimate concerns, then we have a subject who has the personal resources to make an authentic commitment to others. This commitment is truly theirs (it is not the product of socialisation) and it is a real commitment (it is not a device which cloaks self-interest).

Another way of putting these same two points about creativity and commitment is that the subject, thanks to his or her personal powers, has that which is needful for personal autonomy. On the other hand, because their environment (natural, practical and social) reflexively plays such an

important part in both what and whom the person is, we have not constituted some monads whose properties are independent from the context
in which they live and move and have their being. This personal autonomy enables them to have rich private lives which are not internalised
mimetics of external reality. Much of the inner conversation will
undoubtedly be *about* the three orders of reality, but we now have a robust
subject with the wherewithal to reflect *upon* the outside world as object.
Certainly they employ the public linguistic medium in their private
ruminations, and are thus constrained by the things which can and
cannot be said within any natural language, but not in what they chose to
think about within it. Human persons have been left with their souls.
These have neither been evacuated into society's conversation nor impoverished by confinement to a selfish felicific calculus. This inner life is not
just a processing mechanism for arriving at our ultimate concerns (which
is what was abstracted in chapter 7). *We are also persons who are concerned
about our concerns*: this is what commitment means. Most of our inner life
is a dwelling upon them which is prayer and poetry, or perhaps both
together. The mountaineer savours his great climbs and dreams of doing
the 'Big Seven'. The artist exults in a patch of canvas which worked and
agonises over how to complete the effect. The parent silently wonders
over her child's being, as vivid hopes and fears intertwine about the
future. My close family and friends deeply people this book, because I
cannot write in abstraction about human concerns without reflecting and
revealing something of those concerns which concern me.

This is the 'inner directed' face of the ongoing interior dialogue, which
does not leave our private lives hermetically sealed and completely
hidden. On the contrary, prayer and poetry may be matters of deep
inwardness, but they have their outworkings. One of the most important
is that they spill over onto how we are towards other people and things
and how other people find us. They mark and charge what we make out of
our every encounter (natural, practical and social), including what we
ourselves bring to our own personification of our social roles, precisely
because of what we are. However, there is a more explicitly 'outer
directed' aspect to the interior conversation. Part of being concerned
about our concerns is also internally to interrogate ourselves about
whether *we* are doing *them* justice. This is not simply a matter of persons
asking themselves, 'if I am dedicated to x, then am I dedicated enough?'
There is also a judicious question, which is partly an instrumental one, of
how 'I' should act so as best to promote my concerns to the best possible
effect. This can be answered very differently, for the same kind of
concern, by different people, precisely because they are unique persons.
In other words, life is not just a process of learning Wittgensteinian rules

about how to 'go on': it is a much more ethical, creative and personalised reflection about how far should we go, and what do we judge to be the best way to do it. When homeless Jim comes to the door for the second or third time that week, the householder does not just consult the informal norm of charity (which he might well conclude had been satisfied by his generosity on the first occasion), but internally has to ask and answer questions like, 'Can I really send him away empty handed?' 'Won't he just go straight to the pub?' 'What about the others to whom I also owe charity?' Jim represents a commitment, one unsought and inconvenient, but his demands mean that the inner conversation goes on about how this commitment will be lived out.

Perhaps the easiest way of capturing the outworkings of our person-hood is to present them analytically as a second tour around the four quadrants – as if this were a new morphogenetic cycle, which indeed it can be. In reality, life can be pictured as an endless circling around this square, but what I would like to pick out in conclusion are the generic transformations which our *powers as persons* can induce as we re-visit, as it were, each Quadrant in turn. This is the sense in which the mature emergent person (at T4, which is also the new T1), then inspects the 'I', the 'Me', the 'We', and the 'You', which have been part of his or her personal morphogenesis, and then applies his or her autonomous personal powers to pursue their replication or transformation.

To talk of re-visiting the four Quadrants is obviously an analytical contrivance, which is justified because each presents distinct problems and we also have the personal powers to give them our selective attention.

(i) Quadrant 1 is very much the space of introspection. There our continuous and reflective self-consciousness has, as it were, a new item to address, namely the personal and social self which 'I' have become. 'I' therefore turn inwards and examine 'myself' in a subject to subject dialogue, which is made possible by the passage of time. 'I' have become something (or many things) through the concerns which 'I' in the past have adopted and the kind of social actor that I have become. But the 'I' is continuous and thus can take stock of these developments, as well as entering into them, and of course monitoring them with an eye to the future. At this point the 'I' surveys the 'You' with some amazement, because being continuous, it registers surprise when it confronts the way in which its own incremental decisions have cumulated into someone with pronounced form and characteristics. Perhaps we are most acutely aware of this process on those key days when we first acquire such characteristics in the outside world – 'So I'm now a graduate, licensed to drive a car, a married woman, a parent, someone who has climbed Mont Blanc . . .'

The 'I' and 'myself' have the most intimate of all relationships. They have insider information and legitimately engage in insider dealing. Thus they share their uncertainties and self-doubts of which the world may be oblivious. Perhaps a few readers will recognise the internal reaction, 'Well, you may have fooled the driving test examiner, but you're not safe to let on the road.' Furthermore, the 'You' has given the 'I' something to live up to (or live down), but necessarily to live with: and 'I' have to be a collaborator in my own life because 'I' have been there all along, shaping what it has become. But 'I' am an active collaborator because the future still has to be made, and these acquired characteristics do not determine its making. The 'I' cannot remain fixated on the thought, 'Hasn't she come a long way': the day after graduation or ordination or parturition, the 'I' has to pick up the baton and take the responsibility for living out the identities it has developed. The 'I' and the 'You' have their intense and unseen life: only they share their private anxieties, joys, sorrows, courageousness and cowardice. For 'You' have become what you have with my accord, but 'I' must now be the executor. 'You' succeeded in becoming the Lecturer, and we agreed upon its priority in our cluster of ultimate concerns, but 'I' have to give the first and succeeding lectures.

This is the space where *commitment to oneself* takes place: the self has been forged but now has to go forward in the world. Without intra-personal solidarity this cannot occur, even though for most of us it takes place with trepidation and self-doubt. Our feelings of unworthiness can be profound, but without this solidarity we could not live out our concerns – we would back out of them. In the process, and through these dialogues about our tentativeness, our personification of the actors we have become gradually take further shape and become recognisable in the outside world. We may very well not think that our personifications approximate to our ideals of how a teacher or a parent should be, but they are what we, in solidarity, can produce and what others will find to recognise as our unique productions. It must, of course, be allowed that we can back-out, because reality may present challenges which the internal conversation fallibly presumed would be manageable. There are plenty of people with a driving licence who do not become motorists. Indeed, the living out of every concern depends upon a moment by moment re-commitment of the 'I', to carry forward the development of the 'You'. Internally we can fail, fall and pick ourselves up again, but without the solidarity of the 'I' and the 'You', confessing, absolving and resolving within the internal forum, then personal identity will be lost (which is not to say it will not be regained), and this will declare itself socially in the form of defective or stuttering role performances. In Scriptural terms, this commitment to oneself is spelt out very clearly: unless I can love myself, then I lack what it takes to love my neighbour.

(ii) 'Re-entering' Quadrant 2, now as a bearer of a personal identity and a social identity, I find 'I' have a place, and perhaps a new position, upon society's distribution of resources. The developed 'Me' has been assigned her own life-chances and these are not entirely involuntary for anyone who has achieved both identities, because, as active subjects, they have actively collaborated in making themselves *what* they are, even though this was accomplished within the constraints and enablements of our initial involuntary placements. Yet now, 'I' can reflect upon 'my' positioning, as subject reflecting upon object, and can compare 'my' life chances with those of other people. Even more, 'I' can reflect about the nature of the resource distributions themselves. 'I' can deem 'myself' fortunate or unfortunate, a victim or a victor. Because of *what* 'I' am and *whom* 'I' have become, 'I' will also evaluate these distributions as fair or unfair. Depending upon my personal and ultimate concerns, 'I' will judge that certain kinds of people and their activities are not being given their due, be it appropriate recognition or an appropriate allocation. Individuals can judge distributions to be too steep, or too flat, or too skewed. However, in 're-visiting' Quadrant 2, the 'Me' whom they encounter there is again a Primary Agent: one amongst others similarly placed. *Qua* Primary Agent we are still confined to unitary acts which may or may not aggregate into something consequential.

One action, however, which can have efficacy is our personal judgement on the positioning of the 'Me'. 'I' can be content or acceptant that 'I' now have these resources – remuneration, representation and repute – at my disposal, or resent where 'I' now find 'myself'. 'I' can regret the combination of circumstances and deliberations which have placed 'Me' there or resent the exclusion, discrimination and reproduction which have left 'Me' there. Provided the agent does not see herself as condemned to passivity, this inspection can trigger a new cycle of the internal conversation, in which the subject strives to narrow the gap between that which they have become and that which they would be. From this nexus originates the mature student, the career change, the late vocation, certain 'elderly prima gravidas' and those divorcees who cluster in the early years of marriage. How they will fare depends on the same factors and contingencies which were characterised in the first cycle of the inner conversation, plus the effects of any social bonuses or penalties which have been accumulated *en route*.

(iii) It is in Quadrant 3, that the outcomes of those normative judgements about the fairness or appropriateness of resource distributions (made in

Quadrant 2) will have a tendential effect upon subsequent collective action. Those making strong judgements about 'justice' or 'injustice' will tend to find themselves as 'members' of opposing groups of Corporate Agents, whilst those without strong views are the likely non-participants in these collective struggles. Since those who have achieved social identity are now actors in a clearly defined role structure, there are the obvious courses of action they can take to promote their groupings – from joining the professional association/union, engaging in political lobbying, to demonstrating or direct action.

Equally, because we have personal identity which is a distillation of our concerns in all three orders of reality – natural, practical as well as social – then it is *likely* that our occupancy of social roles does not exhaust our personal self-investment. Therefore, as was argued in chapter 7, many will be found belonging to social movements which have no direct connection with their role incumbency. Moreover, as was maintained in section two of the last chapter, global morphogenesis works to maximise the differences which can be promoted through the disengagement of new Corporate Agents. By definition, these movements have their lifetimes too: they succeed and become incorporated, they mutate strategically, they fail and amalgamate, regroup or disband. This is not the place to discuss the why's and wherefore's of these outcomes for such agencies, but rather to highlight some of their effects for participant agents.

What this means upon re-visitation, is that every such person has acquired a biography as a Corporate Agent, and equally importantly they have to determine the next episode of it. Thus many of us can look back to the days of Aldermaston marching and give a variety of accounts why this is not the way we now pursue nuclear disarmament; we can recount why we switched from one Party or faction to another; we can recall our welcoming of new movements or hesitancy about supporting certain new promotive groupings. In doing this, we are reviewing past re-visitations and what we determined about our commitments at those times. On each 'visit', we do the same thing: we re-monitor our commitments and re-determine *how* we will stand and with *whom* in solidarity. Because we change as persons and so do Corporate agents as organisations, then a series of re-commitments is inescapable. The continuity of our personal identities depends upon the continuous nature of our concerns (which must not be taken as given over time). Yet, in so far as an identity is retained, then dedication to its defining concerns will prompt many to sustain their commitments precisely by reflectively adjusting the groupings with which they can work in solidarity.

(iv) It is in Quadrant 4 that this continuity of personal and of social identity alike is scrutinised. It is not hyperbole to say that each day we revisit our role commitments and have to make an act of re-commitment, because our daily wakening confronts us with yesterday's on-going concerns. These we not only have (effectively) to re-endorse, but also (effectively) to re-determine how this re-endorsement will be personified. The 'I' and the 'You' have the day-to-day task of determining what kind of 'You' they will project forward into the future. Today can always be the day of either reversal or renewal of our commitments to the social identities which we have assumed: inexorably each day is one or the other, precisely because personification has to be an active and reflective process about investing ourselves in our existing roles which involves novel and unscripted performances, hour by hour. We are our own script writers, since even the smallest print, which spells out our formal role obligations, cannot tell us how to greet our partners, breakfast the children, get down to a day's research, acknowledge God, or let the dog out. Usually, these will not feel like decisions, except on rare occasions such as 'today I am giving up cigarettes'. They do not do so because we all develop routines for meeting what we have adopted as our routine concerns. Yet in this very routinisation lies our distinctive personification of our roles; recognisable to self and to others and expressive of our continuing commitment.

From the point of view of outside observers, these routine personifications fix what *kind* of parent, teacher, churchgoer or colleague a person is, such that departures from a consistent performance attract attention, even if these in no way constitute breaches of formal role expectations. Comments such as 'It's not like him to be late, to be reluctant to do x or to see y' are judgements upon the *person* and about how their stable personification of a role gradually leads to expectations about the stability of this performance, beyond any strict calls of duty. Yet, internally we all know the fragility of sustaining this stable living out of our commitments. For everyone there are the dull headachy days when doing so is a matter of willing the 'You' to go through the motions of sustaining our personal and social identities. We get through them because the self, in solidarity, acknowledges that the temporary headache is unimportant in relation to the on-going commitment(s). At best we hope to conceal this distraction, and at worst, that we can struggle through without jeopardising ourselves by betraying our ultimate concerns. In contradistinction, real fragility occurs when the personification which has become routine begins to ring hollow internally: when it has indeed become a 'performance' rather than a performative expression of who we are. This can basically happen for two reasons; either the roles in question have changed or we have.

Throughout, roles have been presented as something dynamic because the activities of (corporate) agents transform the role array and because the unscripted personifications of actors also cumulatively transform normative expectations associated with positions. Such transformations have never been presented as matters of consensuality – quite the reverse. Necessarily then, role changes will leave some people 'stranded' in positions which they had initially assumed as vehicles for the expression of their social identity, but which no longer operate in this way. Yet we cannot change most social identities at the drop of a hat or like exchanging hats. There are questions of preparation, of training and of acceptability and there are the constraints made-up of 'sunk costs' in the role(s) we occupy, which come in a variety of currencies. It has been maintained that 'self worth' is the *omnium gatherum* of our social identity, but its objective and subjective facets may now be at war with one another. A position, especially an occupational role, gives us resources, representation and repute: these are both the objective rewards of our incumbency and the external indicators of our social worth. We will repudiate them most reluctantly because the price is heavy and alternatives are always problematic, even if they are available. Moreover, there can even be a dogged fidelity in seeing a commitment through despite such circumstantial changes. However, when our personal identity can no longer be expressed through our social identity, then only bad faith characterises the continuing role incumbent. These are the time servers: they are recognised as such because they have withdrawn their active personification to become passive executors of minimalistic and enforceable expectations, and they know themselves to be such for their self worth no longer derives from this source. Since this is a painful position to be in, the internal conversation will tend to re-engage in a re-prioritisation of concerns to bring about re-alignment of social and personal identities. In this quest for a new 'You', taking a cut in social salary may well be the price of pursuing integrity.

Much the same is true of the person whose own concerns shift and change even though the roles they occupy do not undergo substantial or significant modification. Particularly through our agential involvement in social movements, certain concerns will increase in personal salience, whilst others get demoted through disillusionment. That is only one common process: there are many other ways in which love can grow cold or new fires ignite. Here the key question will be whether the new personal concern can be combined with an existing social identity. The answer is sometimes yes and sometimes no; which it is, turns upon whether a new, but normatively acceptable form of personification can be creatively elaborated, which re-amalgamates personal and social identities. The answer is affirmative, say, for the 'new' feminist lecturer who will change teaching emphasis, revise reading lists, do different kinds of research and consort with different colleagues: but it remains negative for the 'married priest'. This latter is only an extreme example because a choice between roles is entailed, but we all face the generic problem throughout our life-course of how to maintain our integrity by keeping our personal and our social identities in alignment – in a commitment which enhances both and detracts from neither.

Authentic alignment can never be a compromise, because compromising cannot be wholehearted and thus undermines our very selves. By it, we rob ourselves of our personal identity, because compromise is a refusal to prioritise what we care about, which is definitive of who we are. Instead, alignment has to be creative, as do all commitments. That continuous sense of self, the 'I', modified by and modifying the 'Me' and the 'We', has to collaborate with the future 'You' to determine how we will be in society and what part of society will form part of our being. Being human is our gift to society – certainly with society, through society and in society – but it can never be society's gift to us.

Conclusion: the re-emergence of humanity

In conclusion, I want to argue that three of our major problems in social theory are in fact interrelated. These are the 'problem of structure and agency', the 'problem of subjectivism and objectivism' and the 'problem of agency' itself. All hinge, in various ways, upon the causal powers of people, their nature, emergence and efficacy. Bringing real people back in, as robust and stratified beings, presents solutions to these problems which cannot be solved by the alternative strategy of impoverishing humanity. This tackles these issues by simply evacuating agency itself. It is a scenario on which humanity grows weak so that society can grow strong. This currently dominates social theorising and has been shown throughout this book to be no solution at all. On the contrary, it will only be the re-emergence of humanity, meaning that due acknowledgement is given to the properties and powers of real people forged in the real world, which overcomes the present poverty of social theory. The most important of these properties and powers is the 'inner conversation', as the mode of articulation between people and reality. Its exploration represents a new terrain for social theorising to discover, and if it does so it will also make the discovery of the enchantment of humankind. For value rationality is alive and well and flourishes as part of being human.

The problem of structure and agency

To reach the end of this book is also to complete the trilogy which has dealt with culture, structure and agency in turn. The object of the whole exercise has been to link 'structure' and 'agency' by accepting and accentuating the distinctive properties and powers pertaining to each, and then to examine their interplay. This is captured as a morphogenetic sequence in which structure conditions agency, and agency, in turn, elaborates upon the structure which it confronts. Morphogenesis works by employing analytical dualism to delineate cycles of structural conditioning, social interaction and structural elaboration over time, and according to the substantive problem in hand. However, analytical dualism would have no bite unless the causal powers in question were distinct, because they represent different emergent properties, yet ones which can only be examined in combination (SEPs and CEPs in conjunction with PEPs). Without this, it would be impossible to crack the 'vexatious fact of society', namely that we humans form society through our activities, but that we ourselves are also shaped by it. Unless one distinguishes between the emergent properties of the 'parts' and the 'people', nothing determinate can be said about their interplay. Basically, the earlier volumes maintained that approaches which balked at untying 'structure' and 'agency', and insisted instead upon their mutual constitution, merely re-presented this vexation. Thus, Structuration theory's insistence upon 'duality' could not proffer a research methodology for practical analysts of society, which enabled them to disentangle the *interplay* between structure and agency and to say anything precise about it.

Fundamentally, what the assertion of 'duality' balks at is the specification of distinctive causal powers which are *sui generis* to different levels of stratified social reality, especially those which pertain respectively to 'structure' and 'agency'. The same is true of any form of conflationary theorising, for it is the generic defect of conflation to withhold causal powers from either structure or agency. Hence, 'upwards conflation' makes structure the epiphenomenon of agential activities, and 'downwards conflation' renders agents the socialised agents the epiphenomena of socio-cultural systems. Realism is distinctive in according different causal powers to structure (and to culture), which are different again from those pertaining to agents. This does not deny their mutual interdependence. Structural and cultural properties (SEPs and CEPs) only emerge through the activities of people (PEPs), and they are only causally efficacious through the activities of people. The emergence of a structural property like 'centralisation' (e.g. an educational system), results from a long interaction chain of intended and unintended consequences, and it only exerts its powers of constraint and enablement by shaping the situations in which people find themselves (educationally).

However, this property of 'centralisation' is indeed activity-dependent, and retroductively we can specify upon whose activities it depended. Yet once it has emerged, 'centralisation' is a generative power which can belong to things like educational systems, but not to agents themselves, despite the fact that such an institutional form is continuously dependent upon agential activities to keep it going. Each new 'generation' of agents either reproduces or transforms its structural inheritance, but this heritage itself conditions their vested interests in doing so, their aspirations for stasis or for change, the resources they can bring to bear, and the strategies which are conducive to structural morphostasis or further morphogenesis.

The fundamental task of this book has been to give precision to what is meant by the causal powers proper to agency itself. These are the powers which ultimately enable people to reflect upon their social context, and to act reflexively towards it, either individually or collectively. Only by virtue of such powers can human beings be the active shapers of their socio-cultural context, rather than the passive recipients of it. The very notion of morphogenesis is predicated upon such active agents, otherwise there is no legitimate source to which structural or cultural elaboration can be attributed. This means that human beings have the powers of critical reflection upon their social context and of creatively redesigning their social environment, its institutional or ideational configurations, or both. If this book has succeeded at all, this will have consisted in showing how it is possible for human beings to become agentially effective in these ways, that is in evaluating their social context, creatively envisaging alternatives, and collaborating with others to bring about its transformation. These are the personal powers necessary to giving an account of how we contribute to shaping society, and they themselves are dependent upon the realisation of universal human powers, such as self-consciousness. To the extent that this has been successful, then to the same extent have 'structure and agency' been linked in a coherent morphogenetic account. In other words, the problem of how to link the social system with the individual agents, or the macro- with the micro- has a solution which frees us from the vexatious fact of society. Morphogenesis can formulate how we both shape society and are also shaped by it, through examining the interplay of the distinctive sets of causal powers (SEPs, CEPs and PEPs).

The problem of subjectivism and objectivism

However, there are some who claim that any contribution towards solving the 'micro-macro' issue, presumably however successful, would still only have tackled half of the problem posed by 'structure and agency'. Their argument is, fundamentally, that such success as any of us have had, is due to our having 'put together' structural factors and agential factors to tell a coherent story. Yet, it is objected, this cannot be a satisfactory story, because the two elements are not themselves integrated, and cannot be because one is objective and the other subjective. 'Argument about "objective" and "subjective" in short, is as fundamental as argument about "collective" and "individual".[1] Due to the difference between objectivity and subjectivity, any one story about them must always spring apart into two: one told from 'insider' perspective of 'understanding', and the other from the 'outsider' perspective of 'explanation'. Thus, 'there are always two stories to tell, one explanatory and the other interpretative, and they cannot finally be combined'.[2] It is held to follow directly from this that the morphogenetic approach, developed in these volumes, must be defective in accounting for change, 'because what matters is not that structure and agency both determined the outcome, not simply that we need to show how and in what ways and in what combinations they did, rather, the fundamental problem with morphogenesis is that it does not make sense of how we *integrate* structures and agents in a *single* story'.[3]

Now the key point that Hollis and Smith are making obviously cannot be that there are two stories to tell, *merely* because two kinds of causal powers are involved: for every time we give an account of a flower being planted, this does not threaten to split up into the plant's (animate) version and the soil's (inanimate) version. The reason for this is that it can be told as one *explanatory* story. Despite the fact that it integrates two different sets of causal powers, nevertheless the plant's biology and the soil's composition 'simply' interact, precisely because neither of them has a view on the matter. Here we are led back to the vexatious distinctiveness of society and to the supposed conclusion that because the 'people' have subjectivity, whereas the 'parts' do not, that this defies their combination. We must always have two stories, one which seeks to interpret subjective meanings and another which explains objective interconnections in causal terms: 'To understand is to reproduce the order in the minds of actors: to explain is to find causes in the scientific manner.'[4] Certainly, Hollis and Smith agree that we can provide cross-referenced accounts by starting with an individual's subjective choices and calculations, and then fitting in external causes, or we can proceed the other way round, starting with objective structures and fitting in the individual's reflective choices. However, this still leaves two stories which have been 'fitted together', just as morphogenesis is held to work, namely without being able to 'specify how structures and agency are to be combined'.[5]

What leads Hollis and Smith to be so certain that this combination of the objective and subjective must ever lie beyond the grasp of realism, is their denial that 'agents and structures can be placed on the same

[1] Martin Hollis and Steve Smith, 'Two Stories about Structure and Agency', *Revue of International Studies*, 20, 1994, p. 245.   [2] Ibid., p. 244.   [3] Ibid., p. 250.
[4] Martin Hollis and Steve Smith, *Explaining and Understanding International Relations*, Clarendon Press, Oxford, 1990, p. 87.
[5] Martin Hollis and Steve Smith, 'Two Stories', p. 250.

ontological footing, as if they were distinct objects in the social world between which a relation holds'.[6] Now, of course, social realists have never maintained that these are fully *distinct objects*, as opposed to ones possessing *distinctive powers*. There would be no 'vexatious fact of society' for us, if we simply thought of them as 'distinct objects'. Instead, what we are talking about are distinct causal powers, and given our view of stratified reality, social or otherwise, there seems no difficulty about putting them on the same 'ontological footing', *if* what this means is that both sets of powers are real and that there is a relationship between them. As it transpires, Hollis and Smith are not talking about 'ontological footings' at all, meaning that things are either real or not, because the very existence they claim for two stories does depend upon the *reality* of both the objective and subjective domains. What their distinction turns upon is the ontological difference between the 'people' and the 'parts' of society. The 'stuff of their social worlds'[7] consists either of rules and meanings for the 'people' (which are subjectively apprehended and hermeneutically understood), and of an independent structured environment made up of the 'parts' (which are objectively apprehended and causally explained).

Now, the problem of objectivism and subjectivism is rather like an accordion. Depending upon their conceptualisation, 'science' and 'culture' can be held wide apart or folded together. The Hollis and Smith version constitutes the widest gap between them: Science is basically Humean[8] and Culture is basically Wittgensteinian. It is then no surprise at all that 'constant conjunctions' are held to be absent in the cultural domain, and that the operation of causality is doubted to work there, if cause is defined in this Humean way. Conversely, realist theories of 'science' and of 'culture' minimise this gap, as is made explicit in their defence of the possibility of naturalism. Causal powers are held to be generative mechanisms which are at work in both of these open systems, and human reasons are one category of causes. Hence, the possibility of naturalism and the end of a self-standing hermeneutics, for in realism 'understanding' becomes a matter of grasping the causal efficacy of 'people'. Realism is thus 'concerned with actions which are practical, not just symbolic: with *making* (poesis), not just *doing* (praxis), or rather with doing which is not, or not only *saying*'.[9] Instead, to Hollis and Smith, subjectivity is rooted in the *sayings* and *meanings* of a Wittgensteinian 'form of

---

[6] Ibid., p. 244.

[7] Martin Hollis and Steve Smith, *Explaining and Understanding International Relations*, p.6.

[8] Ibid., p. 4. Scientific explanation is equated with 'claiming that similar effects always occur in similar conditions', which is in complete contradistinction to the realist theory of science.

[9] Roy Bhaskar, *The Possibility of Naturalism*, Harvester Wheatsheaf, London, 1989, p. 146.

life', replete with games and understandings of the rules and norms, which 'is clearly not one of causal interplay'.[10] Yet, if reasons are causes, as the realist maintains, then this difference between objectivism and subjectivism does not preclude examining the *interplay* between the causal powers of the 'people' and the 'parts'.

Bhaskar challenged their Humean conception of science and the fact that it leaves *hermeneutics as something entirely different and incommunicado*.[11] Similarly, in *Culture and Agency*, I challenged their conception of culture, as forming part of the 'myth of cultural integration', of which the 'form of life' is a latter-day example. Instead, causality is far from being foreign to culture. There are crucial causal relations between the level of the Cultural System, with its contradictions and complementarities (CEPs), which profoundly condition Socio-Cultural interaction, just as Socio-Cultural doings causally modify the constitution of the Cultural System over time. In short, realist accounts of science and culture were based on the *same model of causal powers*, operative in the two domains, and despite their *sui generis* differences. These powers are *necessarily* intertwined because actions, their conditions and consequences, span the two realms and thus cannot be divorced.

Exactly the same has been maintained throughout this book. An account of the causal powers of human beings (PEPs) has been given in which our subjectivity derives from our engagement with the world, and not through our involvement in 'society's conversation', the local 'form of life', or any other solely discursive order. As Hollis and Smith admit, the problem of linking objectivity and subjectivity, or explanation and understanding, would indeed evaporate and their combination 'would be easy in principle if the world-from-within were somehow lodged in an external world which held the causal key to it'.[12] Although the last phrase implies a form of reductionism which should be resisted, for it would merely reinstate 'downwards conflation', nevertheless, the idea of structures and agents being lodged in the same world is indeed what enables a single story to be advanced here. It is the story of how our human powers (PEPs) are emergent from our relations with the world as a whole, and how they react back upon reality as a whole. Since structures are part and parcel of the world which human beings confront, with which they interact, which they have the power to transform, yet which transform them themselves as they do so, only one story can be told. Two separate versions are actually untellable, for each would contain large gaps, either

---

[10] Martin Hollis and Steve Smith, 'Two Stories. . .', p. 245.
[11] See Roy Bhaskar, *The Possibility of Naturalism*, pp. 132–52.
[12] Martin Hollis and Steve Smith, *Explaining and Understanding International Relations*, p. 91.

about the conditioning circumstances under which agents live, act and develop or about their transformatory consequences for structures, which otherwise must be matters of structural parthenogenesis.

In conclusion, I want to signal how parts II, III and IV of this book do *show* that subjectivity and objectivity are quintessentially intertwined, therefore vindicating the ability of the morphogenetic approach to combine them and to tell its single story.

(1) Part II dealt with the emergence of our subjectivity itself and its interdependence with objective reality. Self-consciousness is the obvious predicate of subjectivity: unless we have a continuous sense of being one and the same person over time, then we may indeed have fleeting subjective impressions, momentary inclinations etc., but these would lack the continuity which furnishes the 'stuff' from which stories are told. The emergence of self-consciousness, our prime human PEP, was held to depend upon our active engagement with the world, through which the very distinction between the subjective and the objective (self and otherness) was formed. The primacy of practice was defended here: it was from our embodied practical relations that emerged our selfhood, reflexivity, memory and thought. In other words, all the elements, which are indispensable to our subjectivity, entailed work in the world and response to its properties and powers. Our own primary human power is thus only disengaged because constituted as we are, we necessarily relate to the causal powers of the world, constituted as it is. The very emergence of our subjectivity is therefore inexplicable, unless it is seen as emerging from human embeddedness in objective reality.

The primacy of practice was also held to undermine any notion of our exclusively cultural constitution. Our causal powers, which derive from our sense of self, are as real as the real world in which they emerged. Our selfhood is not a theory appropriated from the discursive cultural realm, but is a real and causally efficacious property, emergent from practical action in a material context. Thus *realism uncouples the bases of human subjectivity from dependency upon any 'form of life', and links them instead to the categorial structure of the world.* So far, we only have 'one story', but it is about two distinctive sets of causal powers, the human subjective ones only emerging through our embodied interplay with the objective world.

(2) Part III turned to the exercise of these human powers and the part played by our reflexivity in the emergence of our personal identities. Identity was held to hinge upon our concerns in the world, and the dilemma facing every human being was that inescapably each one of us has concerns in the natural order (about physical well-being), in the prac-

tical order (about performative competence) and in the social order (about self-worth). Each concern entails intentionality; it is *about* features of the world. Since it is the prioritising of our ultimate concerns, and the accommodation of other concerns to them, which gives us our unique personal identities, then who we are subjectively depends upon our involvement with the objective world.[13]

The reflective powers which give us our capacity to acquire personal identities are dependent upon our ability to prioritise our concerns *in* the world, including the social world whose considerations of self-worth, however, exercise no hegemony. If our personal identity represents our unique subjectivity, then *who we are* is formed by our, admittedly fallible, reflections upon the world, meaning its natural, practical and social orders. Once again, there can only be one story if our singular subjectivities are formed by our reflections upon objective reality. Our power of reflexivity enables us to prioritise what we care about most in the world (natural, practical and social), but reflection is about the world and therefore cannot be independent from the way the world is. We are not free to construe it as we please, as the epistemic and linguistic fallacies would have it, because the world's powers in relation to our own prevent us, for example, from taking threats to the body as unthreatening (rather than their being of less concern than other commitments). Therefore, *part of our subjective human story is itself shaped and constrained by the causal powers of objective reality.* Certainly, the martyr can regard his cause as more important than his death, but in determining this, part of his act of dedication is the acceptance of the objective fact that he will indeed die. To understand him hermeneutically, we cannot just attend to his subjective priorities, we must also attend to the objective fact of his death, which he has had to take into his own personal account – thus subverting the possibility of any purely subjective interpretation alone.

(3) When social identity was discussed in part IV, which is where the full brunt of the 'structure and agency' problem is encountered, then yet again, if structure stands for objectivity and agency for subjectivity, the two are found to be inextricably intertwined (though not analytically inseparable). Acquisition of a social identity, that is of a role or roles in which we can invest ourselves, was not a matter of a subjective contract, for we are not free to become any social self whom we choose. The only way of making role incumbency possible *for* an agent, and reasonable *to*

---

[13] Here, it is of course perfectly true that we can only know the world under our particular descriptions, derived from natural language. Yet this is true of all knowledge, and every such description is corrigible. This does not serve to claw us back into 'Society's Being' or to make our social 'form of life' pivotal.

an individual, was to invoke the causal powers of structures. These have effected the involuntary pre-grouping of collectivities with objective life-chances, and also conditioned the possibilities of access to different parts of the extant role array for different sections of the population. Thus it is maintained that the Agent is literally the parent of the Actor. We cannot tell the story of how some of us can find subjective satisfaction in a role without reference to the objective structural factors in which the role is embedded in the first place and which enabled its holder to have access to it in the second place.

Nor in personifying our roles, and thus achieving strict social identity, are we bound by a subjective conventionalism. Our human powers are not confined to the confines of the extant role array – to how we merely live out that which we have become in society at a given time. Equally, we can reflect upon the role array itself (and its wider institutional and systemic context), as a subject reflects upon an object, and we have the human power to commit ourselves to others in the pursuit of structural trans-formation. Without subjective feelings of grievance about objective oppression, subjective discontent about objective discrimination, or sub-jective resentment about objective inequalities, none of the familiar struc-tural changes would ensue in society. Yet, if we do succeed in this objective transformational activity, then we will have created new objec-tive positions in which different tracts of the population have the chance to acquire a social identity – to express their subjectivity, because now objectively able to do so.

Therefore, *role-taking* could conceivably be a thin hermeneutic tale told from within a 'form of life', and confined to the present tense: but *role-making* must be a thick account of the objective intertwining with the sub-jective, thus combining two sets of causal powers which are embedded in the same world. Realism tells only one story because dualism is only analytical – which does not mean it can ever be dispensed with. Emergence is about interdependence: just as water remains constituted by the hydrogen and oxygen atoms from which it emerges, and has prop-erties different from its constitutive elements, so are objectivity and sub-jectivity part and parcel of one another, where the emergence of our social identities is concerned. The social identity of each human being who achieves one is not only made *under* circumstances which are not of their own choosing, but is partly made *out* of them, which is why some can fail to attain such a social identity if circumstances are objectively unpropi-tious.

Central importance has been given in this book to the 'inner conver-sion' in making us who we are, because of the ultimate concerns we endorse and the manner in which we then live them out. That we do have a rich interior subjectivity is precisely what has been defended against those who impoverish our hidden lives by reducing them to a process of instrumental rationality or to permutations upon society's discourse. However, the 'inner conversation' is not subjective solipsism. We do not, and cannot tell *ourselves* an 'insider's' story about how we take the world to be, independently of how it is. If we did, we would not survive, let alone, thrive, and nor could any 'form of life', in all its meanings. Instead, the 'inner conversation' is a matter of referential reflexivity in which we ponder upon the world and about what our place is, and should be, within it. Social reality enters objectively into our making, but one of the greatest of human powers is that we can subjectively conceive of re-making society and ourselves. To accomplish this entails objective work in the world by the self and with others. The story to tell is about the confluence of causal powers – those of external reality, and our own which emerge from our relations with it: the two ultimately being mediated through the 'internal conversation'. It is the only story really worth telling, for it is about the transcendental power of human beings to transform the social world and themselves: that they can simultaneously change meanings is only one chapter of it.

In defence of humanity

The implications of revindicating human powers go far beyond the intricacies of resolving the problem of structure and agency or of reuniting subjectivism and objectivism. As I signalled in the Introduction, this is also a defensive operation because humanity is besieged on all sides by those who want the new Millennium to open as the aftermath of the Death of Man. Their disenchantment of the world would then have been accomplished in two stages. Firstly, the Death of God was brought about by evacuating him of all his powers and re-bestowing them on humankind, whose anthropocentric projection he was held to be. Secondly, humanity itself was next to be evacuated of all its powers which were then to be accredited to disembodied texts, the abstract interplay of signs, and the vacuity of eternally deferred meanings. Hence the prospect of a lunar landscape, with non-referential signs blowing in the wind and of humankind as mere nodal points through which indeterminate messages passed on their way through the ether.

It is a temptation to lay the culpability for all of this at the door of postmodern philosophy, even though some of those who had pushed it wide open did eventually recognise the need to 'bring the men back in'. However, that distribution of responsibility ignores the strenuous complicity of social theory. Sociological imperialists had laboured long and hard with a vacuum pump on humankind, sucking out the properties and powers of our species-being, to leave a void behind to be filled with social forces. Even the human shell has not been immune and has started to implode as its contents were evacuated. Thus the body, which might have been thought to be the organic stopping-point, represented no terminus. Indeed, during the last decade, fascination with 'the body' has actually been the final chapter in the project of demolishing humanity. Bodies are no longer respected as something non-reductively material, which mediate our traffic with the world, but only as a permeable medium which takes the ideational impress. The residual cells, molecules and neurones can then be assigned to those playing the 'natural science game'. This is not even a new and robust statement of the impossibility of naturalism. Instead, all are playing equally privileged and incommensurable language games in a world where 'all that remains is to play with the pieces'. What also remains, however, is idealism's territoriality. Each discipline must corner enough pieces to have a thoroughly good game. Our human susceptibility to competitiveness is the one unremarked human characteristic which allows this game-playing to go on. What has changed is that the incentives are no longer material but ideal.

Hence sociological imperialism: for the less that is left to humankind, the larger the terrain for social theorising. Substantively, I have structured this book around two great swathes of social theory which have evacuated human inner-being to this end. On the one hand, the protraction of the Enlightenment project has pared us down to the bone in the model of 'Modernity's Man'. Stripping away our affectivity and normativity, we are left with instrumental rationality alone, that is the purely mechanical ability to fit means to ends, at which we are probably less proficient than the current generation of computers. Their resulting model of man as a bargain-hunter is a moral nullity, because the ends he pursues are matters where *de gustibus non est disputandum*. This lone mechanistic being, for whom every social relationship is commodified, owes nothing of what he is to his fellow humans, and is therefore rendered incapable of a genuine act of commitment to them or solidarity with them. Since his inner life had been stripped down to one mechanical feature, he himself is perfectly uninteresting, compared with the public outworkings of his choices and the game of fitting how they summed to the equations.

On the other hand, 'Society's Being' is also someone who has been subjected to the evacuation of her humanity, but the resulting void has been refurnished with social fittings. We became 'cultural artefacts' whose every property is begged or borrowed from society. Yet there is no one who actually does the begging or borrowing, since even the notion of being a self was a theory appropriated from society. There was once an ironic cartoon of the educational process, where a pupil sat with a funnel in her head through which were being poured information and values. Now and without irony, into the human figure is funnelled a social foam which penetrates every nook and cranny. All she is left with are her molecules: society supplies her with her meanings – and there is nothing between the two. She has no inner life, and she again is perfectly uninteresting in her absence of properties and powers. What she may mistake as such are simply social appropriations. Consequently, there is the same turn from the inner to the outer. Ultimately it is the things that happen to her from outside which rivet attention.

In so far as a minority in the sociological tradition has acknowledged that we do have both inner as well as outer lives, they have erected a brick wall between them. Thus I have already touched upon those defenders of an incommunicado hermeneutics, who demand that separate accounts be given, which make understanding and explanation into two discrete stories that at most can be cross-referenced. Similarly, but less obviously, Goffman intrigued us for two decades with the outer doings of his feisty subject, who insouciantly disported himself in the interstices of society. But the presentation of the self was all about *presentational acts* in everyday life and the account was confined to these public outworkings, for the shutters came down on the self whose inner deliberations generated these performances. Goffman left us with two questions. How could subjects perform socially with such virtuosity if society were merely a stage-setting for the conduct of their private business, and who was the mysterious self who could set up and impose this private agenda? His origins, properties and powers remained immured behind the brick wall. Goffman owed us an account of the self, but left the bill unpaid, for the sources of the self remained completely shrouded.

Thus, even those theorists who accepted that we had both inner and outer lives refused to explore the interchanges between the two, treating them instead as hermetically sealed domains. At most, powers were imputed to people that required a distinct interpretive understanding, but the question hung on the air as to where this hermeneutic capacity of a self came from. At worst, the inner recesses and resources of people were so inaccessibly private that, for all intents and purposes, a 'no trespassing' sign was posted on their inner lives.

The object of this book has been the reverse. It has sought to revindicate our inner lives and to rescue humanity from impoverishment, but it has torn down the privacy sign because what we are is forged between our potential species' powers and our encounters with the world, in which they are developed if we are to survive and to thrive. Hence the emergence of our prime emergent power, self-consciousness, was firmly lodged in our fully material embodiment and our ineluctable interaction with an equally material world. Our concrete practices were accorded primacy in the emergence of our selfhood and these same practices were held to be pivotal to our knowledge of the world. This made the sense of self, reflexivity, thought, skill and discursive ability itself, all fully activity-dependent upon how we made out in confronting reality. Yet reality itself was constituted of irreducible natural, practical and social domains, which represented multiple sources of the self and allowed the social its part in our constitution, without making all that we are the gift of society. Indeed, it was the fact that we have to accommodate to all three realms which made our personal identities greater than that one sub-set of them represented by our social identity. Since each one of us has the problem of how to prioritise our concerns in natural, practical and social reality, our singular solutions were what secured our strict identities as unique persons. As persons we thus had explicable inner and outer lives which interacted. The brick wall had come down. On the far side of it stood robust human beings. Simultaneously, what opened-up was the excitement of being able to explore the ceaseless interplay between their inner deliberations and their public outworkings.

The enchantment of being human

The 'inner conversation' is how our personal emergent powers are exercised on and in the world – natural, practical and social – which is our triune environment. This 'interior dialogue' is not just a window upon the world, rather it is what determines our being-in-the-world, though not in the times and the circumstances of our choosing. Fundamentally, the 'inner conversation' is constitutive of our concrete singularity. However, it is also and necessarily a conversation *about* reality. This is because the triune world sets us three problems, none of which can be evaded, made as we are. It confronts us with three inescapable concerns: with our physical well-being, our performative competence and our self-worth. The world therefore makes us creatures of concern and thus enters through three separate doorways into our constitution. Yet we react back powerfully and particularistically, because the world cannot dictate to us what to care about most: at best it can set the costs for failing to accommodate a given concern.

It is we human beings who determine our priorities and define our personal identities in terms of what we care about. Therefore we are quintessentially evaluative beings. There is nothing in the world which dictates how we list our priorities, although there are plenty of forces inducing us this way and that, not least of which are the discursive powers of the social order. Yet we are also fallible beings, for neither is there anything in the world which can insist that we love in due order. Instead, through external information and internal deliberation, all who achieve personal identity work out their own distinctive constellation of values. It is then through dedicating ourselves to the subjects and objects of our caring that we make our mark upon reality – natural, practical and social.

Thus the natural attitude of being human in the world is fundamentally evaluative. Value-rationality can never pertain only to some restricted historical period, for it is by means of it that every real person navigates their way through the world. Were disenchantment the case, then no one could be going anywhere because they would have lost the power to care about anything: only those with no concerns can be literally aimless. We can substantiate this if we attend to the 'internal conversation', as the mode of articulation between people and reality. We can only distort the quintessentially evaluative quality of humanity if the space where the 'inner conversation' takes place is voided by theory or bricked up by methodology. Demolish it, impoverish it, evacuate it, ignore it, or fill it up with social hard-core, and we will have as much difficulty in comprehending our social subjects as we would in making one day of our own personal doings intelligible to ourselves, if, *per impossibile*, we could switch off the mental commentary which always precedes, accompanies and reflects upon our actions. Open out the 'internal conversation' and we discover not only the richest unmined research field but, more importantly, the enchantment of every human being.

Index